LEARN MICROSOFT® WORD FOR WINDOWS™ NOW

Special Edition

MODEL DISKS INCLUDED

Microsoft PRESS®

MICHAEL BOOM

PUBLISHED BY
Microsoft Press
A Division of Microsoft Corporation
One Microsoft Way
Redmond, Washington 98052-6399

ISBN 1-55615-297-3

Printed and bound in the United States of America.

1 2 3 4 5 6 7 8 9 FGFG 4 3 2 1 0

Dedication

To Lynn, for the times when words fail me.

Acknowledgments

Writing a book about software under development is always a tricky process that requires special help and understanding from both the software developer and the book publisher. As I wrote about Microsoft Word for Windows during its development, I was fortunate to work with a software developer and a book publisher who were both tremendously cooperative on all counts, not only because they're part of the same company (which, I will admit, doesn't hurt!), but because they're thorough professionals.

I want to express my appreciation to the very talented development team at Microsoft who created Word for Windows; to the equally talented staff of Microsoft Press who suggested this book and helped me shape it; and to Russell Borland, the Word for Windows pundit equally at ease in both groups, who was always ready to answer my questions about Word's most obscure corners. Thank you all for helping this writer write about an important tool of his trade.

Contents

INTRODUCTION

Sitting down to learn a new word processor can be as frustrating as moving to a new city. Until you learn the terrain and begin to feel at home, everything takes more time than you think it will. Fortunately, Microsoft Word for Windows is easy to learn and enjoyable to use. And you'll find this book to be a useful guide for learning to use Microsoft's revolutionary new software.

The two enclosed disks contain a Working Model version of Microsoft Word for Windows. This book was written for use with the full retail version of Microsoft Word for Windows, but if you don't have that version, you can use this Working Model instead—the Working Model includes a "run-time" version of Microsoft Windows that allows you to run the program. For instructions on installing and using the Working Model with this book, refer to the section at the end of this Introduction titled "Using the Working Model Disks."

WHY WORD FOR WINDOWS?

Microsoft Word for Windows does more than other word processors and is very straightforward to use. It runs under Microsoft Windows, which gives you the ease of using intuitive drop-down menus and dialog boxes, as well as the ability to display more than one document—or different views of the same document—at one time.

Learn Microsoft Word for Windows Now takes you straight to the heart of Word for Windows' most used and useful features so that you can quickly get down to business. Before you start reading, however, you should at least be familiar with the basic operations of your computer and know how to perform simple tasks such as turning your computer on and off, inserting disks in the drives, formatting disks, loading and saving files, and changing directories.

HOW THIS BOOK IS ORGANIZED

Learn Microsoft Word for Windows Now is divided into four sections, each addressing a different level of experience. The first section addresses users who are completely new to word processing; the second covers the fundamentals of Word for Windows; the third is for users who want to learn to create more complex documents; and the fourth introduces some of Word for Windows' most advanced features. Find the section that sounds appropriate to your level of experience and start there. If you have any trouble understanding the material in that section, it's a simple matter to move back to the previous section.

Each chapter contains practical examples that teach you the concepts presented in the chapter. You'll find a sample document at the beginning of the chapter that shows you what you can accomplish, followed by exercises with numbered steps that re-create the sample document. Try out the exercises! You'll learn much better if you teach your fingers as well as your mind. If you aren't up to typing all the text in the sample document, feel free to abbreviate liberally or leave out text. And finally, have some fun and take the time to play around with Word for Windows as you read.

Section One gets you going with a minimum of effort. In Chapter 1, you find a description of the hardware and software you need to run Word for Windows, as well as a quick tour through Windows. Chapter 2 introduces you to Word for Windows and shows you around the program. And in Chapter 3, you get down to business, creating a standard business letter and learning the five basic stages of document creation.

When you know your way around Word for Windows well enough to create a simple document, you can read Section Two to get a solid grounding in Word for Windows basics, learning skills necessary for creating more complex documents. Chapter 4 shows you how to enter and format characters by adding italic, boldface, and other forms of emphasis. Chapter 5 shows you how to import pictures into your text, and Chapter 6 introduces you to the editing tools that make it easy to move quickly through your document and replace text. In Chapter 7, you learn to format paragraphs by adjusting indents, alignment, and line spacing; and in Chapter 8, you see how to add tab stops to your paragraphs to align columns of text easily. The last three chapters in the section (9, 10, and 11) show you how to add headers and footers to a document; how to control the way Word for Windows breaks a document into pages; and how to save, open, and print documents using special document-retrieval techniques and multiple print options.

The third section is for Word for Windows users who want to know more than just how to get around. Chapter 12 introduces the thesaurus, the Calculate command, and the glossary. Chapter 13 introduces list sorting, spelling checking, and hyphenation. Chapter 14 shows you how to add footnotes to a document, and Chapter 15 introduces styles, a fast and comprehensive method of formatting your documents. Chapters 16 and 17 teach you how to lay out text and graphics on the page—first by creating columns and controlling headers, footers, and footnotes; and then by creating document templates that give you a running start on each new document you create. Chapter 18 teaches you how to store and retrieve documents by creating summaries and by using the File Find command for searches. Chapter 19 describes printing on different sizes of paper and using the print spooler for printing efficiency.

In the last section, you learn the secrets of some of Word for Windows' most powerful and advanced features. Chapter 20 teaches you how to use annotations and revision marks to share documents among Word for Windows users, and Chapter 21 shows you how to use Word for Windows' multiple document views to move quickly and easily through a document, to help with page layout, and to create quick outlines. Chapter 22 introduces you to tables and shows you how to use them to easily arrange complex information. Chapter 23 explains using macros to execute complex tasks with a single keystroke, and Chapter 24 introduces you to fields, a way to program Word for Windows for advanced work. Chapter 25 shows you how to create form letters.

The Appendix offers a complete list of Word for Windows' keyboard shortcuts. Following the Appendix is a comprehensive index to help you quickly find information on any topic covered in this book.

USING THE WORKING MODEL DISKS

The disks bound into the back of this book contain the Working Model of Microsoft Word for Windows. The Working Model has a few restrictions built into it. See "Additional Features in the Full Retail Version of Microsoft Word for Windows" later in this Introduction for a list of additional features you receive when you buy the full retail version of Microsoft Word for Windows. **Because this book was written for the full retail version of Word for Windows, some parts of the book do not apply to the Working Model.** See "Text Differences for the Working Model" (also later in this Introduction) for a list of the topics in the book that do not apply to the Working Model. And see "Visual Differences for the Working Model" for a list of visual differences between the Working Model and the full retail version.

Hardware Requirements for the Working Model

All versions of Microsoft Word for Windows require at least 640 kilobytes of conventional memory (RAM). You need about 1.5 megabytes of free space on your hard disk to install the Working Model version. The Working Model of Word for Windows includes a limited version of Windows specially set up for either an EGA display with high-resolution color (an EGA card with 256 kilobytes of video memory on it) or a VGA display, and, optionally, for a Microsoft Mouse or compatible. Printer drivers are included for only the HP LaserJet series and Epson 9-pin printers, and the Working Model of Word for Windows assumes that the printer is connected to LPT1. Note that most 9-pin dot-matrix printers emulate the Epson FX; therefore, if you're using a dot-matrix printer, the Epson printer driver will probably work for you. If you do not have a printer or if you have a different printer, choose the HP LaserJet during setup, so that you get better-looking fonts on the screen. Note that you can only install one of the two drivers at a time; to change to the other driver, you have to run the Setup program again.

Setup Instructions for the Working Model

To set up the Working Model version of Microsoft Word for Windows, you use the Setup program on the Setup disk. Setup creates a directory named TRYWORD on your hard disk and copies the Word for Windows files and a run-time version of Microsoft Windows from the floppy disks to that directory.

To run the Setup program, insert the Setup disk in a high-density 5¼-inch floppy-disk drive. Change to either the floppy drive containing the Setup disk or the hard drive where you want the Working Model set up. Type the appropriate Setup command for the arrangement of disk drives you are using. The following table provides examples of what to type for various situations:

To start Setup from prompt for drive	*When the Setup disk is in drive*	*Type this command and press Enter*
A	A	*setup*
C	A	*a:setup*
C	B	*b:setup*
D	A	*a:setup*
D	B	*b:setup*

Starting the Working Model

If you have just finished setting up the Working Model on your hard disk, the Setup program automatically starts the Working Model. You see a screen displaying two choices: Explore Working Model and Exit. Point to your choice with the mouse and click the left mouse button. Or, press the key for the underlined letter in your choice (*W* to run the Working Model; *x* to quit).

When you quit the Working Model the first time, you will see a message asking if you want to remove the run-time version of Windows. If you have a full version of Windows 286 or 386, choose Yes. Otherwise, choose No. (If you choose Yes, you can also remove the files with the extension .DRV and .FON from the TRYWORD directory to free up space on your hard disk.) The next time you want to start the Working Model, type:

```
CD \TRYWORD
```

and press the Enter key. Next, type:

```
WINWORD
```

and press the Enter key.

If you had Windows 386 installed prior to installing the Working Model, type:

```
CD \TRYWORD
```

and press the Enter key. Next, type:

```
WIN386 WINWORD
```

and press the Enter key.

If you want to change printers after installing the Working Model, delete all the files in the TRYWORD directory, and run the Setup program again.

Note for Full Windows Users

If you have a full version of Microsoft Windows installed prior to installing the Working Model, you can run the Working Model of Microsoft Word for Windows from Windows, as described in Chapter 2, ''A Tour of Word for Windows.'' Doing so enables you to run multiple applications at the same time, so that you can cut and paste from Microsoft Excel, from Windows Paint, and from any other Windows program. You can also see how Word formats text according to your printer's abilities.

Note that for the Working Model and the full retail version of Word for Windows to perform correctly, you need to have Windows version 2.11. This version requirement applies to both Windows 286 and Windows 386. All versions of Word for Windows (full retail and Working Model) run under earlier versions of Windows, but are not guaranteed to run correctly for all operations.

Additional Features in the Full Retail Version of Microsoft Word for Windows

You get the following additional features when you purchase the full retail version of Microsoft Word for Windows:

- Ability to create documents as large as you have disk space to store. In the Working Model, you cannot store and print documents of more than 7,000 characters. If your document is longer, the Working Model displays a message to this effect. Delete text until the document is 7,000 or fewer characters and then try again.
- Ability to print on all the printers that Microsoft Windows supports. In the Working Model, you can print on only the HP LaserJet series and Epson 9-pin printers and those that emulate it.
- Ability to convert files to and from the most popular word processors. This feature is not included with the Working Model.
- Ability to import graphics files from popular graphics programs and scanner files. This feature is not included with the Working Model.
- Access to the on-line Tutorial, on-line Help, spelling checking, the thesaurus, and hyphenation. These features are not included with the Working Model.
- Ability to view the contents of the clipboard and access to the Windows Control Panel. These features are not included with the Working Model.
- Access to a set of example docment templates and to a variety of useful macros. These resources are not included with the Working Model.
- Product documentation.
- Product support from Microsoft. Microsoft's Product Support Department and Microsoft Press are not staffed to answer questions about the Working Model software.

Text Differences for the Working Model

In the Working Model, AutoSave is set to High, and Background Pagination and Prompt for Summary Info are turned off. In the full retail version, AutoSave is turned off, and Background Pagination and Prompt for Summary Info are turned on. Also, the Author name in the Utilities Customize and Edit Summary Info dialog boxes is set to Microsoft. In addition, the following chapters and sections of *Learn Microsoft Word for Windows Now* do not apply to, or are different for, the Microsoft Word for Windows Working Model:

- Chapter 2, ''A Tour of Word for Windows''
  ''Word's First Appearance''—The Working Model does not ask you for your name and initials. Also, see ''Visual Differences for the Working Model'' later in this Introduction.
  ''The Status Bar''—To view the Status Bar in the Working Model you must choose Status Bar from the View menu.
- Chapter 5, ''Adding Pictures''
  Because the Working Model includes neither the graphics conversion files nor a full version of Windows, you cannot insert pictures into documents with the Working Model. You can, however, insert an empty picture frame into a document.
- Chapter 11, ''Saving, Opening, and Printing a Document''
  ''File Formats''—The File Save As dialog box does not list word-processor formats beyond the ones listed in this section because other formats are not available in the Working Model.
  ''Opening Documents from Other Programs''—The Working Model does not provide the conversion programs for other word processors.
  ''Using the List Box and Pathname''—The Working Model uses the \TRYWORD directory.
  ''The Find button''—This feature does not work in the Working Model.
- Chapter 12, ''Writing Tools''
  ''The Thesaurus''—The Working Model does not provide the thesaurus.

- Chapter 13, "More Editing Tools"
  "Checking Spelling"—The Working Model does not provide spelling checking.
  "Hyphenation"—The Working Model does not provide hyphenation.
- Chapter 19, "Printing Variations"
  "Batch Printing Using Spooler"—Spooler is not supplied with the Working Model.
- Chapter 23, "Macros: Repetitive Tasks Made Simple"
  "Editing a Macro"—Do not edit the macros that come with the Working Model. A message appears when you choose the Macro Edit command, advising you not to edit the macros. You can, however, safely create your own macros and edit them.

Visual Differences for the Working Model

The following differences are noticeable between the Working Model screens and the screen illustrations in this book and the full retail version of the software:

- The title bar shows "(Demo)" following the usual "Microsoft Word" title.
- Dialog-box lists of available fonts and point sizes, documents, directories, templates, macros, styles, and glossary entries are different from the lists shown in this book.
- The status bar will often appear different on the screen from the book illustrations.

Other Information About the Working Model

The Microsoft Word for Windows Working Model is also available on 3½-inch disks, directly from Microsoft. To order, call 1-800-541-1261 and ask for Department MSP. The price of the disks is $9.95.

If you have a question or comment about the text or examples in *Learn Microsoft Word for Windows Now,* or if one of the disks in your package is defective, write to Microsoft Press, Attn: Learn Word for Windows Now Editor, One Microsoft Way, Redmond, WA 98052-6399. No phone calls, please.

SECTION ONE

Beginnings

This section starts you on Word for Windows: You verify that your computer is set up to run Word, you learn Windows fundamentals, and you sit down to create your first Word document.

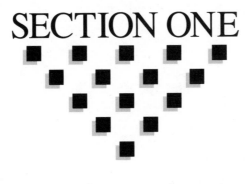

Chapter 1

Setting Up Word for Windows

If you have the Special Edition with disks included, consult the Introduction

In this chapter, your introduction to Microsoft Word for Windows, you learn about Word's working environment—the minimum equipment, enhanced equipment, and software your computer system must have before you run Word. You also learn how to install Windows on your system and how to use Windows to install Word.

If you're setting up a new computer system to run Word, this chapter lists the necessary hardware and software you need. Be sure to consult your computer dealer or computer service department as you put together the system. If you already have a computer system set up, read this chapter to be sure you have everything necessary to run Word.

HARDWARE

Word runs on IBM personal computers and compatible computers (often called "MS-DOS computers" because of the system software they run). MS-DOS computers come in many configurations and have varying levels of power. The minimum computer system Word for Windows can run on has the following:

- An 80286 CPU (central processing unit)
- 640 kilobytes of RAM (random-access memory)
- A graphics display card that supports a 640 × 350 display

- A hard-disk drive of at least 10-megabyte capacity
- A floppy-disk drive
- A keyboard
- A monitor capable of displaying 640 × 350 graphics

Of course, you also want a printer. Figure 1-1 shows a typical computer system set up to run Word.

If you wish, you can use hardware that goes beyond Word's minimum requirements to create a system that makes Word faster and easier to use.

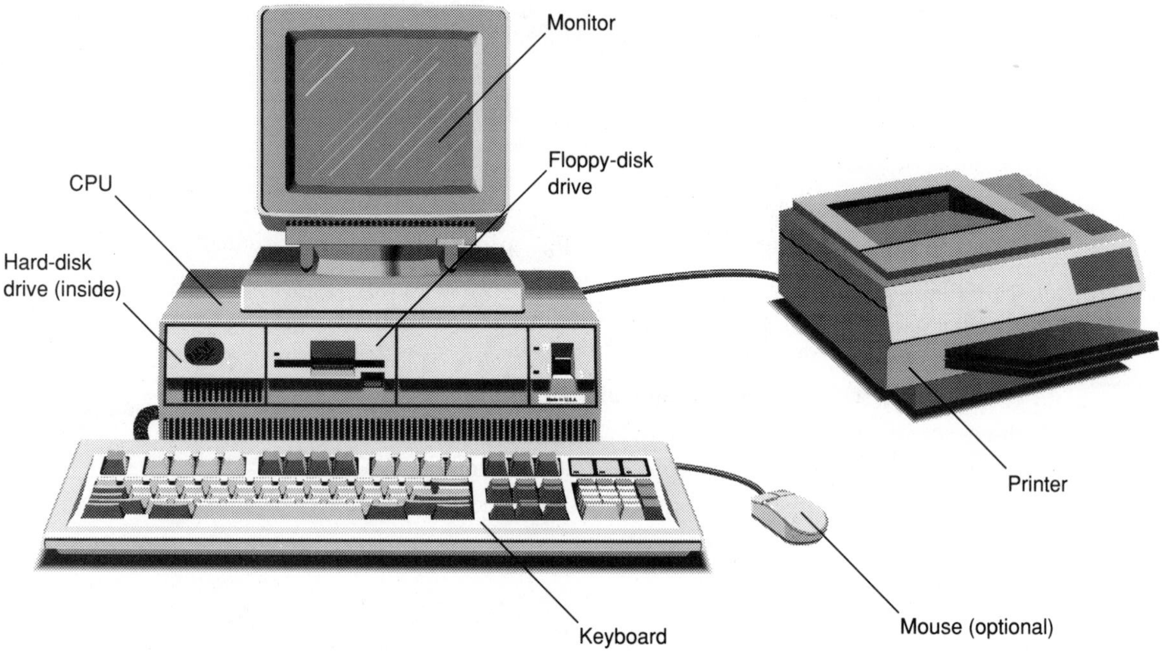

Figure 1-1. *A complete personal computer system.*

The Computer

Computers that run with an 80286 CPU or the more powerful 80386 CPU all run Word. Models in the IBM family of personal computers that use the 80286 CPU are listed on the following page.

- The PC/AT
- The PS/2 Model 50
- The PS/2 Model 60

The PS/2 Model 80, which uses the 80386 CPU, runs Word faster.

Of course, compatible computers and those that exceed the power of these IBM models can also run Word. For example, Word runs well on the Compaq 386, a computer with an 80386 CPU.

Be aware that some early IBM personal computers—the PC, PC/XT, and PCjr—won't run Word because their CPUs lack the necessary power.

RAM

Most computers sold today come with 512 or 640 kilobytes of RAM. If your computer has fewer than 640 kilobytes, you must ask your dealer or computer service department to install extra RAM for you.

To go beyond the minimum necessary RAM, you can add expanded memory boards to your computer. These boards expand available RAM up to 4 megabytes. Word uses the extra RAM to keep more of its working data and your document in memory at one time, which speeds up its operations considerably.

The Graphics Display Card

The IBM PS/2 computers all have built-in graphics display cards that work well with Word. The IBM PC/AT and IBM-compatible computers are sold with different graphics features—they might or might not come with the graphics display card you need. Any cards that work with Microsoft Windows (version 2.03 or later) also work with Word. They include the following:

- The Hercules Graphics Card
- The Hercules Graphics Card Plus
- The IBM Enhanced Graphics Adapter (the EGA card)
- The IBM Video Graphics Array (the VGA card)

Just as there are IBM-compatible computers, there are also graphics display cards compatible with those listed above. These compatible cards should work with Word.

Two graphics display cards found in many computers *won't* work with Word:

- The IBM Monochrome Display
- The IBM Color/Graphics Monitor Adapter (the CGA card)

Disk Drives

Many IBM and IBM-compatible computers come with built-in hard-disk drives. Others don't, but your dealer can easily install a hard-disk drive of your choice. The minimum capacity of a hard-disk drive is usually 10 megabytes. Some models have 20, 40, 80, or even more megabytes. Any of these works with Word.

The floppy-disk drive that comes with your computer, whether 5¼-inch or 3½-inch, should work with Word. You need only one floppy-disk drive in your computer system, but you might find two convenient if you copy disks frequently.

The Keyboard

There are two standard types of keyboards: 10-function-key and 12-function-key. Word works with both these types, but it uses the two extra function keys when they're available on the 12-function-key keyboard.

The Monitor

Word works with any monitor attached to your system as long as the monitor works with your graphics display card. If you use an EGA card, the IBM Enhanced Color Display monitor works well. Computers with VGA cards can't use the Enhanced Color Display monitor but work well with the IBM Personal System/2 Color Display monitor. IBM-compatible monitors work just as well with various graphics display cards. Be sure that your dealer or computer service department matches your monitor with the graphics display card in your system.

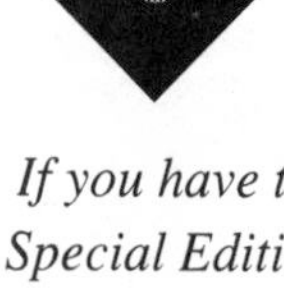

If you have the Special Edition with disks included, consult the Introduction

Printers

Literally hundreds of printers work with Word—expensive laser printers, budget dot-matrix printers, daisy-wheel printers, ink-jet printers, and more. Word works with any printer that connects to your computer system, although not all printers allow Word full use of its features; even Word can't print graphics on a printer that doesn't have graphics capabilities, such as a daisy-wheel printer.

The Mouse

A mouse isn't required for running Word, but adding one to your system makes Word easier and faster to use. Microsoft, IBM, and other companies make mice that work with Word. Be sure that the mouse you use is compatible with either the Microsoft Mouse or the IBM Mouse.

SOFTWARE

In addition to the hardware in your system, you need the following software to run Word:

- MS-DOS version 3.0 or later
- Windows version 2.03 or later, Windows/386, or the run-time version of Windows included with Word
- A printer driver to match your printer
- Microsoft Word for Windows

If you have the Special Edition with disks included, consult the Introduction

MS-DOS

MS-DOS (short for Microsoft Disk Operating System) is the computer's primary system software, necessary to take care of the computer's basic functions. MS-DOS has undergone many revisions, and each revision has its own version number—the higher the number, the later the version. Word works with any version of MS-DOS numbered 3.0 or higher. If you have an earlier version of MS-DOS, you can buy a later version from your computer dealer. (To check your version number, turn on your computer and start MS-DOS. Next, type the command *ver* and press Enter. MS-DOS will then display its version number on your monitor.)

Windows

Windows, another Microsoft product, is an extension of the MS-DOS system software that adds a *graphics interface* to your system. A graphics interface mixes pictures and text on your monitor to present tasks you can accomplish.

You choose the task you want with the keyboard or the mouse. This is usually easier than using the MS-DOS *command line interface,* in which you type commands and see only text in reply.

Like MS-DOS, Windows is updated and given a new version number from time to time. Word works with Windows versions 2.03 and later, Windows/386 (a version for computers with 80386 CPUs), and the run-time version of Windows included with Word. Run-time Windows is a pared-down version of Windows designed to run only Word.

Printer Drivers

If you have the Special Edition with disks included, consult the Introduction

A printer driver is a small piece of software that translates Word's commands into commands your printer can understand. Both Windows and Word include a large set of printer drivers that you can choose from to match the printer in your system. (You choose the driver when you first install Windows on your computer, as discussed later in this chapter.) If you have an unusual printer, be sure your dealer provides you with an appropriate printer driver.

Microsoft Word for Windows

The final piece of software you need, of course, is Microsoft Word for Windows. The software package includes the disks and manuals you need to install Word on your hard-disk drive.

SETTING UP YOUR SYSTEM

When you have all the hardware and software you need to run Word, be sure they're set up properly to run. If your computer system is not yet set up to run, have your dealer or computer service department check that

- All the cards, disk drives, and other internal equipment are installed in the central unit of the computer
- The central processing unit is connected by data cables to all the external components (monitor, keyboard, mouse, and printer)
- All the components that need direct electrical power (central unit, monitor, and printer) are plugged into an AC outlet
- MS-DOS is installed on your hard disk

With all the other elements in place, you can then install Word on your hard disk. When you install Word, it includes its own run-time version of Windows. If you plan to run Word and other software (such as Microsoft Excel or Aldus PageMaker) at the same time, you must buy a full version of Windows and install it on your hard disk before installing Word.

It's possible that your dealer or service department has already installed Word and Windows on your system. If not, it's a simple task that you can do yourself.

Installing Word

Install Word and its version of Windows by running the Setup program that comes on the Word disk labeled Word Setup:

If you have the Special Edition with disks included, consult the Introduction

1. Turn on your computer system (including the central unit and the monitor) and wait for your computer to boot. When the MS-DOS prompt appears (usually *C:>*), the computer is ready for you to install Word.
2. Insert the disk labeled Word Setup in the floppy-disk drive. (If you have two drives, put it in the upper, or A, drive.)
3. Type *a:* and press Enter to make the A drive the active drive.
4. Type *setup* and press Enter.

When Setup runs, it asks you questions about your system, so you need to know the kinds of equipment you have—the mouse, the graphics display card, the type of computer, the brand and model of printer, and so on. (If you aren't familiar with your equipment, ask your dealer or service department what you have in your system.) After you answer the questions, Setup copies all the necessary information from the Word floppy disks onto your hard-disk drive. Setup also determines if there is a full version of Windows on your hard disk. If it finds none, Setup copies the run-time version of Windows. Word is then fully installed on your hard-disk drive.

Installing Windows

If you decide to install a full version of Windows, you'll find complete instructions at the front of the manual included with the Windows package. Installing Windows is almost exactly the same as installing Word: You insert a disk labeled Setup Disk into the floppy-disk drive and then run a program called Setup. Setup asks questions about your equipment and prompts you to insert different disks as it copies information from the floppy disks to the hard-disk drive. When Setup is finished, Windows is installed on your hard-disk drive.

When you're finished installing Word and Windows on your computer system, you can eject any floppy disks still in the drive, shut your system off, and then store the original floppy disks in a safe place. If anything happens to the versions of Word or Windows on your hard-disk drive, you can use the floppies to reinstall them.

A QUICK SUMMARY

In this chapter, you prepared to run Word by checking all your computer's components—the RAM, graphics display card, disk drives, keyboard, monitor, printer, and, of course, computer—to be sure they provide the power necessary to run Word. You also learned which versions of MS-DOS and Windows are necessary to run Word and saw how to install Word and Windows on your system. With all the parts in place, you're ready to move on to the next chapter, where you'll start Word for the first time.

Chapter 2

A Tour of Word for Windows

In this chapter, you start Word for Windows and take a look around. You see the different parts of the Word window and learn how to use Word's menus. You also peek inside the menus to see the commands you can use. Most important, you become familiar with Word's environment—the vocabulary and features you should become comfortable with as you continue to use Word.

STARTING WORD FOR WINDOWS

To start Word, you must turn on your system and start the Winword.exe program from either the MS-DOS command line or from within Windows.

If you have the Special Edition with disks included, consult the Introduction

If you plan to use only the run-time version of Windows (included with Word), you can start Winword.exe only from MS-DOS. Winword.exe then automatically runs the abbreviated version of Windows before it starts Word.

1. Turn on all your equipment.
2. At the first MS-DOS prompt, type *cd \winword* (or the name of whichever directory Word for Windows is in) and press Enter.
3. At the second MS-DOS prompt, type *winword* and press Enter.

If you plan to run the full version of Windows and then run Word with it, first run Windows and then run Winword.exe.

1. Turn on all your equipment.

2. At the first MS-DOS prompt, type *cd \windows* (or whichever directory Windows is in) and press Enter.
3. At the second MS-DOS prompt, type *win* and press Enter.
4. When Windows appears, press the Backspace key to leave the Windows directory.
5. Select Winword (or whichever directory Word for Windows is in) from the list of names in the MS-DOS Executive window, and press Enter to see the contents of the Word directory.
6. Select Winword.exe from the new list of names that appears, and press Enter to run Word.

Word's First Appearance

If this is the first time you've run Word, a dialog box asks you to enter your name and initials. Type your name, using the Backspace key to correct mistakes as you type.

If you have the Special Edition with disks included, consult the Introduction

Word extracts the initials from your name and fills in the Initials text box. When you finish, press Enter, and the dialog box disappears.

Word stores the name and initials you entered to use later as a "name stamp." It adds a small data file to any document you create, identifying you as the author. Don't worry if you think you might want to change the name; you'll learn how to do this later.

THE PARTS OF WORD

Shortly after you start Word, the Word window (shown in Figure 2-1) appears. Each program that runs under Windows appears in its own window. If you're using run-time Windows, only the Word window appears on the screen, and you won't be able to run any other programs. If you're using the full version of Windows, you can often see several windows on the screen at once, each running its own program. In fact, if you started Word using the full version of Windows, then the Word window you now see covers a window underneath it. That window contains MS-DOS Executive, the program that works with files on your disk drive and launches programs such as Word.

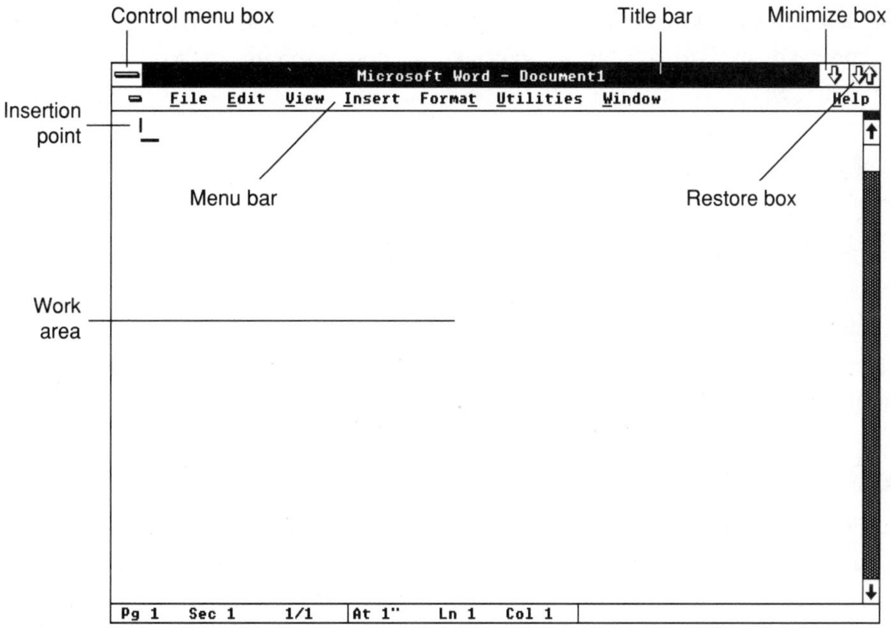

Figure 2-1. *The standard elements of the Word window.*

Standard Window Features

Each window that appears on the Windows screen includes standard elements common to most windows. Figure 2-1 labels the parts of the Word window that are common window elements:

- The *title bar* displays the name of the program running in the window—in this case, "Microsoft Word."
- The *menu bar* shows menu names that you choose to display the program's commands.
- The *Control menu box* offers you special commands that control the window. In the Word window, this is called the *Word Control menu box.*
- The *restore box* shrinks the window if it is full-screen size. The *maximize box* replaces the restore box if the window does not take up the full screen.
- The *minimize box* reduces the window to an *icon,* a tiny symbol tucked away in the corner of the screen.

- The *work area* is the large interior section of the window that the program uses to display its data and special symbols. In Word's window, the work area is called the *text area.*

The Text Area

Word's text area is the area in Word's window that you fill with characters as you type. In its upper left corner is a small, blinking vertical line, the *insertion point.* It marks the spot where you enter text. Try typing something now, and watch the insertion point as you type. It moves across the document window from left to right, leaving characters as it moves. You'll learn more about how to enter text in the next chapter.

The Ruler and the Ribbon

Word offers two important features in the document window that you can use to control the appearance of characters and paragraphs. They are the *ruler* and the *ribbon.* To see these features, turn them on by choosing menu commands. (If you don't know how to do this, see the next section, "Using Menus.")

1. Choose Ribbon from the View menu. The ribbon appears at the top of the document window.
2. Choose Ruler from the View menu. The ruler appears below the ribbon.

The ruler

The ruler, shown in Figure 2-2, has inch markings that progress from left to right and includes a box labeled Style on the left side as well as a row of icons. You use the box, icons, and inch markings to control the appearance of paragraphs in Word documents.

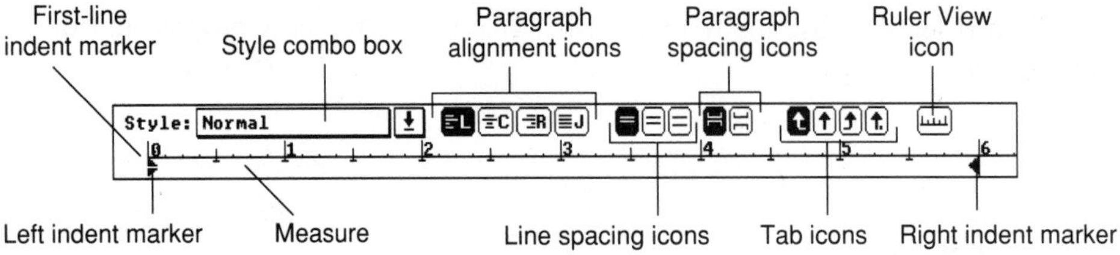

Figure 2-2. *The parts of the ruler.*

The *measure* is the line with inch markings stretching along the ruler. It measures the width of the page area you're typing in. Notice the three markers along the measure, two on the left and one on the right. They show the left, first-line, and right indents of the paragraph you're typing. Moving the markers in and out (as you'll learn to do in Chapter 7) changes the paragraph indents.

The box labeled Style is a *combo box,* a Word control that effectively mixes a menu and a text box. You can type in it or select it to pop down a list of styles. This particular combo box puts one of Word's most powerful features at your command: the ability to control the general appearance of one or several paragraphs by choosing a single style name. You'll learn more about styles in Chapter 15.

Next to the Style combo box are four *paragraph alignment icons.* These icons control the way Word fits text to the indents of the paragraph. They can move text to the left indent (leaving a ragged right indent), center text halfway between the indents, move text to the right indent (leaving a ragged left indent), or fit text on a line so that both left and right indents look smooth (justified text).

The *line spacing icons* control the spacing between the lines you type. You can choose single spacing, "one-and-one-half" spacing, or double spacing. Next to the line spacing icons are the *paragraph spacing icons,* which control the amount of spacing between paragraphs. You can choose no blank lines or one blank line.

The *tab icons* set tab stops along the measure. Special tabs let you align columns of words by their left edges, center columns of words around the tab stop, align columns of words by their right edges, or line up columns of numbers on their decimal points.

The last icon is the *Ruler View icon,* which changes the ruler to show paragraph indents, page margins, or column widths.

You'll learn to use many of the ruler features in the next chapter and in Chapter 8.

The ribbon

Just above the ruler is the ribbon (shown in Figure 2-3 on the following page), which controls the appearance of the characters you type.

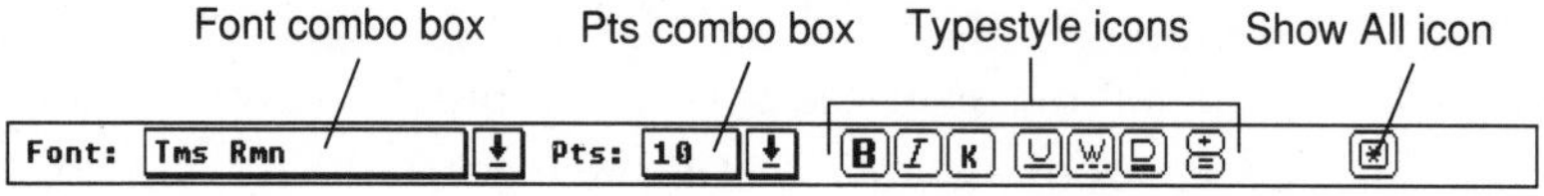

Figure 2-3. *The parts of the ribbon.*

The combo box at the left of the ribbon is the *Font combo box.* It offers you different type styles for characters you type on the screen and print in your documents. To the right of this box is the *Pts combo box,* which controls the size of the characters.

Eight icons to the right of the combo boxes control emphasis you add to your characters: bold, italic, small capitals, three different kinds of underlining, superscripting, and subscripting. These are the *typestyle icons.* One other icon at the far right of the ribbon, the *Show All icon,* makes normally invisible characters (such as paragraph marks) visible for easier editing.

If you have the Special Edition with disks included, consult the Introduction

The Status Bar

At the bottom of the document window is the *status bar,* shown in Figure 2-4. Notice that it is divided into three sections.

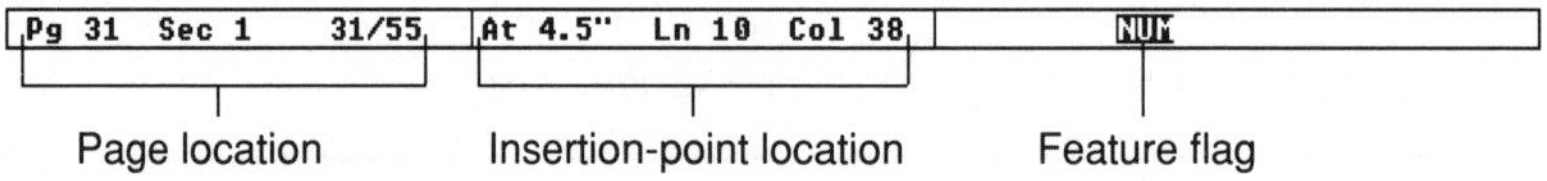

Figure 2-4. *The parts of the status bar.*

The left section shows your page location in a large document. Word documents can comprise hundreds of pages and can be divided into different sections. This part of the status bar shows the section you're looking at, the page number of the text, and the total number of pages in the document.

The middle section of the status bar shows the location of the insertion point in the current page. It lists the distance from the top edge of the page to the insertion point and the line and column number at which the insertion point is located. When you ask Word not to display your document as it will be printed (as you'll learn to do in Chapter 4), this section shows only the column number and doesn't display the distance from the top edge and the line number.

The right section shows the *feature flags.* A feature flag is a small symbol that appears in this part of the status bar when you turn on a Word feature. Feature flags are convenient, especially for features that aren't obvious when they're on. An example of a feature flag is the NUM flag, which appears when you turn on Number Lock on your keyboard. The flag disappears when you turn off Number Lock.

The status bar has a fourth function: presenting messages from Word. For example, as you move through menu commands using the cursor keys, each command you select brings up a short message in the status bar describing the command's function. This message temporarily replaces the normal contents of the status bar and then disappears as soon as you close the menu.

The Scroll Bar

The long vertical bar on the right side of the document window (shown in Figure 2-5) is the *vertical scroll bar.* It serves two purposes: to show you roughly where you are in a document and to let you quickly move your viewpoint from one place to another.

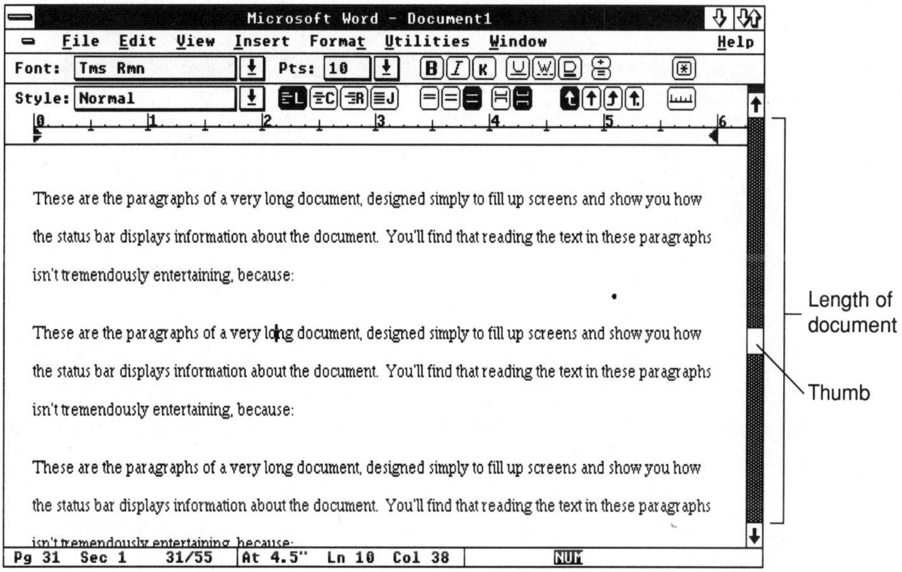

Figure 2-5. *The parts of the scroll bar.*

The shaded bar represents the length of the entire document in the text window. The rectangular box in the bar (called the *thumb*) represents your current location in the document. The thumb can move from the top to the bottom of the shaded bar, representing different locations in the document. You'll learn in Chapter 3 how to move the thumb and use the direction arrows at each end of the scroll bar to choose a new viewpoint location.

USING MENUS

You use the elements of Word's window to control Word quickly and visibly. These controls are convenient, but they offer only a fraction of Word's features. You'll find many more features—both simple and advanced—within Word's menus.

Choosing Commands from Menus

Word's menus function like menus in other Windows programs—each menu lists a set of commands from which you can choose using either the mouse or the keyboard. First, choose the menu you want to open, and then choose the command you want from the menu. Figure 2-6 shows an open Word menu.

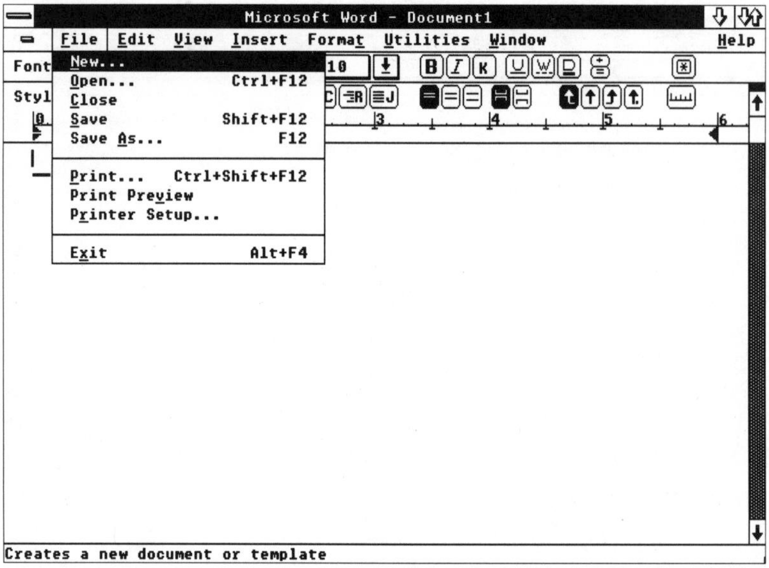

Figure 2-6. *The File menu lists commands you use to store and print Word documents. Note the information given in the status bar about the selected command.*

If you haven't used Windows menus before, a quick lesson should make you comfortable with them.

Choosing a command using a mouse

To open a menu and choose a command using a mouse, move the pointer to a name on the menu bar (or to the Document Control or the Word Control menu box), and click the left mouse button. When the menu drops down, move the pointer to the command you want, and click the left mouse button again. Try choosing the About Word command from the Help menu:

1. Choose Help from the menu bar.
2. Choose About from the menu that drops down.
3. A small box appears with information about Word and the currently available memory and disk space. Move the pointer to OK, and click the left mouse button to clear the box from the screen.

Choosing a command using the keyboard

To open a menu and choose a command using the keyboard, press Alt to select the Document Control menu box in the menu bar. Then press the right cursor key to select the other menu names. Press Enter to open the selected menu. Or use an even faster method: Each menu name has an underlined letter. Press Alt and then the underlined letter. The menu drops down, and the first command is highlighted. To open the Word Control menu (which has no underlined letter), press Alt and then the Spacebar. To open the Document Control menu (labeled with a "-"), press Alt and then the hyphen.

To choose a command from a menu, use the down cursor key to select it, and then press Enter. The menu closes, and the program executes the command. A faster method is to press the underlined letter of the command you want to use. Word executes the command and closes the menu.

Try choosing the About command from the Help menu:

1. Press the Alt key.
2. Press the H key to open the Help menu.
3. Press the A key to choose the About command.
4. A small box appears with information about Word and the currently available memory and disk space. Press Enter to clear the box from the screen.

More Menu Tips

When a menu command is impossible to give (for example, the Cut command when you don't have a text block selected), the command appears dimmed (less bold than the other commands) and is impossible to choose. Some menu commands available have an ellipsis (...) at the end of the command name. This means the command opens up a dialog box. There are times when you want to close a menu without choosing a command. To close with the mouse, simply click outside the menu. To close with the keyboard, press Esc.

A LOOK AT WORD'S MENUS

Word's menus contain different families of commands you use in working with documents. By opening each menu and looking at its contents, you can get a good overview of Word's features. To get an idea of what each command does, use the down cursor key to highlight the commands in the open menu. The status bar displays a short message telling you the function of the highlighted command.

The Document Control Menu

The Document Control menu at the left end of the menu bar is much like the Word Control menu above it. The commands in the Document Control menu are window manipulation commands similar to those in the Word Control menu. The difference is that Document Control menu commands affect only the document window, an area within the Word window, while Word Control menu commands affect the entire Word window.

The File Menu

The three sections of commands in the File menu are separated by horizontal lines. The first group controls document storage. These commands save your documents on disk, recall them later, and start new documents. The second group comprises printing commands. They choose a printer, show how your document will look on paper before you actually print, and print a document when you're ready. The Exit command constitutes the third section. Exit closes Word and returns you to Windows.

The Edit Menu

The commands in the Edit menu let you remove, copy, and move blocks of text in your document with ease and search documents for specific words. They also let you jump to a specific page or location in a long document, create and change text to place at the top and bottom of each printed page, and alter the layout of tables.

The View Menu

One of Word's most powerful features is its ability to show you different views of the same document. The commands in the View menu let you see a document as a condensed outline, as bare-bones text with no special formatting or fancy appearance, or as each page would look when printed. These commands also tailor Word's on-screen appearance by controlling the parts of the document window you see. They can add or remove the ribbon or ruler (special document window tools), open a special area where you can work with footnotes, or change the appearance of the menus.

The Insert Menu

The Insert menu commands offer you items to insert in a document that you can't insert as simple text from the keyboard. These items include footnotes, special location markers, tables designed to align information as you type, and page numbers, among others.

The Format Menu

Use the Format menu commands to control the appearance of your document and the text within. Its commands perform many functions that the ribbon and ruler do. In addition, they let you set special tabs and table layouts so that you can easily align information on the page as you type.

The Utilities Menu

The Utilities menu commands give you a spelling checker, a thesaurus to help you find words as you write, and a function that calculates numbers in your text and inserts the result in another part of your document.

The Window Menu

The commands in the Window menu help you create and handle multiple document windows within the Word window. They arrange document windows in orderly columns and rows and let you easily find a document window covered up by other document windows.

The Help Menu

Come to this menu for information about Word's features. Its commands bring up text telling you about a feature in question and also run tutorials that teach you how to use Word.

If you have the Special Edition with disks included, consult the Introduction

Menu Variations

Word's menus aren't set in stone—you can change their contents to fit your needs. The commands you see in the menus now aren't the full set of available commands. These *short menus* are limited to the most useful and simple Word commands so that they're less confusing to beginning Word users. Later you'll switch to *full menus,* which offer all available Word commands. In Chapter 24, you'll learn an advanced Word feature that lets you create your own custom commands and add them to Word menus.

QUITTING WORD

When you finish your first look at Word, you can quit the program in one of three ways:

- Choose the Close command from the Word Control menu.
- Choose the Exit command from the File menu.
- Double-click on the Word Control menu box.

If you've entered any text, Word asks whether you want to save your work on disk as a document. If you change your mind about quitting, choose the Cancel button by clicking on it or by pressing Tab twice and then pressing Enter. The dialog box disappears, and Word continues to run. To quit now, choose the No button by clicking on it or by pressing Tab once and then pressing Enter. Word quits without saving your work. (You'll learn to save your work in the next chapter.)

If you used Word with the run-time version of Windows, you see the MS-DOS prompt on the screen. You can now turn off your computer, monitor, and printer.

If you used the full version of Windows, you should see the MS-DOS Executive window on the screen, which shows that Windows is still running. Before you turn off your computer system, you should first quit Windows with one of the same three methods you used to quit Word:

- Choose the Close command from the MS-DOS Executive's Control menu.
- Choose the Exit command from the MS-DOS Executive's File menu.
- Double-click on the MS-DOS Executive's Control menu box.

When a dialog box appears and informs you that this will end your Windows session, press Enter. The window closes and you see the MS-DOS prompt once again. You can now turn off your computer system.

A QUICK SUMMARY

You had a quick tour of Word in which you learned about the text window, the ruler, the ribbon, and the status bar. You also learned how to use menus and took a peek at Word's menus to see the different families of commands. Now that you're familiar with Word's environment, you're ready to move on to the next chapter, where you'll create and print a Word document.

Chapter 3

Creating a Document

In this chapter you do your first real work on Word for Windows—you create and print a document. In the process, you learn how to use the computer keyboard, the scroll bar, the Clipboard, the ruler, the ribbon, and the dialog boxes. You also learn how to close a document, how to start a new document, and how to open a document you worked on previously.

THE FIVE STAGES OF DOCUMENT CREATION

You create a Word document in five stages:

- **Entering**—typing the text
- **Editing**—correcting mistakes and revising the text
- **Formatting**—setting the appearance of characters and paragraphs and designing the printed pages of your document
- **Saving**—capturing your document on disk
- **Printing**—sending your document to a printer for output

You don't necessarily go through the stages in the above order. You might print the document before you go back to edit it; you might set formatting as you enter text; and you might (and should) save a document many times as you work on it.

Look closely at the document in Figure 3-1 on the following page. Paragraph indents vary; some text lines are centered; and some words are boldface, italic, or underlined. In this chapter, you'll use the five stages of document creation to re-create this document.

9/9/90

Mr. Orloff Petruchio
General Manager
Typecast, Inc.
4526 Ardentia Lane
Heater, CA 93265

Dear Mr. Petruchio:

I just received the first shipment of 10,000 videotape packages you printed for us. We have a problem. The first paragraph on the back of the package should read:

Helltax!

A Horror Film for the Entire Family...

> When IRS auditor Nicholas Axolotl is possessed by demons, a week of terror begins for the hapless Trunhill family. As blood oozes from stones, each family member must endure merciless and probing questions from disembodied voices about recent spending habits. Realistic portrayals of disallowed deductions and dire fiscal consequences will raise hairs on the back of every viewing adult while putting the kids to sleep. A perfect film for families with overactive children. Rated PG-13.

You mistakenly printed "A perfect film for families with radioactive children" in the last sentence. This severely limits the market for this movie, so we must have the entire run reprinted with corrections at your expense. I've tried to contact you by phone, but have had no luck. Your secretary tells me you're negotiating contracts at the Fresno Film Festival. Please call me immediately when you come back. We ***must*** fix this problem now.

Yours sincerely,

Pieter Geestliefde
Marketing Director
Goretax Films
Oakland, CA 94601

Figure 3-1. *This letter shows Word's ability to format text and paragraphs.*

ENTERING TEXT

You enter text from your computer keyboard. As you type, characters appear in the document window at the insertion point, which moves from left to right. Your keyboard has a standard set of character keys as well as extra keys that you use to perform special functions.

The Keyboard Layout

Figure 3-2 shows the two standard keyboards that most IBM and IBM-compatible computers use.

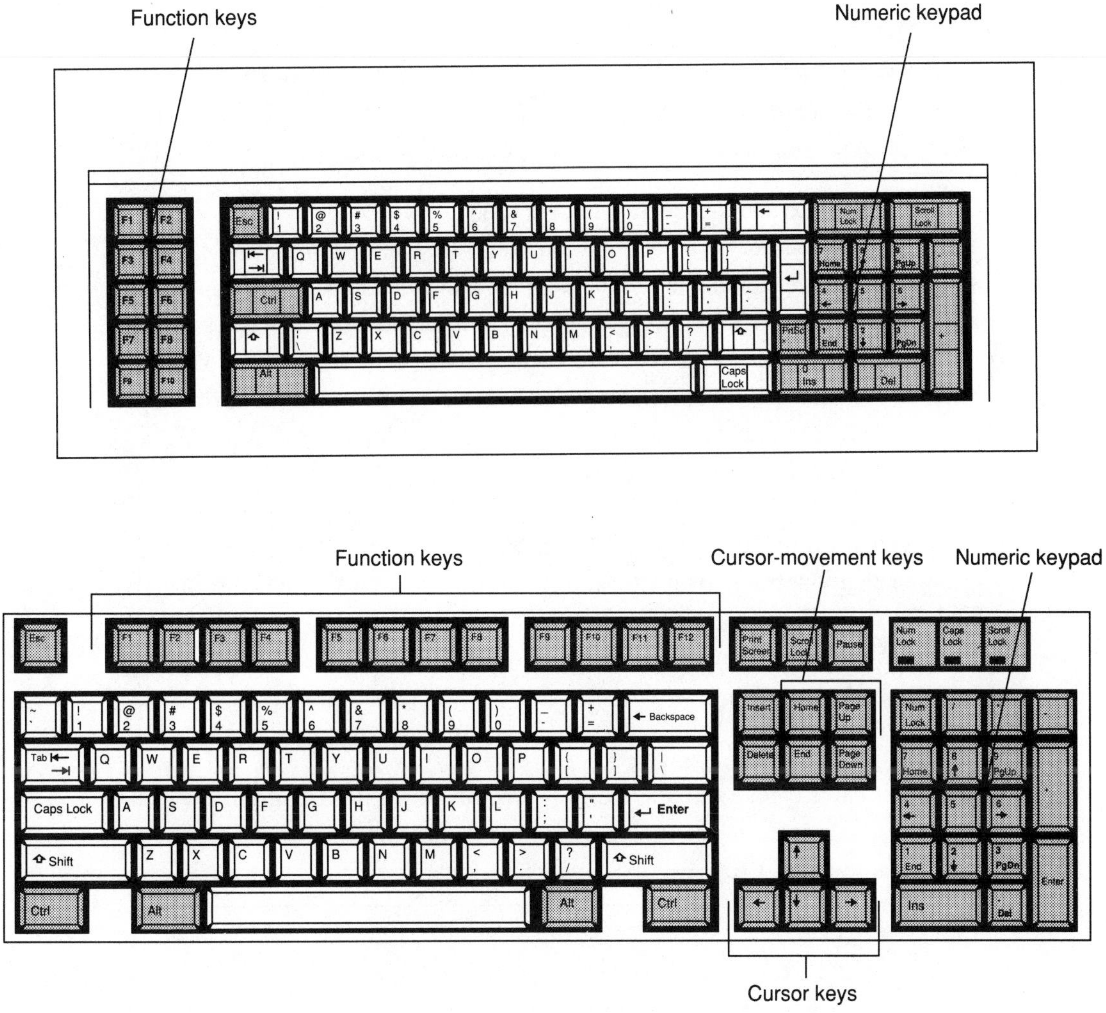

Figure 3-2 *The keys as they appear on a 10-function-key keyboard (top) and on a 12-function-key keyboard (bottom).*

The character keys

When you press a character key, you enter a character in your document. Typical characters are uppercase and lowercase letters, numerals, and symbols. The space is also a character; to enter it, press the Spacebar.

The Tab key

To move the insertion point to the next tab stop to the right, press Tab. When you first start Word, tab stops are at half-inch intervals. (You'll learn to set tab stops in Chapter 8.)

The Shift, Caps Lock, Ctrl, and Alt keys

You use these four keys in combination with other keys. For example, to produce capital letters and the symbols above the numerals in the top row of keys, hold down Shift and press a letter or a numeral key. If you press Caps Lock once, all letters you type are capitalized. (You must still hold down Shift to produce the symbols above the numerals, however.) To turn off the Caps Lock feature, press Caps Lock a second time. A feature flag—CAPS—appears in the status bar when Caps Lock is turned on.

To use Ctrl or Alt, hold down the key and press another key. In this book such keyboard combinations are shown with a hyphen. For example, Ctrl-B indicates that you hold down Ctrl and press B. Shift-Ctrl-F4 indicates that you hold down Shift and Ctrl and press F4 (a function key). In effect, keyboard combinations are shortcuts in Word; you can use them instead of choosing a command from a menu.

The Esc key

You press Esc to leave (escape from) a process you started but don't want to finish. For example, if you open a menu and then decide not to choose a command, simply press Esc.

The Delete and Backspace keys

Use Delete and Backspace to correct errors as you type. Backspace deletes the character to the left of the insertion point and moves the insertion point one position to the left. Delete erases the character to the right of the insertion point; the insertion point stays where it is. (The Delete key on a 10-function-key keyboard is part of the numeric keypad described later.)

The Enter key

Pressing Enter sends the insertion point to the beginning of a new line. In Word, you press Enter to begin a new paragraph, not to begin a new line. Word starts a new line without the Enter key when you type to the right edge of the page. You'll see how this works later in the chapter as you enter the text of the sample document.

The cursor keys

Cursor keys are marked with arrows. When you press a cursor key, the insertion point moves in the direction of the arrow: up, down, left, or right. On 12-function-key keyboards, a set of four cursor keys is located between the numeric keypad and the character keys; 10-function-key keyboards use the 2, 4, 6, and 8 keys of the numeric keypad as cursor keys.

Cursor-movement keys (found above the cursor keys on 12-function-key keyboards and on the numeric keypad on 10-function-key keyboards) move the insertion point in larger jumps:

- *Home* moves the insertion point to the left end of the current line.
- *End* moves the insertion point to the right end of the current line.
- *PgUp* moves the insertion point up one full screen of text and scrolls the document down one screen so that you can see the new text.
- *PgDn* moves the insertion point down one full screen of text and scrolls the document up one screen.

Cursor keys move the insertion point only through text already entered, not out of text and into blank areas of the screen.

The numeric keypad

You can use the numeric keypad to enter numbers as you would with a calculator, but the keys on your computer's numeric keypad also double as cursor and editing keys.

You use the Num Lock key to turn the Number Lock feature on and off. When Number Lock is on, the flag NUM appears in the status bar, and pressing keypad keys enters numbers. When Number Lock is off, the flag disappears, and the keypad controls the insertion point.

Arrows on the keys indicate the direction in which the keys move the insertion point. Home, End, PgUp, and PgDn work like the equivalent cursor-movement keys on a 12-function-key keyboard. Delete erases characters as described earlier, and Insert inserts blocks of text in the text window. You'll learn to use Insert later.

The function keys

You use function keys to perform functions with a single keystroke—for example, to edit text or insert special text. Because function keys initiate actions that can alter your document, don't press a function key unless you know what it does. A complete list of these functions and keyboard shortcuts is in the Appendix.

Entering the Sample Text

First, turn on your computer and start Word. When the document window appears, be sure the ruler and the ribbon appear at the top of the window. If they do not, choose Ruler from the View menu to turn on the ruler and Ribbon, also from the View menu, to turn on the ribbon. When the insertion point appears in the upper left corner of the text area:

1. Type the date and address you see in Figure 3-3. Press Enter at the end of each line. (Press Enter twice to create a blank line.)
2. Type *Dear Mr. Petruchio:* Now press Enter twice and stop.

   If you make mistakes as you type, use Backspace to delete the incorrect characters and then type the correct text. Notice that the text you type doesn't look like the finished document—you'll edit and format later to make it match. Now continue with your letter.
3. Type the first paragraph of the letter body, press Enter twice at the end of the paragraph, and stop. (Don't use Enter to end lines within the paragraph.)

Notice that when you type to the end of a line, Word moves the insertion point and the word you're typing to the beginning of the next line. This feature is called *word wrap;* it lets you type without worrying about running off the edge of the page or splitting words. (You may get different line breaks than those in the examples; Word considers the capabilities of your printer when displaying text.)

9/9/90

Mr. Orloff Petruchio
General Manager
Typecast, Inc.
4526 Ardentia Lane
Heater, CA 93265

Dear Mr. Petruchio:

I just received the first shipment of 10,000 videotape packages you printed for us. We have a problem. The first paragraph on the back of the package should read:

Helltax!

A Horror Film for the Entire Family...

When IRS auditor Nicholas Axolotl is possessed by demons, a week of terror begins for the hapless Trunhill family. As blood oozes from stones, each family member must endure merciless and probing questions from disembodied voices about recent spending habits. Realistic portrayals of disallowed deductions and dire fiscal consequences will raise hairs on the back of every viewing adult while putting the kids to sleep. A perfect film for families with overactive children. Rated PG-13.

You mistakenly printed "A perfect film for families with radioactive children" in the last sentence. This severely limits the market for this movie, so we must have the entire run reprinted with corrections. I've tried to contact you by phone, but have had no luck. Your secretary tells me you're negoshiating contracts at the Film Fresno Festival. I can't believe you did this to me, you poltroon! Please call me immediately. We must fix this problem now.

Yours sincerely,

Pieter Geestliefde
Marketing Director
Goretax Films
Oakland, CA 94601

Figure 3-3. *Enter the text as it appears in this example.*

When you press Enter, Word moves the insertion point to the beginning of the next line—whether or not you're at the end of a line—and interprets Enter as the end of a paragraph. For example, the first lines of the letter you are typing are each separate paragraphs because you pressed Enter at the end of each line.

The content of a paragraph is anything you've typed since the last time you pressed Enter (or since the beginning of the document). For example, the first paragraph of your document is "9/9/90." The second paragraph has no content: It's a blank line you created by pressing Enter twice. This definition of a paragraph is an important word-processing concept. You'll realize its importance later, when you format paragraphs in a document. Continue now with your letter.

1. Type the rest of the document to the end of "Yours sincerely,". Be sure to include any misspellings in the text (you'll correct them later), and remember not to press Enter until the end of each paragraph.
2. To create blank space for a signature, enter four blank lines before the sender's name and address.

Notice that as the window fills up, text at the top of the screen disappears so that you can enter new lines at the bottom of the screen. In the next section, you'll learn how to scroll back to see the text at the top of your document.

EDITING TEXT

After you finish typing your document, you can go back to correct spelling and typing errors. You can also change wording or rearrange ideas. A simple way to change text is to move the insertion point to the characters you want to change, use Backspace and Delete to erase characters, and then type new text. Another way is to select a section of text and use menu commands to edit it.

Moving the Insertion Point

You can use the cursor keys or the mouse to move the insertion point. To use the mouse, point to a new position in the document window and then click the left mouse button. If you click on a spot outside the text, the insertion point goes to the text nearest the pointer. You can't use the mouse to point to text not visible in the window. Instead, use the scroll bar to move to the section of the document you want, and then point and click.

Using the Scroll Bar

Word keeps your entire document in memory, including the sections that are out of sight above and below the window. Because you can see only one part of the document at a time, you must change the view to see another part. To change your view of the document, you can use the cursor keys or the scroll bar.

Moving the thumb of the scroll bar up scrolls your view to an earlier part of the document; moving the thumb down scrolls the view to a later part. To move the thumb with the mouse, point to the thumb and then drag it to a new position along the shaded area of the scroll bar. (To drag, hold down the left mouse button while you roll the mouse and then release the button when the thumb is at the desired position.)

If you have not changed the view since you finished typing our sample document, the bottom part of the letter appears in the text window. Because Word always follows the end of a document with one screen of blank space, the view you see is actually the middle of the document. The scroll bar reflects this: It shows the thumb near the middle of the bar, not at the bottom. Use the scroll bar to move to the top of the document:

1. Move the mouse pointer to the thumb.
2. Hold down the left mouse button.
3. Move the pointer to the top of the scroll bar's shaded area.
4. Release the left mouse button.

The thumb moves to the top of the scroll bar, and the window shows the top of the document. To move the view to any other section of the document, drag the thumb to the approximate location along the scroll bar.

You can move the thumb in two other ways:

- Click on the up or down arrow of the scroll bar, which scrolls the view up or down one line.
- Click on the shaded section of the scroll bar above or below the thumb, which scrolls the view up or down a full screen.

Whenever you use the scroll bar to move the view, the insertion point does not move. To move the insertion point into the document window, point to a character in the window and click with the mouse pointer. If you start to type with the insertion point out of sight, Word switches the view to the location of the insertion point and changes the thumb location to match.

Making Simple Text Corrections

If you typed the letter exactly as it is shown in Figure 3-3, it contains several mistakes. Use the insertion point to correct them, starting with the misspelled word "negoshiating" in the last paragraph of the letter:

1. Use the cursor keys or the scroll bar to move the view to the end of the letter. You must be able to see the last full text paragraph before the closing paragraph.
2. Place the insertion point between the "h" and the "i" of the word "negoshiating" in the last paragraph.
3. Delete the "s" and the "h" by pressing Backspace twice.
4. Type *t* to replace the "s" and "h".

The text moves left to fill in when you delete characters and right to give more space when you type new characters. You can insert as much text as you want; Word pushes following text to the right (and then down to the beginning of the next line when necessary). Insert the phrase "at your expense" at the end of the second sentence in the last paragraph:

1. Place the insertion point between the letter "s" and the period in the sentence that ends "with corrections."
2. Type a space and then type *at your expense*.

The rest of the text in the paragraph moves to the right and then down to following lines to accommodate the inserted phrase.

Selecting Text

Moving the insertion point is an effective way to correct small mistakes, but it's not an easy way to delete or move large sections of text. Word's editing commands are more efficient. To use them, you must first *select* the section of text you want to work on. The easiest way to select text is to indicate both ends of the text by using the insertion point.

Selecting text using the mouse

Move the pointer to the beginning (or end) of the text you want, and then drag the pointer (by holding down the left mouse button) to the other end of the text. Word highlights the text as you drag. When you release the mouse button, the text remains highlighted. This highlighted text is a *text block*. To drag the text selection into an area above or below the current view, move the pointer to the top or bottom border of the document window; Word scrolls up or down in the indicated direction.

Selecting text using the keyboard

First, move the insertion point to the beginning (or end) of the text you want. Next, hold down the Shift key and move the insertion point to the other end of the text. Then release the Shift key. As you move the insertion point, Word highlights the text block. The highlight remains when you release Shift.

Deselecting Text

To *deselect* a block of text (remove the highlight), simply move the insertion point to a new location using the mouse or keyboard.

Using Editing Commands

Once you select a block of text, you can use Word commands to act on that text. Figure 3-4 on the following page shows a block of text selected for deletion. The commands in the Edit menu move and delete blocks of text from your document. Try them now on your letter.

The first block of text you want to change is the sentence "I can't believe you did this to me, you poltroon!", which now seems a bit strong. To delete the sentence, you must first select it. To use the mouse:

1. Move the pointer to the spot immediately before the "I" at the beginning of the sentence.
2. Drag the pointer (holding down the left mouse button) to the spot immediately before the "P" at the beginning of the following sentence and release the button.

To use the keyboard:

1. Use the cursor keys to place the insertion point immediately before the "I" at the beginning of the sentence.
2. Hold down the Shift key and use the cursor keys to place the insertion point immediately before the "P" at the beginning of the following sentence.
3. Release the Shift key.

> You mistakenly printed "A perfect film for families with radioactive children" in the last sentence. This severely limits the market for this movie, so we must have the entire run reprinted with corrections at your expense. I've tried to contact you by phone, but have had no luck. Your secretary tells me you're negotiating contracts at the Film Fresno Festival. I can't believe you did this to me, you poltroon! Please call me immediately. We must fix this problem now.

Figure 3-4. *The highlighted sentence is a text block to be deleted.*

With the sentence selected as shown in Figure 3-4, you can cut it out of your letter.

■ Choose the Cut command from the Edit menu.

The sentence disappears from your letter, and the text following it moves to the left and up.

Now try the Cut and Paste commands to move a word from one location to another. The phrase "Film Fresno Festival" in the last paragraph should be "Fresno Film Festival." To move the word "Film" to a new location behind the word "Fresno":

1. Select the word "Film" and the space following it.
2. Choose the Cut command from the Edit menu. The word "Film" disappears from the letter.
3. Move the insertion point to the spot before the letter "F" of "Festival."
4. Choose the Paste command from the Edit menu. Word inserts "Film" between "Fresno" and "Festival."

The Clipboard

When you use the Cut command, Word removes the selected text from the document and stores it in a part of memory called the *Clipboard.* The Copy command is similar: It creates a copy of the selected text and puts the copy on the Clipboard without removing the original text from the document. The Paste command inserts the contents of the Clipboard into the document at the insertion-point location.

The Clipboard retains only one block of text at a time. When you use Cut or Copy on a new block of text, the old block on the Clipboard is removed from memory and disappears forever! You can use Cut, Copy, and Paste to edit small or large blocks of text, limited only by the amount of memory available to the Clipboard.

FORMATTING TEXT

After you enter and edit text, you can change its appearance to add emphasis and make the document easier to read. This is called *formatting*. Two simple and effective types of formatting you can use are character formatting and paragraph formatting.

Character Formatting

Character formatting changes the appearance of characters. It works in much the same way as editing: You first select a text block and then choose a formatting command to change the appearance of that text. Word offers many kinds of character formatting. The kind likely to work on most printers is *typestyle*. Typestyle is a character style such as italic, boldface, or underlining.

Using boldface

The first word you want to emphasize is the film title "Helltax!" in the middle of the letter. To put it in boldface using the mouse, do the following:

1. Select the word "Helltax!" (including the exclamation mark).
2. Select the B button on the ribbon (located below Utilities in the menu bar).

The word "Helltax!" is now in boldface, which you can easily see when you deselect the word. (If it isn't in boldface, your printer might not support boldfacing. Word knows your printer's capabilities and shows only character formatting your printer supports.)

To put "Helltax!" in boldface using the keyboard:

1. Select the word "Helltax!" (including the exclamation mark).
2. Choose the Character command from the Format menu.

   A dialog box (shown in Figure 3-5 on the following page) opens. It contains the character-formatting options you can select.
3. Press the Tab key three times to select the Bold option.
4. Press the Spacebar once to turn on the Bold option. An X appears in the box.
5. Press Enter.

The dialog box disappears, and "Helltax!" now appears in boldface.

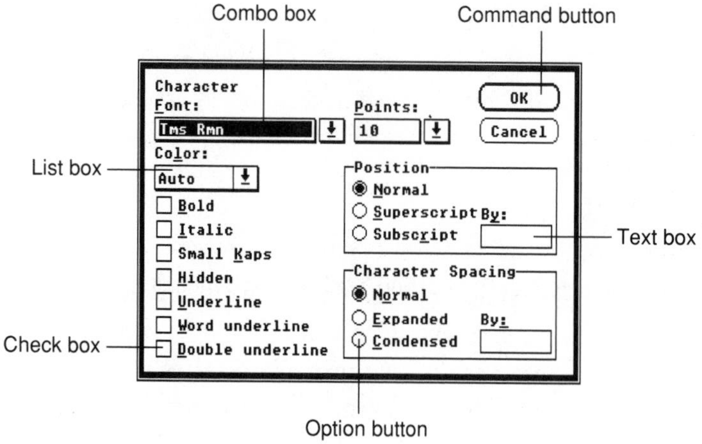

Figure 3-5. *The Format Character dialog box offers character-formatting options.*

Note that although these examples use the mouse with the ribbon and the keyboard with a menu command and dialog box, you can use the mouse to choose commands and work with dialog boxes, and you can also use the keyboard with the ribbon and the ruler. You'll find examples of both uses throughout later chapters in this book.

Using a dialog box

The Format Character dialog box is one of many you'll work with as you use Word. Each dialog box offers options (such as Bold and Italic) that you choose to control the way Word works. Many options are grouped together in a labeled section of the dialog box called an *area.* To move from option to option (or from area to area) with the mouse, you simply click on the option you want. To move with the keyboard, press Tab. Each press moves the selection from one option to the next. (You see the selection either as highlighted text or as a dotted box around the option.)

There are many different types of options. You set each type in a different way:

- An *option button* is a small round button you can turn on and off. These options are found grouped together in an area; you can turn on only one of the option buttons in an area at a time. (For example, the Normal, Expanded, and Condensed options of the Format Character dialog box are all option buttons.) When an option button is turned on, the button is filled with a dot; when turned off, the button is empty. To turn on an option button with the mouse, simply click on it. To turn on an option button with the keyboard, use Tab to move to the option area, and then use the cursor keys to select the option button you want. By selecting it, you turn it on. Press Tab to leave the area.

- A *check box* is an option preceded by a square box. When the option is turned on, the check box is filled with an X; when it's turned off, the box is empty. To turn the check box on and off with the mouse, simply click on it. To use the keyboard, select the option by pressing Tab, and then press the space bar to turn the option on and off.
- A *text box* is a rectangle sometimes filled with text, sometimes empty. You can change the contents or enter new text with the keyboard. To change the contents of a text box, first select it with the mouse or the Tab key. Use the cursor keys, Delete, and Backspace to edit the text in the text box. If any copy in the text box is selected as a text block (as it is when you select the text box with the Tab key or drag over its contents with the mouse pointer), then any typing you do deletes the selected text and replaces it with what you type.
- A *list box* looks like a text box with a down arrow added to its right side. (For example, the Color option in the Format Character dialog box is a list box.) You can't type new text in a list box; instead, you choose from a list of options. To see those options, click on the down arrow with the mouse pointer or select the option with the Tab key, and then press the down cursor key. A list of options opens. To select an option, click on it with the mouse pointer or use the cursor keys to move to it; then press Enter. The list closes, and your new selection appears in the list box.
- A *combo box* looks like a list box with the down arrow slightly detached from the right side. (For example, the Font option in the Format Character dialog box is a combo box.) A combo box combines the functions of a list box and a text box: You can select a combo box and enter text in it, as you do in a list box, or you can click on the down arrow (or use your cursor keys) to open a list of options that you choose from.

- A *command button* is a round-cornered rectangle with a command inside. When you choose a command button, you ask Word to perform a task. (For example, the OK button is a command button that asks Word to close the dialog box and implement all the options you set.) Some command buttons open new dialog boxes (these use an ellipsis [...] in the button); others close the current dialog box. To choose a command button, simply click on it with the mouse or use Tab to select it and press Enter.

Once you set the options you want in a dialog box, choose the OK button (or press Enter) to close the dialog box and put the options into effect. If you decide not to use the options you set, choose the Cancel button or simply press Esc to close the dialog box. Now that you understand dialog boxes, let's go back to the example.

Using underline

Underlining a word is similar to boldfacing, as you can see by underlining the word "radioactive" in the last paragraph:

1. Select the word "radioactive."
2. Click on the U button on the ribbon if you have a mouse, or turn on the Underline option in the Format Character dialog box. (Choose Character from the Format menu, press Tab seven times, press the Spacebar once, and then press Enter.)

"Radioactive" is now underlined.

Combining typestyles

You can combine typestyles for more effect, as you can see by putting the word "must" in the last paragraph into boldface italic:

1. Select the word "must."
2. If you have a mouse, click on the B button and then the I button on the ribbon. To use the keyboard, choose Character from the Format menu, turn on the Italic and Bold options, and press Enter to close the dialog box.

The word now stands out in boldface italic.

Paragraph Formatting

Paragraph formatting changes the indents, line spacing, and other paragraph attributes. To use paragraph format commands, first select one or more paragraphs. Paragraph format commands affect complete paragraphs (remember the definition of a paragraph) whether the entire paragraph or only part of it is selected. If you select a block of text that starts in the middle of one paragraph, includes another full paragraph, and ends in the middle of a third paragraph, any paragraph-formatting command changes the appearance of all three paragraphs, including the parts of the paragraphs not selected. This means that you can select a single paragraph simply by moving the insertion point into it.

Setting indents

The ruler (shown in Figure 3-6) shows you the left and right indents of the paragraph you have selected. The left indent marker is the bottom of two small wedges at the left of the ruler. The top wedge is the first-line indent marker, which shows the left indent of the first line of the paragraph. (This indent can be different from the left indent of the rest of the paragraph.) The large wedge at the right of the ruler is the right indent marker.

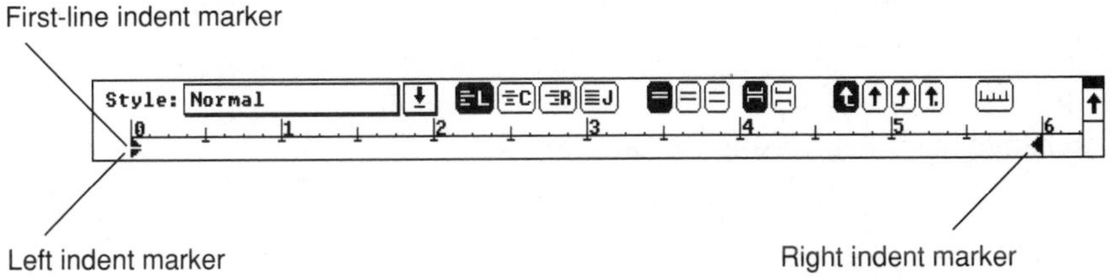

Figure 3-6. *The ruler shows the indents of selected paragraphs.*

You can drag any of these markers using the mouse, or you can use a formatting command to set new paragraph indents. The inch markings on the ruler are measured from the overall document margins, which are normally 1¼ inches from the right and left edges of an 8½-inch-by-11-inch sheet of paper. In other words, the 0 marking on the ruler starts 1¼ inches from the left edge of the paper, and the 6 marking starts 1¼ inches from the right edge.

Setting the left indent. Change the left indent of the paragraph "9/9/90" so that it starts in the middle of the page.

To change the indent setting using the mouse:

1. Move the insertion point into the paragraph so that the ruler shows the paragraph's indent settings.
2. Drag the left indent marker in the ruler from the 0 mark to the 3 mark. The first-line indent marker moves with the left indent marker as you drag it.
3. Release the mouse button. The date moves to the middle of the screen to start at the new left indent setting.

To change the indent setting using the keyboard:

1. Move the insertion point into the paragraph so that the ruler shows the paragraph's indent settings.
2. Choose the Paragraph command from the Format menu. The Format Paragraph dialog box appears.
3. The option Indents From Left is already selected. Type *3* and press Enter to set the new left indent and close the dialog box.

Setting left and right indents. Now try changing both left and right indents in the paragraph describing the movie. A half-inch indention on both sides sets off the paragraph from the rest of the letter as a quotation.

To change the indents using the mouse:

1. Place the insertion point anywhere in the paragraph that begins "When IRS auditor...."
2. Drag the left indent marker in the ruler from the 0 mark to the ½ mark (between the 0 and 1 marks).
3. Drag the right indent marker from the 6 mark to the 5½ mark (between the 5 and 6 marks).

To change the indents using the keyboard:

1. Place the insertion point anywhere in the paragraph that begins "When IRS auditor...."
2. Choose the Paragraph command from the Format menu to open the Format Paragraph dialog box.

3. Type *.5* in the From Left box.
4. Press Tab to move to the From Right box.
5. Type *.5*.
6. Press Enter to close the dialog box and set the new indents.

Setting alignment

While you're working on this paragraph, you can change its alignment to further set it apart from the rest of the text. Paragraphs usually appear *left-aligned;* that is, the left edge of the text lines up evenly, while the right edge is uneven, or ragged. If you use full justification (called simply "justified" in Word), the program fits the words in each line so that both the left and right indents are aligned. To set full justification using the mouse:

- Click on the Justified alignment button in the ruler. It's the fourth button from the left (following the Style combo box) and shows lines of fully justified text.

To set full justification using the keyboard:

1. Choose Paragraph from the Format menu.
2. When the dialog box opens, press Shift-Tab to select the alignment box. (Pressing Shift-Tab moves the selection backward; pressing Tab moves it forward.)
3. Press the right cursor key three times to select Justified.
4. Press Enter to close the dialog box.

Centering a paragraph

You can center each line of a paragraph on the page. For instance, the short paragraphs "Helltax!" and "A Horror Film for the Entire Family..." would look better centered.

To use the mouse to center the paragraphs:

1. Select a text block starting in the middle of "Helltax!" and stretching down to the middle of the word "Film." (Even though both paragraphs aren't fully contained in the text block, they're both fully selected for paragraph formatting.)

2. Click on the Center button on the ruler (the second button from the left, showing centered lines of text).

To use the keyboard to center the paragraphs:

1. Select a text block starting in the middle of "Helltax" and stretching down to the middle of the word "Film." (Even though both paragraphs aren't fully contained in the text block, they're both fully selected for paragraph formatting.)
2. Set Center alignment in the Format Paragraph dialog box. (Press Shift-Tab to select the alignment box, press the right cursor key once to select Center, and press Enter to close the dialog box.)

That's it—you've finished formatting your letter! It should now look much like the original document in Figure 3-1 at the beginning of the chapter.

SAVING A DOCUMENT

Once the document is in its final form with editing and formatting completed, it's wise to save it on disk before you print it. It's even wiser to save a document every 15 minutes as you work on it. If anything fatal happens to your document—the power fails, someone turns off the computer, or something else equally undesirable happens—you can always restart Word and open the latest saved version of the document. Saving every 15 minutes ensures that you will never lose more than 15 minutes' worth of work.

Using the Save Command

The letter has yet to be saved. You can tell by looking at the title bar of the Word window: The document is untitled because you haven't saved it. Saving requires giving the document a name.

Choosing a document name takes some thought. The name must be no longer than eight characters and can contain only letters, numbers, and these symbols: ! @ # $ % & ( ) - _ { }. Try to choose a name that reminds you of the contents of your document.

To save your sample letter:

1. Choose the Save command from the File menu. A Save dialog box appears.

2. Type *petruch* as the name to remind you of the letter's recipient.
3. Press Enter.

Another dialog box appears, in which you can type additional information about the document. For now, press Enter to save the document without additional comments. The dialog box disappears, the status bar indicates that you're saving a document, and the name in the title bar changes to PETRUCH.DOC. Word saves your document on your hard disk in the Winword directory. It appends the extension DOC to the filename, so your letter is stored as PETRUCH.DOC.

If you have the Special Edition with disks included, consult the Introduction

Using the Save As Command

The Save dialog boxes appear only the first time you save a document using the Save command. If you revise your document and choose Save again, Word saves the document under the same filename, erasing the last version and replacing it with the current one. To save a new version without erasing the previous one, use the Save As command on the File menu. It always opens the Save dialog box so that you can enter a new document name. Word then saves your document under the new filename, leaving the previous version stored intact under the old filename. The title bar shows the new name, and each time you use the Save command for this document, Word saves the revision under the new name.

PRINTING A DOCUMENT

The last step in creating a document is printing it on paper. Before you start printing:

1. Be sure your printer is turned on.
2. Be sure your printer is *on line,* ready to accept information from your computer.
3. Be sure the paper is in position to print. The printing mechanism (print head, laser, ink jet, or whatever you have) must be set to start printing at the very top of the page. Your printer manual or dealer can tell you how to set up your paper correctly.

When your printer is ready, you can print your document. Try it now on the letter you created:

1. Choose the Print command from the File menu. A Print dialog box appears.
2. Press Enter to close the dialog box.

The status bar shows that you're printing, and your printer starts to print. The finished printout should look like Figure 3-1 at the beginning of the chapter, with some possible variations: Because the characters a printer uses can differ greatly from printer to printer, your printout may contain characters in a size or typeface different from those in the sample document, which was printed on a laser printer. For example, if your printer normally uses smaller or larger characters, the lines of text may not break at the same points as those in the example. In addition, if your printer doesn't support boldface or underlining, you won't see the emphasis you added to text in the letter. You'll learn in later chapters how to use Word *before* you print to see how your document will look when it comes off your printer.

STARTING A NEW DOCUMENT

When you finish one document and want to start another, use the Close and New commands to close the document you're working on and open a new one. Try it now:

1. Choose the Close command from the File menu. If you've never saved the document, or if you've made changes or printed since you last saved, a dialog box appears, asking whether you want to save changes.
2. To close the dialog box, press Enter to save changes; choose the No button to close without saving. (Choose the Cancel button to keep the document from closing.) When the document closes, the document window disappears from the Word window.
3. Choose the New command from the File menu to open a new document. A dialog box appears.
4. Press Enter to close the dialog box.

A new document window appears.

Opening a Previously Saved Document

To work on a previously saved document, use the Open command:

1. Choose the Open command from the File menu. A dialog box appears.
2. If you know the name of your document, type it in the Open File Name text box and press Enter. The document opens in a new window.

If you don't know the name of your document, the Files box shows the available documents. Choose one by pointing to it and double-clicking with the mouse or by pressing Tab once, using the cursor keys to highlight the name, and pressing Enter. The document opens in a new window.

An easier method is to choose your document from the File menu. Word keeps the filenames of the last four documents you worked on at the end of the File menu. When you choose the filename, Word opens the document in a new window.

Quitting Word

When you ask Word to quit, it always asks you whether you want to save work you haven't already saved. If you've already saved everything, Word quits without the save query.

A QUICK SUMMARY

In this chapter, you took a big step and learned to create and print a document. You went through the five stages of document creation: entering text, editing to correct mistakes and change order, formatting to change the document's appearance, saving the document on disk for later recall, and printing the document on paper. You also learned how to open and close documents. You can use what you learned here to create your own documents, but you've hardly scratched the surface of Word's features. Read the next section of this book to learn more features and see how to create more complex documents with ease.

SECTION TWO

Basics

This section teaches you the basic features of Word for Windows. You learn how to enter and format characters, insert graphics, and edit your work. You also learn how to work with long documents, how to use the full power of paragraph formatting, how to set tabs and add page numbers to your documents, and how to fully control Word's printing and pagination.

Chapter 4

Entering and Formatting Characters

In the previous chapter, you learned to type characters, select a block of text, and change the character formatting of the selected block. This chapter teaches you how to format characters as you type—how to add character to your characters as the inspiration arises! This chapter also shows you how to enter special characters not usually available on your keyboard, explains invisible characters, and shows the ways you can use different fonts, character sizes, and types of emphasis to give your documents distinction.

SETTING UP WORD

Before you start working, set up Word so that you have full menus, so that the ruler, ribbon, status bar, and scroll bar are visible in the document window, and so that the window shows more character varieties:

1. If you haven't done so, turn on your computer and start Word.
2. Choose the Full Menus command from the View menu. (If you find the Short Menus command in the View menu instead of Full Menus, Full Menus is already in effect.)
3. Open the View menu and look at the Ribbon, Ruler, and Status Bar commands. If any of these commands does *not* have a check before it, choose that command. (A check before a menu command shows that its feature is turned on.)

4. Choose the Preferences command from the View menu.
5. When the Preferences dialog box opens, look at the Vertical Scroll Bar option. If the check box is empty, select Vertical Scroll Bar and put a check in the box.
6. Turn off the Display as Printed option (remove the check from its box) and then close the dialog box by using the OK button.

The Display as Printed option restricts the characters you see on the screen to the same type styles your printer can print. If your printer can print only a limited number of type styles, Word can show only those type styles on the screen while Display as Printed is on. When you turn this option off, Word can display a wider variety of type styles on the screen. This lets you try all the examples in this chapter, even if your printer has a limited set of type styles. You might not be able to print the styles you use, but that's not important for our purposes here.

When you quit Word, Word saves your settings on disk. The next time you run Word, it uses the settings you previously had in effect. As you work through the chapters in this section, you don't need to reset commands such as Full Menus—they remain in effect until you turn them off.

ENTERING SPECIAL CHARACTERS

Most of the characters you enter are lowercase letters, numerals, and punctuation marks. You use the Shift key in combination with other keys to produce capital letters and common symbols such as the dollar sign and the percent sign. Word goes even further and offers you a way to produce additional characters—foreign characters and special symbols.

Foreign Characters and Special Symbols

A *character set* is a complete grouping of alphabetic, numeric, and other characters that have a common design. A typical character set includes approximately 190 characters—many more than you can produce by combining Shift with the standard letter and numeral keys. The extra characters are special symbols such as math symbols and editing marks or foreign characters that supplement the Roman alphabet—for example, vowels with umlauts (used in German) and foreign currency marks.

To enter special characters, you first find the character you want in a table listing the full character set. You can find the ANSI character set, the most common set used with Word for Windows, in Appendix C of the *User's Reference*.

To type special symbols, hold down Alt, use the numeric keypad (be sure Number Lock is turned on) to type a 0 followed by the three-digit number for the character you want, and then release Alt. The character you want appears on the screen. (If the character you want has a two-digit number, you must type an extra 0 before the number so that it has three digits in all.)

You can type the sample memo in Figure 4-1 to learn how to enter special characters and use character formatting. The memo contains a sentence with a cent sign, a special character.

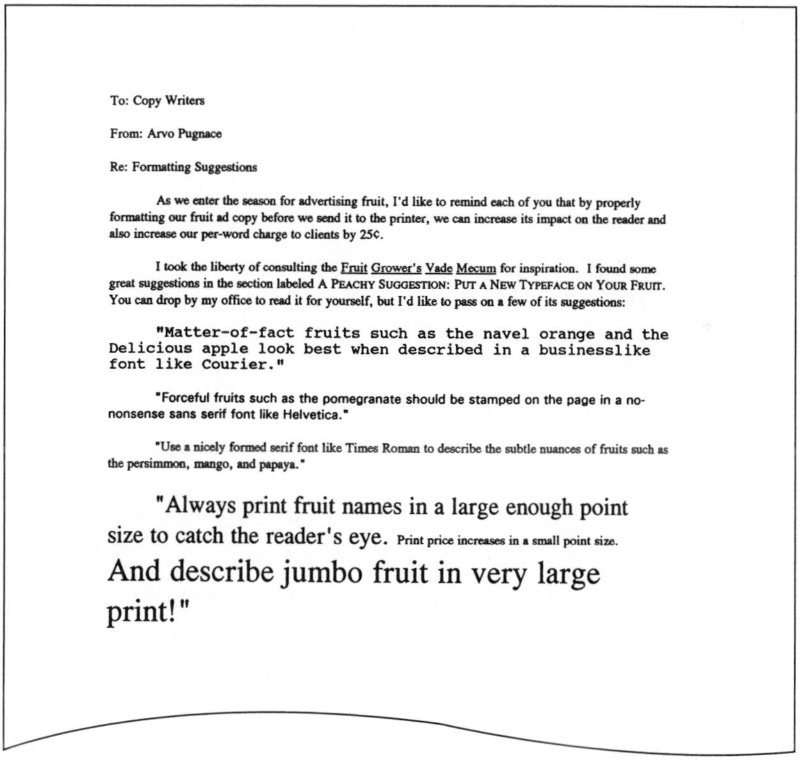

To: Copy Writers

From: Arvo Pugnace

Re: Formatting Suggestions

As we enter the season for advertising fruit, I'd like to remind each of you that by properly formatting our fruit ad copy before we send it to the printer, we can increase its impact on the reader and also increase our per-word charge to clients by 25¢.

I took the liberty of consulting the Fruit Grower's Vade Mecum for inspiration. I found some great suggestions in the section labeled A PEACHY SUGGESTION: PUT A NEW TYPEFACE ON YOUR FRUIT. You can drop by my office to read it for yourself, but I'd like to pass on a few of its suggestions:

"Matter-of-fact fruits such as the navel orange and the Delicious apple look best when described in a businesslike font like Courier."

"Forceful fruits such as the pomegranate should be stamped on the page in a no-nonsense sans serif font like Helvetica."

"Use a nicely formed serif font like Times Roman to describe the subtle nuances of fruits such as the persimmon, mango, and papaya."

"Always print fruit names in a large enough point size to catch the reader's eye. Print price increases in a small point size. And describe jumbo fruit in very large print!"

Figure 4-1. *This sample memo shows special characters and character formatting.*

When you look up the cent sign in the ANSI chart, you find its number: 162. To enter it, first type the text up to the cent sign:

1. Type the sentences in the memo and press Enter twice at the end of each paragraph.
2. Press Tab once at the beginning of each indented paragraph to create the indention.
3. Continue typing the text up to the cent sign, and then stop.
4. Hold down Alt.
5. Type *0162* using the numeric keypad.
6. Release Alt.

When you enter special characters, Word treats them as it treats standard characters. You can select them, format them, and edit them exactly as you would normal characters.

Invisible Characters

Invisible characters are those you enter normally with the keyboard but that don't appear in the text window. The simplest invisible character is the space. Each time you press the Spacebar, the insertion point on the screen moves to the right and leaves a blank space behind it. Although nothing appears on the screen, Word treats that space as a character.

The tab is another invisible character. Each time you press Tab, the insertion point jumps to the right or to the next line if it's at the end of a line. Although nothing appears on the screen, Word treats that tab space as a character.

The paragraph mark is yet another invisible character. When you press Enter at the end of a paragraph, Word places a paragraph mark (¶) at the insertion point's location and then moves the insertion point down to the beginning of a new line. Although the paragraph mark isn't visible, you can select and edit it just as you can the other invisible characters.

It's much easier to select and edit invisible characters if you can see them. To see the invisible characters in the text you typed:

1. Choose the Preferences command from the View menu.

2. When the Preference dialog box appears, check the Show All option.

3. Choose the OK button to close the dialog box.

You now see some previously invisible characters (shown in Figure 4-2).

Spaces in the text appear as dots between other characters, tabs appear as right-pointing arrows, and paragraph marks appear as the traditional proofreader's paragraph mark. Notice that a paragraph mark follows the cent sign even though you didn't press Enter there. Word always starts a new document with a single paragraph mark that follows the end of anything you're typing. A paragraph mark must appear at the end of each document. You cannot delete this mark.

If you no longer want to see the invisible characters, turn off the Show All check box in the Preferences dialog box. If you have a mouse, simply select the small star icon (the Show All icon) at the far right of the ribbon to turn the invisible characters off.

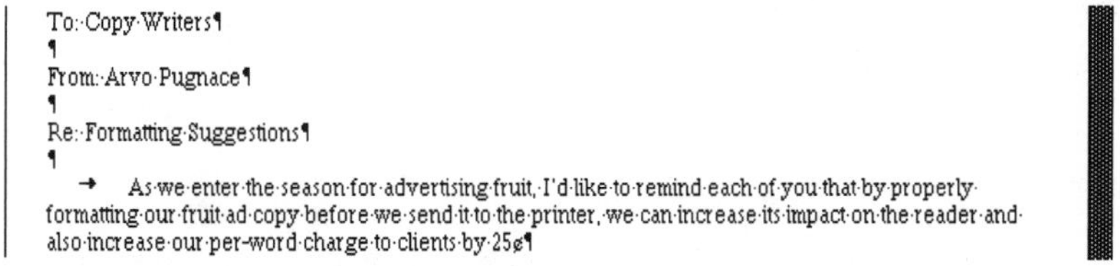

To:·Copy·Writers¶
¶
From:·Arvo·Pugnace¶
¶
Re:·Formatting·Suggestions¶
¶
→ As·we·enter·the·season·for·advertising·fruit,·I'd·like·to·remind·each·of·you·that·by·properly·formatting·our·fruit·ad·copy·before·we·send·it·to·the·printer,·we·can·increase·its·impact·on·the·reader·and·also·increase·our·per-word·charge·to·clients·by·25¢¶

Figure 4-2. *The text you entered earlier now shows all the invisible characters that are present.*

CHARACTER FORMATTING

You already know how to apply some character formatting to text—you applied italics, boldface, and underlining in the previous chapter. These formats are only one type of character formatting—typestyle. Word offers three ways to format typeface characters:

- Changing fonts (the typeface of characters used to display and print text)
- Setting character size (the height and width of the characters)
- Applying typestyles (formats such as underlining and boldface)

Applying Formatting

In the previous chapter, you first entered text, next selected a block of text, and then applied formatting to the selected text. It's often more convenient, however, to apply character formatting as you enter text. To do so, you choose a format, type what you want using that format, and then turn off the format. As long as you have a formatting option turned on, everything you type appears in that format.

For example, to type the sentence "There were two of them!", you would type the text up to the word "two" and then turn on underlining. When you typed "two," it would appear underlined. Before you continued typing, you would turn off underlining so that the rest of the sentence wouldn't be underlined.

Whether you apply formatting as you type or later on selected text, you use any of three application methods:

- The ribbon
- The Format Character command
- Keyboard shortcuts

The ribbon

You use the parts of the ribbon to change character formatting using a mouse. The Font combo box changes fonts; the Pts combo box changes point size. (You learn to use both combo boxes later in the chapter.) The eight icons to the right of the Pts box set typestyles, and the last icon on the right is the Show All icon.

The Format Character command

When you choose the Character command from the Format menu, the Format Character dialog box (shown in Figure 4-3) opens. You use the options there to control character formatting. The Font combo box changes fonts, the Points combo box changes point size, and the Color list box changes the color of characters displayed on a color monitor or printed with a color printer. The seven check boxes turn different typestyles on and off. The buttons in the Position area control superscript and subscript, and the By text box controls the distance above or below the line. The buttons in the Character Spacing area control the spacing on the screen of the characters you enter, and the By text box controls the amount of spacing added or deleted.

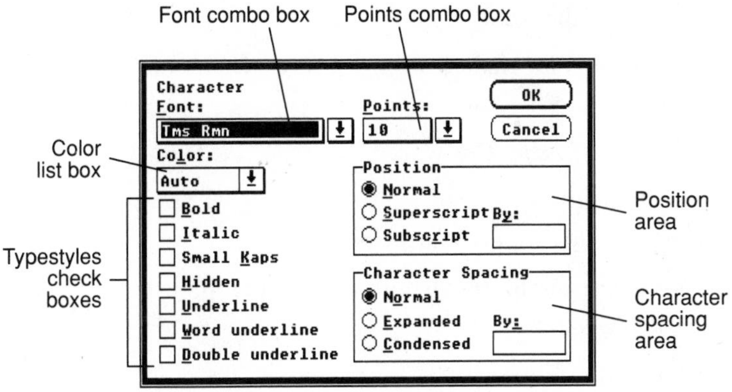

Figure 4-3. *The Format Character dialog box.*

Keyboard shortcuts

Keyboard shortcuts offer most of the formatting power of the ribbon and the Format Character dialog box but allow you to change formats quickly, without your hands leaving the keyboard. Each keyboard shortcut is a combination of Ctrl and a letter key. When you press the key combination, you turn a type of formatting on or off.

Applying Typestyles

Typestyle is the simplest type of character formatting you can apply. It is also the type of character formatting most likely to work with a variety of printers. The memo you started earlier contains a paragraph (shown in Figure 4-4) that demonstrates some typestyles available in Word.

Continue entering the memo to practice applying typestyles as you type. (The invisible characters are visible in the figure. Use them to see where to press Enter, Tab, and use the Spacebar. They don't need to be visible in your document.)

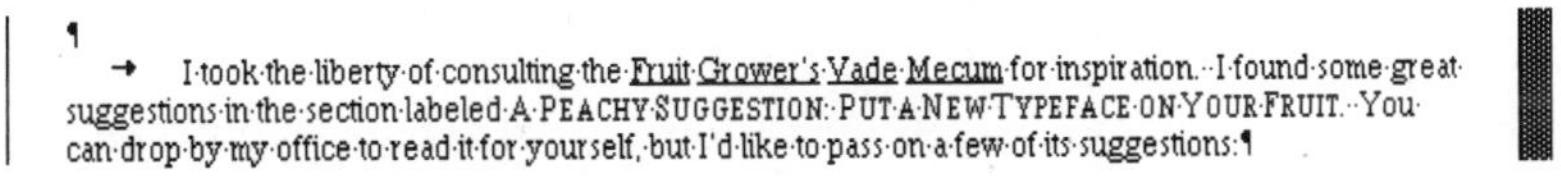

¶
→ I·took·the·liberty·of·consulting·the·Fruit·Grower's·Vade·Mecum·for·inspiration.··I·found·some·great·suggestions·in·the·section·labeled·A·PEACHY·SUGGESTION:·PUT·A·NEW·TYPEFACE·ON·YOUR·FRUIT.··You·can·drop·by·my·office·to·read·it·for·yourself,·but·I'd·like·to·pass·on·a·few·of·its·suggestions:¶

Figure 4-4. *Different typestyles available in Word change the appearance of portions of the text.*

1. Type up to the beginning of the word "Fruit."
2. Press Ctrl-W to turn on Word Underline. (The icon W on the ribbon reverses in color.)
3. Type *Fruit Grower's Vade Mecum.* The words are underlined, but the spaces between them are not.
4. Press Ctrl-W a second time to turn off Word Underline.
5. Type the second sentence up to the beginning of the phrase "A PEACHY SUGGESTION."
6. Press Ctrl-K to turn on Small Kaps.
7. Type *A Peachy Suggestion: Put a New Typeface on Your Fruit.* (Be sure to use uppercase and lowercase letters.)
8. Press Ctrl-K a second time to turn off Small Kaps.
9. Finish typing the rest of the paragraph.

Using a keyboard shortcut as you type is the easiest way to turn typestyles on and off, but it's not the only way. If you forget the key combination you need, you can use the ribbon or the Format Character dialog box to do the same job. Table 4-1 shows the different typestyles you can use as well as the part of the ribbon, the option in the dialog box, or the keyboard shortcut that turns the typestyles on and off.

Note that color typestyles print only on color printers. To set color in the Format Character dialog box, choose any one of eight colors—black, blue, cyan, green, magenta, red, yellow, or white—from the Color list box. If you choose "auto," Word chooses your printer's default color (most likely black). To set color with a keyboard shortcut, press Ctrl-V and then type in the color you want and press Enter when the status bar asks you for a color. (A word of warning: If you choose the same color as the screen's background color, you won't see any of the characters you enter in the text window.)

Hidden text

Hidden text hides text. When you turn it on, any characters you type or have selected become invisible—they don't show up on the screen, even though Word stores them in your document.

Typestyles	*Ribbon Icon*	*Format Character Dialog Box Option*	*Keyboard Shortcut*	*Explanation*
Boldface	B	Bold	Ctrl-B	Makes each character thicker and more emphatic
Italic	I	Italic	Ctrl-I	Slants the top of each character to the right
Small caps	K	Small Kaps	Ctrl-K	Turns lowercase letters into small capital letters; leaves uppercase letters all full height
Underline	U	Underline	Ctrl-U	Places a single line under everything you type, including spaces
Word underline	W	Word Underline	Ctrl-W	Underlines words you type, but not spaces
Double underline	D	Double Underline	Ctrl-D	Places a double line under everything you type, including spaces
Superscript	+	Superscript	Ctrl-=	Reduces size of characters and raises them 3 points
Subscript	=	Subscript	Ctrl-Shift-=	Reduces size of characters and lowers them 3 points
Color	None available	Color	Ctrl-V	Turns characters any one of eight colors

Table 4-1. *Word offers many typestyles.*

To turn hidden text on or off, use either the Hidden option in the Format Character dialog box or the Ctrl-H key combination. There is no button on the ribbon to turn hidden text on and off. To *see* hidden text, select the Hidden Text or Show All option in the View Preferences dialog box or use the Show All icon on the ribbon. Word displays hidden text as characters underlined with a dotted line.

When you print a document that contains hidden text, Word doesn't print the hidden text unless you specifically ask it to. This makes hidden text a useful tool for adding confidential information such as salaries or financial projections to a document. You can print one version of the document that doesn't show hidden text for general release and another, private version that includes the hidden text.

Changing Fonts

A font is a family of characters that have the same design. You can see in this book that the characters in the main body of the text belong to the same font (called a typeface in traditional typesetting). Although you see many different characters and sections of text that are italic or boldface, a stylistic unity ties all the characters in one family together.

To change fonts, you select the new font by its name. In the sample memo, a new font starts at the beginning of the third full paragraph of text. The font you've used so far is listed as Tms Rmn in the Font combo box on the ribbon. It is the first font Word uses when you start a new document. To try choosing a new font, use either the ribbon or the Format Character dialog box at the beginning of the third paragraph.

To use the ribbon if you have a mouse:

1. Click on the down arrow of the Font combo box on the ribbon.
2. When the combo box opens, select the Courier font. (Use the up and down scroll arrows to scroll through the font names. The list will vary depending on how you set up Word and which printer you are using.) The box closes and displays the name of the selected font.
3. Type the paragraph that begins "Matter-of-fact...."

To use the Format Character dialog box:

1. Choose the Character command from the Format menu to open the dialog box. The Font combo box is already selected.
2. Press Alt-down cursor key to open the combo box.
3. Use the up and down cursor keys to scroll through the font names.
4. Select the Courier font and press Enter to close the dialog box.
5. Type the paragraph that begins "Matter-of-fact...."

The paragraph appears in the Courier font.

You can also use a keyboard shortcut to change fonts. Ctrl-F selects the combo box on the ribbon, where you can type the font name or press Alt-down cursor to open the combo box and select a font name. Then press Enter to change to that font. Try it now to change to the Helv font:

1. Press Ctrl-F to select the ribbon's Font combo box.
2. Type *Helv* and press Enter to switch to the Helv font.
3. Type the paragraph that begins "Forceful fruits...."

Now that you've entered two paragraphs using different fonts, switch to the Tms Rmn font for the rest of the memo.

- Choose Tms Rmn from either the ribbon or the Format Character dialog box.

Choosing a Point Size

Changing the point size changes the size of the characters you enter. Character size is measured in *points,* a traditional typesetting unit of measurement equal to approximately 1/72 inch. The point size of a character refers to its height. For example, a 14-point character is taller (and correspondingly wider) than a 10-point character.

Changing the point size is like changing fonts: You choose a size from the Pts combo box on the ribbon or from the Points combo box in the Format Character dialog box. To use a keyboard shortcut, press Ctrl-P to select the Pts combo box on the ribbon so that you can type your own point size.

The last two paragraphs of the memo (shown in Figure 4-5) use text in different point sizes.

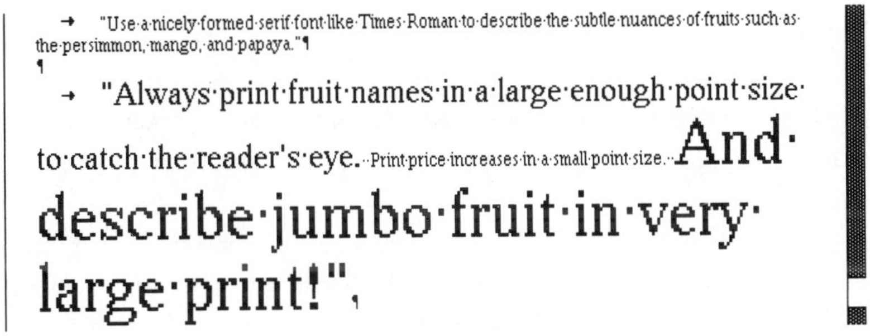

Figure 4-5. *Changing the point size lets you type characters of different sizes.*

To enter this section:

1. Type the first of the two paragraphs using the default 10-point character size.
2. Choose 18 from the Pts combo box on the ribbon or from the Points combo box in the Format Character dialog box.
3. Type the first sentence of the next paragraph.
4. Choose a point size of 8.
5. Type the second sentence.

Notice as you use the 18-point font that Word moves the line of text far enough down to accommodate the larger characters. As you type different-size characters in one line, Word moves the line down far enough from the previous line (or from the top of the document) to make room for the largest characters in the line.

Word has eight point sizes you can use while typing in the Tms Rmn font. To type characters in a point size other than the ones you're offered in the combo box, type the point size directly into the combo box. Try this on the third sentence of the paragraph:

1. Click on the Pts combo box on the ribbon or select the Points combo box in the Format Character dialog box. A blinking insertion point appears in the combo box, and the number in the box is highlighted.
2. Type *36* in the box (to replace the current value) and press Enter to change to a 36-point character size.
3. Type the third sentence.

If you have the Special Edition with disks included, consult the Introduction

If you enter a point size that isn't offered in the size list of the Points combo box, the text you enter using that point size may look particularly jagged. If your printer supports the font and point size you use, however, the characters will be smooth when printed regardless of their appearance on the screen.

As you do the examples in this chapter, note that the fonts and point sizes you use in the text window might not work should you try to print them on a printer that does not support them. Each printer has its own set of fonts that should appear in the Font combo box if you (or your dealer) installed your printer properly in Windows. The "Printers" section of your Word documentation lists all the printers that Word supports. Find your printer there and see what fonts and point sizes it supports. To ensure proper printing of your own documents, use only those fonts and point sizes as you format characters.

Combining Fonts, Sizes, and Typestyles

You can use almost any combination of font, point size, and typestyle to get exactly the effect you want. Although you're limited to one font and one size at a time, you can combine typestyles. For example, you can use a 24-point Helv font with bold, italic, and underline turned on to make an emphatic statement.

Some typestyles, however, can't be combined. You can use only one underline typestyle at a time; choosing any underline typestyle turns off any other underline typestyle. Likewise, you can't use superscript and subscript simultaneously. If you turn one on, the other turns itself off.

Inserting Characters in Formatted Text

After you type text, you can move the insertion point back to the middle of the text and insert more text. When you do, Word applies to your inserted text the formatting—the font, size, and typestyle—of the character immediately to the left of the insertion point. This can save you work as you insert and delete text. For example, move the insertion point to the middle of the phrase "A Peachy Suggestion" and type some text. The text you type will also be in small caps. Move the insertion point to the middle of the word "Vade" and type some text. This text will be underlined to match the text surrounding it.

A QUICK SUMMARY

In this chapter, you learned how to type special characters and change the character formats as you type. You also learned how to use the ribbon, the Format Character dialog box, and keyboard shortcuts to change three types of formatting: font, point size, and typestyles. In the next chapter, you learn how to add flair to your documents by inserting graphics.

Chapter 5

Adding Pictures

If you have the Special Edition with disks included, consult the Introduction

In this chapter, you learn how to add pictures to your documents. If you run Word for Windows under a full version of Windows, you learn how to run Windows Paint, a graphics program, simultaneously with Word. You then see how to store Windows Paint pictures on the Clipboard to insert later in a Word document. If you run Word with its own run-time version of Windows, you learn how to import a TIFF file containing a picture created with another graphics program or a scanner. The chapter goes on to show you how to change the size of a picture in a document, how to trim off excess portions, how to add a border for emphasis, and how to position it in your document.

SETTING UP WORD

In the previous chapter, you turned on full menus, the ruler, the ribbon, and the status bar from the View menu and turned off the Display as Printed feature in the View Preference dialog box. Those settings remain the same for this chapter. In addition, you need to turn on the Pictures option:

1. Turn on your computer and start Word if you haven't done so already.
2. Choose the Preferences command from the View menu to display the View Preferences dialog box.
3. Select the Pictures option if it isn't already turned on (if there is no check in the box).
4. Choose the OK button to close the dialog box.

USING PICTURES

Word can use pictures from many different sources. It can use pictures created in Windows Paint, included with the full version of Windows, or it can use any pictures saved as a TIFF file. TIFF stands for Tagged Image File Format; it is the standard file format used for pictures created with a scanner, a piece of equipment that turns a photograph into the digitized picture used in a computer. Many popular graphics programs can also save their images as TIFF files. TIFF files are usually named with a TIF extension, so they're easy to recognize.

The sample document for this chapter (shown in Figure 5-1) was created using two pictures drawn in Windows Paint: the fancy letter "M" at the beginning of the report and the pie chart in the middle of the report. To create the document, you first run Paint, draw the two pictures, and then transfer

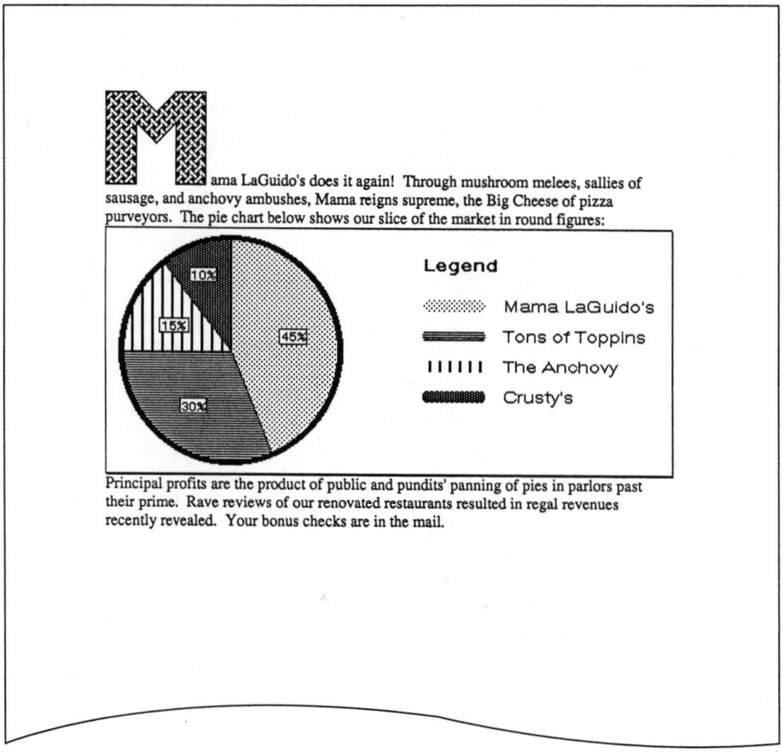

Figure 5-1. *This Word document includes pictures that enhance the text.*

them to Word by selecting them, pasting them into the Clipboard, and inserting them into your document. As you duplicate this report, you'll learn the techniques for importing pictures into your own documents.

If you don't have Windows Paint, you won't be able to recreate the report exactly, but you can approximate it if you have a TIFF file on hand. Instead of creating the "M" pictured and inserting it in the document as described, simply type in a very large boldface M at the beginning of the first sentence. When it comes time to insert the pie chart picture, follow the instructions for inserting a TIFF file. Your TIFF picture will be completely different from the pie chart, and you may not be able to follow the example exactly when it comes to resizing, cropping, and bordering the picture, but you can at least get a general idea of how to work with pictures in Word.

Running Windows Paint

Because Paint runs under Windows, you can run Paint at the same time as you run Word. To start Paint:

1. Press Alt-Esc until you see the MS-DOS Executive window. (If only the MS-DOS Executive icon appears, press Alt-F5 to restore it to full size.)
2. Move to the directory that contains the filename PAINT.EXE. (PAINT.EXE is located in the Windows directory if you installed Windows using the Windows Install program.)
3. Start Paint by selecting PAINT.EXE and pressing Enter or by double-clicking on the filename.
4. When the Paint window opens, click on its Maximize box (or choose the Maximize command from the Control menu) so that Paint fills the entire screen.
5. Open the Options menu and select the For Printer option. For Printer ensures that the graphics you create have the right proportion and resolution to work with your printer. If you use the For Screen option instead, the pictures you create and add to your documents might not print correctly.

Once Paint is running in its own window, you can switch back to Word and MS-DOS Executive by pressing Alt-Esc, which brings open windows to the top of the screen. For now, use Paint to create the two pictures you need.

Creating a Picture

If you don't know how to use Paint, read the Paint section of the Windows manual. It describes Paint's tools and commands and includes a sample picture you can create. That picture is the pie chart you'll use in the report.

The first picture you create, however, is the capital "M" in the report's first line. Although it looks like an elaborate font, it's actually a picture. To create the letter:

1. Use the Line tool to create an outline of the letter "M."
2. Choose the Patterns command from the Palette menu to open the Palette box.
3. Choose a crosshatch pattern and close the Palette box.
4. Use the Fill tool to fill the "M" with the crosshatch pattern.
5. Save your picture on disk as BIGM. (Windows adds the extension MSP for you.)

The second picture you must create is the pie chart in the middle of the report. You can try it on your own or follow the instructions in the Paint section of the Windows manual. When you finish, save your chart on disk as PIECHART.

Transferring a Picture to the Clipboard

To transfer a picture to the Clipboard, you first select a section of the picture. You can do this using either the Selection Rectangle or the Selection Net, both of which are located at the far left of Paint's Tool palette. Use the Selection Rectangle to draw a rectangle around a section and select everything within the rectangle. Use the Selection Net to draw a freehand boundary around an object without inadvertently selecting nearby objects.

After you select a section of a picture, use either the Cut or the Copy command on the Edit menu to transfer your selection to the Clipboard. The Cut command removes the selected section from the picture, while the Copy command leaves the selected section in the picture.

To transfer the "M" you created to the Clipboard:

1. Open the file BIGM.MSP you created earlier.
2. Use the Selection Net to draw a circle around the "M."

3. Choose the Copy command from the Edit menu to transfer the "M" to the Clipboard.

When you used the Selection Net, it pulled the borders of the area you selected tightly around the "M" to include the smallest amount of blank space possible. If you had used the Selection Rectangle, it would have included any blank space you surrounded with the rectangle. Using the Selection Net helps you do less trimming after you bring the picture into Word.

As long as you're in Paint, why shouldn't you put the pie chart on the Clipboard, too? Because the Clipboard holds only one object at a time, whether it's a block of text or a section of a picture. If you put a block of text on the Clipboard by using the Cut or Copy command in Word and then moved to Paint and put a picture on the Clipboard, the Clipboard would erase your block of text. If you moved back to Word and cut or copied a block of text, the Clipboard would erase your picture. Be careful to use the Clipboard for only one element at a time.

ADDING A PICTURE TO A DOCUMENT

Now that you have a picture on the Clipboard, you can return to Word, where you use the Paste command to add the picture to a document. You can then use Word's picture editing features to trim unwanted sections of the picture, resize the picture to fit your document, add a border, and position the picture the way you want.

Pasting Pictures

To return to Word and insert the "M" in the report:

1. Press Alt-Esc until the Word window returns to the screen.
2. Choose the Paste command from the Edit menu. The "M" appears at the beginning of the new document, and the cursor appears to its right.
3. Set the type size to 12 points.
4. Press the Spacebar to add some room between the "M" and the text that follows, and then type the text of the document. Stop after pressing Enter at the end of the first paragraph. Figure 5-2 on the following page shows the text with the paragraph marks.

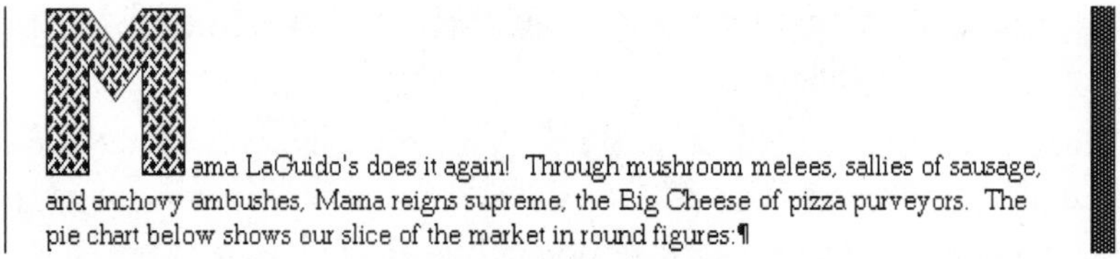

Figure 5-2. *The first paragraph of the report with paragraph marks made visible.*

Notice that Word pushes down the line of characters containing the picture to accommodate the height of the picture, as it does to accommodate the height of large fonts.

Now insert the pie chart into the report. (If you don't have Windows Paint, skip to the instructions for inserting a TIFF file.)

1. Press Alt-Esc until the Paint window returns to the screen.
2. Open the file PIECHART.MSP for the pie chart picture.
3. Use the Selection Rectangle to select the pie chart and the four pizza parlor names to its right. (You don't want the "Market Share" label below it.)
4. Choose the Copy command from the Edit menu to copy the selection to the Clipboard.
5. Choose the Close command from the Control menu to close Paint. (You don't need to use Paint anymore, and closing it frees up memory that Word can use.)
6. Press Alt-Esc if necessary to return to Word.
7. Choose Paste from the Edit menu. The pie chart appears.
8. Press Enter to start a new paragraph.
9. Finish typing the document, using Figure 5-3 as a guideline.

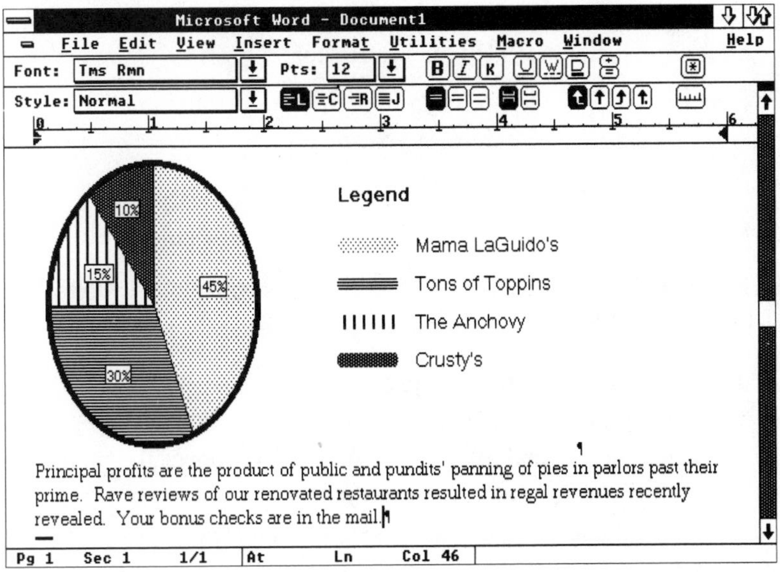

Figure 5-3. *The end of the report with paragraph marks made visible.*

Inserting a TIFF file

If you don't have Windows Paint but have a TIFF picture you can use in place of the pie chart, try importing it.

1. Choose Picture from the Insert menu to open the Insert Picture dialog box (shown in Figure 5-4).

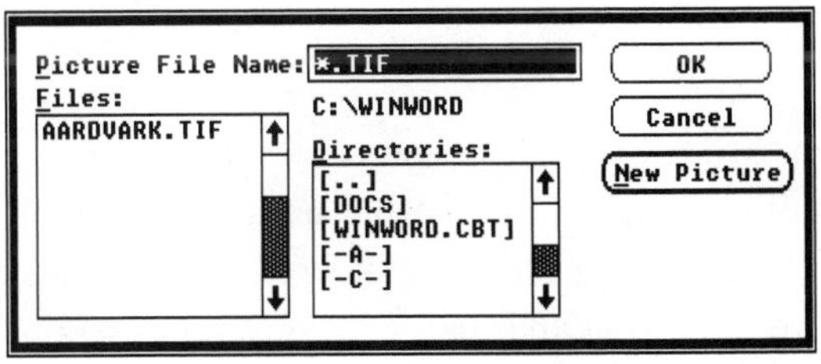

Figure 5-4. *Use the Insert Picture dialog box to insert TIFF pictures or to create empty areas or boxes in a document.*

2. Use the Directories scrolling list, if necessary, to change to the directory where your TIFF picture is stored.
3. Select your TIFF picture from the scrolling list and press Enter to close the dialog box and insert your picture.
4. Press Enter to start a new paragraph.
5. Finish typing the document, using Figure 5-3 as a guideline.

Chances are that your picture isn't the same size as the pie chart, but you can still use it as a rough example in the steps that follow.

Notes about pasting and inserting pictures

When you insert a picture in a document, Word treats it as a single character. You can type text before and after the picture; Word moves the picture in the paragraph as you change the text preceding it. Because you pressed Enter immediately after inserting the pie chart, you created a paragraph with a single character: the pie chart picture. You'll format the paragraph later in this chapter to center the picture.

A quick sidelight on inserting pictures: You can insert an open space in your document by choosing the Picture command from the Insert menu and choosing the New Picture option. This procedure inserts a blank picture measuring one inch by one inch into your document. You can move this picture around, change its size, and add a border. Use the Insert Picture command to create open areas or empty boxes in your document without using Windows Paint.

Formatting Pictures

After you insert a picture in a document, you can select the picture in the same way as you select a single character. You can then use Word's picture formatting features to *scale* the picture, a process that stretches or shrinks the picture, or to *crop* the picture, a process that trims off unwanted sections of the picture or adds empty space around its edges. You can also add different kinds of borders to the picture.

Selecting

You can select a picture in a document in three ways: *1)* Drag the mouse pointer across it from left to right (or right to left), *2)* click in the middle of the picture, or *3)* position the insertion point to the right or left of the picture and hold down Shift as you use a cursor key to move the insertion point across the picture.

Select the pie chart picture so that you can practice cropping and scaling:

- If you're using a mouse, click the mouse pointer in the middle of the picture.
- If you're using the keyboard, Move the insertion point to the left of the picture, and hold down Shift as you press the right cursor key.

When the picture is selected, you see it surrounded by a frame (shown in Figure 5-5) that has eight small squares along its borders. These squares are called *sizing handles*. You drag the sizing handles with the mouse to scale and crop the picture.

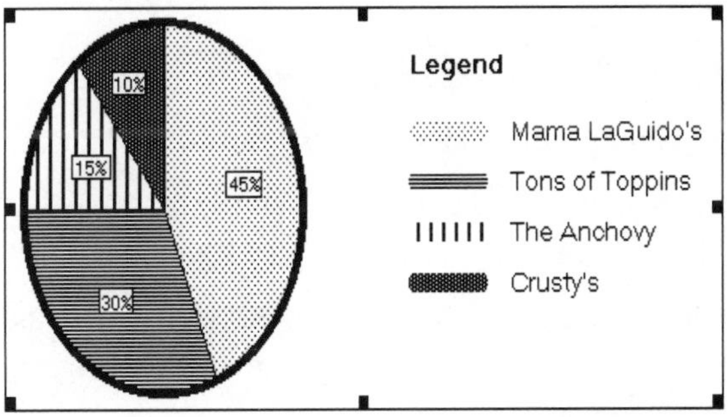

Figure 5-5. *When a picture is selected, it shows a border frame with sizing handles.*

Cropping

You can use either of two methods to crop a selected picture. You can use the mouse and the sizing handles, or you can use the Format Picture command.

To crop a picture using the mouse, you drag any sizing handle to move the picture's border to a new location. Dragging toward the center removes part of the picture, and dragging away from the center adds space to the picture. Each sizing handle on the *side* of a border drags its side inward and outward. Each sizing handle in a *corner* drags two borders at once. As you drag the sizing handles, the status bar tells you by how many inches you're cropping the border(s).

To crop a picture using the keyboard, choose Picture from the Format menu. The Format Picture dialog box (shown in Figure 5-6) appears. The four boxes labeled "Crop From" control cropping. You can select any boxes and enter a value in inches to move the border of the picture toward the center by that distance. For example, if you selected the Top box and entered a value of *0.5*, Word would strip the top half inch off the picture. If you entered a negative value, such as *–0.5*, Word would add a half inch to the top of the picture.

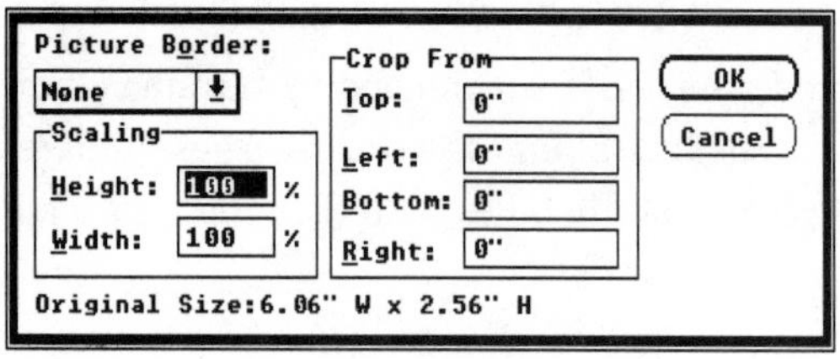

Figure 5-6. *The Format Picture dialog box.*

If you have a mouse, try cropping the picture using the sizing handles:

1. Drag the right border's sizing handle to the left until the status bar reads Cropping: 2" Right. This crops the pizza parlor names.
2. Drag the right border's sizing handle back to the right until the status bar reads 0" Right. This returns the picture to its original size and restores the pizza parlor names.
3. Drag the sizing handle in the lower right corner up and to the left. This crops two borders at once.
4. Drag the lower right corner's sizing handle back to its original position (until the status bar reads 0" and 0"). The picture returns to its original size.

Now try cropping the pie chart using the Format Picture command:

1. Choose the Picture command from the Format menu to open the Format Picture dialog box.
2. Press Shift-Tab four times to select the Right cropping box.
3. Enter *2* to crop 2 inches from the right side of the picture.
4. Choose the OK button to close the dialog box. The right side of the pie chart is cropped so that the pizza parlor names no longer appear.

5. Return the picture to its original state by opening the dialog box again, entering *0* in the Right cropping box, and closing the dialog box using the OK button.

Whenever you crop a picture, Word retains the entire picture in memory and on disk when you save the document. You can crop the picture again anytime to restore contents you previously trimmed.

Scaling

You scale (stretch or shrink) a picture using the same controls as those you use to crop: the sizing handles and the Format Picture dialog box. If you hold down Shift and drag the sizing handles, you scale the picture instead of cropping it.

The Format Picture dialog box contains two boxes (labeled Scaling) that control the amount of horizontal or vertical "stretch." You enter a percentage value in these boxes: values less than 100% shrink the picture, and values greater than 100% stretch the picture.

If you have a mouse, try shrinking and then stretching the pie chart by using the sizing handles:

1. Hold down the Shift key and drag the right border's sizing handle toward the center of the picture. The picture shrinks horizontally as the status bar reports the percentage.
2. Hold down the Shift key and drag the upper right corner's sizing handle away from the center. The picture stretches equally in vertical and horizontal directions while the status bar reports the amount.
3. Use the Shift key and sizing handles to return the picture to its original dimensions. (The status bar should read 100% vertical and 100% horizontal when you finish.)

Now try shrinking and stretching using the Format Picture dialog box:

1. Choose Picture from the Format menu to open the dialog box.
2. Choose the Height Scaling box and enter *75*.
3. Choose the Width Scaling box and enter *50*.

4. Close the dialog box using the OK button. The picture shrinks to 75% of its original height and 50% of its original width.
5. Open the dialog box again and enter scaling height and width values of 100. Close the box using the OK button. The picture reappears in its original size.

Notice that as you scale the picture, its elements become distorted, especially the lettering. Some pictures respond well to scaling, while others might become too distorted to use.

Adding a border

Sometimes you need a border around a picture to keep it from looking "lost" on the page. To add a border, you first set the picture boundaries, if necessary, by cropping. You then use the Border combo box in the Format Picture dialog box. Try adding a border to the pie chart:

1. Crop the picture so that the borders are evenly spaced around the pie chart and labels.
2. Open the Format Picture dialog box.
3. Select the combo box labeled Border.
4. Choose the Shadow option and then close the dialog box using the OK button.

The picture now has a border with a shadow effect along the right and bottom. To see the border more clearly, deselect the picture. The other options in the Border combo box offer borders of a single thin line, a single thick line, double thin lines, or no border at all. You can choose any of these to fit the style of your document.

Positioning

You can move a picture to a different position in a document by selecting the picture and then using Cut, Copy, and Paste to move it as you would move a word or a single character. If you create a paragraph containing only the picture, you can position the picture as you would a paragraph. To add space above and below the picture, you use Enter to add blank lines. To move the picture from left to right, you can change either the indents or the alignment of the paragraph.

The pie chart paragraph is currently aligned flush left, so that the picture is against the left indent. When you change the indent, you change the horizontal location of the picture:

1. Select the pie chart paragraph if it's not currently selected.
2. Use the ruler or the Format Paragraph dialog box to change the first-line indent to 2 inches. (The first-line indent controls the picture location because there is only one line in the paragraph.) The picture moves so that its left border is 2 inches from the left margin of the document.
3. Reset both indents to 0. The picture returns to its original position.

Setting the left indent when the picture is aligned flush left is a convenient way to position the picture in the precise horizontal location you want. To center the picture, you can simply choose center alignment:

- Click on the center alignment button in the ruler or choose the Center Alignment option in the Format Paragraph dialog box. The picture moves to the horizontal center of the document.

A QUICK SUMMARY

In this chapter, you learned to transfer a picture from Windows Paint to Word via the Clipboard. You saw that Word treats an inserted picture as a single character you can cut, copy, and paste as you would other characters. You also learned how to scale and crop pictures, how to add a border for emphasis, and how to position a picture where you want it in the document. In the next chapter, you learn to use special tools to edit the characters and pictures in your documents.

Chapter 6

Editing Tools:

Text Selection, Search and Replace, Bookmarks, and Go To

This chapter is about the tools that Word for Windows offers to help you edit your documents. In it, you learn more fundamentals of editing in Word—moving the view and the insertion point and selecting sections of text. You also learn to use some new editing tools: the Search and Replace commands, which let you change words, phrases, or formatting throughout a document; the Bookmark command, which helps you mark text for later reference; and the Go To command, which lets you jump to a specific location in a long document.

SETTING UP WORD

You can use the examples in this chapter without changing any of the Word settings in effect from the previous chapter. Those settings include:

- Full menus
- A text window that shows the ruler, ribbon, and status bar
- The Display as Printed option turned off and the Pictures option turned on (in the View Preferences dialog box)

The examples in this chapter require a long document that you can scroll through and edit. With some help from the Copy and Paste commands, you can duplicate the paragraph in Figure 6-1 to create a long document with a minimum of typing:

→ One: Bold people often embolden their words with **bold characters** to imbue a sense of solid strength. Other people use italic to add flair and sophistication to their writing. They hint that their content is *outstanding, something you really want to know!* Many people prefer to use underlines, often with the effect of pointing a finger at you as they speak: "You'd better pay attention or there will be dire consequences!" I prefer to mix styles of emphasis to ***thoroughly confuse everybody*** .¶
¶
¶

Figure 6-1. *Type this paragraph to start the sample document.*

1. Set the character size to 12 points.
2. Type the paragraph shown in Figure 6-1. Use formatting—boldface, underlining, and italic—wherever you see it. The invisible characters show you where to press Tab and Enter. Be sure to press Enter twice at the end of the paragraph to create a blank line following the paragraph.
3. Select a block of text extending from the first character of the paragraph to the end of the blank line.
4. Choose the Copy command from the Edit menu to place a copy of the text block on the Clipboard.
5. Move the insertion point to the end of the document.
6. Choose the Paste command from the Edit menu 20 times to insert 20 copies of the paragraph into the document (or press Shift-Ins as a shortcut for the Paste command). Each paragraph should be separated from the next by a blank line.
7. Save the document under the name LONGTEXT.

You now have a four-page document to use with the editing examples in this chapter.

MOVING THE INSERTION POINT

In Chapter 3 you learned to move the insertion point a character or line at a time by using the cursor keys. In longer documents you'll find this a slow process. You can speed up the process by using keyboard shortcuts that move the insertion point through larger sections of text—a word, sentence, paragraph, window of text, or even the entire document.

Table 6-1 shows the keys and key combinations that move the insertion point. Try them on your sample document:

Insertion-Point Movement	*Key or Key Combination*
Single character forward	Right cursor
Single character backward	Left cursor
Single line up	Up cursor
Single line down	Down cursor
Beginning of the current line	Home
End of the current line	End
Beginning of the current word	Ctrl-left cursor
Beginning of the next word	Ctrl-right cursor
Beginning of the current paragraph	Ctrl-up cursor
Beginning of the next paragraph	Ctrl-down cursor
Beginning of the document	Ctrl-Home
End of the document	Ctrl-End
Up one window of text	PgUp
Down one window of text	PgDn
Beginning of the current window of text	Ctrl-PgUp
End of the current window of text	Ctrl-PgDn

Table 6-1. *Keyboard shortcuts for moving the insertion point.*

Use these keys and key combinations to move the insertion point to a new location. For example, if you typed a sentence and noticed that you forgot to capitalize the first letter of the paragraph, you would press Ctrl-up cursor to jump back to the beginning of the paragraph, where you could correct your mistake. Pressing Ctrl-End would return the insertion point to the end of the document, where you could resume typing.

As you work with a document, you'll sometimes need to move the insertion point to a distant location and then return to your previous location. Press Shift-F5 to move the insertion point to its previous location.

SELECTING TEXT

You learned in Chapter 3 to select text by holding down Shift as you use the cursor keys or by dragging the pointer across text. Word offers faster ways to select text.

Using Mouse Shortcuts

Word gives you mouse shortcuts for accurate text selection. These shortcuts make use of double-clicking and an area of the text window called the *selection bar*. The selection bar is a thin, vertical, blank area of the document window immediately to the left of the text. When you move the pointer to the selection bar, the pointer becomes a right-pointing arrow. Figure 6-2 shows the pointer resting in the selection bar.

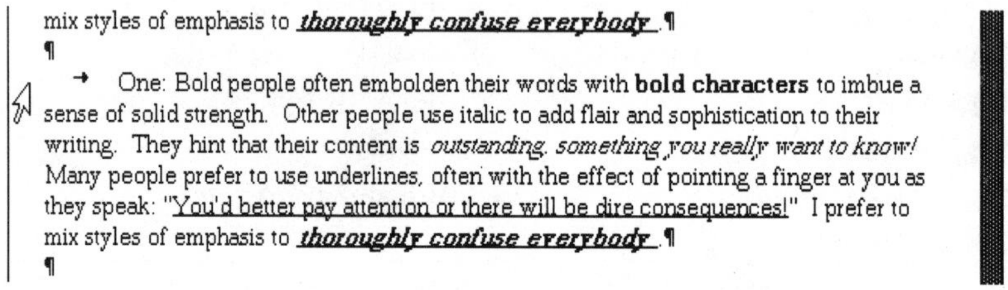
mix styles of emphasis to ***thoroughly confuse everybody***.¶
¶
→ One: Bold people often embolden their words with **bold characters** to imbue a sense of solid strength. Other people use italic to add flair and sophistication to their writing. They hint that their content is *outstanding, something you really want to know!* Many people prefer to use underlines, often with the effect of pointing a finger at you as they speak: "You'd better pay attention or there will be dire consequences!" I prefer to mix styles of emphasis to ***thoroughly confuse everybody***.¶
¶

Figure 6-2. *The pointer changes to a right-pointing arrow when it is in the selection bar.*

Different shortcuts select specific blocks of text:

- To select a word: Place the pointer in the word and double-click the left mouse button.
- To select a sentence: Place the pointer in the sentence, hold down Ctrl, and click the left mouse button.
- To select a line: Place the pointer in the selection bar immediately to the left of the line and click the left mouse button.
- To select a paragraph: Place the pointer in the selection bar immediately to the left of the paragraph and double-click the left mouse button.
- To select the entire document: Place the pointer anywhere in the selection bar, hold down Ctrl, and click the left mouse button.

Using Keyboard Shortcuts

To select text using keyboard shortcuts, hold down Shift as you use the shortcuts from Table 6-1 to move the insertion point. You could, for example, select a word you just typed by pressing Shift-Ctrl-left cursor. Or you could use Ctrl-Home to move the insertion point to the beginning of the document and then press Shift-Ctrl-End to select the entire document.

Word also lets you "expand" your current selection from a single insertion-point location up to the entire document. Each time you press F8, your selection grows by one step. If you press F8 and have no text selected, the Extend mode is turned on. Press F8 a second time, and Word selects the current word. Keep pressing F8 to expand the selection to the current sentence, the current paragraph, the current section (if there is one—you'll learn how to create sections in a later chapter), and finally the entire document. Press Shift-F8 to shrink the selection by the same amounts, going from the entire document down to the insertion-point location.

One more selection shortcut is to press Ctrl-5 (using the 5 on the numeric keypad) to select the entire document.

A Selection Example

Because the sample document you created has so many identical paragraphs, you might want to number each paragraph by changing its first word to the paragraph number. That way, you'll know where you are as you scroll through your document:

1. Press Ctrl-Home to move the insertion point to the beginning of the document.
2. Move the insertion point to the beginning of the next text paragraph by using the mouse or by pressing Ctrl-down cursor twice.
3. Move the cursor past the tab characters by pressing the right cursor key.
4. Select the first word of the paragraph by double-clicking or by pressing Shift-Ctrl-right cursor and press the Del key.
5. Type *Two* to replace the deleted word "One."
6. Use the same procedure to move to the next paragraph and replace the word "One" with *Three*. Continue through all the paragraphs, numbering them up through Twenty-one.

SEARCHING FOR CHARACTERS AND FORMATTING

To find specific words or formatting in a document, you can search through the document yourself, scrolling page by page with an observant eye—if you have a short document. If you have a long document, it's easier to use the Search command.

Searching for Characters

The most common type of search is for text. For example, if you tend to overuse the word "really," you can search for each location of "really" and decide whether you really need to use "really" in that location.

To specify the characters you want to find, choose Search from the Edit menu to open the Search dialog box (shown in Figure 6-3).

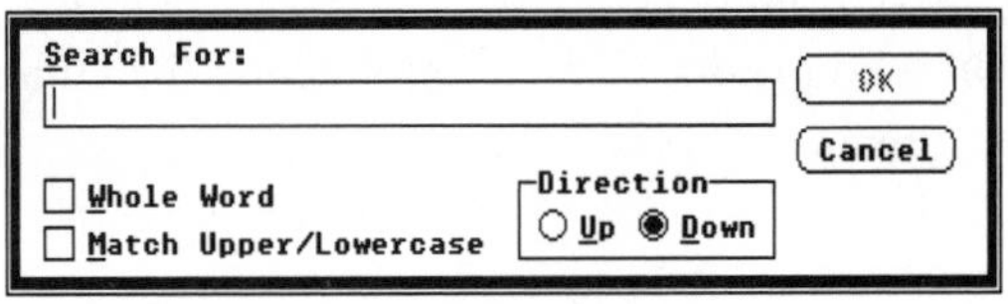

Figure 6-3. *The Search dialog box.*

Type the characters you want to find using the text box labeled Search For. You can type a longer string of characters than the text box shows; if you do, Word scrolls your string to the left so that you can continue typing. You can use a maximum of 256 characters as search text.

After you type your search characters, choose the OK button to start. Word searches from the insertion point forward to the end of the document. If it finds your search characters, it selects them, moves the view to show their location, and closes the dialog box. If Word doesn't find the characters, it opens a dialog box to ask whether you want to continue searching from the beginning of the document. If you choose Yes, Word continues searching until it either finds your search characters or reaches the end of the document again. If you choose No, Word stops the search.

Try searching for the word "bold" in your document:

1. Move the insertion point to the beginning of the document to start the search there.

2. Choose Search from the Edit menu to open the Search dialog box.
3. Type *bold* in the Search For text box.
4. Choose OK to start the search. When Word encounters the first "Bold," it closes the dialog box and selects the word.
5. Choose Search again to continue searching. The Search dialog box opens again, with the word "bold" already entered in the text box.
6. Choose OK to start the search. Word continues searching from the location of the selected word, closes the dialog box, and selects the characters "bold" in the middle of the word "embolden."

Searching for whole words

Word selected the letters "bold" even though they were a part of another word. Search doesn't normally distinguish between whole words and parts of words. To look for a whole word only (that is, a string of characters with a space on each end), turn on the Whole Word option in the Search dialog box:

1. Choose Search once more to continue searching. The Search dialog box opens.
2. Turn on the Whole Word option. (It shows a check when it's on.)
3. Choose OK to start the search. Word finds the next occurrence of "bold" and selects it.
4. Press Shift-F4, a shortcut, to continue the search without reopening the dialog box. Word uses the characters and options you last entered in the dialog box. It finds the word "Bold" in the next paragraph and selects it.
5. Press Shift-F4 once more to continue searching. Word skips the word "embolden" and finds the word "bold" that follows it.

Matching case

Word now searches for whole-word occurrences of "bold," but it doesn't distinguish between "Bold" and "bold." To tell it to match the case of the characters in the Search For text box, turn on the Match Upper/Lowercase option:

1. Choose Search to open the Search dialog box.
2. Turn on the Match Upper/Lowercase option.

3. Choose OK to continue the search. The dialog box closes, and Word selects the next occurrence of "bold."
4. Press Shift-F4 to continue the search. Word moves to the next "bold," skipping "Bold" and "embolden." It is now looking for "bold" only as a whole word in lowercase characters.
5. Continue pressing Shift-F4 until you reach the end of the document. Word continues to select the word "bold" as it finds it. When you reach the end, a new dialog box opens, asking whether you want to continue from the beginning of the document. Choose No.

Changing the search direction

To change the direction so that Word searches from the insertion point back toward the beginning of the document, change the Search Direction in the Search dialog box to Up:

1. Choose Search to open the Search dialog box.
2. Select the Up button at the bottom of the box.
3. Choose OK. Word searches backward through the document until it encounters the previous "bold," which it selects.
4. Continue the search by pressing Shift-F4 until you reach the beginning of the document. Word searches backward, selecting "bold" as it finds it.
5. When you reach the beginning, a dialog box asks whether you want to continue searching from the end of the document. Choose No to stop the search.

Using wildcards

To search for strings without specifying all the characters, use wildcard characters. A wildcard holds a place in a string but doesn't specify any particular character. Type a question mark in the Search For text box to specify an indeterminate character. For example, to find all four-letter words that start with "fl," you would type *fl??* in the Search For text box. Word would then look for "f" and "l" followed by any two characters and select all four characters when it found them. Typing *fl??* would find "flag," "flit," "flop," and other similar strings, but not "foot" (doesn't start with "fl"), "floor" (has too many letters), or "fly" (has too few letters).

Using wildcard characters works best when you have the Whole Word option turned on. If the option isn't on, Word finds your search string in words of any length, not the length you defined using the wildcards.

Searching for special characters

To search for special characters such as tabs and paragraph marks, use a code to enter them in the Search For text box. The code is a caret (^) followed by a single letter. These codes search for special characters you learned to use in previous chapters:

- ^w—a white space
- ^t—a tab
- ^p—a paragraph mark

For example, typing *^tThree* would make Word search for a tab followed by the word "Three." Because Word interprets question marks and carets as wildcards or code starters, you use special codes to search for literal occurrences of them:

- ^?—a question mark
- ^^—a caret

You can find codes for other special characters (section marks and optional hyphens, for example) in the *User's Reference*. You'll learn to use some of these special characters in later chapters.

Searching for Formatting

It's often useful to search for formats rather than characters. For example, you might want to see every italicized word in a document to review important concepts. To search for formatting, open the Search dialog box and use keyboard shortcuts to turn on search formatting. Most character formatting uses the keyboard shortcuts you use to apply the formatting within the document—Ctrl-I, for example, turns on italic, and Ctrl-B turns on boldface—but there are some differences. Consult the *User's Reference* for a full list of keyboard combinations.

Each time you press a format key combination, the Search dialog box turns a message on or off in the space below the Search For text box. When you initiate the search, Word searches for the formatting you turned on. For example, pressing Ctrl-I (the italic formatting shortcut) displays the Italic message. If you search with this message displayed, Word looks for occurrences of italic formatting. To turn off formatting, press Ctrl-Spacebar.

Try looking for boldface formatting in the document:

1. Move the insertion point to the beginning of the document to start the search there.
2. Choose Search to open the Search dialog box.
3. Press the Del key to erase the text in the Search For text box. (You want to look for formatting alone, not characters.)
4. Change the Search Direction to its original setting: Down.
5. Press Ctrl-B to turn on the Bold message. The word "Bold" appears below the text box. (If you press Ctrl-B again, "Bold" disappears. Press it once more to turn it on again.)
6. Choose OK to start the search. Word closes the dialog box and selects the phrase "bold characters," which is formatted in boldface.

Word searches for paragraph formatting as well as for character formatting. To turn paragraph formatting on and off in the Search dialog box, you use key combinations, usually the same combinations you normally use to apply paragraph formatting in the document's text. For example, to look for centered text, press Ctrl-C. (The other paragraph formats and their keyboard shortcuts are in Chapter 7. The *User's Reference* also shows a full list of key combinations for paragraph formats in the Search dialog box.) When you start the search, Word looks for a paragraph that contains the formatting you specified and selects the entire paragraph when it finds one.

Searching for Combinations of Characters and Formatting

You can combine characters and formatting to narrow the search specifications. For example, you could search for all occurrences of the word "kumquat" in underlined italic contained in centered paragraphs by typing the word in the Search For text box, turning on the Whole Word option, and then turning on the Underline, Italic, and Centered messages.

REPLACING CHARACTERS AND FORMATTING

The purpose of most searches is to locate characters or formats and replace them with different characters or formats. Use the Replace command from the Edit menu to tell Word what to search for and what to use as a replacement. The Replace dialog box (shown in Figure 6-4) offers all the features of the Search dialog box except the Direction option buttons and adds the Replace With text box and the Confirm Changes option.

```
┌─────────────────────────────────────────────────────────┐
│ Search For:                                               │
│ ┌───────────────────────────────────┐    ( OK )          │
│ │                                    │                     │
│ Replace With:                             ( Cancel )       │
│ ┌───────────────────────────────────┐                     │
│ │                                    │                     │
│                                                            │
│ ☐ Whole Word                                               │
│ ☐ Match Upper/Lowercase      ☒ Confirm Changes             │
└─────────────────────────────────────────────────────────┘
```

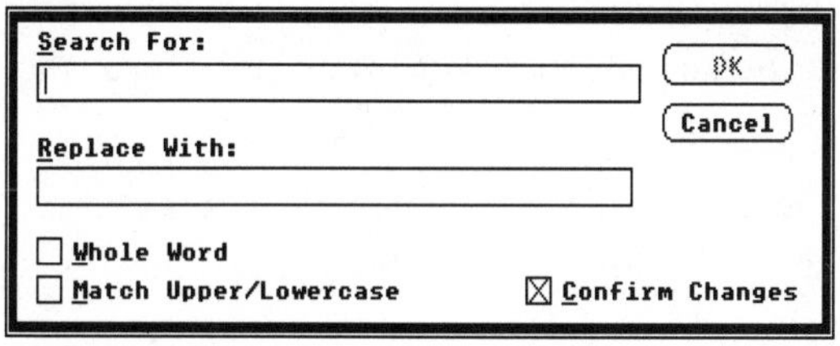

Figure 6-4. *The Replace dialog box.*

The Search For text box and the Whole Word and Match Upper/ Lowercase options work the same as they do in the Search dialog box. You use the Replace With text box to enter a string of replacement characters and to choose replacement formatting. Once you set both the search and replacement specifications, you start the search. As Word finds each occurrence of your search entry, it replaces it with your replacement entry, working through to the end of the document. If you have the Confirm Changes option on, Word stops to show you each occurrence and asks whether you want to replace it. If the option is off, Word replaces all occurrences without asking you.

The sample document has the word "outstanding" listed throughout in italic. Replace it with the word "sensational" in boldface:

1. Move the insertion point to the beginning of the document to start the search and replace operation there.

2. Choose Replace from the Edit menu to open the Replace dialog box.

3. Type *outstanding* in the Search For text box.

4. Press Ctrl-I to turn on the Italic message under the Search For text box.

5. Select the Replace With text box, and type *sensational*.

6. Press Ctrl-B to turn on the Bold message below the Replace With text box.
7. Turn on the Confirm Changes option if it isn't already on.
8. Choose OK to start the operation. Word closes the dialog box, selects the first italicized "outstanding" it finds, and opens a dialog box asking whether you want to make the replacement.
9. Choose Yes. Word closes the dialog box, replaces "outstanding" with a boldface "sensational," and finds the next italicized "outstanding." Word asks again whether you want to make the replacement.
10. Choose No this time. Word closes the dialog box, leaves the selection as it is, finds the next italicized "outstanding," and asks whether you want to replace it.
11. Choose Cancel to stop the operation.

Notice that the Confirm option is also available in the confirmation dialog box. If during your search you decide not to check each change, you can turn this option off and select Yes. Word then continues through the rest of the document, changing all occurrences without asking you each time.

SETTING BOOKMARKS

To mark a location so that you can easily jump to it later, use a bookmark. The bookmark is a Word feature that marks a location or a section of text and gives it a name. Later, you use the Go To command to jump to any bookmark you have set.

To set a bookmark, first select a block of text or move the insertion point to a location that you want to mark. Then choose Bookmark from the Insert menu to open the Bookmark dialog box (shown in Figure 6-5). Type a name

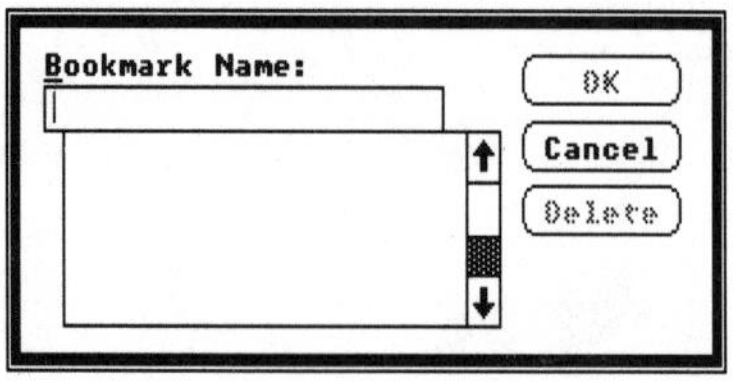

Figure 6-5. *The Bookmark dialog box.*

for your bookmark in the Bookmark Name text box. The bookmark name must have between 1 and 20 characters, start with a letter, and consist of only letters, numbers, and underscores (_). Choose OK to set the bookmark and close the dialog box.

Try assigning bookmarks to the sample document:

1. Move to the end of the document and select the entire last paragraph of text.
2. Choose Bookmark from the Insert menu to open the Bookmark dialog box.
3. Type the name *last_paragraph* in the Bookmark Name text box.
4. Choose OK to define the bookmark as the paragraph you selected.
5. Press Ctrl-Home to place the insertion point at the beginning of the document's first paragraph.
6. Choose Bookmark to open the Bookmark dialog box.
7. Type the name *middle* in the Bookmark Name text box.
8. Choose OK to define the insertion-point location as a bookmark.
9. Move the insertion point to somewhere around the middle of the document.
10. Choose Bookmark one more time. The list box below the Bookmark Name text box lists the bookmarks you set.
11. Redefine the middle bookmark by selecting it in the list box: double-click on "middle" with the mouse, or use the down cursor key to select it. Then press Enter. The dialog box disappears, and the new insertion-point location is defined as the bookmark named "middle." Word forgets the old location.

As you set bookmarks, you build a list of bookmark names in the list box. You can redefine these bookmarks as you did above, assigning them new locations or new sections of text. You can delete a bookmark by selecting it in the list box and then choosing the Delete button in the Bookmark dialog box.

JUMPING TO BOOKMARKS, PAGES, AND OTHER LOCATIONS

The Go To command in the Edit menu opens the Go To dialog box (shown in Figure 6-6), where you can choose to jump to a bookmark or to a specific page, line, or other location.

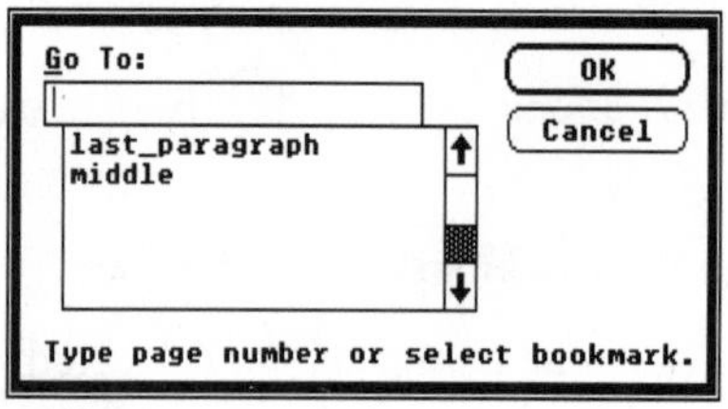

Figure 6-6. *The Go To dialog box.*

Jumping to a Bookmark

To jump to a bookmark, select the bookmark name from the list box below the Go To text box, and then choose OK (or simply double-click on the name). Word moves the insertion point to the bookmark location or selects the block of text that is defined by the bookmark. The view changes to show you the new insertion-point location or text selection.

Jumping to Pages and Lines

To jump to a specific page, type a page number in the Go To text box, and then choose OK. Word moves the insertion point and the view to the beginning of the specified page. To move by lines rather than pages, type *L* followed by the number of lines you want to move forward, and then choose OK. Entering a negative number moves you backward. For example, entering *L37* moves the insertion point to the beginning of the line 37 lines below the current location. Entering *L-6* moves the insertion point to the beginning of the line six lines above the current location.

To combine pages and lines, enter both the page number and the line number in the text box. Type the letter *P* in front of your page number. For example, entering *P6L21* jumps to line 21 of page 6. Entering *P10L-3* jumps to a location three lines before the beginning of page 10.

Jumping by Percentage

Use the Go To dialog box to move the insertion point a specified percentage forward or backward through the document. If you type a percent sign (%) followed by a number, Word jumps through to the location at that percentage of the document. For example, entering *%50* moves the insertion point to the middle of the document.

A Go To Example

Use Go To now to move to different locations throughout your document:

1. Choose Go To from the Edit menu to open the Go To dialog box.
2. To jump to the last_paragraph bookmark, double-click on the bookmark name or select the name using the down cursor key and press Enter. The dialog box closes, the view jumps to the last paragraph of the document, and the paragraph is selected.
3. Choose Go To again. The Go To dialog box opens.
4. Type *P2L5* in the text box.
5. Choose OK to close the dialog box. The insertion point and view jump to the beginning of the fifth line of page 2.
6. Press F5 to use a shortcut. "Go to:" appears on the status bar.
7. Type *middle* and press Enter to jump to the bookmark named middle.

The last jump used the Go To shortcut. The F5 key lets you type your new location on the status bar without opening the Go To dialog box. You can enter the same locations as you can in the Go To text box, or you can type the name of an existing bookmark.

A QUICK SUMMARY

You saw in this chapter how to use Word's editing tools. You started by learning how to move the insertion point using key combinations and how to select text easily. You went on to learn four Word editing commands—Search, Replace, Bookmark, and Go To—to make your way through long documents, search for text and formatting, and replace them with new text or formatting. In the next chapter, you learn much more about formatting paragraphs.

Chapter 7

Paragraph Formatting:

Indents, Alignment, and Line Spacing

Paragraph formatting, perhaps more than any other type of formatting, controls your document's overall appearance. In this chapter, you learn to shape paragraphs by setting indents, changing alignment, controlling line spacing, and adding borders. You also learn about paragraph marks: how they store formats and mold paragraphs, and how you can cut, copy, paste, and insert them. You'll also see how to protect paragraphs from being split apart by page breaks during pagination.

SETTING UP WORD

To use the examples in this chapter, start Word for Windows and be sure you have the same settings in effect as you used in the last chapter. These include:

- Full menus
- A text window that shows the ruler, ribbon, and status bar
- The Display as Printed option turned off and the Pictures option turned on (in the View Preferences dialog box)

The sample document for this chapter, shown in Figure 7-1 on the following page, is a simple collection of paragraphs using different formats. You create these paragraphs as you work through the examples that follow.

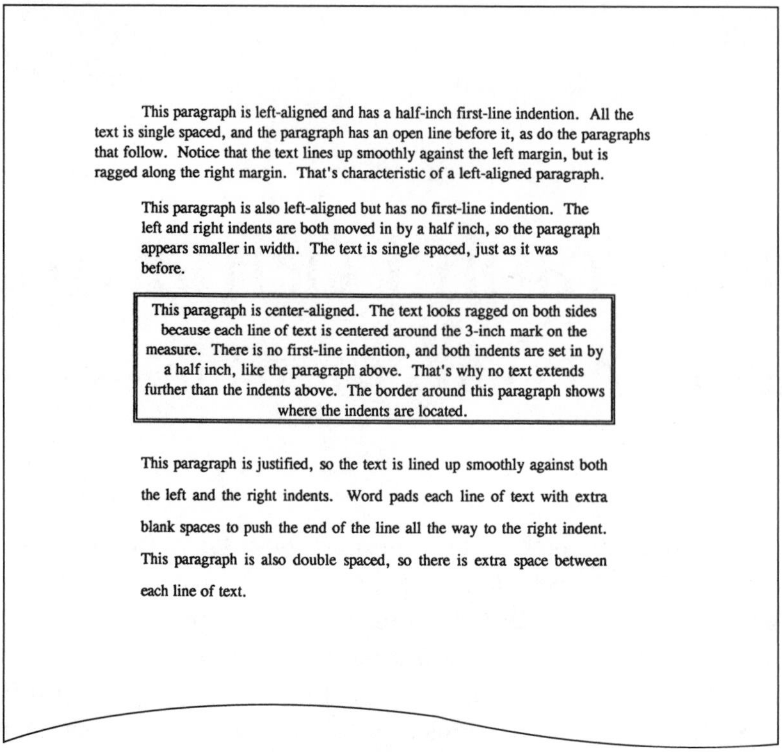

This paragraph is left-aligned and has a half-inch first-line indention. All the text is single spaced, and the paragraph has an open line before it, as do the paragraphs that follow. Notice that the text lines up smoothly against the left margin, but is ragged along the right margin. That's characteristic of a left-aligned paragraph.

This paragraph is also left-aligned but has no first-line indention. The left and right indents are both moved in by a half inch, so the paragraph appears smaller in width. The text is single spaced, just as it was before.

This paragraph is center-aligned. The text looks ragged on both sides because each line of text is centered around the 3-inch mark on the measure. There is no first-line indention, and both indents are set in by a half inch, like the paragraph above. That's why no text extends further than the indents above. The border around this paragraph shows where the indents are located.

This paragraph is justified, so the text is lined up smoothly against both the left and the right indents. Word pads each line of text with extra blank spaces to push the end of the line all the way to the right indent. This paragraph is also double spaced, so there is extra space between each line of text.

Figure 7-1. *This sample document uses different kinds of paragraph formatting.*

PARAGRAPH MARKS

You learned in Chapter 3 that you enter a paragraph mark (an invisible character) each time you press Enter in a document. The paragraph mark does more than mark the end of a paragraph, however. It also contains the paragraph's formatting specifications—its indents, alignment, line spacing, border type, and other information.

Think of each paragraph mark as a text "mold" for the paragraph. Any text you type before a paragraph mark conforms to the shape determined by the mark's formatting. For example, if you enter text before a paragraph mark that is set to be left-aligned and double-spaced, Word starts each line against the left margin and puts a blank line between lines.

Because any text you enter must have a paragraph mark to control its paragraph formatting, Word starts every new document with a paragraph mark containing default formatting. When you type, the text follows the paragraph mark's formatting. When you press Enter at the end of the first paragraph, Word duplicates the paragraph mark and all its formatting, leaves it at the end of the paragraph, and keeps the original mark at the end of the document. This original mark remains at the end of the document; you can't delete it, but you can change its formatting.

CHANGING PARAGRAPH FORMATS

To apply new paragraph formats, you first select one or more paragraphs. You learned in Chapter 3 to select a single paragraph for formatting by placing the insertion point anywhere in the paragraph. This means that the paragraph you are typing is always selected for formatting. You also learned that when you select a text block for paragraph formatting, Word formats all the paragraphs that are part of the text block, even if some of those paragraphs are only partially selected.

Paragraph Formatting Methods

Once you select a paragraph, you can change formats using one of three methods:

- The ruler
- The Format Paragraph command
- Keyboard shortcuts

An overview of each method should give you a general idea of the way the method works.

The ruler

The ruler (shown in Figure 7-2 on the following page) lets you use the mouse to change paragraph formatting. The four icons in the middle of the ruler set paragraph alignment. The next three icons to the right set line spacing, and the two icons that follow open or close a blank line before each paragraph. You use the measure, located below the icons, to set paragraph indents.

You learn about the remaining parts of the ruler, such as the Style combo box and the icons for setting tab stops, in later chapters.

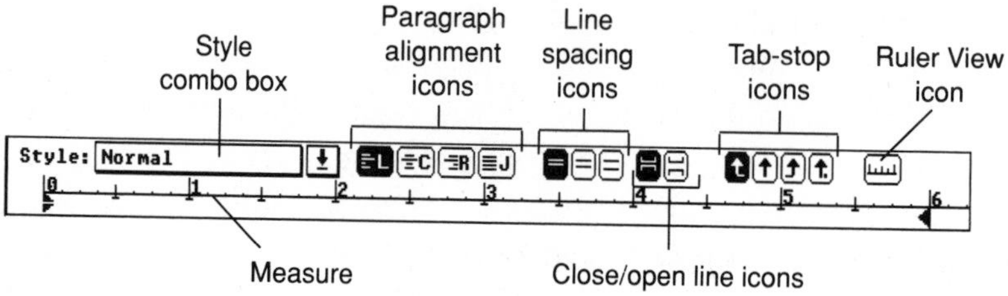

Figure 7-2. *The ruler.*

The Format Paragraph command

The Paragraph command on the Format menu opens the Format Paragraph dialog box, shown in Figure 7-3. The four Alignment buttons set the paragraph alignment, and the Indents text boxes below set the paragraph indents. The Spacing text boxes to the right of the indent settings control the line spacing in the paragraph. Below them are the Border and Pattern list boxes, which set paragraph borders.

The section labeled Keep Paragraph and the check box labeled Page Break Before control the way Word treats a paragraph when it sets page breaks. The Line Numbering check box sets an option that numbers each line in the paragraph. The Style combo box sets styles, and the Tabs button takes you to another dialog box, where you set tab stops.

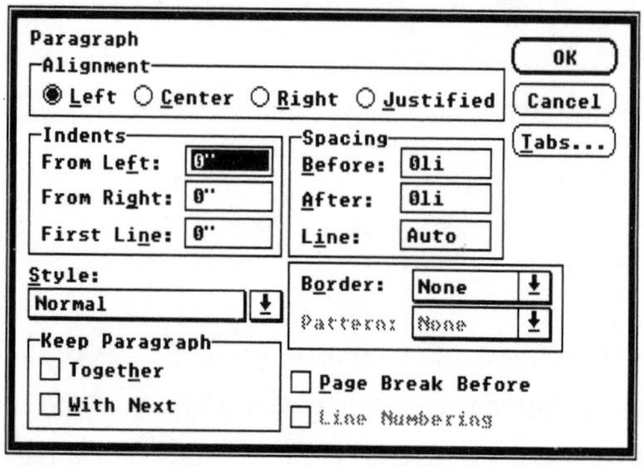

Figure 7-3. *The Format Paragraph dialog box.*

Keyboard shortcuts

Keyboard shortcuts offer most of the paragraph formats you can set on the ruler and in the Format Paragraph dialog box. The shortcuts, listed throughout this chapter, are a combination of Ctrl plus a letter or number key.

SETTING PARAGRAPH INDENTS

Each paragraph has three indent settings: left, right, and first line. Word measures each indent from the margins of the document. The margins default to 1¼ inches for the left and right margins and 1 inch for the top and bottom margins. (You'll learn how to change the margins in Chapter 17.)

A paragraph's left indent controls the left edge of all lines except the first. The indent is measured in from the left margin. If the left indent is 0, it rests exactly on the left margin—1¼ inches from the left edge of the page. If the left indent is 1 inch, it rests an inch to the right of the left margin—2¼ inches from the left edge of the page.

A paragraph's right indent controls the right edge of all lines in the paragraph. The way you measure the indent depends on whether you use the ruler or the Format Paragraph dialog box. On the ruler, the right indent is measured in terms of the left margin. When the right indent is set to 6 inches, it rests 6 inches to the right of the left margin—7¼ inches from the left edge of the page (or 1¼ inches from the right edge of the page). In the Format Paragraph dialog box, the right indent is measured in from the right page margin. If the right indent is 0, it rests on the right margin—1¼ inches from the right edge of the page. If the right indent is ¾ inch, it rests ¾ of an inch to the left of the right margin—2 inches from the right edge of the page.

The first-line indent controls only the left edge of the paragraph's first line. You use the first-line indent to create an indention for the paragraph. On the ruler, it is measured in from the left margin. In the Format Paragraph dialog box, setting the first-line indent to a positive number indents the first line to the right of the following lines. Setting it to a negative number moves the first line out to the left of the following lines, creating a "hanging indent."

Setting Indents Using the Ruler

You can set indents on the ruler using either a mouse or a keyboard. Both methods move the indent markers to new settings along the ruler's measure.

Using the mouse

To set indents on the ruler using the mouse, you drag the appropriate indent marker to the position you want and then release the mouse button. Figure 7-4 shows and labels the three indent markers. Note that when you move the left indent marker, the first-line indent marker moves with it. This keeps the first-line indention you set as you change the left indent. You can move the first-line indent marker individually to change its indention.

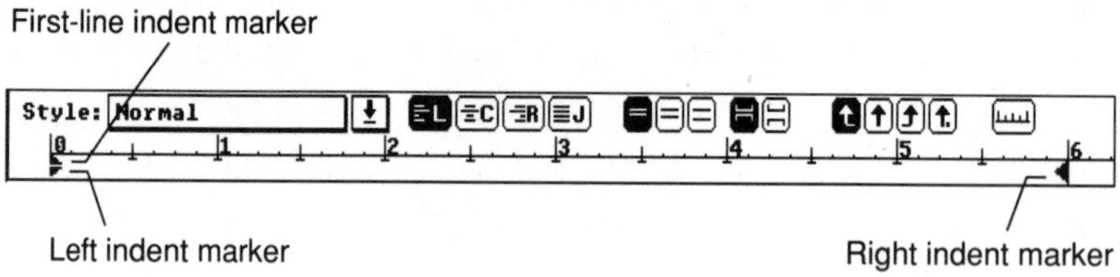

Figure 7-4. *The ruler's three indent markers.*

Using the keyboard

To set indents on the ruler using the keyboard, press Ctrl-Shift-F10 to turn on the ruler mode. The small, square *ruler cursor* (shown in Figure 7-5) appears below the measure.

First, move the ruler cursor to a position along the measure using the right and left cursor keys. (To move the ruler cursor in large increments, use Ctrl-right cursor and Ctrl-left cursor.) When the cursor reaches the position you want, press one of these keys to tell Word which indent to set:

- L sets the left indent.
- R sets the right indent.
- F sets the first-line indent.

When you finish setting indents, press Enter to apply the indents and turn off the ruler mode. (Pressing Esc turns off the ruler mode without applying the indents.)

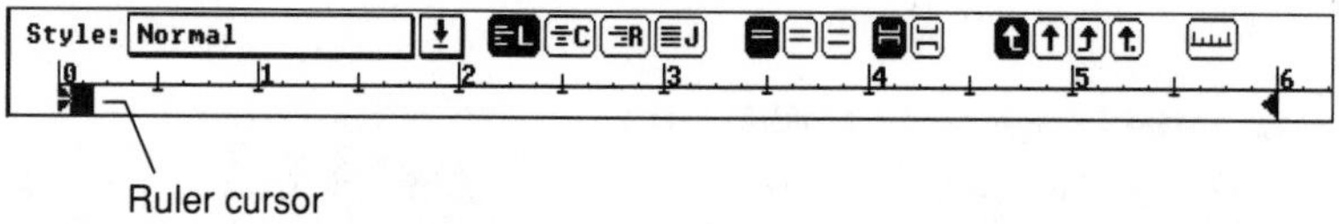

Figure 7-5. *The ruler cursor appears when you turn on the ruler mode.*

Setting Indents Using the Format Paragraph Dialog Box

To set indents in the Format Paragraph dialog box, you first choose Paragraph from the Format menu. When the dialog box opens, you select the appropriate Indents text box: From Left for the left indent, From Right for the right indent, and First Line for the first-line indent. Enter the amount of indention you want, and then press Enter to close the dialog box and apply the indent.

Setting Indents Using Keyboard Shortcuts

Four keyboard shortcuts let you change indents:

- Ctrl-N moves the left and first-line indents to the right ½ inch (a process called *nesting*).
- Ctrl-M moves the left and first-line indents out to the left ½ inch.
- Ctrl-T moves the left indent to the right ½ inch.
- Ctrl-G moves the left indent to the left ½ inch.

An Indent Example

Try setting indents as you type the sample document shown in Figure 7-1:

1. Before you type the first paragraph, set the first-line indent to ½ inch by using the mouse to drag the first-line indent marker to the ½-inch position along the measure. Or press Ctrl-Shift-F10, use the right cursor key to move the ruler cursor to the ½-inch position, press F, and then press Enter. This creates a first-line indention.
2. Set the point size to 12, type the first paragraph, and press Enter when you finish.
3. Type the second paragraph but stop before you press Enter. Notice that the indention you created in the first paragraph is duplicated in this paragraph.
4. Choose Paragraph from the Format menu to open the Format Paragraph dialog box.
5. Enter *.5* in the From Left text box, *.5* in the From Right text box, and *0″* in the First Line text box.

6. Press Enter to close the dialog box and apply the new margins. The text moves in on both sides by ½ inch, and the first-line indention disappears.
7. Press Enter to end the paragraph.

SETTING PARAGRAPH ALIGNMENT

Word can align paragraphs in four ways:

- Left alignment, in which all text lines align against the left indent, leaving a ragged right edge.
- Right alignment, in which all text lines align against the right indent, leaving a ragged left edge.
- Centered alignment, in which all text lines are centered exactly between the left and right indents, leaving ragged edges on both sides.
- Justified, in which all text lines align against both the left and right indents to create smooth edges. Word adds spaces between words to create full justification.

You can apply each type of alignment using the ruler, the Format Paragraph dialog box, or keyboard shortcuts.

Setting Alignment Using the Ruler

To align a paragraph using the ruler, simply click on the appropriate alignment icon. All the text in the selected paragraph(s) conforms to the alignment you choose.

Setting Alignment Using the Format Paragraph Dialog Box

To align a paragraph using the Format Paragraph dialog box, open the box by choosing Paragraph from the Format menu. Select the appropriate button in the Alignment section. Then press Enter to close the box and apply the alignment to the selected paragraph(s).

Setting Alignment Using Keyboard Shortcuts

These keyboard shortcuts align selected paragraphs:

- Ctrl-L applies left alignment.
- Ctrl-R applies right alignment.
- Ctrl-C applies centered alignment.
- Ctrl-J applies justified alignment.

An Alignment Example

Try the different methods of applying alignment to paragraphs:

1. Type the third paragraph of the document, stopping before you press Enter.
2. To center the text in this paragraph, click on the ruler's centered alignment icon, or press Ctrl-C.
3. Press Enter to start a new paragraph, and then type the fourth paragraph, again stopping before you press Enter.
4. Choose Paragraph from the Format menu to open the Format Paragraph dialog box.
5. Press Shift-Tab to select the Alignment box and use the right cursor key to select the Justified button.
6. Press Enter to close the dialog box and apply the justification. The text in the paragraph aligns smoothly along both the left and right indents.

SETTING LINE SPACING

Line spacing is the amount of space between lines of text in a paragraph. Word measures this space in points, the same unit of measurement it uses to measure the height of fonts. It measures from the bottom of one line of text to the bottom of the line above it. The bottom of a line of text is determined by the length of the *descenders* used in a font, as shown in Figure 7-6 on the following page. Descenders are "tails" on characters such as j and p.

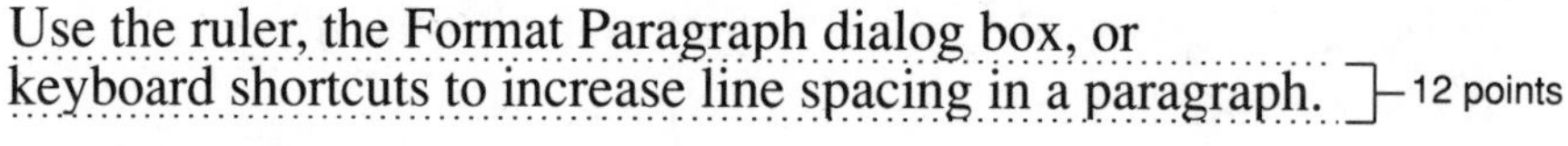

Figure 7-6. *Word measures line spacing from the bottom of one line to the bottom of the line above it.*

Word sets the default line spacing to one line, a unit of measurement that Word interprets as 12 points. If you use characters larger than 12 points in size, Word adjusts the line spacing to several points greater than the largest character in the line. This means that if you set line spacing to 18 points and then type using a 24-point font, Word sets the line spacing for that line to approximately 30 points so that the top of the tallest character doesn't run into the line above it. However, if you set line spacing to 18 points and then use a 10-point font, Word doesn't decrease the spacing to match the small font. Line spacing remains at 18 points. You can use the ruler, the Format Paragraph dialog box, or keyboard shortcuts to increase the line spacing in a paragraph and add more empty space between lines of text.

Setting Line Spacing Using the Ruler

The ruler includes three icons that set line spacing:

- Single space (12 points between lines)
- One-and-one-half space (18 points between lines)
- Double space (24 points between lines)

Because these spacings have fixed point sizes, they work best with 12-point or smaller fonts. If you use larger fonts, such as 24 points, these line spacing settings have no effect.

To set line spacing, select the appropriate icon on the ruler using the mouse. Figure 7-7 identifies the icons.

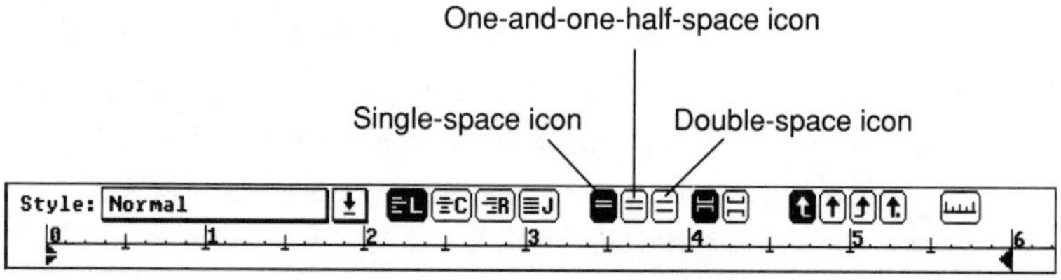

Figure 7-7. *The line spacing icons on the ruler.*

Setting Line Spacing Using the Format Paragraph Dialog Box

To change line spacing using the Format Paragraph dialog box, choose the Format Paragraph command to open the box. Use the Line text box in the Spacing section to enter spacing in line increments. For example, entering *2 li* specifies line spacing of 24 points. You can also enter the distance between lines in points. Type *pt* following the number so that Word knows you mean points and not lines. If you want Word to set line spacing automatically, enter *auto*. Word increases or decreases line spacing to match the largest font in each line.

Setting Line Spacing Using Keyboard Shortcuts

Three keyboard shortcuts set the same line spacing distances as the ruler icons set:

- Ctrl-1 sets single spacing (12 points).
- Ctrl-2 sets double spacing (24 points).
- Ctrl-5 sets one-and-one-half spacing (18 points).

When you use one of these keyboard shortcuts, the spacing you choose appears on the ruler.

Setting an Open Line Before and After Each Paragraph

In addition to controlling spacing between lines, Word controls spacing between paragraphs. Two icons on the ruler (shown in Figure 7-8 on the following page) control space before paragraphs but not after. Clicking on the open line icon adds 12 points of space before each selected paragraph, and clicking on the close line icon removes the space before each selected paragraph.

Entering a line or point measurement in the Before text box in the Format Paragraph dialog box adds that much space *before* each selected paragraph. Entering a measurement in the After text box adds that much space *after* each selected paragraph.

Two keyboard shortcuts duplicate the actions of the ruler icons:

- Ctrl-O opens 12 points of space before each selected paragraph.
- Ctrl-E closes any space before each selected paragraph.

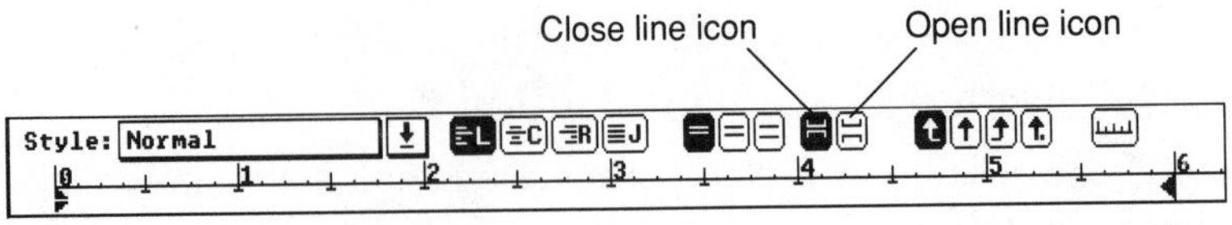

Figure 7-8. *The paragraph spacing icons on the ruler.*

A Spacing Example

Change the spacing of the last paragraph you typed:

1. Select the fourth paragraph of the sample document.
2. Open the Format Paragraph dialog box by choosing Paragraph from the Format menu.
3. Type *36 pt* in the Line text box, and press Enter to apply the spacing. All the lines in the paragraph are separated by 36 points.
4. Click on the double spacing icon on the ruler, or press Ctrl-2. The line spacing reduces to 24 points (two lines).

Now try adding a single line before all the paragraphs in your document:

1. Select the entire document by pressing Ctrl-5 on the numeric keypad.
2. Click on the open space icon on the ruler, or press Ctrl-O. An empty line appears before each paragraph in the document.

ADDING A PARAGRAPH BORDER

In Chapter 5 you learned to add different kinds of borders to pictures. You use the Format Paragraph dialog box to add similar borders to paragraphs. Try adding a border around the third paragraph:

1. Move the insertion point into the third paragraph.
2. Choose Paragraph from the Format menu to open the dialog box.
3. Select the Border list box and choose the option labeled Box.
4. Select the list box labeled Pattern and choose the option labeled Double.

5. Press Enter to apply the border. A double-lined box appears around the paragraph.

The Border list box offers you a selection of borders that set off selected paragraphs, and the Pattern list box lets you choose the type of line used in the border. You can see examples of different options in Figure 7-9.

When you add a border to a paragraph, you set the border size by changing the left and right indents of the paragraph and the spacing above and below it. The sides of the box are set by the left and right paragraph indents, and the vertical bar is set by the left paragraph indent. The top and bottom of the box are set by the spacing before and after the paragraph, as are the horizontal lines above and below.

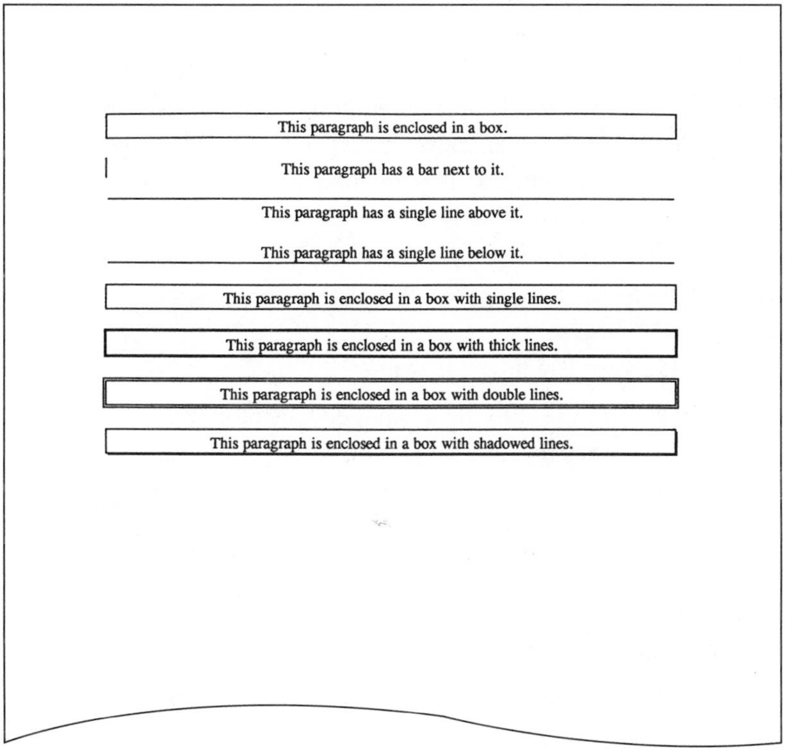

Figure 7-9. *Examples of different types of paragraph borders.*

SPLITTING AND COMBINING PARAGRAPHS

As you cut, copy, paste, and insert blocks of text, you find yourself including paragraph marks along with the rest of the text. Because paragraph marks contain formatting for their paragraphs, you might get unexpected results. Simple explanations of two basic paragraph operations—splitting a paragraph and combining two paragraphs—show you the effect of editing on paragraphs.

Splitting a Paragraph

The simplest way to split a paragraph is to move the insertion point to the location where you want the split and then press Enter. The paragraph mark you insert splits the paragraph into two new paragraphs. Both have the same paragraph formatting because Word copies the formatting from the paragraph mark at the end of the original paragraph into the inserted paragraph mark.

If you cut or copy a text block containing a paragraph mark and then paste the block into another paragraph (the target paragraph), the target paragraph splits into two paragraphs. The two new paragraphs might have different formats. If the pasted paragraph mark contains different paragraph formatting from that of the target paragraph mark, the pasted paragraph mark formats the first of the split paragraphs, and the second of the split paragraphs retains its original formatting.

An example shows you how this works:

1. Select a block of text in the sample document extending from the beginning of the word "border" in the third paragraph to the end of the word "justified" in the fourth. This block contains the paragraph mark at the end of the third paragraph, which holds centered paragraph formatting.

2. Select Copy from the Edit menu to copy the text block to the Clipboard.

3. Move the insertion point to the middle of the first paragraph, and choose Paste from the Edit menu to paste the text block into the middle of the first paragraph.

The first paragraph splits into two paragraphs. The first of the split paragraphs is now centered because it ends with the paragraph mark copied from a centered paragraph. The second of the split paragraphs retains its original paragraph formatting because it ends with the original paragraph mark.

Combining Paragraphs

To combine two paragraphs, you remove the paragraph mark at the end of the first paragraph. Word adds all the text of the first paragraph to the text in the second paragraph; if the two paragraphs had different paragraph formatting, the formatting of the first paragraph is lost (with its paragraph mark).

The simplest way to remove a paragraph mark between two differently formatted paragraphs is to place the insertion point at the beginning of the paragraph following the paragraph mark and press Ctrl-Backspace. You can also select the paragraph mark (you might need to make it visible first) and use Cut to remove the mark. Try combining the third and fourth paragraphs of the sample document:

- Place the insertion point at the beginning of the fourth paragraph and press Ctrl-Backspace.

The two paragraphs combine, and the formatting of the third paragraph changes to match that of paragraph four: justified and double-spaced.

PARAGRAPHS AND PAGINATION

When Word prints a document, it breaks the document into pages. If Word reaches the end of a page in the middle of a paragraph, it splits the paragraph in two with a page break. To keep a paragraph from being split by pagination, use the options in the lower left corner of the Format Paragraph dialog box.

When you turn on the Together option (in the Keep Paragraph section), any selected paragraphs are locked so that Word cannot split them in two with a page break. If a locked paragraph is too long to fit at the end of a page, Word moves the entire paragraph to the beginning of the next page.

The With Next option in the Keep Paragraph section binds two paragraphs together so that Word won't split them with a page break. When you turn on this option, Word binds the selected paragraph to the paragraph immediately following it. If both paragraphs won't fit at the end of a page, Word moves them both to the beginning of the next page.

The Page Break Before option next to the Keep Paragraph section does the opposite of With Next: It inserts a page break before the selected paragraph. Page Break Before guarantees that the selected paragraph will appear at the top of a page.

A QUICK SUMMARY

In this chapter you learned how a paragraph mark acts as a text mold by holding paragraph formatting information. You saw how to use the ruler, the Format Paragraph dialog box, and keyboard shortcuts to apply paragraph formatting, and you used these methods to set paragraph indents, alignment, and line spacing. You also learned how to add a border to a paragraph, how to work with paragraph marks as you edit text blocks, and how to control page breaks within and between paragraphs. In the next chapter, you learn to set and use tab stops to align columns of text.

Chapter 8

Tabs

Tabs in Word for Windows help you align text and columns in your documents. In this chapter you learn how to set tab stops, use the Tab key to align text with tab stops, and change existing tab stops. You learn how to align columns of text and numbers in different ways and how to add leaders before text. By following the examples in this chapter, you create a restaurant menu that shows you practical applications for tabs.

SETTING UP WORD

To use the examples in this chapter, start Word and be sure to use the same settings you've used in the past few chapters:

- Full menus
- A text window that shows the ruler, ribbon, and status bar
- The Display as Printed option turned off and the Pictures option turned on (in the View Preferences dialog box)

Throughout the chapter you use tab techniques to create the menu shown in Figure 8-1 on the following page. Tabs align the columns of items and prices, create the leaders that tie items and prices together, and help align the parts of the menu heading.

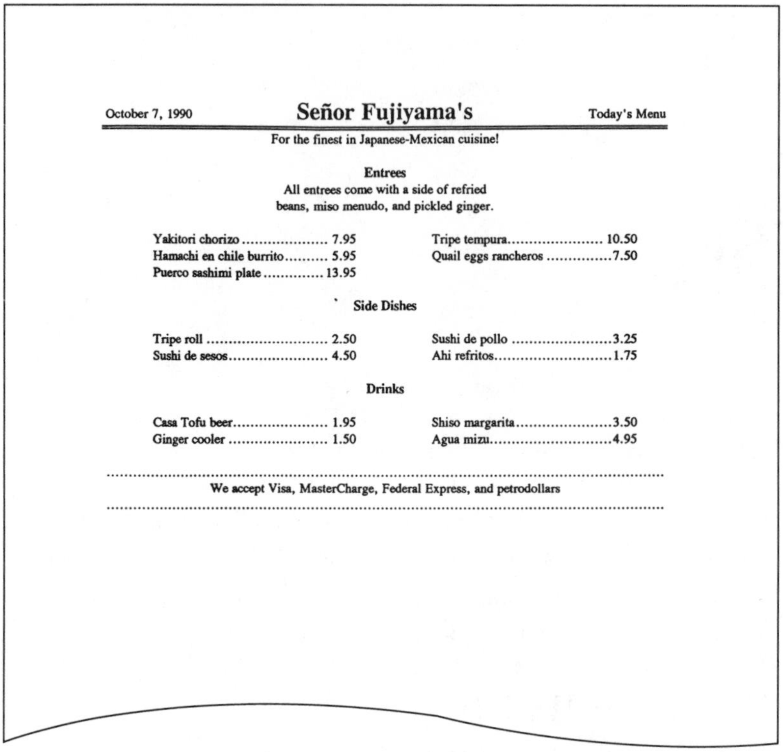

October 7, 1990 **Señor Fujiyama's** Today's Menu

For the finest in Japanese-Mexican cuisine!

Entrees

All entrees come with a side of refried beans, miso menudo, and pickled ginger.

Yakitori chorizo	7.95	Tripe tempura	10.50
Hamachi en chile burrito	5.95	Quail eggs rancheros	7.50
Puerco sashimi plate	13.95		

Side Dishes

Tripe roll	2.50	Sushi de pollo	3.25
Sushi de sesos	4.50	Ahi refritos	1.75

Drinks

Casa Tofu beer	1.95	Shiso margarita	3.50
Ginger cooler	1.50	Agua mizu	4.95

We accept Visa, MasterCharge, Federal Express, and petrodollars

Figure 8-1. *This menu uses tabs to align columns and position information within lines.*

TAB STOPS

As you learned in previous chapters, pressing Tab moves the insertion point to the right. The new stopping point is called a *tab stop*. Tab stops are markers; when you press Tab, the insertion point moves to the right along the current line to the next tab stop. If no tab stops remain before the end of the line, the insertion point moves to the next line and stops at the first tab stop in that line.

Each tab stop performs three functions:

- It marks a location where the insertion point stops when you press Tab.
- It controls the alignment of the text you type after you press Tab.

- It adds a leader of dots, dashes, or a solid line over the space you jumped by pressing Tab. (It can also omit the leader if you wish.)

Because setting tab stops is a type of paragraph formatting, each paragraph has its own set of tab stops. Any tab stops you set are stored in the paragraph mark and duplicated in the next paragraph when you press Enter.

In previous chapters you used the Tab key to jump to tab stops without setting them at all. You used *default tab stops,* which Word creates in paragraphs when you set no tab stops. Default tab stops appear every half inch along the ruler. You can see them in Figure 8-2; they are marked with small horizontal lines.

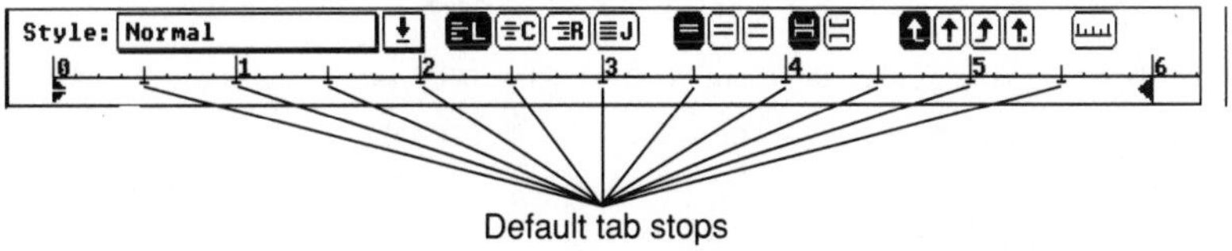

Figure 8-2. *Default tab stops appear every half inch along the measure.*

Setting a tab stop is a simple matter of inserting a tab-stop marker on the ruler. Word offers four different types of tab stops: left, center, right, and decimal. Figure 8-3 shows the ruler icon for each type of tab stop.

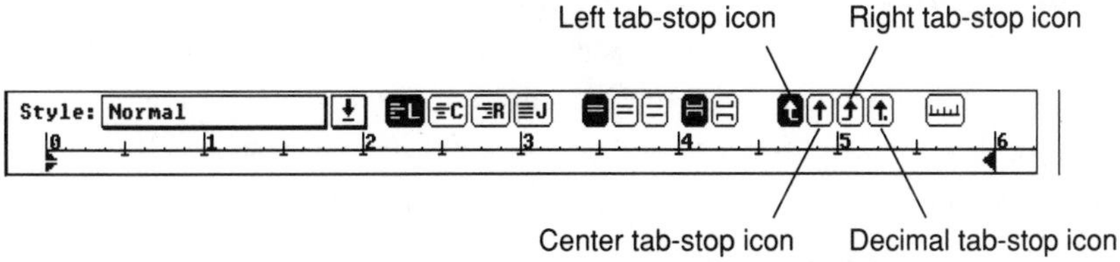

Figure 8-3. *The four tab-stop icons of the ruler.*

Tab stops control the alignment of text you type after you press Tab. Figure 8-4 on the following page shows how the four types align text.

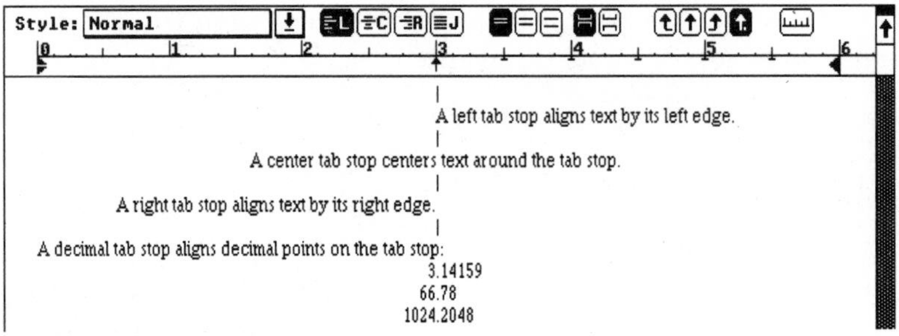

Figure 8-4. *The four types of tab stops align text differently.*

SETTING A TAB-STOP POSITION

To set a tab stop, you select a paragraph or group of paragraphs, as you would for paragraph formatting, and then use the ruler or the Format Tabs command. When you set a tab stop, all the default tab stops to the left of the new tab stop are removed.

Using the Ruler

You can set tab stops on the ruler using either the mouse or the keyboard. Both methods put tab stops along the measure.

The mouse method

To set a tab stop using the mouse, select one of the tab-stop icons on the ruler. Then point to a position along the measure and click the left mouse button. A tab stop using the alignment you chose appears in that position. If you have a mouse, set a tab stop for the first paragraph of the menu:

1. Select the center tab-stop icon.
2. Move the pointer to the spot below the 3 mark of the measure and click the left button. A center tab-stop symbol appears there.

The keyboard method

You can also set tab stops along the measure using the keyboard. First, turn on the ruler mode (Ctrl-Shift-F10). Next, move the ruler cursor to the position you want along the measure and press one of the keys listed below to choose the kind of tab stop you want. Finally, press Ins to set the tab stop there. The four keys that choose types of tab stops are:

- 1—Left tab stop
- 2—Center tab stop
- 3—Right tab stop
- 4—Decimal tab stop

When you finish setting tab stops on the ruler, press Enter to apply the stops and turn off the ruler mode.

If you don't have a mouse, use the keyboard now to set a center tab stop:

1. Press Ctrl-Shift-F10 to turn on the ruler mode.
2. Press the right cursor key until the ruler cursor moves to the spot on the measure under the 3 mark.
3. Press 2 to select a center tab stop and Ins to insert the stop. A center tab-stop symbol appears on the ruler.
4. Press Enter to apply the tab stop and turn off the ruler mode.

Using the Format Tabs Command

To use the Format Tabs command to set tab stops, you open the Format Tabs dialog box (shown in Figure 8-5) by choosing Tabs from the Format menu.

To set a tab in the Format Tabs dialog box, first choose one of the tab-stop types in the Alignment section and then use the Position text box to enter a position in inches along the ruler. Choose the Set button at the bottom of the box to set the tab stop and start work on a new one. When you finish setting tab stops, choose the OK button to close the box and apply your tab stops to the selected paragraphs.

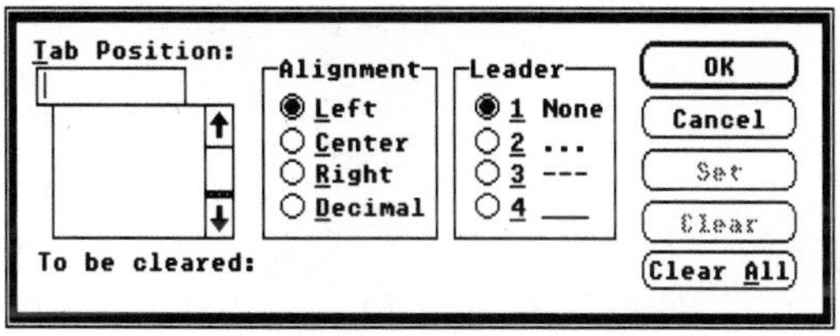

Figure 8-5. *The Format Tabs dialog box.*

Use the Format Tabs dialog box to set a second tab stop for the first paragraph of the menu:

1. Choose Tabs from the Format menu to open the Format Tabs dialog box.
2. Select the Right button in the Alignment section to choose a right tab stop. (Press Tab once and the down cursor key once.)
3. Select the Tab Position text box and enter the value *6* to set the tab stop at the 6 mark on the ruler.
4. Choose the Set button to set the tab stop. (Press Tab until you select the button, and then press Enter.)
5. Choose OK to close the box and apply the tab stop. The box closes, and a right tab-stop symbol appears at the 6 mark on the ruler, superimposed on the right margin marker of the paragraph.

Typing Text at a Tab Stop

Now you can try typing text at the tab stops you set and then enter the first few paragraphs of the menu:

1. Type *October 7, 1990* and press Tab to jump to the center tab stop.
2. Change the font size to 18 and set bold text formatting.
3. Type *Señor Fujiyama's.* (To enter the "ñ," hold down Alt, type *0241* on the numeric keypad, and then release Alt. Be sure that Num Lock is on when you do this.) The name centers on the tab stop.
4. Press Tab to jump to the right tab stop.
5. Reduce the font size to 10 and turn off bold formatting.
6. Type *Today's Menu.* The phrase appears flush against the right tab stop (and the right margin). Figure 8-6 at the end of this example shows the results.
7. To emphasize the text you entered, use the Format Paragraph command to add a double-line border below the paragraph.
8. Press Enter to start a new paragraph. Turn off the border and change the paragraph alignment to centered.

9. Type *For the finest in Japanese-Mexican cuisine!* and press Enter twice.
10. Turn on bold character formatting, type *Entrees*, and press Enter.
11. Turn off the bold character formatting. Use the Format Paragraph command to set the left paragraph indent to 1.75 inches and the right indent to 4.25 inches (1.75 inches from right).
12. Type *All entrees come with a side of refried beans, miso menudo, and pickled ginger.*
13. Press Enter twice. Figure 8-6 shows the results of your work. (Tab and paragraph marks are visible to help you see where you should press Tab and Enter.)

Notice that the tab stops you set in the first paragraph allowed you to align text left, right, and centered, all in the same left-aligned paragraph.

Figure 8-6. *The center and right phrases of the first line are positioned by tab stops. Notice the tab-stop markings along the measure of the ruler.*

ADDING TAB LEADERS

You use the Format Tabs dialog box to add a leader to a tab stop. If you have a mouse and want to open the box without using a menu command, simply double-click on a tab marker along the ruler measure. The Format Tabs dialog box opens.

On the left side of the dialog box, below the Position text box, is the tab list. It shows all the tabs set in the selected paragraph, listed in order of their positions on the ruler. To add a leader to one of these tabs, select it in the tab list, click on button 2, 3, or 4 in the Leader section of the dialog box (button 1 turns off the leader), and then select the Set button. The Leader buttons show the types of leaders they add: dotted line, dashed line, or solid line. After you set the leaders you want, choose OK to close the dialog box and apply the leader settings.

The menu has a section that lists the food prices. Set the tabs and leaders for that section:

1. Reset the paragraph indents to 0 and 6 inches, set the paragraph alignment to left, and clear all tab stops from the ruler. (To clear them, choose Tabs from the Format menu, select the Clear All button in the Format Tabs dialog box, and press Enter to close the box.)
2. Set a left tab at 0.5 inch.
3. Set a decimal tab at 2.5 inches.
4. Set a left tab at 3.5 inches.
5. Set a decimal tab at 5.5 inches. (Open the Format Tabs dialog box afterwards if it isn't already open.)
6. Select the 2.5-inch tab in the tab list box, turn on leader number 2 (the dotted line), and choose the Set button.
7. Select the 5.5-inch tab in the tab list box, turn on leader number 2, and choose the Set button.
8. Choose OK to close the dialog box and apply the tab settings.
9. Press Tab and then type the first line of the menu, pressing Tab between each item of text: *Yakitori chorizo*, Tab, *7.95*, Tab, *Tripe tempura*, Tab, *10.50*. Figure 8-7 shows where each tab mark appears.
10. Press Enter to start a new paragraph, and enter the next two lines of the menu using the same techniques. (Use Figure 8-7 for the text to type.) Press Enter twice at the end of the "Entrees" section.

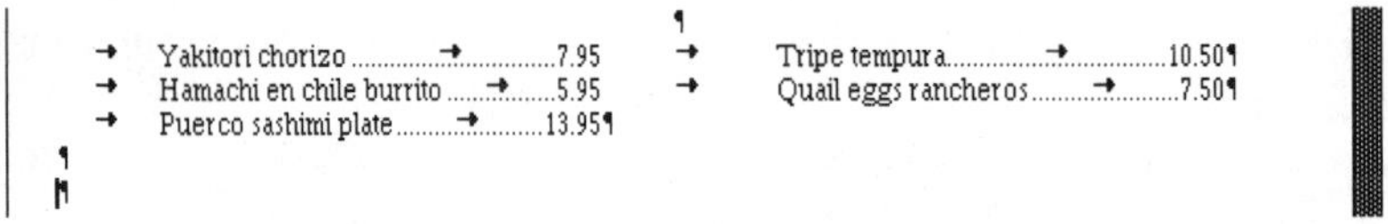

Figure 8-7. *Menu items and prices are tied together by tab leaders.*

Notice that each time you press Tab to jump to a tab stop that has a leader, a dotted line stretches from the old insertion-point location to the new insertion-point location.

CHANGING TAB STOPS

You can easily change tab stops after you've inserted them. As you do, you change the text aligned with them. You change the location of text you've entered by moving tab stops to new positions. You change the text alignment by changing the type of tab stop, and you change the type of leader by choosing a new leader for the tab stop. You can also entirely remove a tab stop from the ruler. Any text aligned with that tab stop moves right to the next tab stop.

Removing a Tab Stop

To remove a tab stop using the mouse, you drag the tab stop from the ruler to the main document window and drop it there. The tab stop disappears. To remove a tab stop using the keyboard, you turn on the ruler mode, center the ruler cursor over the tab stop you want to remove, press Del, and then press Enter to turn off the ruler mode.

To remove a tab stop using the Format Tabs dialog box, you open the dialog box, select a tab stop from the tab list box, choose the Clear button, and then choose OK to close the box and remove the tab stop. The Format Tabs dialog box offers another removal option that you used in the previous example. If you choose the Clear All button, Word removes every tab stop from the selected paragraphs and then adds default tab stops.

Changing a Tab-Stop Position

To change a tab-stop position using the mouse, simply drag a tab-stop marker on the ruler from one position to another; any text aligned with that tab stop moves with the tab to its new location. To change a tab-stop location using the keyboard (both on the ruler and in the Format Tabs dialog box), you must first remove the tab stop from its current location and then place a new tab stop at the new location. Try moving a tab stop in the last three paragraphs you entered:

1. Select the three lines of menu items (starting with "Yakitori," "Hamachi," and "Puerco").

2. Move the left tab stop at the 0.5 mark on the ruler to the 0.25 mark. All the text in the first column moves with the mark.
3. Return the tab stop to the 0.5 position. All the text moves back to its original position.

Once you align columns of text around a tab stop, you can move the columns by moving the tab stop.

Changing Tab-Stop Alignment

To change the text alignment of a tab stop on the ruler, first remove the tab stop and then replace it with a different type of tab stop. You can do this using either the mouse or the keyboard. To change text alignment in the Format Tabs dialog box, select the tab you want to change from the tab list, turn on a new alignment option in the Alignment section, choose the Set button, and then choose OK. As soon as you change the alignment, all the text aligned to that tab stop changes its position in the text line.

Changing a Tab-Stop Leader

To change a tab-stop leader, you must use the Format Tabs dialog box. Select the tab stop you want from the tab list box, turn on a new leader option in the Leader section, choose the Set button, and then choose OK when you finish. If you select option 1 (None), you turn off the leader completely. Once you change a tab-stop leader, all leaders tied to that tab stop change to the new type of leader.

Finishing the Menu Example

To finish the menu, enter the next two sections of text as you did the first section, and finish off by using a new tab technique:

1. Turn on bold character formatting and change the paragraph alignment to centered.
2. Type *Side Dishes* and press Enter twice.
3. Turn off the bold character formatting and change the paragraph alignment to left. Type the next two lines of text, pressing Tab where you see the tab marks in Figure 8-8.

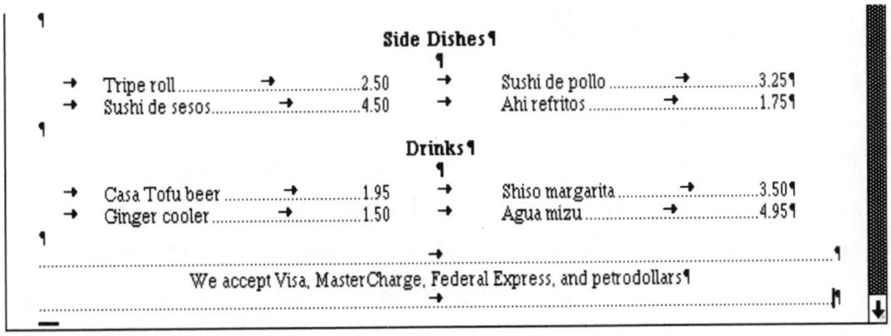

Figure 8-8. *The last section of the menu uses tab leaders to create two dotted lines across the page.*

4. Press Enter twice to finish the "Side Dishes" section.
5. Enter the next section, "Drinks," as you entered the previous one. When you finish, press Enter twice.
6. Clear all tab stops from the ruler and then set a single right tab stop at the 6 mark. (If you do this using the mouse, you have to insert the tab stop to the left of the margin mark and then drag it over to the 6 mark. You cannot insert a tab stop directly on a margin marker.)
7. Use the Format Tabs dialog box to turn on tab leader number 2 (the dotted line) for the tab stop you inserted.
8. Press Tab. A dotted line appears across the page.
9. Press Enter to start a new paragraph, and set the paragraph alignment to centered.
10. Type the last sentence and press Enter.
11. Set the paragraph alignment to left and press Tab to enter a dotted line across the page.

You finished Señor Fujiyama's menu using a tab stop as a convenient way to add dotted lines across the page. Using tab leaders this way gives you alternatives to the line patterns offered as paragraph borders.

A QUICK SUMMARY

You learned in this chapter that tab stops are a type of paragraph formatting. Each tab stop sets a stopping position, text alignment, and type of leader. You saw how to set tab stops using the ruler and the Format Tabs command, and you learned how to move, remove, and alter existing tabs to control the appearance of columns and lines of text. In the next chapter, you learn to add headers and footers, two Word features that number and identify pages in your documents.

Chapter 9

Headers and Footers:

Topping (and Bottoming) Your Work

A document of more than one or two pages needs identification on each page to tie the pages together and to help readers find their way through the document. Word for Windows identifies pages with headers and footers, two features that label the top and bottom of each page you print. In this chapter, you learn how to create headers and footers that include page numbers, the date and time, and any other text you care to add. You learn how to set header and footer positions on the page, suppress them on the first page, and create different headers and footers for alternate pages. You also learn how to view headers and footers on your monitor before you print your document.

SETTING UP WORD

To use the examples in this chapter, start Word and be sure you have the same settings in effect as you used in the past several chapters:

- Full menus
- A text window that shows the ruler, ribbon, and status bar
- The Display as Printed option turned off and the Pictures option turned on (in the View Preferences dialog box)

Because headers and footers are intended for documents of many pages, the sample document for this chapter is a three-page report. The content of the document is unimportant, so use Cut and Paste to duplicate a single paragraph 20 times for the body of the document. Start by entering a title:

1. Set paragraph alignment to centered and character formatting to bold, 24-point text, and then type *Reiteration Report.* Press Enter to start a new paragraph.
2. Set paragraph formatting to include an open line before each paragraph.
3. Reduce the character size to 10 points and type *by Randall Redux.* Press Enter.
4. Set paragraph alignment to left and line spacing to double. Turn off bold character formatting.
5. Type the text of the paragraph shown in Figure 9-1 and press Enter at the end of the paragraph.
6. Select the paragraph you typed and choose Copy from the Edit menu.
7. Move the insertion point to the blank line following the paragraph.
8. Press Shift-Ins 20 times to paste 20 copies of the paragraph into the document.

The resulting document should be three pages long.

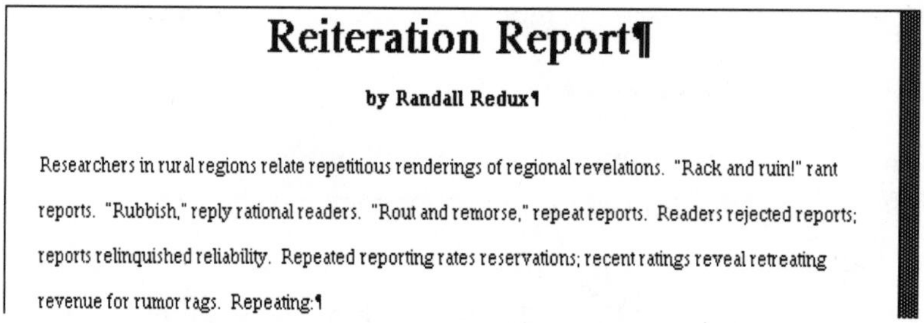
Reiteration Report¶

by Randall Redux¶

Researchers in rural regions relate repetitious renderings of regional revelations. "Rack and ruin!" rant reports. "Rubbish," reply rational readers. "Rout and remorse," repeat reports. Readers rejected reports; reports relinquished reliability. Repeated reporting rates reservations; recent ratings reveal retreating revenue for rumor rags. Repeating:¶

Figure 9-1. *Enter the paragraph beneath the heading and duplicate it 20 times.*

After you add headers and footers to this document using the examples that follow, the finished document looks like the one shown in Figure 9-2.

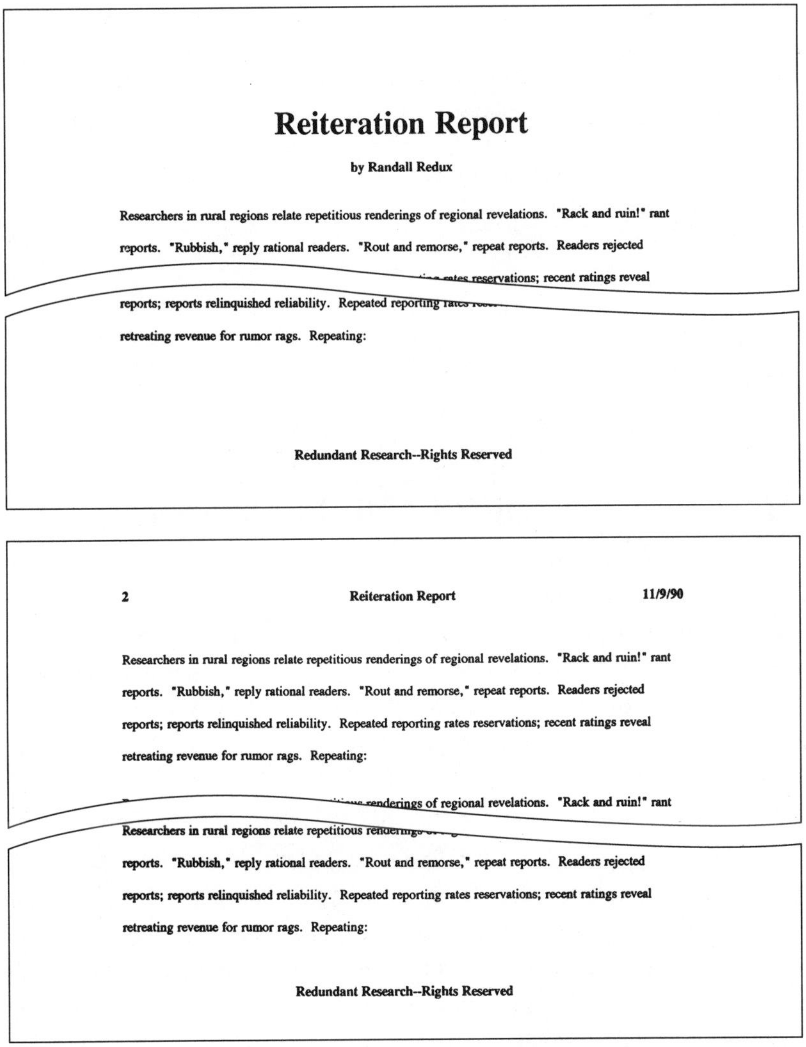

Reiteration Report

by Randall Redux

Researchers in rural regions relate repetitious renderings of regional revelations. "Rack and ruin!" rant reports. "Rubbish," reply rational readers. "Rout and remorse," repeat reports. Readers rejected ...ations; recent ratings reveal

reports; reports relinquished reliability. Repeated reporting ... retreating revenue for rumor rags. Repeating:

Redundant Research--Rights Reserved

2 **Reiteration Report** **11/9/90**

Researchers in rural regions relate repetitious renderings of regional revelations. "Rack and ruin!" rant reports. "Rubbish," reply rational readers. "Rout and remorse," repeat reports. Readers rejected reports; reports relinquished reliability. Repeated reporting rates reservations; recent ratings reveal retreating revenue for rumor rags. Repeating:

...renderings of regional revelations. "Rack and ruin!" rant

Researchers in rural regions relate repetitious ...

reports. "Rubbish," reply rational readers. "Rout and remorse," repeat reports. Readers rejected reports; reports relinquished reliability. Repeated reporting rates reservations; recent ratings reveal retreating revenue for rumor rags. Repeating:

Redundant Research--Rights Reserved

(continued)

Figure 9-2.
The finished report has headers and footers added to its printed pages.

Figure 9-2. *continued*

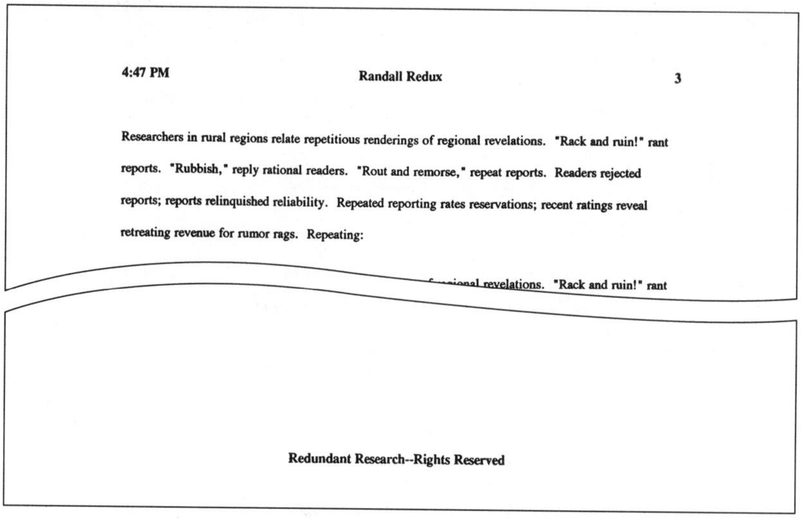

4:47 PM Randall Redux 3

Researchers in rural regions relate repetitious renderings of regional revelations. "Rack and ruin!" rant reports. "Rubbish," reply rational readers. "Rout and remorse," repeat reports. Readers rejected reports; reports relinquished reliability. Repeated reporting rates reservations; recent ratings reveal retreating revenue for rumor rags. Repeating:

regional revelations. "Rack and ruin!" rant

Redundant Research--Rights Reserved

WHAT ARE HEADERS AND FOOTERS?

A *header* is a banner of text at the top of each page of a printed document. A typical header includes the name of the document, the page number, and other information such as the author's name or the date of the document creation. A header in Word can be as short or as long as you like, from a lone page number to a full page of text. You can add character formatting to create distinctive text and paragraph formatting to shape text in the header. You can also add graphics if you like.

A *footer* serves the same purpose as a header but lies at the bottom of each page. Some documents use footers in place of headers, putting page numbers and title information at the bottom of each page. Other documents use footers in addition to headers, printing additional document information such as copyright notices or company names. Word footers—like headers—can use formatted text and graphics. You can create long or short footers, and you can include both a footer and a header on the same page.

Footers and headers don't normally appear in the main document window on your monitor because they break up the body of your text and make editing difficult. To create and edit headers and footers, you open a separate section of the document window called a *pane*.

CREATING HEADERS AND FOOTERS

To open a pane for a header or footer, you choose the Header/Footer command from the Edit menu. It opens the Header/Footer dialog box shown in Figure 9-3.

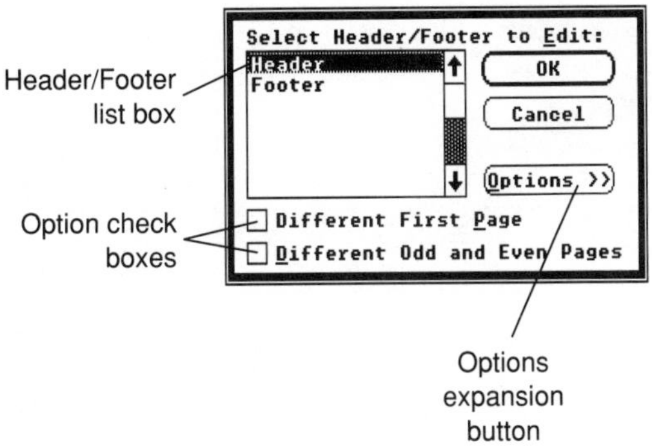

Figure 9-3. *The Header/Footer dialog box.*

The Header/Footer Dialog Box

The list box in the upper left corner of the dialog box shows the types of headers and footers you can edit. At the moment, two are available: Header and Footer. When you use header and footer options discussed later in the chapter, additional choices appear in the list box.

The two check boxes at the bottom of the dialog box offer options that add choices to the list box: a separate header and footer for the first page, and different headers and footers for odd and even pages. The top two buttons on the right—OK and Cancel—are standard, but the third button—Options—is not. It expands the dialog box to offer more options that you learn to use later in the chapter.

Creating a Header

To create a header, use the mouse to double-click on the header name in the list box or use the keyboard to select the name (if it isn't already selected). Choose the OK button to close the dialog box. The header/footer pane (shown in Figure 9-4 on the following page) opens in the bottom of the window.

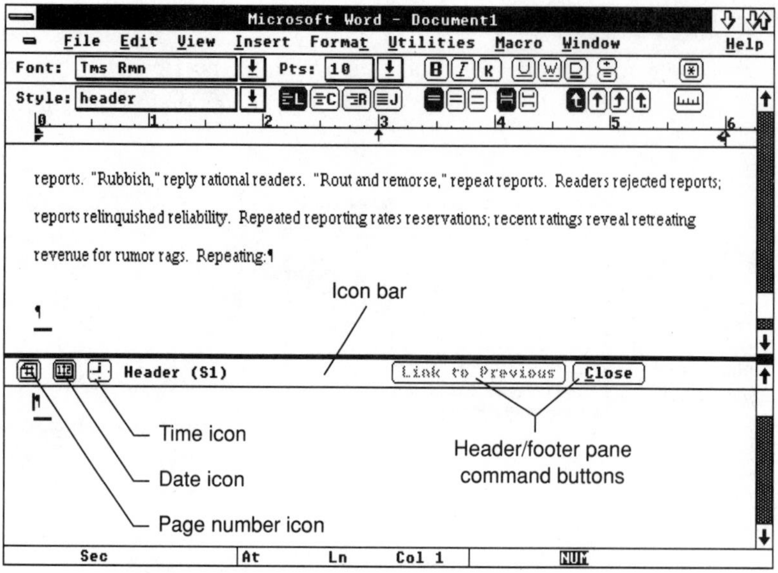

Figure 9-4. *The header/footer pane opens in the bottom of the document window.*

The bar at the top of the header/footer pane is the *icon bar*. The three icons on its left side insert the page number, today's date, or the current time in the header. Next to these icons is the type of header or footer being edited (Header) and the section of the document the header affects (S1). The Link to Previous button is for use in documents containing more than one section. You don't need to use it here. The last button in the icon bar, Close, closes the header pane when you finish creating a header.

The empty area below the icon bar contains the insertion point and an end-of-document mark like those in the main document window. As you type in the header pane, you're entering text that becomes part of the header, not part of the body of the document.

Entering text

You enter text in the header/footer pane the same way you do in the main document window. You can apply character and paragraph formatting by using the ribbon and the ruler or by using commands on the Format menu. Note that Word sets two tab stops for you: a centered tab stop in the middle of the measure and a right tab stop at the right end of the measure. Use these tab stops to center text or to align it flush right. If you prefer, you can remove these tab stops and set your own.

Entering page numbers, date, and time

To enter a page number, the date, or the time in the header, move the insertion point to the location you want and select either the page number, date, or time icon to insert a *field.* A field tells Word to perform an action at the insertion-point location. The different fields you insert using the header-pane icons tell Word to perform these actions:

- The page number field tells Word to insert the appropriate page number at the field's location when Word prints the document.
- The date field tells Word to insert the day's date at the field's location when Word prints the document. Word reads the date from your computer's built-in clock.
- The time field tells Word to insert the current time at the field's location when Word prints the document. Word reads the time from your computer's built-in clock.

Fields are one of Word's most powerful features. These are only three of more than a hundred fields available in Word. Other fields perform calculations, insert author names, compile indexes, and much more. You'll learn more about fields in Chapter 24.

To select a field icon using the mouse, simply point to the icon and press the left button; Word inserts the field at the insertion-point location. To insert a field using the keyboard, press Shift-F10, and then press a single letter key for the icon field you want: P for the page number field, D for the date field, or T for the time field.

Enter a header now for your document:

1. Choose the Header/Footer command from the Edit menu to open the Header/Footer dialog box.
2. Press Enter to open the header/footer pane. (Header is already selected in the list box, so pressing Enter opens the pane to edit the header.)

3. Turn on bold character formatting.
4. Insert a page number field by selecting the page number icon or by pressing Shift-F10 followed by P. The number 1 appears in boldface at the left side of the header.
5. Press Tab to jump to the centered tab stop in the middle of the line and type *Reiteration Report*. It appears centered on the line.
6. Press Tab to jump to the right tab stop at the end of the line, and insert a date field by selecting the date icon or by pressing Shift-F10 followed by D. Today's date appears flush against the right end of the line.
7. Close the pane by using the mouse to select the Close button in the icon bar or by pressing Shift-F10 followed by C (for Close).

Creating a Footer

Creating a footer works exactly like creating a header except that you open the header/footer pane by selecting Footer in the list box and that once you open the pane, the icon bar reads Footer instead of Header. You insert text, time, date, and page numbers exactly as you do in the header. Add a footer to your document:

1. Choose Header/Footer from the Edit menu to open the Header/Footer dialog box.
2. Choose Footer from the list box and then choose OK (or press Enter) to open the header/footer pane.
3. Press Tab to move to the centered tab stop, turn on bold character formatting, and type *Redundant Research--Rights Reserved.*
4. Close the header/footer pane by selecting the Close button or by pressing Shift-F10 followed by C.

Note that when you create a header or a footer, you should not press Enter at the end of the last line. If you do, you add a blank line below the last line of text; that blank line increases the height of the header or footer and takes space from the main body of the text.

VIEWING HEADERS AND FOOTERS

When you close the header/footer pane, Words remembers the header or footer you created and applies it when you print the document. The header or footer doesn't appear in the main document window. To see how headers and footers look before you print the document, use Page View. To turn on Page View, choose Page from the View menu.

When you use Page View, the document window changes. The scroll bar adds a small icon at each end of the scroll bar, the measure on the ruler changes slightly, and you see each page as it will print out. Page View works differently from the normal view you've used up to this point; Chapter 21 details its workings. To view your headers and footers, you need only know how to scroll through the pages of your document: To scroll up, press the up cursor key; to scroll down, press the down cursor key.

To view the headers and footers you just created:

1. Choose Page from the View menu to turn on Page View.
2. Press Ctrl-Home to move to the first line of the document, and then press the up cursor key to move up one line to the header. You see the blank margin at the top of the page and the header line you created earlier.
3. Press PgDn to move the insertion point one screen down the page. Keep pressing (slowly) until you come to the end of the page. You see the footer there, followed by the blank margin at the bottom.
4. Press PgDn twice to jump to the top of the next page, and then press PgUp to see the top of the page. You see the second page header there, with the page number showing page 2.
5. Continue scrolling with PgUp or PgDn until you see how the headers and footers are set on each page.
6. To turn off Page View, choose Page from the View menu.

HEADER AND FOOTER OPTIONS

You might want to use different headers and footers for different pages of your document. For example, the title page of the report would look better if you eliminated the header above the report title. Word offers optional headers and footers you can turn on in the Header/Footer dialog box.

Creating Headers and Footers for a Title Page

To create a special header and footer for a title page, turn on the Different First Page option in the Header/Footer dialog box. This adds two entries to the list box—First Header and First Footer. Your document now has two headers and two footers: First Header and First Footer contain the header and footer that appear on the first page of the document. Header and Footer contain the header and footer that appear on all subsequent pages.

To create the first-page header, select First Header in the list box and press Enter to open the header/footer pane. It's empty at first. You enter text and fields in this pane the same way you did when you created the regular header and footer. Close the pane when you finish. Anything you enter appears as the header on the first page only. If you enter nothing in the pane, no header appears on the first page.

You create the first-page footer by selecting First Footer in the list box. Any footer you create in the opened pane appears only on the first page.

Create a special blank header for the title page of the report and set the title-page footer to match the regular footer:

1. Choose Header/Footer from the Edit menu to open the Header/Footer dialog box.
2. Turn on the Different First Page option. First Header and First Footer appear in the list box.
3. Select First Footer and press Enter to open the header/footer pane.
4. Duplicate the footer used in the rest of the document: Turn on bold character formatting, press Tab once to center the text, and then type *Redundant Research--Rights Reserved.*
5. Close the pane by selecting Close or by pressing Shift-F10 and then C.

Notice that you didn't need to select First Header to create a header for the first page. The first header is blank until you fill it in—you wanted to leave it blank, so you could simply go on to the footer. The first footer is also blank, so you had to open it and duplicate the footer used in the rest of the document. To see the results of your first-page header and footer, turn on Page View and scroll through the document. When you have finished, turn off Page View.

Creating Headers and Footers for Facing Pages

If you create a Word document designed to print facing pages (to be copied later onto both sides of the paper and bound), you can use separate headers and footers for even-numbered and odd-numbered pages. Separate headers and footers make it possible to keep the page number in the outer corner of each page—on the right side of odd-numbered pages and on the left side of even-numbered pages. Separate headers and footers can also include different information, such as the document title on even-numbered pages and the section title on odd-numbered pages. The sample printout at the beginning of the chapter shows how headers and footers work on facing pages.

To create headers and footers for facing pages, turn on the Different Odd and Even Pages option in the Header/Footer dialog box. When you do so, the Header and Footer entries in the list box are replaced with Even Header, Even Footer, Odd Header, and Odd Footer. Even Header and Even Footer contain the header and footer for even-numbered pages. Odd Header and Odd Footer contain the header and footer for odd-numbered pages. To enter text and fields for these new headers and footers, you select them, open the header/footer pane, and type or use the icon bar as you do to create other headers and footers.

Note that when you create odd and even headers and footers, Word retains the contents of the standard header and footer (not the first-page header and footer) in the odd header and footer, and it leaves the even header and footer blank.

Set up the headers and footers in the report so that they work for facing pages: Create odd and even headers and footers, edit the odd header so that it looks good on an odd page, and then fill in the even header and footer.

1. Choose Header/Footer from the Edit menu to open the Header/Footer dialog box.
2. Turn on the Different Odd and Even Pages option. Odd and even header and footer entries appear in the list box.
3. Choose Odd Header in the list box and press Enter to open the header/footer pane.
4. Delete the text currently in the pane.

5. Turn on bold character formatting (if it isn't already on) and then choose the time icon to enter a time field.
6. Press Tab to move to the center of the line, and type *Randall Redux.*
7. Press Tab to move to the right end of the line, and choose the page number icon to enter a page number field.
8. Choose Header/Footer from the Edit menu to open the Header/Footer dialog box, choose Even Header, and then press Enter to show the even header in the header/footer pane.
9. Turn on bold formatting, and then insert a page number field by selecting the page number icon. The number "1" appears in boldface at the left side of the header.
10. Press Tab to jump to the center tab stop in the middle of the line, and type *Reiteration Report.* It appears centered on the line.
11. Press Tab to jump to the right tab stop at the end of the line, and insert a date field by selecting the date icon. Today's date appears flush against the right end of the line.
12. Choose Header/Footer from the Edit menu to open the Header/Footer dialog box, choose Even Footer, and then press Enter to show the even footer in the header/footer pane.
13. Press Tab to move to the center tab stop, turn on bold character formatting, and type *Redundant Research--Rights Reserved.*
14. Close the pane.
15. Use Save As (from the File menu) to save this report under the name REDUNREP. You'll use the report as a sample document in the next chapter.

You now have an odd-numbered page header with the time of printing in the upper left corner of the page, the author's name in the middle, and the page number in the upper right (outer) corner of the page.

To see the results of your new headers and footers, turn on Page View and scroll through the pages. The headers and footers should look like the ones shown at the beginning of this chapter. Turn off Page View when you have finished.

CONTROLLING PAGE NUMBERS

When you insert a page number field in a header or footer, Word numbers pages starting at page 1 and counting up, using Arabic numerals. To start numbering using a number other than 1 or to use letters or Roman numerals to number the pages, you can change page numbering in the Header/Footer dialog box.

Setting the Starting Number

To change page numbering, you first open the Header/Footer dialog box and then choose the Options button. The dialog box expands to display the extra controls shown in Figure 9-5.

To set the starting page number for a document, select the Start At text box, type the starting number, and press Enter to close the dialog box. For example, if you entered *6* in the Start At box, Word would number the first page 6 (even if there were no page number set to print on that page) and continue by numbering the following pages 7, 8, 9, and so on.

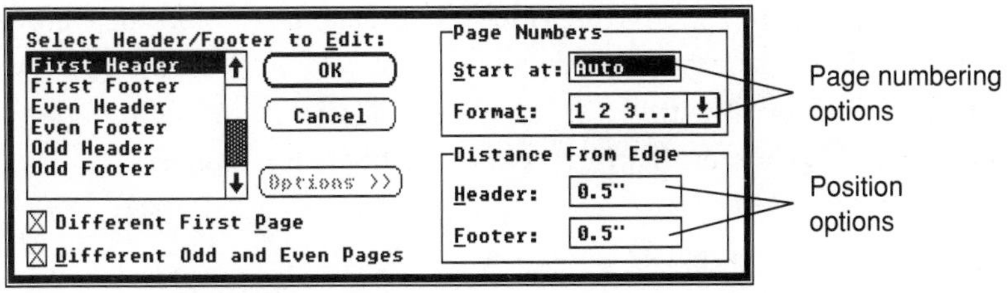

Figure 9-5. *These header and footer options control page numbering and header and footer positions.*

Choosing a Numbering Format

The Format list box offers a selection of numbering systems to choose from: the normal Arabic system, lowercase letters, uppercase letters, lowercase Roman numerals, and uppercase Roman numerals. Choose the system you want by opening the list box and selecting the appropriate system. Once you select, press Enter to close the dialog box.

SETTING HEADER AND FOOTER LOCATIONS

Word's normal header location starts ½ inch from the top edge of the page and continues as far as you have text and graphics in the header. Word's normal footer location starts ½ inch from the bottom edge of the page and continues up far enough to hold all the text and graphics you entered in the footer. You can change the locations by opening the Header/Footer dialog box, choosing the Options button to expand the box, and changing the values in the Header and Footer text boxes.

The values you enter measure the distance in inches from the top or bottom of the page to the beginning of the header or footer. For example, if you entered *2* in the Header text box, all headers in the document (including the first header and odd and even headers) would start 2 inches from the top of the page. Entering *1.5* in the Footer text box would position all footers in the document 1½ inches from the bottom of the page.

As you move headers and footers toward the middle of the page, you shrink the main text area so that Word can't fit as many words of the main text body on each page. You can set the headers and footers to appear closer to the top and bottom of the page, which gives each page more text area, but be careful if you use a laser printer and set a distance less than ½ inch. Most laser printers can't print within ½ inch of the page edge and might ignore the part of the header or footer that falls within the ½-inch boundary.

A QUICK SUMMARY

In this chapter you learned to create headers and footers by using header and footer panes. You learned how to insert date, time, and page number fields in your headers and footers and how to control the way Word numbers pages. You also saw how to create headers and footers for a title page and for facing pages by using header and footer options. In the next chapter you learn more about the way Word creates document pages.

Chapter 10

Creating Pages

As you learned in previous chapters, Word for Windows breaks long documents into pages before printing, a process called *pagination*. In this chapter, you learn how to control Word's pagination: to insert your own page breaks, protect parts of a document from page breaks, and choose how Word sets page breaks during pagination. You also learn how to preview and adjust Word's page breaks before you print.

SETTING UP WORD

To use the examples in this chapter, start Word and be sure that these settings are in effect:

- Full menus
- A text window that shows the ruler, ribbon, and status bar
- The Display as Printed option turned off and the Pictures option turned on (in the View Preferences dialog box)

The report you created and saved in the preceding chapter is suitable for using in this chapter to work with pagination. Open the report using the Open command on the File menu. It should appear under the filename REDUNREP.DOC.

HOW WORD SETS PAGE BREAKS

Word treats a long document stored in the computer's memory as one very long page through which you can scroll. When you print, Word can no longer maintain the document as one long page; it must break the document into separate pages to fit on sheets of 8½-inch-by-11-inch paper.

To calculate where to place each page break, Word first determines the amount of vertical space available for each page. It looks at the top and bottom page margins—usually one inch each—and subtracts them from the main text space. It checks for footnotes (or other, similar page additions, which you learn about in Chapter 14), computes their total depth, and subtracts that from the main text space as well. Word then knows how much vertical space it can use for the main text on each page and begins pagination.

To paginate a document, Word starts at the beginning and reads down until it reaches the maximum number of lines it can fit in the main text area of the first page. It inserts a page break at this location, which appears in your document as a dotted line across the screen. Word starts reading again, and when it reaches the end of the text it can fit onto the second page, it inserts another page break there. And so it continues, until it reaches the end of the document—inserting page breaks so that each page has as much text as possible but not so much that the text overruns headers, footers, footnotes, or margins.

Soft Page Breaks

Word's page breaks aren't anchored to specific locations in the document; they're flexible. If you edit or format the document after page breaks are in place—perhaps by inserting or cutting text in the middle of a page—there might be too much or too little text per page. Word must repaginate the document by moving the page breaks before it prints the document. These flexible page breaks are called *soft page breaks*.

Automatic Background Pagination

Because it's convenient to see where Word inserts page breaks as you type (so that you can watch for page breaks in bad locations), Word uses *background pagination* to constantly repaginate the document. When you enter enough text to fill a page, Word inserts a page break on the screen. If you change the document, Word relocates the page breaks to fit the changes.

If you don't want to see page breaks appear and change as you work, you can turn off background pagination by choosing Customize from the Utilities menu. This opens the Customize dialog box (shown in Figure 10-1), where you can turn off the Background Pagination option. Once the option is off, Word stops inserting page breaks as you enter text. Any page breaks already in your document remain where they are, regardless of editing and formatting changes, until you print your document or use the Repaginate Now command.

Try adding text to the report to see the results of background pagination:

1. Scroll through the report until you find the page break at the end of the second page.
2. Move the insertion point a couple of lines above the page break, and type two or three lines of text. (Anything will do.) Word moves the page break up several lines to accommodate the new text you entered.
3. Choose Customize from the Utilities menu to open the Customize dialog box.
4. Turn off the Background Pagination option and choose OK to close the box.
5. Enter several more lines of text.

Notice that the page break on the screen no longer changes its position as you add new lines to the page.

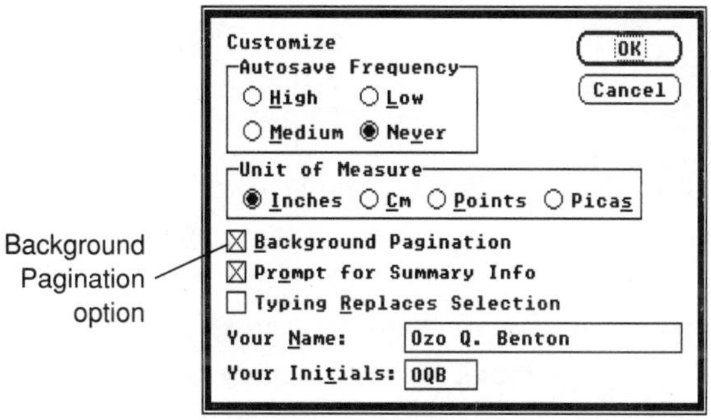

Figure 10-1. *The Customize dialog box.*

The Repaginate Now Command

Repaginate Now, on the Utilities menu, tells Word to repaginate the document. It resets all the page breaks to fit the current document contents. Although you don't need to use Repaginate Now if you have background pagination turned on, you can use it before you print to see where page breaks occur when background pagination is turned off. Try it on the report:

- Choose Repaginate Now from the Utilities menu.

The page break on the screen moves up several lines to accommodate the new lines you previously entered. Now turn background pagination back on for the rest of the examples in the chapter:

1. Choose Customize from the Utilities menu to open the Customize dialog box.
2. Turn on the Background Pagination option and choose OK to close the box.

SETTING YOUR OWN PAGE BREAKS

When Word paginates, the page breaks don't always occur where you want them. For example, if you create a document with several chapters, you might want to start each chapter on a new page, leaving the last page of each chapter less than full if necessary. Because Word tries to fill each page as it paginates, the beginning of a chapter might appear in the middle of a page if the last page of the previous chapter isn't full. You can insert your own page breaks, called *hard page breaks,* in a document. Hard page breaks don't move during repagination; they force Word to start a new page whether or not the previous page is full.

Inserting a Hard Page Break

To insert a hard page break, move the insertion point to the location you want (the beginning of the line you want to appear at the top of the page) and press Ctrl-Enter. A hard-page-break line appears on the screen. The hard page break differs from the soft page break in appearance: the hard page break is a closely spaced dotted line, while the soft page break is a "stretched-out" dotted line.

To insert a page break using the menus, choose Page Break from the Insert menu if you're using short menus or Break from the Insert menu if you're using full menus. The Page Break command immediately inserts a hard page break at the insertion point. The Break command opens the Insert Break dialog box (shown in Figure 10-2), where you choose the Page Break option and the OK button to insert a hard page break.

To delete a page break (hard or soft), simply move the insertion point to the beginning of the line following the page break and press Backspace.

Try adding hard page breaks to the report:

1. Move the insertion point to the beginning of the line immediately above the soft page break.
2. Press Ctrl-Enter. A hard page break appears above the line and the soft page break moves down to a new location, a full page after the new hard break.
3. Move the insertion point to the beginning of the line above the hard page break you entered and then press Ctrl-Enter to insert a new hard page break. A second hard page break appears.

The line between the two hard page breaks will appear alone on its own page when you print the document.

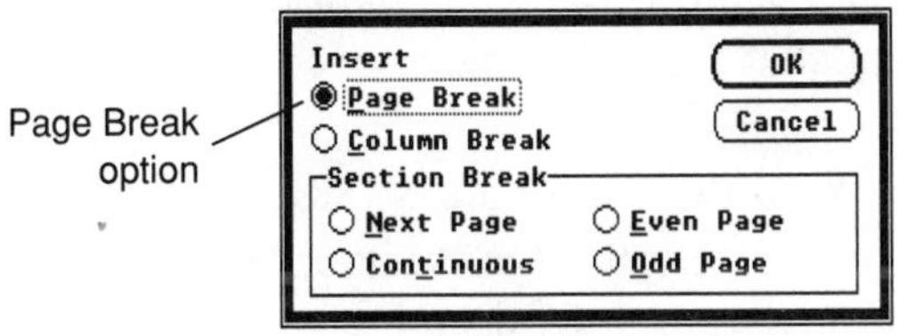

Figure 10-2. *The Insert Break dialog box.*

Specifying Word's Page Breaks

Inserting a hard page break forces Word to start a new page at that location. An alternative is to select a paragraph and specify that Word insert a soft page break before or after that paragraph when it paginates.

A paragraph at the top of a page

You learned in Chapter 7 one way to specify a soft page break using the Paragraph command in the Format menu: When you turn on the Page Break Before option in the Format Paragraph dialog box, Word inserts a soft page break before the selected paragraph when it paginates the document. To remove the soft page break, select the paragraph and turn off the option.

A paragraph on its own page

To set a paragraph so that it appears on its own page, simply insert two hard page breaks, one before and one after the paragraph.

AVOIDING BAD PAGE BREAKS

A document might have several parts you don't want split by a soft page break. You can control where Word places its page breaks by protecting parts of the document using the Format Paragraph command or by setting the method you want Word to use to determine page breaks within paragraphs.

Widow and Orphan Control

When Word paginates a document, it checks to be sure it doesn't leave *widows* and *orphans*. A widow is a single line split from the end of a paragraph and placed alone at the top of the next page. An orphan is a single line split from the beginning of a paragraph and left standing alone at the end of the preceding page.

To avoid widows and orphans, Word looks at the lines it creates when it splits a paragraph. If Word sees an orphan, it moves the page break up one line, moving the orphan to the beginning of the next page so that it rejoins the paragraph. If Word sees a widow, it moves the page break up one line, moving a second line of the paragraph to join the widow on the next page. Note, however, one important fact: Word can't protect paragraphs of two or three lines against widows and orphans. No matter how you split the paragraph, a widow, an orphan, or both occur.

If you don't want Word to check for widows and orphans, you can turn off this feature by choosing Document from the Format menu to open the Format Document dialog box, shown in Figure 10-3. Turn off the option labeled Widow Control in the lower right corner of the dialog box and choose OK to close the dialog box.

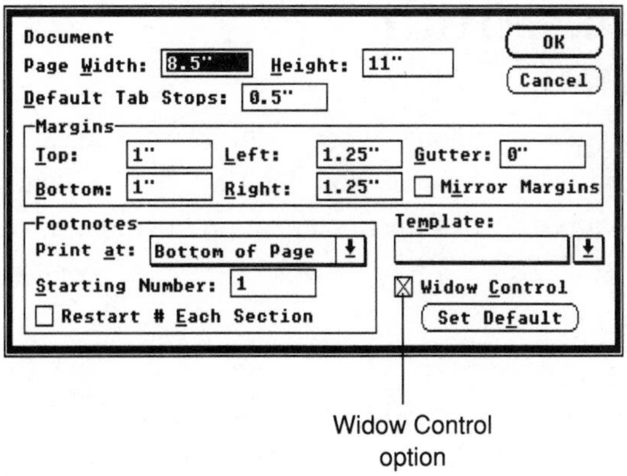

Figure 10-3. *The Format Document dialog box.*

Protecting Blocks of Text from Page Breaks

You learned in Chapter 7 that the Keep Paragraph Together option (in the Format Paragraph dialog box) protects a paragraph from being split by a page break. You also learned that the Keep Paragraph With Next option (also in the Format Paragraph dialog box) binds a selected paragraph to the following paragraph so that Word won't insert a page break between them.

You can combine these options to protect large parts of a document from page breaks. For example, if you select three paragraphs and turn on both options, you create a block of three paragraphs that Word can't split or separate from each other. In addition, you bind the third paragraph to the one following so that Word can't insert a page break between them.

Using this method, it's possible to protect a block so large that it won't fit on a single page. In that case, Word has no option but to split the protected block with a page break.

Protecting Pictures from Page Breaks

Word never splits a picture using a page break because it treats the picture as a single character. Many pictures, though, have captions that might be separated from them by a page break. To bind a picture and a following caption together and protect them from page breaks, select the picture and then set the Keep Paragraph With Next option in the Format Paragraph dialog box. (This works only if the picture and caption are two separate, adjacent paragraphs.)

SEEING THE PAGE LAYOUT BEFORE YOU PRINT

Word shows you in the document window where page breaks occur, but it doesn't show you how the page layout looks. You don't see headers and footers or page margins. To see a preview of the document on the monitor before you print, use Print Preview.

Print Preview

When you choose Print Preview from the File menu, the text window shows a preview (similar to that in Figure 10-4) of your document as it will appear when printed. You see the pages reduced in size to fit in the window. Because the text size is reduced, you might not be able to read all the words in the document, but you can see how and where the body, headers, footers, and footnotes appear on the page. If the page layout doesn't look the way you want, you can quit Print Preview and change page breaks, headers, footers, and formatting to get the results you want. (In Chapter 17, you'll learn how to change margins, page breaks, and header and footer locations directly in Print Preview.)

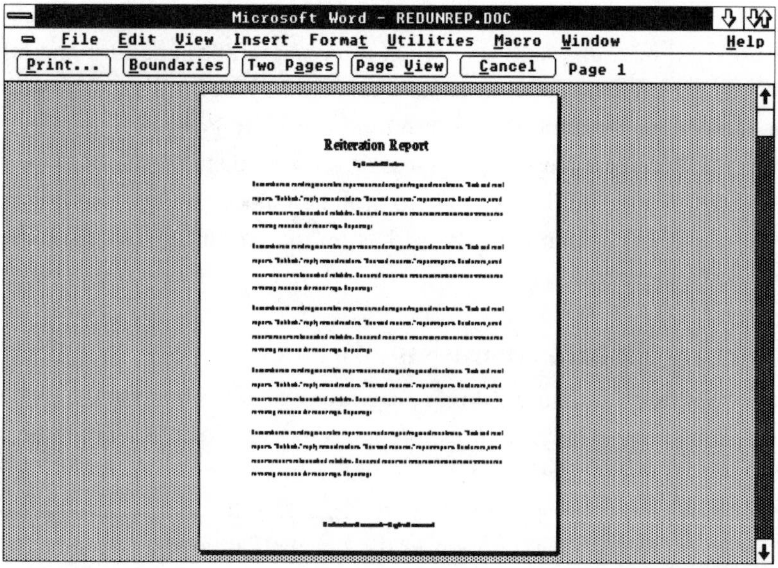

Figure 10-4. *The Print Preview screen.*

Paging through the document

To page through the document in Print Preview using the mouse, use the scroll bar on the right side of the window. Click on the down arrow or the gray area below the thumb to move to the next page; click on the up arrow or the gray area above the thumb to move to the preceding page. The page number you're viewing appears on the right side of the icon bar. To use the keyboard, press PgDn to see the next page or PgUp to see the preceding page.

One-page and two-page displays

When you first use Print Preview, it shows you one page of the document at a time. You can see two pages at a time by choosing the Two Pages button on the icon bar or by pressing the A key. To return to a one-page display, choose the One Page button or press A.

Quitting Print Preview

To quit Print Preview, press Esc, choose the Close or Cancel button, or choose Print Preview from the File menu.

Viewing the sample report

Use Print Preview now to view your report:

1. Choose Print Preview from the File menu. The first page appears in the text window.
2. Click on the down arrow of the scroll bar or press PgDn. Page 2 appears in the window.
3. Click on the Two Pages button or press A. Two pages of the report appear at the same time in the window.
4. Use the scroll bar or the PgDn and PgUp keys to page through the document. You should see the page containing the single line that you set earlier by inserting two hard page breaks.
5. Quit Print Preview by pressing Esc.

A QUICK SUMMARY

In this chapter you learned how Word paginates documents. You learned the difference between soft and hard page breaks and how to control Word's pagination through background pagination and by using the Repaginate Now command. You also learned how to insert and delete your own page breaks. The chapter taught you how to use paragraph formatting to specify soft page breaks before or after a paragraph, to protect paragraphs from page breaks, and to bind two paragraphs into a protected group. The final part of the chapter showed you how to use Print Preview to see pages before you print them. In the next chapter—the last chapter of this section—you learn new techniques for saving, opening, and printing documents.

Chapter 11

Saving, Opening, and Printing a Document

If you have the Special Edition with disks included, consult the Introduction

This chapter discusses activities important to finishing a Word for Windows document: saving and retrieving your work and printing your document. You learn useful details about saving documents in different directories or on different disk drives; saving documents so that you can use them in other programs; and setting Word to periodically save as you create a document. You also learn how to search different drives and directories and how to retrieve saved documents using wildcard characters. You even learn to load documents created on other word processors.

The last section of this chapter teaches you printing options. You learn how to limit the number of pages you print, how to print several copies of a document, how to set Word to work with different types of paper feeds, and how to print additional information about your document.

SETTING UP WORD

Because you're going to print a document in this chapter, you must change the Word settings you used in the preceding chapter so that the document window shows what you print. Start Word, and be sure you have the following settings in effect.

- Full menus
- A text window that shows the ruler, ribbon, and status bar
- The Display as Printed and Pictures options turned on (both in the View Preferences dialog box)

To use the examples in this chapter, you need a multipage document. Open the report you created and saved in Chapter 9, REDUNREP.DOC. Notice that the report doesn't look the same as it did before. Because you have the Display as Printed option turned on, the characters in the document change to match the characters your printer can print. These characters might be smaller or larger than the characters you used in creating the report, so the paragraph lengths and pagination might change.

SAVING A DOCUMENT

As you learned in Chapter 3, saving a document is an important safeguard. It ensures that all your work won't disappear in a flash of interrupted electrical power. For effective protection, you should save frequently as you work. Saving a document is also necessary whenever you turn off your computer. You can open your saved document later to continue your work, or you can recall previously finished documents to reuse them in a slightly altered form (a boon to teachers who use the same multiple-choice tests year after year!).

The Save and Save As Commands

Save and Save As are both commands that save documents. You learned earlier that Save opens the Save dialog box only the first time you use it on a document. Once you save the document and give it a name, using Save again saves the document to disk without opening the dialog box. Word simply replaces the disk file you last saved with the new version. Save As, on the other hand, opens the Save dialog box every time you use the command so that you can rename your document or change any option that is available in the dialog box.

The Save dialog box

When you choose Save As to open the Save dialog box, it looks like the one in Figure 11-1.

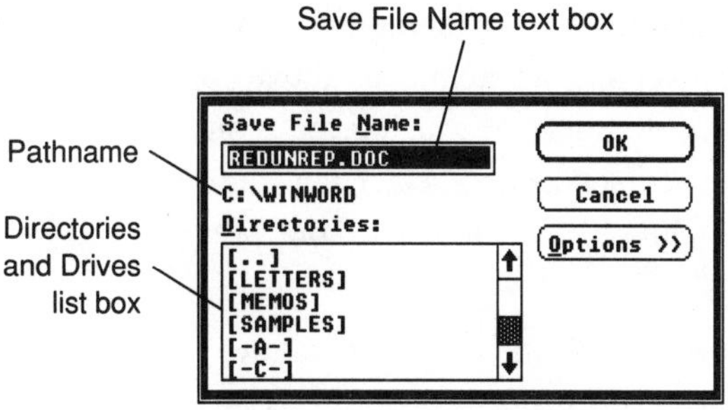

Figure 11-1. *The Save dialog box.*

Word proposes the name REDUNREP.DOC in the Save File Name text box because the document was previously saved with that name. The Save File Name text box would be blank if this were the first time the document was saved.

Use the dialog box to enter a filename and choose the directory and disk drive where you want to save the document. Enter the filename in the text box labeled Save File Name. The pathname beneath the text box tells you the current drive and directory, and the list box under the pathname offers you a selection of directories and disk drives to which you can move.

Changing Drive and Directory

To change drives and directories in the Save dialog box, it's important that you understand files, disk drives, directories, and pathnames. If you need help, you can find it in both the MS-DOS documentation and the Windows manual.

Using the list box and pathname

If you save a document by simply typing a filename and choosing OK, Word saves the document file in the directory and disk drive currently selected—usually the directory and disk drive in which Word is located. You can read the current drive and directory in the pathname below the Save File Name box. For example, the Save dialog box in Figure 11-1 shows the pathname C:\Winword. This means that any documents you save are stored in the Winword directory (shown with a backslash as \WINWORD) on the hard-disk drive (C:).

If you have the Special Edition with disks included, consult the Introduction

The items in the list box below the pathname are different disk drives and directories to which you can move. By selecting an item, you move to that drive or directory. (To select an item, double-click on it using the mouse or select the box using Tab, press the down cursor key to select the item, and then press Enter.) The following items choose disk drives or the previous directory:

- [..] (the parent-directory item) moves you to the directory "above" the current one. For example, if you are in C:\Winword\Letters, selecting [..] moves you back one directory to C:\Winword.
- [-A-] moves you to the first (or only) floppy-disk drive on your computer.
- [-B-] moves you to the second floppy-disk drive on your computer.
- [-C-] moves you to the C hard-disk drive.
- [-D-] (or any other letter) moves you to the D (or other letter) section of the hard disk.

Drive letters appear in the list box only if you have the specific hardware for each letter. Other entries in the list box are subdirectories of the current directory. If you select one of them, you move to that directory, and the pathname changes to show your new location. For example, if you are currently at C:\Winword and choose the subdirectory [Letters] from the list box, your new location appears as the pathname C:\Winword\Letters. Whenever you select a new directory or drive, Word changes the contents of the list box to show any subdirectories in the new drive or directory.

Please note that if you use the list box to change to a floppy-disk drive, you must have a formatted disk in the drive. If you don't, Word won't let you change to that drive. If you have no formatted disks on hand, you can format disks using MS-DOS or, if you have the full version of Windows, the MS-DOS Executive program.

To format a disk with MS-DOS, you must quit Word (saving your work first) and then use the format command described in your MS-DOS manual to format the disk. You can also create new directories on the disk if you want. You then start Word again, open your document, and proceed to use your formatted disk.

If you're using the full version of Windows, you can press Alt-Esc to change to the MS-DOS Executive. There you can use the commands in the Special menu to format a disk and create directories on the disk if you want. When you're finished, press Alt-Esc to return to Word.

One important note: Formatting erases the contents of a disk, so be sure the disk you format is empty or contains nothing useful.

Save Options

Choosing the Options button in the Save dialog box expands the box to include several new options shown in Figure 11-2. Set these options to save your document in different formats or to create a backup file. When you choose OK, Word uses the options you set as it saves your document.

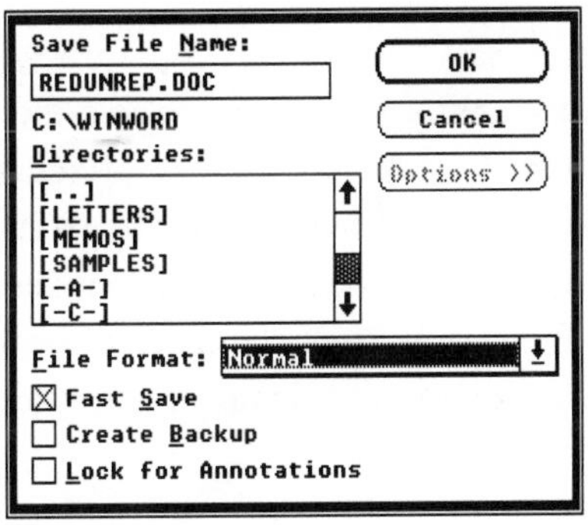

Figure 11-2. *The expanded Save dialog box.*

Fast save

When you first save a document, Word stores all the characters and formatting in a disk file. If you then add text to the document or otherwise revise it, Word uses a feature called *fast save* the next time you choose Save. Fast save saves only additions or changes to the original document, appending them to the document's disk file. This makes saving to disk much faster than using a *full save,* which saves the entire document.

Word uses fast save automatically when you use Save more than once on a document. It continues to use fast save until the accumulated changes become too much for it to handle. Word then uses a full save to incorporate all the changes and resave the entire document. To specify either a fast save or a full save, turn the Fast Save option on or off in the Save dialog box, and choose OK.

Create Backup

The Create Backup option creates two saved versions of your document: the most recently saved version and the previously saved version. This is how it works: When you first save a document with Create Backup turned on, Word saves it in a single disk file under the name you choose. The second time you save the document (using either Save or Save As), Word saves the full document in a second disk file and then adds the extension BAK to the original filename. The third time you save, Word erases the first document file, replaces it with a full save of your document, and then changes the name of the second document file to end in BAK.

Word continues swapping the two document files so that you always have two versions of your document: the most recently saved version and the version previous to that. You can find both documents in the same directory—the most recent version with the extension DOC and the previous version with the extension BAK. A backup is useful when you make extensive changes to a document, save it, and then realize you don't want those changes. You can always open the BAK file to retrieve the version of your document that doesn't contain the changes.

Lock for Annotations

Lock for Annotations is an option that, when turned on, prevents anyone who later opens the document from adding annotations to it. Annotations is an advanced feature discussed in Chapter 20 that lets other document users add their comments to the document.

File formats

The File Format list box lists the different formats Word can use to save your document. In Word's usual format, labeled Normal, Word saves all characters and formatting in a form that it can quickly and easily read when you open the document again. Because not all programs can use this format, if you save a Word document in this format and then open the file in another word processor (such as the Notepad program in Windows), the program is likely to read the file as gibberish. You can save your document using different formats to make the document compatible with other programs:

- Document Template saves a document as a template, a type of framework you can use within Word to create similar documents. (This feature is discussed in Chapter 17.)
- Text Only saves a document as characters only, without any formatting. It uses a single paragraph mark at the end of each paragraph.
- Text+Breaks saves a document as characters only, without any formatting. It uses a single paragraph mark at the end of each line.
- Text Only (PC-8) saves a document as characters only, without any formatting, and puts a single paragraph mark at the end of each paragraph. It saves data in an 8-bit format so that you don't lose diacritical marks or special European characters when you save the document.
- Text+Breaks (PC-8) saves a document as characters only, without any formatting, and puts a single paragraph mark at the end of each line. It also saves data in an 8-bit format to preserve European characters and diacritical marks.
- RTF saves a document in a Microsoft format called "Rich Text Format," a format that saves characters along with some formatting and graphics.
- Various word-processor formats are listed in the File Format list box. Each of these formats saves a document so that it can be read by the word processor it names.

Use Text Only and Text+Breaks to save documents for use with simple programs like Notepad or with telecommunications programs. You might find that some programs need a paragraph mark at the end of each line to avoid treating each paragraph as a single long line that runs off the right side of the screen. Most telecommunications programs need these *returns,* sometimes called CRs (carriage returns). Use Text+Breaks to save documents for use with these programs. Some programs (particularly Microsoft programs) can swap documents saved in the RTF format, which allows interchange between such different computers as the IBM and the Macintosh.

The other file formats are used by word processors other than Word. To give a document on disk to someone who uses another word processor, you can save the document using the appropriate word-processor format. When the other person opens the document, it retains as much formatting and graphics as the other word processor can support.

Try changing directories in the Save dialog box and then save REDUNREP using the Text Only format:

1. Choose Save As from the File menu. The Save dialog box opens.
2. Choose Option to expand the dialog box.
3. Move up one directory by selecting [..] from the Directories list box.
4. Move back to the original directory by selecting its name from the Directories list box.
5. Choose Text Only from the File Format list box.
6. Enter the name *REDUNREP.TXT* in the Save File Name text box. (Adding the TXT extension will remind you later that it's a Text Only file.)
7. Choose OK to save the document. Word saves it in Text Only format in the original directory.

The Summary Sheet and Statistics

When you save a document for the first time using the normal Word format, Word opens a second dialog box—the Summary Info dialog box (shown in Figure 11-3)—where you can enter information about the document. This information includes a document title, the subject, the author's name (already filled in from the information you entered when you first set up Word), keywords (single words describing key aspects of the document), and any comments you care to add. You can search through document summaries later to find a specific document on disk. Chapter 18 gives you details on creating summaries and using them to open documents.

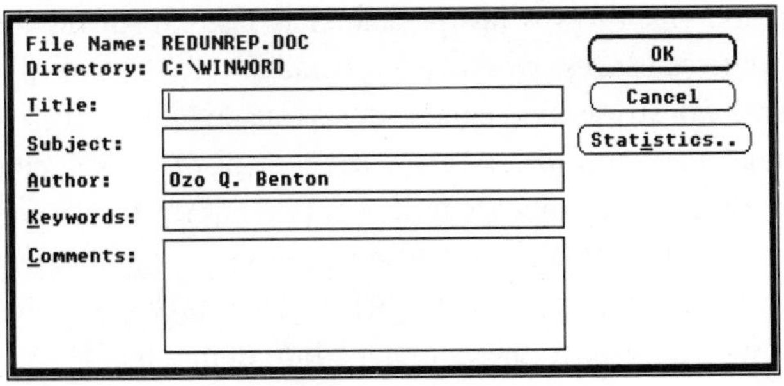

Figure 11-3. *The Summary Info dialog box.*

You can leave the Summary Info dialog box without filling in any information. Choosing OK saves the document, appending any summary information you entered to the file, and then closes the dialog box. Choosing Cancel stops the save process and closes the dialog box. Choosing Statistics opens the Statistics dialog box (shown in Figure 11-4), in which you can read some interesting information about your document.

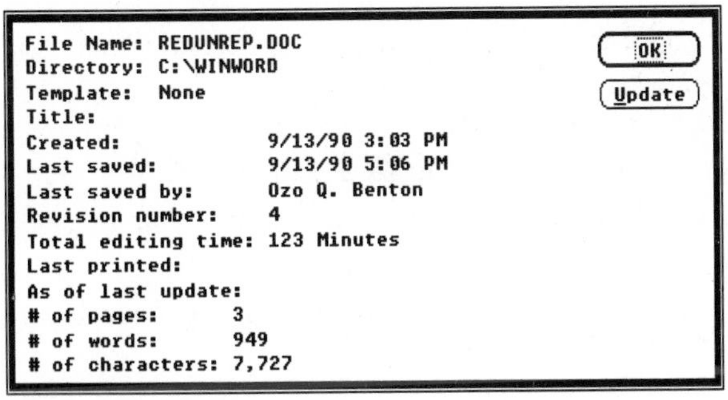

Figure 11-4. *The Statistics dialog box.*

The Statistics dialog box

The Statistics dialog box shows the state of your document. It tells you the filename and lists the directory in which the document is saved. It shows you the name of the template used to create the document (if any) and lists the title you entered in the Summary dialog box (if any). It also gives the date and time the document was started, the date and time the document was last saved, who saved it, the number of times it was revised, the length of time you spent editing it, and when it was last printed. The last part of the dialog box tells you the number of pages, words, and characters the document contains. (Word counts each string of characters surrounded by spaces as a word.) Choose the Update button to read the current state of your document (not the last saved state that first appears in this dialog box). Choose the OK button to close the box and return to the Summary Info box.

Try looking at the statistics for REDUNREP. Because you've already saved this document, you must open the Summary Info dialog box to see this information:

1. Choose Summary Info from the Edit menu to open the Summary Info dialog box.
2. Choose the Statistics button to open the Statistics dialog box and read the information about REDUNREP.
3. When you finish, choose OK to close the Statistics dialog box and return to the Summary Info dialog box.
4. Choose Cancel to close the Summary Info dialog box.

Using Autosave

Although it's a good idea to save a document periodically as you write, it's easy to get involved in writing and forget to save until you finish your Word session. You can use Word's autosave feature to remind you to save frequently: Choose Customize from the Utilities menu to open the Customize dialog box (shown in Figure 11-5), where you can turn on this feature.

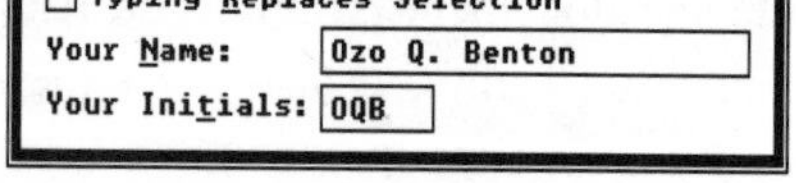

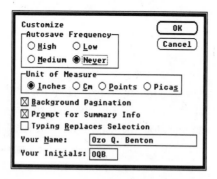

Figure 11-5. *The Customize dialog box.*

The Autosave section of the dialog box contains four options: High, Medium, Low, and Never. These options determine the amount of time between reminders: High waits from 10 to 30 minutes between reminders, Medium waits from 20 to 45 minutes, Low waits from 30 to 60 minutes, and Never turns off the autosave feature. The amount of text entry or editing you do determines whether autosave waits the minimum or maximum number of minutes. The more work you do, the more often Word reminds you to save. To turn on the autosave feature, select High, Medium, or Low and choose the OK button to close the dialog box.

After autosave is on, it periodically beeps and opens a dialog box that asks, Save Now? The Yes button is already selected, so if you choose OK, the dialog box closes, and Word saves your document. Choosing the Cancel button also closes the dialog box, but Word doesn't save your document. You have a third option: If you turn on the Postpone option, enter a number of minutes, and then choose OK, the dialog box closes and doesn't open again until the set number of minutes passes.

OPENING A DOCUMENT

Saving a document is of no use by itself: You must be able to retrieve what you save. The Open command on the File menu is your retrieval tool. You use it to open files in different directories and disk drives and, among other options, to open documents created and saved in other word processors.

The Open Dialog Box

Choosing Open from the File menu opens the Open dialog box, shown in Figure 11-6.

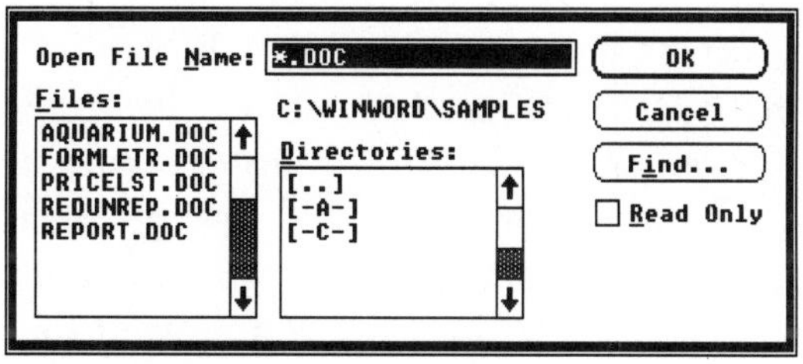

Figure 11-6. *The Open dialog box.*

Use the dialog box to determine the file you want to open. You can type the name of a document file in the text box labeled Open File Name if you know the exact name. Choosing OK then opens that document if Word finds it in the current drive and directory. To search for a filename, use the Files list box, which shows all the document files in the current directory. You can change directories or drives by selecting items in the Directories list box. It works in the same way as the Directories list box in the Save dialog box. The pathname above the list box always shows your current location.

Finding Word Documents in a Directory

The Files list box displays the names of any files in your current directory that end with the extension DOC, the standard extension Word appends to document filenames. The list box doesn't show filenames that have different extensions or no extensions because the filename in the Files text box specifies that the list box show only DOC files. To search for files you want to see, replace the filename with one that uses *wildcards.*

Using wildcards

A wildcard is a character that can stand for any other character or group of characters in a filename. You insert the wildcard in a filename as a substitute for characters that are irrelevant to the search.

You can use two wildcard characters in Word:

- * (asterisk) stands for one or more undetermined characters.
- ? (question mark) stands for a single undetermined character.

Use the asterisk when you don't care about the total number of characters in a filename. For example, if you want to look for all the documents in the current directory that start with "BU," type the filename *BU*DOC.* Word then locates filenames of any length that start with "BU": BURRITO.DOC, BUM.DOC, BULLET.DOC, BUDDHIST.DOC, and so on.

You can use an asterisk before or after the period that separates a filename from its extension to search for filenames that have specific extensions or specific base names. For example, if you use **.DOC*, Word finds all filenames that end with the extension DOC. If you use *AQUA.**, Word finds all filenames with the base name AQUA, regardless of their extensions.

The question-mark wildcard holds the place of a single character in a filename. Use it when the overall length of the filename is important. For example, use *R?NT* to search for all four-letter filenames starting with "R" and ending with "NT." Typing *R?NT* would find RENT and RANT but not RECENT.

To use a filename containing wildcards to search for documents, enter the filename in the Open File Name text box and press Enter. Word displays in the Files list box all the files in the current directory that match the wildcard filename. Notice that Word already uses the wildcard filename *.DOC to show all the files ending with the DOC extension. Changing that wildcard filename changes the files you see in the list box.

Try opening the Text Only version of REDUNREP you saved earlier. You'll need to use a different wildcard filename to display REDUNREP.TXT in the list box:

1. Choose Open from the File menu to open the Open dialog box.
2. Select the Open File Name text box if it isn't already selected. Notice that you don't see REDUNREP.TXT listed in the Files list box because the *.DOC wildcard filename in the Open File Name text box shows only files ending with the DOC extension.
3. Type **.** and press Enter to replace the *.DOC wildcard. The Files list box changes to show all the files in the current directory. (*.* is the standard wildcard that shows all filenames regardless of their base names or extensions. You could also have typed *.TXT to limit the list to files with the TXT extension.) REDUNREP.TXT should be one of the filenames.
4. Select REDUNREP.TXT in the list box and choose OK. The dialog box closes, and a new dialog box appears, asking you from what format you want to convert. The Text format is already selected.
5. Choose OK to close the dialog box. The document appears in the document window. Notice that all the character formatting is stripped from the document and that the headers and footers appear at the end of the document.
6. Choose Close from the File menu to close REDUNREP.TXT. It closes, and REDUNREP.DOC appears on the screen once more.

The Find button

The Find button in the Open dialog box opens a second dialog box, where you can search for a specific document using the information you entered in the Summary Info dialog box. This advanced feature is discussed in Chapter 18.

If you have the Special Edition with disks included, consult the Introduction

The Read Only Option

You might want to open a document to read it without revising it. To protect the document from accidental alteration, turn on the Read Only option in the Open dialog box. Once the option is on, any document you open appears in the document window, where you can alter it as you would any other document. If you try to save the altered document, however, Word refuses to let you save it under the same name. You can, if you like, save it under a different name. This protects the original document file from alteration.

Opening Documents from Other Programs

If you receive a document on disk created by a word processor other than Word or a file of text saved by a program other than a word processor, you can open it as you would any other document provided it was saved in a format that Word recognizes. Word recognizes the following formats:

- DCA/RFT (files created by DisplayWrite and DisplayWriter)
- Microsoft Excel BIFF (text files saved by Microsoft Excel)
- Microsoft Windows Write
- Microsoft Word for DOS
- Microsoft Works word-processing files
- Microsoft Multiplan and Multiplan BIFF (text files saved by Multiplan)
- MultiMate 3.3, Advantage, and Advantage II
- RTF (Rich Text Format, files saved by Microsoft Word for the Macintosh and other Microsoft programs)
- Text Only (text files saved with no formatting)
- WordPerfect 4.1, 4.2, and 5.0
- WordStar 3.3, 3.45, 4.0, 5.0, and 5.5

Before Word opens a document saved in a file format other than its own, it opens a dialog box with a list of possible file formats. Select the document's format from the list, and then choose OK to close the dialog box and open the document. Word tries to match the document's formatting to its own as closely as possible. If the other word processor uses formatting radically different from Word's, all the formatting might not translate perfectly.

PRINTING A DOCUMENT

After creating and saving a document, the big payoff is turning on your printer and printing the document on paper. In Chapter 3, printing was a simple matter of choosing the Print command, choosing the OK button in the Print dialog box, and waiting for your printer to print the document. This section shows you some useful alternatives that make printing more flexible and convenient.

The Print Dialog Box

When you choose Print from the File menu, Word opens the Print dialog box. Like other Word dialog boxes, this dialog box includes an Options button that you can choose to expand the dialog box to include additional options. Figure 11-7 shows the expanded Print dialog box with the available options.

Set the printing options you want to use in this dialog box, and then choose OK to close the box and start printing.

Figure 11-7. *The fully expanded Print dialog box.*

Printing Document Additions

The Print list box at the top of the dialog box offers you a choice of printing the document or various additions to the document. The default choice, Document, prints the contents of the document you see in the text window. The other choices—Summary Info, Annotations, Styles, Glossary, and Key Assignments—print additions that aren't part of the document's actual contents. For example, if you choose Summary Info in the Print list box and choose OK to start printing, Word prints any summary information you entered in the Summary dialog box when you saved the document. Annotations, Styles, Glossary, and Key Assignments are all additions to a document created by advanced features that you learn to use in later chapters.

Printing Several Copies

To print more than one copy of a document or document addition, enter the number of copies you want in the Copies text box.

Printing a Range of Pages

The section of options labeled Pages controls the range of pages that Word prints. The default option is All, which prints all the pages. To print a limited range of pages, you select the From To option. You then enter the beginning page number in the From text box and the ending page number in the To text box. To print a single page, enter the same page number in both the From and To text boxes. To print from a page in the middle of the document to the end of the document when you don't know the final page number, enter *9999* in the To box. Word will print to the end of the document and stop, unless your document happens to have 10,000 or more pages!

To print part of a document that doesn't begin or end neatly at a page break, first select as a text block the part you want to print, and then choose the option labeled Selection before you print. Word prints only the section you have selected and repaginates so that the beginning of the selected section starts at the top of the first page.

Reversing Print Order

Word normally prints a document from the first page to the last page. If you have a printer that prints on separate sheets and stacks the printed pages face up as it prints, your printed document is stacked in reverse order: The last page is on the top, and the first page is on the bottom. To print so that the pages appear in their proper order, turn on the Reverse Print Order option. Word then prints from the last page to the first page.

Setting Draft Quality

Most printers offer at least two qualities of print: final and draft. Final-quality (sometimes called near-letter-quality) printing is slower than draft quality, but the printed characters look smoother and better formed than draft-quality characters. Draft-quality characters usually look rough, but they print much faster than final-quality characters. To print a speedy draft-quality version of your document, turn on the Draft option before printing. (Note that draft quality might not reproduce some of the character formatting—such as boldface or italic—that final quality does.)

Setting Paper Feed

A printer can offer different methods of feeding blank paper into its rollers for printing. Dot-matrix printers can accept a single sheet at a time from your hands (useful for letterhead or other special paper) or print continuously on sheets of fanfold paper fed through the rollers by the printer's tractors. Laser printers print on single sheets that feed into the printer's rollers from a paper bin. Some laser printers have more than one bin, so you could keep letterhead paper in one bin, high-quality plain paper in another, and inexpensive paper in a third.

The Paper Feed list box offers printing options for the methods that apply to your printer. If you have a dot-matrix printer, the default setting might be Continuous—Word prints one page after another and lets the printer feed itself new sheets of paper. If you choose Manual, Word prints each page and then stops before printing the next page, displaying a dialog box that asks whether you want to continue. You can then insert a new page by hand and choose Continue to print the next page. You repeat this procedure until you finish printing the document or until you choose Cancel in the dialog box.

If you use a laser printer, the Paper Feed list box might offer the options Bin 1, Bin 2, and Bin 3 to select any of three paper bins for the printer to use. When you choose a bin, Word prints continuous pages, and the printer supplies paper from the bin you choose. If you choose the Mixed option, Word prints the first page of the document on a sheet from bin 1 and the following pages on sheets from bin 2. This option is useful for printing letters if you have letterhead paper in bin 1 and second sheets in bin 2.

Updating Fields for Printing

Recall from Chapter 9 that when you insert a date or time field in a header or footer, Word inserts the current date or time at that location when you print. Other fields don't update when you print a document; they retain the same value until you specifically tell Word to update the field. If you turn on the Update Fields option before you print, Word updates all the fields before printing. (Chapter 24 tells you more about fields.)

Including Additional Information in Printouts

The section labeled Include enables you to print additional information along with your document. Simply turn on any of the four options that you want printed:

- Summary Info prints any summary information about the document on a separate page after the document is printed.
- Annotations prints any annotations that have been added to the document on separate pages at the end of the document. (You learn to add annotations to a document in Chapter 20.) Turning on Annotations also turns on Hidden Text because annotations are formatted as hidden text.
- Hidden Text prints any hidden text inserted in the document as if the text weren't hidden.
- Field Codes prints any fields inserted in the document instead of printing the results of the fields. For example, a date field inserted in a header prints as {date} instead of the current date. Using this option helps you see the structure of a document when you have many fields.

Starting to Print

To start printing after you set the printing options the way you want them, simply choose the OK button. (Be sure you turn on and select your printer, as you learned to do in Chapter 3.) Word begins printing your document using your printing options. The status line at the bottom of the text window tells you which page is printing so that you can track the progress.

Try printing two copies of two pages of REDUNREP in reverse order:

1. Choose Print from the File menu to open the Print dialog box.
2. Choose the Options button to expand the dialog box.
3. Enter *2* in the Copies text box.
4. In the Pages section, select the From To option. Type *2* in the From text box and *3* in the To text box.
5. Turn on the Reverse Print Order option.
6. Choose OK to start printing.

Word prints two copies of pages 2 and 3. The document should print in this order: page 3, page 2, page 3, page 2.

A QUICK SUMMARY

This chapter taught you more about saving a document to disk, opening a previously saved document, and printing a document. You learned how to save documents in any directory and on any disk drive; how to use options that create backups; how to save in formats for other programs to read; and how to save your document at regular intervals while you're entering and editing. You also learned how to open documents in any disk drive or directory, how to use wildcards to display different files in the Open dialog box, and how to use different options to open documents created on other word processors and protect documents you open from alteration. The section about printing showed you how to print additional information about your documents; how to print limited page ranges, use reverse page order, accommodate different page feeding methods, and control the quality of the printout; and how to include normally invisible parts of your document in the printout.

You've now reached the end of the second section of this book and should feel in command of Word for Windows basics. The chapters in the next section take you further: You learn some of Word's unique advanced features. They make much of what you learned to do in this section faster and easier. Read on.

SECTION THREE

Beyond Basics

In this section you learn Word for Windows features that go beyond document basics. These features make your work easier: They help you find the best word to use, they check your spelling, they sort lists and calculate numbers, and they let you apply many formats with one simple command. They also help you create complex documents with footnotes, columnar text, and advanced page layout. Mastering the features described in this section puts you firmly and comfortably in control of Word.

Chapter 12

Writing Tools

If you have the Special Edition with disks included, consult the Introduction

Word for Windows offers you several tools that make the process of writing easier: The thesaurus introduces you to new words and helps you avoid using clichés; the Calculate command performs calculations on numbers in a text block so that you don't have to stop writing to use a calculator; and the glossary creates a collection of frequently used phrases, paragraphs, headings, pictures, and other useful document pieces that you can easily insert with a minimum of typing. This chapter introduces you to these tools and teaches you how to use them to make writing easier.

SETTING UP WORD

The examples in this chapter deal only with text entry; you don't have to print or perform any fancy formatting. Use these settings:

- Full menus
- A text window that shows the ruler, ribbon, and status bar
- The Display as Printed option turned off (in the View Preferences dialog box)

Figure 12-1 on the following page shows the memo you create as you use the examples in the chapter. As conductor of the Beautiful Music Symphonette of Glamour Valley, you'll find that this memo not only motivates your employees to increase their productivity but gives you the opportunity to use Word's writing tools.

**Beautiful Music Symphonette
of
Glamour Valley**

Music That Won't Surprise You

To: All Employees
From: Maestro Edouard Amadeus Thompson
Re: Monthly productivity awards

I want to take this opportunity as conductor and overseer of the Beautiful Music Symphonette of Glamour Valley to tell you the results of this month's productivity survey. The string division has topped the other divisions by playing the most notes per player this concert month, followed by the woodwinds, brasses, and (ahem!) percussion. The table below shows our most productive players with their weekly note tallies:

Week	Bo Longo	Raoul Romero	Tanya Pitchov
One	62,709	55,465	64,012
Two	54,809	49,441	75,545
Three	57,669	58,710	81,003
Four	62,466	60,989	1,079
Totals:	237,653	224,605	221,639

Violist Bo wins a recording of the complete set of Johann Strauss, Jr.'s waltzes as transcribed for flute and harp by Emil Waldteufel--a full 32-compact-disc set donated by the Beautiful Music Symphonette of Glamour Valley Docent Society. Harpist Raoul, a grizzled veteran of the Sugarplum Variations, wins the fully annotated scores of Leroy Anderson's Christmas masses, the famous "Winter Wonder" and "Sleighride of Joy" masses (donated by the Beautiful Music Symphonette of Glamour Valley Junior Auxiliary). Flutist Tanya is, alas, in the hospital recuperating from cruelly chapped lips after her solo performance of *Satyagraha* for the Beautiful Music Symphonette of Glamour Valley Musicians' Relief Fund. We know she'll be back in the running soon.

Good health, Tanya, and thank you, one and all, for a productive month!

Maestro Edouard Amadeus Thompson

P.S. The brass division might have a better notes-per-player-per-week rating if the trombone section would stop reading automobile magazines during long rests.

Figure 12-1. *Use the thesaurus, the glossary, and the Calculate command to help you create this document.*

THE THESAURUS

Word's thesaurus gives you word-finding power. If you're an old hand with a thesaurus in book form, you'll find that Word's on-screen thesaurus helps you keep writing without interruption—you don't have to stop writing to open a book, look up a word in an index, and turn to the word's location.

If you have the Special Edition with disks included, consult the Introduction

If you've never used a thesaurus, using Word's is an easy way to learn the value of a thesaurus for finding synonyms or for finding a word when you know the meaning but not the word. It's a simple matter of selecting a word in your document, choosing the Thesaurus command from the Utilities menu, and looking through the synonyms in the Thesaurus dialog box.

Selecting a Word for the Thesaurus

To select a word for the thesaurus, simply move the insertion point to the right or middle of the word you want. You don't have to select the entire word as a text block (although you can if you want). Because the thesaurus looks at the word immediately to the left of the insertion point, you can easily look up the word you just typed by stopping and choosing Thesaurus. If you select several words as a text block and then choose Thesaurus, the thesaurus looks up the first word in the selection.

Opening the Thesaurus

You open the thesaurus by choosing Thesaurus from the Utilities menu, or more quickly by pressing Shift-F7. Both methods open the dialog box shown in Figure 12-2.

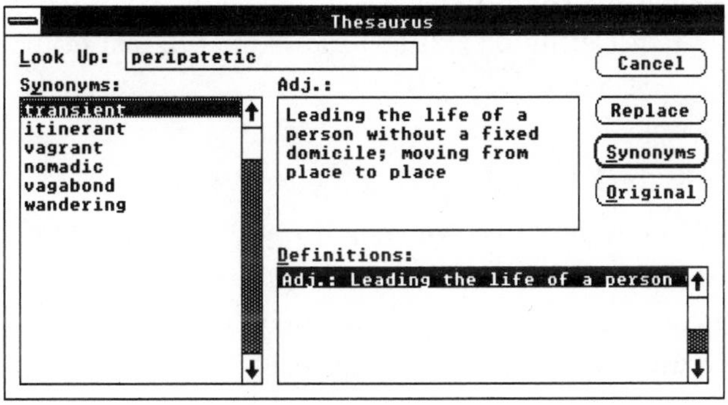

Figure 12-2. *The Thesaurus dialog box.*

The word you selected appears in the Look Up text box. Under that box is the Synonyms list box; here you find words with meanings similar to that of the selected word. To the right of the Synonyms list box is the Full Definition text box, and below that box is the Definitions list box. The Definitions list box shows a listing, in truncated form, of the different definitions (if they exist) for the word in the Look Up text box. One of these definitions is selected; the Full Definition text box shows the full definition. The label of the Full Definition text box shows the type of word the definition describes: noun, verb, adjective, adverb, and so on.

The four buttons on the right side of the dialog box control its actions. Cancel, of course, closes the box without performing any action. You'll learn more about the other buttons as you progress through the chapter.

Reading Synonyms

The Synonyms list box shows synonyms for the word in the Look Up text box. You might find that these synonyms don't match the meaning of the word you selected; Word sometimes presents a list of synonyms based on a different definition of the same word. For example, the word "minute" can be a noun describing a segment of time or an adjective describing something extremely small. The synonym list for the noun is completely different from the synonym list for the adjective. Choosing the appropriate definition is necessary for seeing the appropriate synonym list.

To see synonyms for the correct definition of the selected word, select a new definition from the Definitions list box, which displays different meanings (if any exist) for the word in the Look Up text box. After you select a new definition, the Synonyms list box changes to show synonyms that match the new meaning; the Full Definition text box shows the full text of the new definition you chose.

Replacing the Selected Word with a Synonym

When you see a word you want in the synonym list, you can use it to replace the word you selected in the document; simply select the word in the synonym list, and choose the Replace button. The Thesaurus dialog box closes, and Word replaces the old word with the newly chosen one.

Browsing Through the Thesaurus

One of the pleasures of using a thesaurus is learning new and interesting words by browsing through synonyms, a pastime Word's thesaurus makes easy. Start by opening the Thesaurus dialog box, and then enter an interesting word in the Look Up text box. To see synonyms for that word, choose the Synonyms button. The Definitions box shows you the definition(s) of your word. You can, of course, choose any definition to see an appropriate synonym list.

If you see a particularly interesting word in the synonym box, you can see its definitions and more synonyms by placing it in the Look Up text box. To do this using a mouse, double-click on the word you want. To do this using the keyboard, first select the word in the synonym list, and then choose the Synonyms button. You can use this method to leap from word to word, following your interest.

If you first opened the thesaurus to replace a selected word, it's easy to browse around and forget why you opened the thesaurus in the first place. Use the Original button to redisplay the originally selected word in the Look Up text box so that you can get back to business.

A Thesaurus Example

The first part of the memo (shown in Figure 12-3 on the following page with paragraph marks visible) contains a good place to use the thesaurus. As you write the memo, you want to describe your authority as conductor in no uncertain terms. For some reason, though, the phrase "conductor and dictator" seems too harsh. The thesaurus has some better alternatives.

1. Start the memo as an empty document.
2. Set the paragraph format to center alignment and the character format to 18-point bold (if available).
3. Type the first three lines of the memo. Press Enter twice at the end of the third line.
4. Reduce the character size to 12 points. Then type *Music That Won't Surprise You*, and press Enter twice.

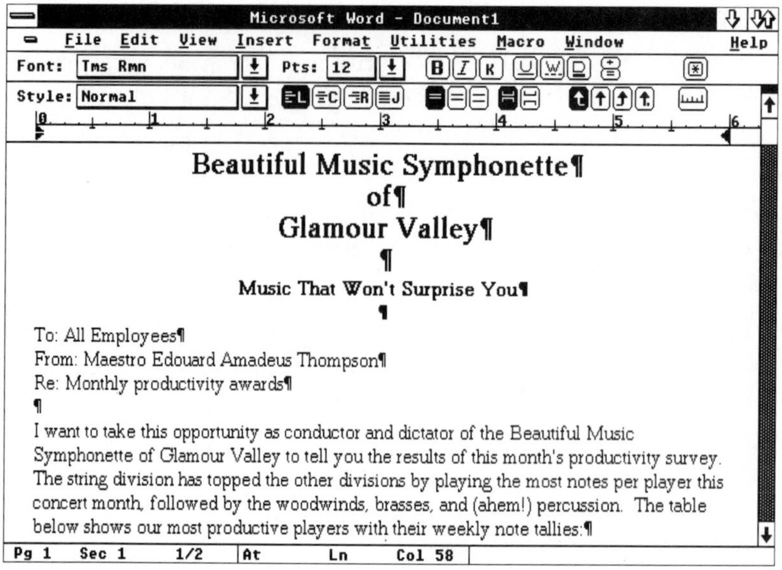

Figure 12-3. *Type the first part of the sample memo using the paragraph marks in this figure as guides for pressing Enter.*

5. Change paragraph alignment to left, and turn off the bold character formatting.
6. Type the next three lines of the memo, and press Enter twice at the end of the third line.
7. Start typing the first paragraph of the body of the memo as it appears in Figure 12-3. Stop typing at the end of "dictator."
8. Choose Thesaurus from the Utilities menu to open the thesaurus. The Thesaurus dialog box appears with "dictator" in the Look Up text box and a list of synonyms in the Synonym list box.
9. The list of synonyms seems harsh; all the synonyms use the definition "An absolute ruler, especially one who is harsh and repressive." Select the second definition, "One who imposes or favors absolute obedience to authority," as one that better describes your position. A new list of synonyms appears.

10. These synonyms also have excessively authoritarian connotations, so you decide to look up synonyms for "manager," a much milder word. Select the Look Up text box, use Backspace and Delete to delete "dictator," and then type in *manager*. Choose the Synonym button. New synonyms and definitions appear.
11. None of these synonyms has the edge you want. Choose the second definition, "Someone who directs and supervises workers." A new synonym list appears.
12. You like the ring of the word "overseer." Select it in the Synonym list box, and choose the Replace button. The dialog box closes, and the word "dictator" is replaced with "overseer."
13. Finish typing the paragraph, press Enter twice, and stop.

THE CALCULATE COMMAND

Some documents contain lists of numbers that need to be added, numeric expressions that need to be resolved, or other mathematics that can force you to stop writing, pull out a calculator, and work out the result before you go back to writing. The Calculate command on the Utilities menu can save you the trouble of reentering all those numbers. You simply select a block of text and choose Calculate. Word performs any simple mathematical functions contained in the text block and puts the result on the Clipboard.

Selecting Text for Calculation

You can select a block for calculation using normal selection techniques, which select text in rows. There are times, especially with figures, when you want to select a column of text for addition (like the columns of note tallies in the memo). If you use normal selection techniques, you can't separate one column from the next because Word selects the entire row before it moves down to select another row. To select a column by itself without selecting text to either side, you use a special selection technique—*column selection.*

To use column selection, position the insertion point at one corner of a column. Press Ctrl-Shift-F8 to start column selection. (The status bar displays a COL flag while column selection is turned on.) Then move the insertion point using the mouse or the cursor keys to the opposite corner of the column.

Word selects all the text in a rectangle between the initial location and the moving insertion point. To turn off column selection, press Esc (or use Ctrl-Shift-F8). The COL flag disappears from the status bar, and the selection process returns to normal. The column selection is also turned off whenever a calculation is executed.

Calculating

Choose Calculate from the Utilities menu to start calculating within a text block. The result is determined by the order in which Word encounters numbers in the text block and the way it uses *mathematical operators.*

Mathematical operators

A mathematical operator is a symbol that tells Word to perform a particular mathematical operation. Word recognizes six operators that add, subtract, multiply, divide, find powers, and set percentages:

- + (or no symbol) for addition
- – for subtraction
- * for multiplication
- / for division
- ^ for "to the power of"
- % for "percent" (the same as dividing the percentage number by 100)

To use an operator, place it directly before a number unless it is a percent sign, in which case you place it directly after a number. For example, /45 means to divide by 45. *34% means to multiply by 34 percent. The symbol ^ can calculate roots as well as set exponents: For example, ^3 means "to the third power"; ^0.5 means "to the ½ power" (the square root). Avoid the exclamation point (!) when calculating; it can throw off the result.

Order of calculation

Word calculates by reading the text block from left to right, top to bottom (as you read a page) and by performing operations in the order in which it encounters them. It ignores any text between numbers and operators. For example, if you select the text block "34 shoulder pads at *$5.00 each multiplied by *15%," Word calculates "34 * $5.00 * 15%," which is 34 multiplied by $5.00 multiplied by 15 percent, or $25.50. The order of calculation can be modified by enclosing operations in parentheses. For example, 2 + (2 * 3) equals 8, while (2 + 2) * 3 equals 12.

Decimals and dollars

When Word calculates, it returns a result with as many decimal places as the number in the text block that contains the most decimal places. For example, the operation 9 * 0.3333333 returns the value 2.9999997. Word uses seven decimal places because 0.3333333 contains seven decimal places. If you use the dollar sign ($) before one of the numbers in the calculation, the result also includes the dollar sign.

Using the Result

After Word calculates, it places the result on the Clipboard and temporarily shows the result on the status bar. To paste the result in the document, place the insertion point where you want the result and choose the Paste command from the Edit menu (or press Shift-Insert).

A Calculation Example

The memo contains three columns of numbers (shown in Figure 12-4), which are lists of the number of notes played by musicians in the orchestra.

Week	Bo Longo	Raoul Romero	Tanya Pitchov
One	62,709	55,465	64,012
Two	54,809	49,441	75,545
Three	57,669	58,710	81,003
Four	62,466	60,989	1,079
Totals:	237,653	224,605	221,639

Figure 12-4. *Use the Calculate command to calculate the sums of these columns of numbers.*

Type in this part of the memo and use Calculate to total the numbers:

1. Set up the heading-line paragraph by placing center-aligned tab stops at 1.75 inches, 3.25 inches, and 4.75 inches.

2. Change character formatting to word underline and bold, and enter the first line shown in Figure 12-4. (The tab characters are visible to show you where to press Tab.) Press Enter at the end of the line.
3. Remove the tabs on the ruler and insert new decimal tabs at 2 inches, 3.5 inches, and 5 inches.
4. Turn off word underline and bold character formatting and enter the next four lines, using Figure 12-4 to see where to press Tab. Press Enter at the end of the last line of figures.
5. Turn on bold character formatting and type *Totals*. Turn off bold formatting, and then press Tab.
6. Select the first column of numbers by placing the insertion point at the beginning of the number "62,709," pressing Shift-Ctrl-F8, and moving the insertion point to the end of the number "62,466."
7. Choose Calculate from the Utilities menu to add the column. The result appears temporarily in the status bar.
8. Move the insertion point back to the end of the line you last typed, and press Shift-Insert to insert the result below the column of numbers.
9. Press Tab to move to the next column.
10. Select the column of numbers under the name "Raoul Romero" as you did in the preceding column, and choose Calculate to add the numbers.
11. Move the insertion point back to the end of the document, and press Shift-Insert to paste the result at the bottom of the second column.
12. Press Tab to move to the next location. Then, select the final column of numbers, calculate their sum, and paste the result as you did previously. Press Enter twice at the end of the line to prepare for entering the rest of the document.

THE GLOSSARY

Many phrases, sentences, and parts of a document often repeat throughout the document. Rather than type each occurrence, you can use Word's glossary to store a repeated piece of text (or a graphic) and insert that piece wherever you want it. To turn text and graphics into a glossary entry, you select the piece you want as a text block, choose the Glossary command from the Edit menu, and then give the piece a short name in the Glossary dialog box. To insert the piece later, you type the glossary entry name in the document and press F3. Word replaces the short glossary entry name with the full contents of the glossary entry.

Creating a Glossary Entry

The first step in creating a glossary entry is to enter the text or graphics you want. Once it is entered, you select it as a text block. You can select all text, all graphics, or a mixture; the glossary stores the entire contents of the block, preserving all graphics and character formatting.

With a text block selected, choose Glossary from the Edit menu to open the Glossary dialog box shown in Figure 12-5. (The Glossary command is not available unless text is selected or there are already entries in the glossary.) The bottom line of the dialog box shows your selection. Because it's only a single line, this description area doesn't show any selected graphics or character formatting. The line can show only the beginning of the selected text if the text is too long to fit on one line.

Enter the name for your glossary entry in the Glossary Name text box. Brevity counts. The shorter your glossary name, the easier it is to type in the document. Of course, being brief can cause problems: A name such as "j" or

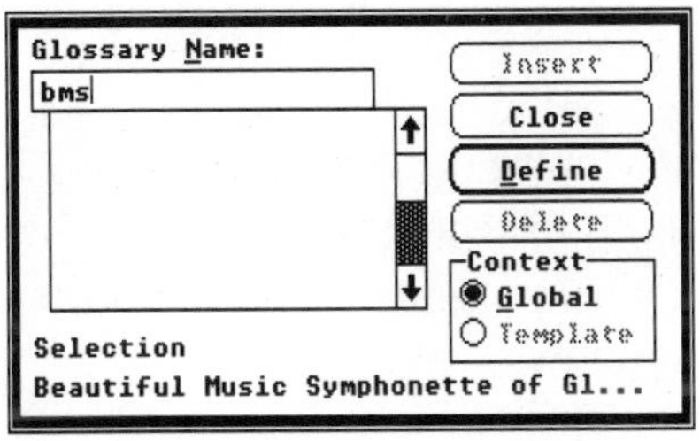

Figure 12-5. *The Glossary dialog box.*

"4" doesn't often remind you of the entry contents. A key word in a phrase, a short word describing a picture, or the initials of a name or the title work well as glossary names.

The context area determines if the Glossary entry will be available to all documents (Global) or only to documents created using a specific template. Templates are discussed in Chapter 17.

With the contents of the entry selected and a name entered, you define your new glossary entry by choosing the Define button. The dialog box closes, and Word adds your entry to the glossary list. To see your entry, open the dialog box again by choosing Glossary from the Edit menu. The list box below the Glossary Name text box lists all available glossary entries.

A glossary definition example

The phrase "Beautiful Music Symphonette of Glamour Valley" occurs often in the rest of the memo. Define it as a glossary entry:

1. Select "Beautiful Music Symphonette of Glamour Valley" as a text block in the first full paragraph of the memo.
2. Choose Glossary from the Edit menu to open the Glossary dialog box. The beginning of the selected phrase appears in the description area.
3. Enter *bms* (the initials of Beautiful Music Symphonette) in the Glossary Name text box.
4. Choose the Define button to add the entry to the glossary list, and close the dialog box.

Inserting a Glossary Entry in a Document

Once you have entries in your glossary, you can insert them in a document in either of two ways:

- Type the name of the glossary entry in the document, and press F3 at the end of the entry. Word replaces the entry name with the full contents of the glossary entry, including graphics and character formatting.

- Open the Glossary dialog box using the Edit Glossary command and select the entry name you want from the glossary list. Choose the Insert button to close the dialog box and insert the contents of the entry you chose.

Directly typing a glossary name in a document is the quickest way to enter a glossary entry. Note that Word ignores uppercase and lowercase characters in a glossary name, so you don't have to use the Shift key as you type the name. If you forget a glossary name you need, opening the Glossary dialog box presents you with a list of entries to jog your memory. As you move through the list, the first part of each entry is displayed at the bottom of the dialog box.

A glossary insertion example

The rest of the memo uses "Beautiful Music Symphonette of Glamour Valley" several times. Use the glossary to insert it:

1. Use the sample document in Figure 12-1 to type the rest of the memo, stopping at the beginning of "Beautiful Music Symphonette of Glamour Valley" in the first paragraph following the "Totals" line.
2. Choose Glossary from the Edit menu to open the Glossary dialog box.
3. Select bms in the glossary list. Then choose Insert to close the dialog box and insert the glossary entry in the memo.
4. Continue typing, stopping at the beginning of "Beautiful Music."
5. Type *bms* and press F3. Word replaces "bms" with "Beautiful Music Symphonette of Glamour Valley."
6. Type the rest of the memo, typing *bms* and pressing F3 to insert the "Beautiful Music" phrase a final time. (It's not important to enter this text verbatim, so abridge it if you like.)

Saving Glossary Entries

Word retains all the glossary entries you create during a Word session. If you close one document and start a new one, the glossary entries you created in the earlier document are available to you. When you close Word, it asks whether you want to save your glossary changes. To save your glossary entries for use in later sessions, answer yes. Word stores the glossary entries on disk under the filename NORMAL.DOT. If you answer no when asked to save the glossary changes, Word deletes the glossary entries you created during the session, so you won't see them in later sessions.

Printing the Glossary List

As you add glossary entries over many sessions, the glossary list can grow quite large. To see it in its entirety, you can print it on a sheet of paper. Choose the Print command from the File menu, and then choose Glossary from the Print list box in the Print dialog box. Choosing the OK button prints the glossary list.

Deleting Glossary Entries

If your glossary list grows too large for comfort or you find that you don't need a glossary entry, you can remove an entry using the Glossary dialog box. Open the dialog box using the Edit Glossary command, select the entry you want to remove from the glossary list, and choose the Delete button. Word deletes the entry from the glossary and closes the dialog box. If, at the end of your Word session, you choose to save your glossary changes, Word deletes from the saved-on-disk glossary all the entries you deleted during the session.

A QUICK SUMMARY

You learned in this chapter how to use some of Word's writing tools to simplify writing and text entry. You learned how to open the thesaurus, look through synonym lists, and replace a selected word with a new word. You saw how Word calculates the result of numbers and operators in a block of selected text and how to paste the result where you want it. In the last part of the chapter, you learned to use the glossary to store frequently repeated text and to insert your stored text by choosing from a list of entries or by directly typing the entry name in a document. In the next chapter, you learn to use Word's editing tools to edit the text you enter.

Chapter 13

More Editing Tools

If you have the Special Edition with disks included, consult the Introduction

The best editing tool is an editor who reads your work, corrects your grammar, organization, and spelling, and returns the document to you in a form that says what you really intended. Because most of us can't afford this kind of editorial luxury, Word for Windows offers editing tools to help the person most sympathetic to your writing—you—make revisions in your text. In this chapter, you learn to use three of these editing tools, all of which are found on the Utilities menu: the Sort command, the Spelling command, and the Hyphenate command.

SETTING UP WORD

The examples in this chapter don't require printing but do use formatting. Use the following settings:

- Full menus
- A text window that shows the ruler, ribbon, and status bar
- The Display as Printed option turned off (in the View Preferences dialog box)

To learn how to hyphenate, sort, and check spelling, you use the examples in this chapter to enter and edit a report from the director of the Wee Tot Petting Farm (shown in Figure 13-1 on the following page). The trade-specific animal descriptions provide a worthy challenge to Word's spelling checker.

Wee Tot Petting Farm

"Fins, Fur, Feathers, and Finances--in Fresno!"

Date: 6/12/90
To: Limited partners
From: J. Wellington Biddlecomb, General Manager

Dear Partners:

I'd like to take this opportunity to report to you on the burgeoning business here at the Wee Tot Petting Farm; the tykes are tumbling through the turnstiles in ever-increasing numbers thanks to our recent improvements.

Many partners have asked me why there were no dividends at the end of last month. The answer is simple: all profits have been reinvested in the facilities at this crucial period. The beginning of the summer is traditionally the time for improvements in the toddler-tactile livestock industry; we have followed suit with spectacular results. The list that follows shows our acquisitions for the month of May followed by favorable comment tallies from the comment box:

Date:	Acquisition:	Favorable Comments:
5/6	3 moomoos	14
5/9	4 oinkoinks	6
5/11	15 cluckclucks	11
5/15	10 quackquacks	18
5/21	2 bowwows	17
5/30	1 hisshiss	0

In order of popularity, our acquisitions are:

Date:	Acquisition:	Favorable Comments:
5/15	10 quackquacks	18
5/21	2 bowwows	17
5/6	3 moomoos	14
5/11	15 cluckclucks	11
5/9	4 oinkoinks	6
5/30	1 hisshiss	0

All our bipedal and quadripedal additions have certainly proved their worth. Unfortu-nately, our lone apedal addition hasn't fared as well, but was still a worthwhile

(continued)

Figure 13-1.
Use the Sort, Spelling, and Hyphenate commands to edit this document.

Figure 13-1. *continued*

addition--at only $100 for a 14-foot anaconda ($7.14 a foot), we got a great deal! As it turns out, he is proving to be an invaluable resource for getting rid of other unpopular petting animals.

I know that you are proud of the priceless toddler-tactile resource we are creating within our great city. Tell your friends with pride, "I invested $50,000 in the Wee Tot Petting Farm." Their comments will be additional payment for your investment.

Yours sincerely,

J. Wellington Biddlecomb
General Manager
Wee Tot Petting Farm

SORTING LISTS

Many documents contain lists of names, instructions, dates, or other items. Often, the information as you first type it is in no particular order; it would be much easier to read if the list were sorted into alphabetic, numeric, or chronological order. Sorting is a tedious process perfectly suited to a computer. Turn it over to Word by using the Sort command on the Utilities menu.

An Overview of the Sorting Process

When Word sorts a list, it actually sorts paragraphs, so it's important that you enter each item as a separate paragraph. Each paragraph is called a *record* (a term borrowed from the world of database software). A record stores a single unit of information in the list. If you organize information the same way within each record (for example, a list of names with each record showing last name, first name, and phone number), each separate piece of information in a record is called a *field* (another term borrowed from database software).

To sort a list of records, first select all the records as a text block. Then choose the Sort command from the Utilities menu and use the Sort dialog box to set sort criteria. You can sort alphabetically, numerically, or chronologically, using forward order, reverse order, and other sorting methods. After you set the criteria and start the sort, Word sorts all the records in the text block according to your directions and replaces the unsorted list with a sorted one. You can use the Undo command if you don't like the new order.

Creating Records and Fields

The Sort command works best if you follow these simple rules as you create records in your document:

- Press Enter at the end of each record to keep records separated.
- Separate each field in a record using a tab or comma. Don't mix tabs and commas as field separators—use only tabs or only commas.
- Enter dates in one of three formats: month/day/year (2/28/89), fully spelled out (September 9, 1957), or day (space) month (space) year (10 Sep 74). Word sorts dates if you omit the year (2/28 or 10 Sep, for example), but be consistent: If you leave the year off one date in your list, leave it off the other dates as well. Also be sure to use a three-letter abbreviation if you abbreviate the names of months: Jan, Feb, Mar, Apr, May, Jun, Jul, Aug, Sep, Oct, Nov, Dec.

Try your hand at entering a list of records. Use the text, paragraph marks, and tab stops shown in Figure 13-2 for guidance. The report contains two lists of recently acquired petting-farm animals. If you enter the first list, you can copy it and use Sort to reorder it according to the popularity of the animals. When you type the first list, separate each record (an animal purchase) with a paragraph mark and each field within a record (date, animal, and number of comments) with a tab.

1. Enter the report up to the list heading and stop. Do not enter the heading. In this example, the font is Tms Rmn. The title line is 18-point text in boldface, with a centered paragraph format. The second line is 12-point text in boldface, also centered. The text that follows is left-aligned, using 12-point regular text (not boldface). Be sure to follow the spelling in the figure exactly. Deliberate mistakes are included for the spelling checker to find later.
2. Move in the left indent by ½ inch.

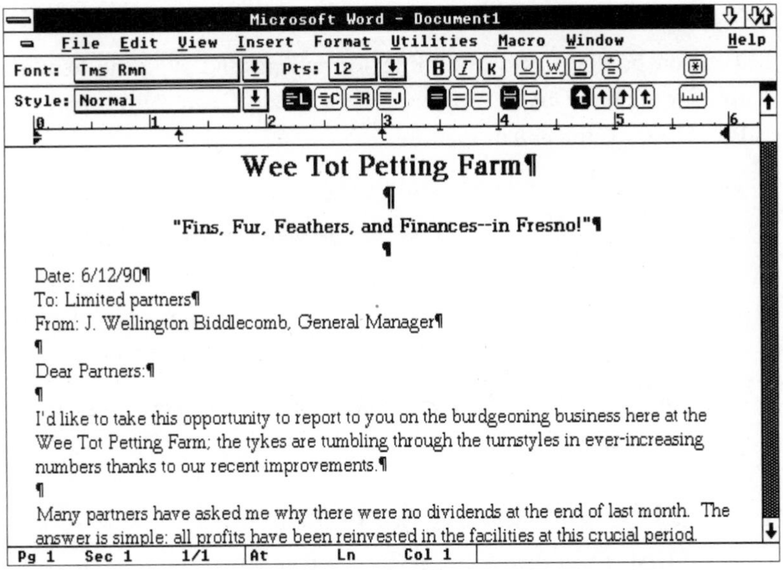

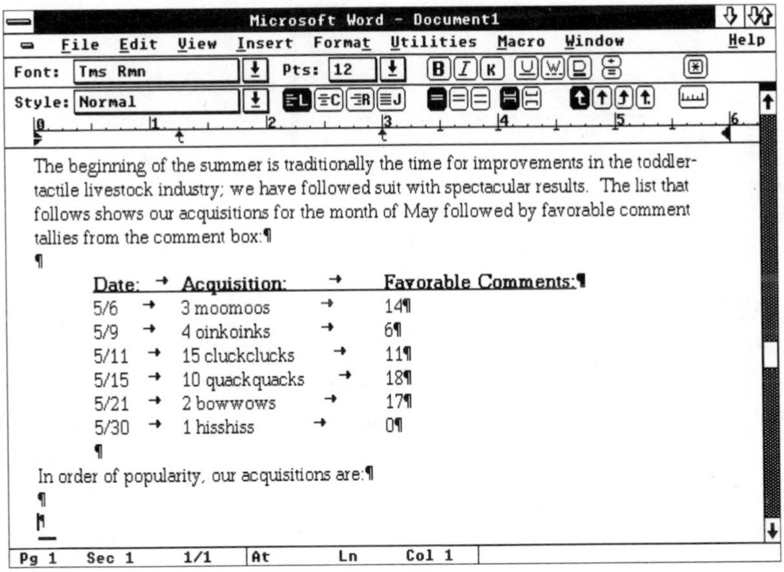

Figure 13-2. *Follow the instructions for entering this text.*

3. Set left-aligned tab stops at 1¼ inches and 3 inches.
4. Turn on boldface and underline formatting and type the heading line for the list: *Date:* (Tab) *Acquisition:* (Tab) *Favorable Comments:*. Press Enter at the end of the line.
5. Turn off boldface and underlining.
6. Enter each line of the list. Press Tab between fields and press Enter at the end of each line.
7. At the end of the last line, press Enter twice and move the left margin to the 0 mark.
8. Enter *In order of popularity, our acquisitions are:* and press Enter twice at the end of the line.

Selecting a List and Setting Sort Criteria

To sort a list, first select the entire list as a text block. Then choose Sort from the Utilities menu to open the Sort dialog box shown in Figure 13-3.

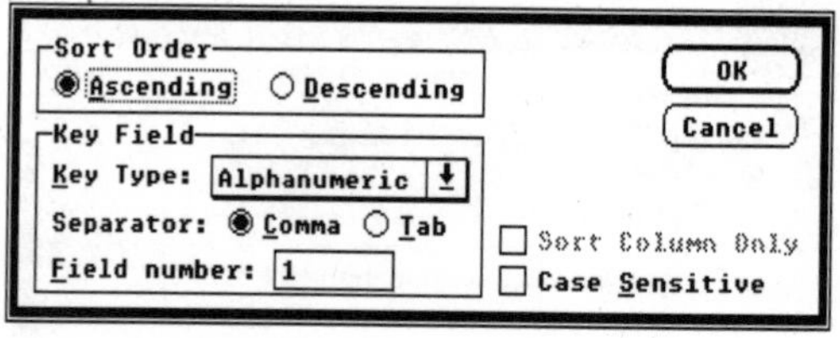

Figure 13-3. *The Sort dialog box.*

Setting the key field

The area labeled Key Field is the primary area you use for setting sort criteria. To understand how to use it, look at the way Word sorts records: Word normally sorts using the first field of each record. For example, if you have records containing the fields "last name," "first name," and "telephone number," Word sorts the records by "last name." To sort by a different field, you change the number in the Field Number text box to the number of the field you want. Thus, if you enter field number 2, Word sorts using the second field—in this case, "first name." The field you use to sort by is called the *key field.*

Choosing a separator

To specify the key field as any field other than the first, you must tell Word the field separator you're using—commas or tabs. Choose either the Comma button or the Tab button in the Separator line to specify the field separator. (Note that if you use tabs as field separators, using commas within fields won't split up those fields. For example, "Biddlecomb, J. Wellington" can be a single field if it's separated from other fields by tabs.)

Choosing the sorting method

Use the Key Type selection box to choose the sorting method you want Word to use. You have three choices:

- Alphanumeric, which sorts the key field in alphabetic order
- Numeric, which sorts the key field in numeric order
- Date, which sorts the key field in chronological order

It's important to choose the right key type. For example, Word places 100 before 20 if it sorts alphanumerically, because in alphanumeric order, 1 comes before 2. If Word sorts numerically, it places 20 before 100.

Setting sort order

The Sort Order area at the top of the dialog box offers two sort orders: ascending and descending. Choose ascending order to sort from the beginning of the alphabet to the end, from the lowest number to the highest, or from the earliest date to the latest. Choose descending order to sort from the end of the alphabet to the beginning, from the highest number to the lowest, or from the latest date to the earliest. After you choose the key field and separator and then set the key type and sort order, choose OK to close the dialog box and start the sort.

Try rearranging the list of animals in order of the number of favorable comments each animal received. This requires you to sort by the third field using descending numeric order. First you must duplicate the list:

1. Select the list along with its heading line as a text block. Be sure to include the paragraph mark at the end of the last record.
2. Choose Copy from the Edit menu.

3. Move the insertion point to the end of the document and choose Paste from the Edit menu to add a copy of the list to the end of the document.
4. Select all the animal records in the second list as a text block. (Don't include the heading line.)
5. Choose Sort from the Utilities menu to open the Sort dialog box.
6. Choose Descending sort order, choose Numeric as the key type, set the separator as Tab, and enter *3* in the Field Number text box to sort by the third field, "Favorable Comments."
7. Choose OK to close the box and start the sort. The dialog box closes, and Word sorts the records in the list in descending numeric order by the number of favorable comments.
8. Finish the sample report. Move the insertion point to the end of the document, press Enter, and enter the rest of the document as shown in Figure 13-4.

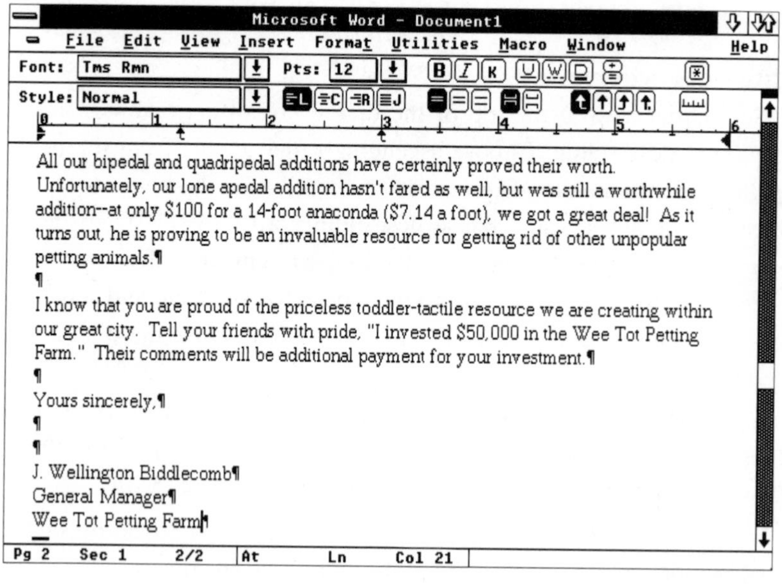

Figure 13-4. *The second half of the report.*

Word's Sort Order

To sort effectively in alphanumeric order, you should know the character order that Word uses to sort records. When Word sorts alphanumerically, it ignores quotation marks, spaces, tabs, and diacritical marks, such as the German umlaut (¨). It then sorts, putting punctuation marks first (sorted by their order in the ANSI character table), followed by numerals in numeric order and then letters in alphabetic order. Word doesn't normally distinguish between uppercase and lowercase letters when sorting. For example, Word arranges "ant, Apple, artwork, Beast" in that order, completely ignoring the capital "A" in Apple. To separate capitalized words from uncapitalized words during a sort, turn on the Case Sensitive option in the Sort dialog box. Word then sorts by placing all uppercase letters before lowercase letters so that all capitalized words appear before uncapitalized words; thus, it would arrange the words as "Apple, ant, artwork, Beast."

CHECKING SPELLING

Everybody makes spelling mistakes; if the inexplicable spelling rules of the English language don't trip you up, then straying fingers on the keyboard do. When you finish a document, Word's spelling checker combs your text for spelling mistakes, typing errors, double occurrences of words ("Paris in the the spring," for example), and capitalization errors.

If you have the Special Edition with disks included, consult the Introduction

An Overview of Spelling Checking

The Spelling command on the Utilities menu starts Word's spelling checker. When Word runs a spelling check, it reads through your document (or any portion you have selected), comparing each word it encounters with a list of 130,000 words it has on the hard disk in its main dictionary file. If it comes across a word it can't find in its dictionary, it shows you the word and asks whether you want to replace it.

You can deal with an unmatched word in several ways. You can replace the word if it's misspelled. If you don't know how to spell a word, Word can suggest alternative spellings for you to choose from. If the word is spelled correctly but isn't included in Word's dictionary, you can tell Word to move on without changing the word and, if you use that word often, to add it to a supplemental user dictionary. Once you add words to the supplemental dictionary, Word looks through both that dictionary and its main dictionary as it runs the rest of the spelling check.

Word's spelling checker has one important limitation: It doesn't check for proper usage. If you use the wrong word in a sentence, Word won't notice the problem if the word is in its dictionary. For example, the sentence "It's reel butter" is wrong, but Word won't alert you because "reel" is a correctly spelled word in its dictionary.

Starting a Spelling Check

Before you start a spelling check, you must decide whether to check the entire document or only a portion of it. You can save time by checking only a newly revised portion if you've already checked the rest of the document. To check a section of the document, select the section as a text block. To check the entire document, be sure no text block is selected.

To start checking, choose Spelling from the Utilities menu to open the Spelling dialog box shown in Figure 13-5.

Use the Word text box at the top of the dialog box to check the spelling of a single word. Simply type the word in the text box and then choose the Check button to tell Word to check its dictionaries for the term. To check the entire document or the text block you selected, choose the Start button. The dialog box closes, and Word checks the document for spelling. The status bar at the bottom of the window tells you that a check is in progress.

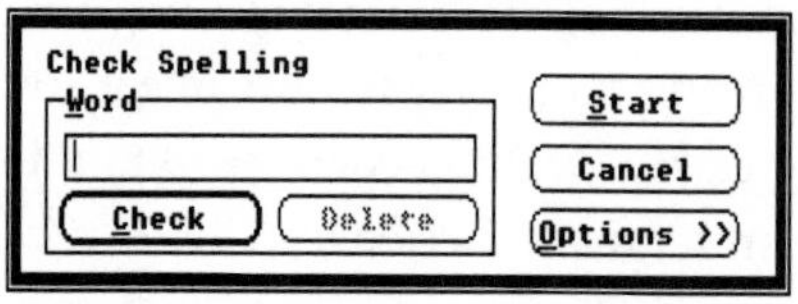

Figure 13-5. *The Spelling dialog box.*

Dealing with Unmatched Words

If you're checking the entire document, Word reads from the insertion-point location to the end, where it pauses and asks whether you want to continue the check from the beginning. If you do, Word reads from the beginning to the insertion-point location, where it stops. If you are checking a text block, Word reads from the beginning to the end of the block. You can quit anytime by pressing Esc; Word operation then returns to normal.

Occasionally, Word can match every word in your document to a word in its dictionaries—it finds no misspellings or typing errors. If so, the spelling check ends, and you can go back to work. More often, however, there are enough errors to keep Word busy. As soon as it finds a word that it can't match in one of its dictionaries, Word stops the check and opens a second Spelling dialog box (shown in Figure 13-6).

The Not In Dictionary box at the top of the dialog box lists the unmatched word. Word also selects the unmatched word in the document to let you read it in context; if the Spelling dialog box is covering the selected word, move the box to a new location by pointing to its title bar with the mouse and dragging or by using the commands in the dialog box's bar menu.

Below is the Change To text box. This box also contains the unmatched word, placed here for you to alter or replace by selecting the word and typing. If you enter a replacement here, choose the Change button. Word then closes the dialog box and replaces the unmatched word in the document with your change. It then continues the spelling check.

If Word points out a misspelling that you don't know how to correct, choose the Suggest button. Word looks through its dictionaries for words that have similar spellings and displays them in the Suggestions list box. Scroll through these suggestions. Chances are you'll find the correct spelling of the

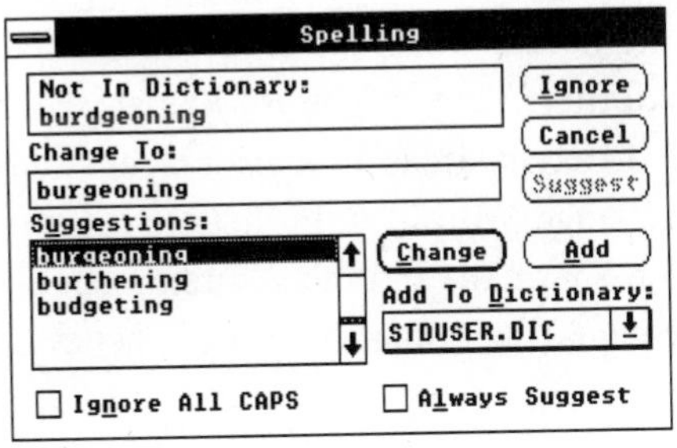

Figure 13-6. *The second Spelling dialog box shows unmatched words. In this figure, the Suggest button has been chosen, so the dialog box shows spelling suggestions for the misspelled word.*

unmatched word. When you do, use it to replace the selected word in the document by double-clicking on it or by selecting it using the cursor keys and then choosing the Change button.

Adding words to a supplemental dictionary

Word sometimes encounters unmatched words that are, in fact, spelled correctly; these are usually words unique to a business or profession or proper names that aren't included in Word's main dictionary. (A main dictionary that included all these words would be too large to use with reasonable speed and would be impossible to keep up to date.) When Word presents you with one of these words, you have two options. You can tell it to ignore the word by choosing the Ignore button—Word then leaves the word alone and continues its check—or you can add the word to your own private dictionary so that Word will recognize it the next time it encounters the word.

The Add To Dictionary list box shows the name of the supplemental dictionary to which you add new words—usually STDUSER.DIC, Word's default supplemental dictionary. When Word presents you with an unmatched word that you want to add to STDUSER.DIC, choose the Add button. Word saves the unmatched word in the STDUSER.DIC file on disk. The next time it encounters the word during a spelling check, it finds the word in this dictionary and passes it without stopping.

Working with Dictionaries

Most people never need to do more than add words to the STDUSER.DIC dictionary to tailor Word to their spelling needs. Other Word users have specific spelling needs that require more flexibility. They might use British spellings, or they might use words found in different areas of business or study. If you're one of these people, you can change Word's main dictionary so that it uses British spellings (or even French, German, and other foreign spellings), and you can create different supplemental dictionaries to use whenever you need them.

Choosing an alternative main dictionary

Word comes with one main dictionary: English (US). This dictionary uses spellings standard to United States English. If you buy an alternative main dictionary—English (UK) for British spellings, for example—and install it on your hard disk, you can then choose between English (US) and your alternative dictionary. Choose Spelling from the Utilities menu, choose the Options button in the Spelling dialog box to see more spelling options, and then use the options in the Dictionaries area (shown in Figure 13-7).

The list box labeled Main shows the main dictionaries you have on your hard disk. You can choose any one of them, but no more; Word uses only one main dictionary at a time. After you select a main dictionary in the list box, choose Start to start a spelling check or Cancel to close the box. Word remembers the main dictionary you chose and will use that dictionary in future spelling checks.

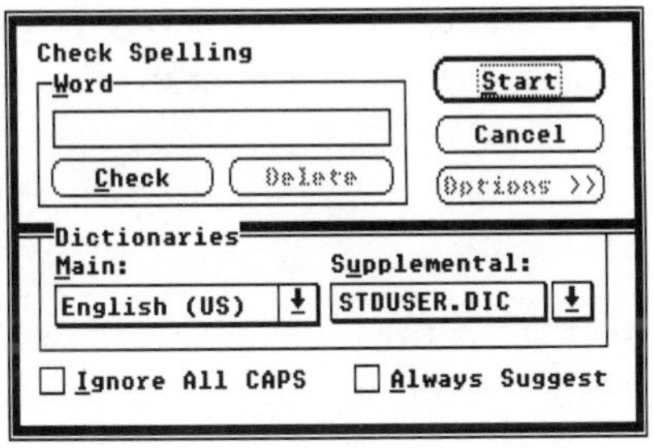

Figure 13-7. *The expanded Spelling dialog box.*

Creating new supplemental dictionaries

When Word checks spelling, it looks through its main dictionary as well as the standard supplemental dictionary STDUSER.DIC. If you create additional supplemental dictionaries, you can add any one of them as a third dictionary for Word to look through. To create a new supplemental dictionary, use the Supplemental list box. Select the name in the text box and replace it by typing a new name using standard filename rules (eight or fewer characters) and the extension DIC. Press Enter. Word recognizes your proposed name as a new dictionary name and asks whether you want to start a new dictionary. When you answer Yes, Word opens a new file using your filename with the extension DIC. When you open the Supplemental list box later, you see the name of your new dictionary.

Once you select a custom dictionary in the Supplemental list box, Word looks through the custom dictionary as a supplement to the main dictionary and STDUSER.DIC as it checks spelling. When you add a word to a supplemental dictionary in the second Spelling dialog box, you can select either your dictionary or STDUSER.DIC in the Add To Dictionary list box. Word adds the new term to the chosen dictionary.

Deleting words and supplemental dictionaries

If you enter a word in a supplemental dictionary and then decide to delete the word, open the Spelling dialog box, type the word in the Word text box, and choose the Delete button. Word removes that word from the supplemental dictionary you have chosen.

To remove an entire supplemental dictionary from Word, return to Windows. Move to the Word directory, select the name of the dictionary you want to remove (it will end in DIC), and use the Delete command on the File menu to erase it from the hard disk.

Spelling Checker Options

When you use the Options button in the first Spelling dialog box, the bottom of the expanded box contains two options: Ignore ALL CAPS and Always Suggest. These options are also available at the bottom of the second Spelling dialog box. Ignore ALL CAPS asks Word to ignore any words spelled in all capital letters. Turn it on to avoid acronyms such as "ASCII," "MIDI," and other jawbreakers that are probably not in Word's dictionaries. Always Suggest saves you the task of choosing the Suggest button when an unmatched word appears. If you turn on this option, Word always offers suggestions when it finds an unmatched word.

To use Word's spelling checker without going through the menus, press F7. This starts a spelling check on any selected block of text without opening the first Spelling dialog box. If the program finds an unmatched word, it opens the second dialog box so that you can replace or ignore the word as you see fit. F7 is especially handy for checking a single word. If you place the insertion point in a word you want checked and press F7, Word checks the spelling of that word. It does not check the entire document as it would if you chose the Spelling command on the Utilities menu.

A Spelling Checker Example

Use Word's spelling checker to check the document for typing and spelling errors. The animal names in the list won't match any words in Word's main dictionary, so you can add them to a custom dictionary—PETFARM.DIC—for later use. (Delete the dictionary from the disk when you finish this example.)

1. Move the insertion point to the beginning of the document to start the spelling check there.
2. Choose Spelling from the Utilities menu to open the first Spelling dialog box.
3. Choose the Options button to expand the dialog box.
4. Select STDUSER.DIC in the Supplemental text box, replace it with the filename *PETFARM*, and press Enter.
5. When Word asks whether you want to create that dictionary, answer Yes. This opens the dictionary file on the hard disk and starts the spelling check. The dialog box closes, and Word searches until it finds an unmatched word. The first one should be the name "Biddlecomb" (unless you accidentally made typing errors in the document). The second Spelling dialog box opens with the name in the top text box. Word also selects the name in the report.
6. Ignore the name by choosing the Ignore button. The dialog box closes, and Word continues its check. The next unmatched word it encounters is "burdgeoning."
7. Choose the Suggest button. Word offers a list of alternatives. Double-click on the correct spelling "burgeoning" (or select it and then choose the Change button). The dialog box closes, the selected word is replaced, and Word continues the check. The next unmatched word is "turnstyles."
8. Choose the Suggest button and use the suggested spelling "turnstiles" to replace the selected word. Word continues its spelling check until it encounters "moomoos." It opens the second Spelling dialog box again.

9. Add "moomoos" to the PETFARM dictionary by choosing the Add button. Word leaves the word intact and continues the spelling check.
10. Add the words "oinkoinks," "cluckclucks," "quackquacks," "bowwows," "hisshiss," "quadripedal," and "apedal" to the PETFARM dictionary using the same technique. Word continues to the end of the document, where it finishes the check and returns the insertion point to the beginning.
11. Test your new dictionary additions by running a second check. Make sure you have PETFARM.DIC selected as the supplemental dictionary. Word picks the word "Biddlecomb" (you ignored it but didn't add it to the dictionary), but it passes all the other petting-farm words as correctly spelled.

HYPHENATION

If you have the Special Edition with disks included, consult the Introduction

Hyphens in text both bind and separate: They can tie two words together as they do in the phrase "toddler-tactile," or they can break words apart at the end of a line. Unfortunately, when hyphens move around during editing, they lose their utility and get in the way. For example, if you split the word "primordial" at the end of a line (so that it reads "primor-" "dial") and then insert text before the word, pushing it down to the next line, you end up with "primor-dial" on one line.

Different Types of Hyphens

Word offers three types of hyphens to help you avoid hyphenation problems:

- The regular hyphen, entered by pressing the Hyphen key
- The optional hyphen, entered by pressing Ctrl-Hyphen
- The nonbreaking hyphen, entered by pressing Ctrl-Shift-Hyphen

The regular hyphen is a standard character that Word treats much like a space. If two words separated by a regular hyphen fall at the end of a line, Word uses the second word to start the next line.

The optional hyphen is an invisible character you can insert to break a word in two. If the word is at the end of a line, Word breaks the word at the optional hyphen's location and displays a hyphen at the break. If revisions move the word down or back to the middle of a line, the hyphen disappears, and the word appears undivided. The optional hyphen remains invisible until further revisions move the word back to the end of a line, where it can once again be broken.

The nonbreaking hyphen appears like a regular hyphen in text. The only difference is that words separated by a nonbreaking hyphen will not be split if they approach the end of a line. Use the nonbreaking hyphen on words (such as "V-neck") that you don't want split between two lines.

You can see the different types of hyphens after you enter them in a document. Turn on the Show All icon on the ribbon, or turn on Show All or Optional Hyphens in the View Preferences dialog box. All regular hyphens appear as they did before; optional hyphens appear as hooked hyphens, and nonbreaking hyphens appear as double-length hyphens.

Automatic Hyphenation

When Word creates lines, it moves any word that doesn't fit at the end of a line to the beginning of the next line. If only the last few letters didn't fit on the line above, Word leaves a hole in that line. If the line is left-aligned, you can see the hole as an especially ragged notch in the right edge of the paragraph. If the line is fully justified, Word fills in for the moved word by inserting space between the words in the line; excessive spacing can make reading the line more difficult. The narrower the paragraph indents, the worse these problems become. Word can help by automatically splitting a large word with an optional hyphen instead of moving the full word to the next line.

To use automatic hyphenation, you first enter text without regard for indents or word spacing. When you finish, choose the Hyphenate command from the Utilities menu to open the Hyphenate dialog box (shown in Figure 13-8). Choose the OK button to start the hyphenation process.

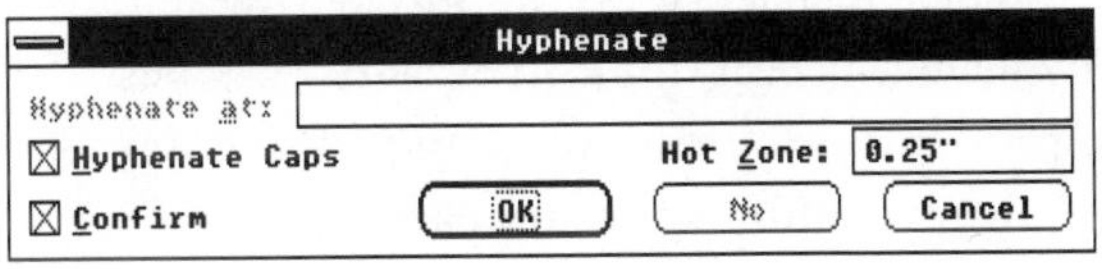

Figure 13-8. *The Hyphenate dialog box.*

The hyphenation process

When Word hyphenates a document, it uses a *hot zone,* a vertical band set against the right indent of the paragraph. The hot zone normally has a width of 0.25 inch. If Word discovers at the right indent (or throughout a line in fully justified text) any holes larger than the hot zone, it hyphenates (if possible) the word that begins the next line, moving up part of the word to fill in the previous line.

When hyphenating a word, Word checks its hyphenation list, a file on the hard disk similar to a dictionary file. The hyphenation list contains a large list of words broken into syllables with acceptable divisions. When Word finds the word it wants to hyphenate in the list, it displays the word in the Hyphenate dialog box, in the Hyphenate At text box. The word appears broken into syllables, and Word highlights the hyphen at the break likely to work best.

If you agree, choose the Yes button. Word adds an optional hyphen at that point and continues the hyphenation process. If you don't like the break, use the left and right cursor keys to move the break to another location and choose Yes to insert an optional hyphen there. If you don't want to split the word at all, choose No to leave the word undivided and continue the hyphenation process. Choose Cancel to stop hyphenation completely.

Setting the hot zone

The size of the hyphenation hot zone is a matter of taste. You might want a setting smaller than 0.25 inch to create smoother margins, or you might want a larger setting to avoid excessive hyphenation. To reset the hot zone size using the Hyphenation dialog box, replace the measurement in the Hot Zone text box with the measurement you want.

Automatic confirmation

If you trust Word's judgment in hyphenation, turn off the Confirm option in the Hyphenate dialog box. Then Word doesn't stop at each word break to ask whether the break is acceptable. Instead, it works through the entire document, inserting optional hyphens where it thinks they will work best. To stop the hyphenation process, press Esc. You can, of course, delete any optional hyphens that Word inserts when you think they are inappropriate.

Hyphenating uppercase words

Word usually hyphenates words whether they're uppercase or lowercase characters. To avoid hyphenating acronyms or other words that use all capital letters, turn off the Hyphenate Caps option in the dialog box before you start the hyphenation process.

A hyphenation example

Try hyphenating the report to smooth out the ragged right margins:

1. Move the insertion point to the beginning of the document.
2. Choose Hyphenate from the Utilities menu to open the Hyphenate dialog box.
3. Choose the OK button to start hyphenation. Word works through the document until it finds the first hot-zone violation—the word "follows" in the second paragraph. It offers the word to you with a suggested break in the Hyphenate At text box.
4. Choose Yes to approve the break and continue hyphenation. Word moves on to "Unfortunately."
5. Choose Yes to approve the break and continue hyphenation. When Word finishes hyphenating, it notifies you in a dialog box. The finished document now has much smoother right margins.

The hyphenation exercise you just tried hyphenates your document as it appears in Word with the Display as Printed option turned off. Because the printer you use may set longer or shorter lines of text when you print the document, the inserted hyphens in the example probably won't appear if you print your document. (For example, the document printout in Figure 13-1 doesn't show the first hyphen that you inserted in the example.) To hyphenate a document as it will appear in a printout, turn on the Display as Printed option in the View Preferences dialog box, and then hyphenate.

A QUICK SUMMARY

In this chapter you learned to use some of Word's most useful editing tools. You learned how to create fields and records and how to sort records according to different criteria. You saw how to use Word's spelling checker to look for misspellings and typing errors and how to create your own supplemental dictionaries. The last part of the chapter introduced you to hyphenation and showed you how to use automatic hyphenation to smooth out the right margins of your documents.

The next chapter introduces you to a single—but very useful—Word feature: footnotes.[1]

---

[1] See the next chapter.

Chapter 14

Creating Footnotes

Many documents require footnotes to provide references or comments for statements in the body of the text. Adding these footnotes without a computer is a challenging task; if the footnotes go at the bottom of each page, you must calculate exactly the number of lines of body text and footnote text that can fit on each page. Word for Windows eliminates all the trouble: You simply insert a footnote marker where appropriate, enter the text of the footnote, and then continue to enter the document. Word does the rest of the work.

In this chapter, you learn not only how to insert footnotes but how to control footnote numbering or use unnumbered footnotes. You learn to edit existing footnotes—changing their location, content, and formatting—and how to control their placement—at the bottom of the page or at the end of a chapter or document.

SETTING UP WORD

The examples in this chapter don't require printing or fancy formatting, so keep the same settings you used in Chapter 13:

- Full menus
- A text window that shows the ruler, ribbon, and status bar
- The Display as Printed option turned off (in the View Preferences dialog box)

The sample document for this chapter (shown in Figure 14-1 on the following page) is a scholarly treatise on the footnote by Waldo Ambergris. It includes enough footnotes per square inch to give you plenty of practice.

The Footnote In History

by

Waldo Ambergris

Many[1] literary historians have neglected the proper place of the footnote in literary history: Some[2] claim that the footnote is only a parenthetical aside to the mainstream of literary thought; others[3] feel that the footnote should be shunted off the center stage of the written word to languish in the wings, far from the spotlight of literary illuminati. It is my contention[4] that the noble footnote deserves better treatment. To that end I now publish the newsletter "The Bottom[5] Line," which elevates the lowly footnote from the nether regions of literary history to the acme[@] of contemporary addenda. I also give you this history to acquaint you with footnote facts.

Why does the footnote deserve an elevated status?[6] Look back with me now to the dimly lit beginnings of the footnote in ancient Rome.

The first recorded reference[7] to a footnote shows us that early Romans used it to support a stone tablet, much as they used the base of a column to support the column.[8] The original text of the footnote was an incantation to the gods asking for textual stability and long shelf life. Space-conscious stone carvers soon discovered that they could add extra comments by getting rid of the incantation and filling the space with text they forgot to include in the tablet above.[9] This practice was soon carried over

---

[1]Or perhaps only quite a few.
[2]Obviously disturbed individuals.
[3]Mostly disreputable persons.
[4] And also my doctoral thesis.
[5]Made you look!
@ Trademark of the Acme Corporation. "We go out of our minds so you won't mind going out!"
[6]Why indeed?
[7]Found within a footnote of Style Guides Of The Ancient Romans.
[8]The characters at the top of the tablet were called, accordingly, "Capital Letters."
[9]For a complete discussion of this substitution, read Useless Trivia For The Academic, by Oliver Ibid, Cider Press, 1984.

(continued)

Figure 14-1.
Use the Insert Footnote command to place footnotes in this document.

Figure 14-1. *continued*

into the world of papyrus and print. Early attempts at multiple footnotes ran into difficulties when the roman numerals used to indicate each footnote grew long enough to fill an entire page. This problem was solved by the introduction of the arabic numbering system and the utilization of imaginary numbers. Freed from the constraints of physically imposed brevity, medieval scholars began to explore the limits of the footnote.[10] It was at this time that the copyright and the trademark were invented. In fact, one of the first characters struck by Johann Gutenberg[11] was the copyright symbol, followed soon by the FBI warning symbol.[12]

Today, of course, we now have computers to help us with footnotes. It has become as easy to enter text in a footnote as it is to enter it in the body of the text, so why not[13] give the footnote its due by subverting the dominant paradigm of the parenthesis and placing all additional comments in footnotes? It is only through concerted effort that we can elevate the footnote to its proper status at the bottom of the page.[14]

[10]Op Cit the Elder writes in his Principia Obscurati of a footnote that lasted for 57 pages. The author's obvious scholarly prestige was boosted even further when readers realized that the body of the text was only two sentences long.
[11]Inventor of the Movable Type, a class of traveling merchants who peddled their wares from town to town.
[12]This symbol later faded into obscurity, but is now being revived by video titlers.
[13]Indeed, why not?
[14]In fact, we might even enter the twenty-first century with video footnotes! As subtitles become more and more prevalent, might we not hope that directors can use them to add to a scene dialog that the actors forgot? Footnotes under all!

AN OVERVIEW OF FOOTNOTES

Footnotes are statements that amplify a remark in a document or provide a reference for verification or further reading. To avoid interrupting the flow of the text, a *footnote marker* informs the reader that a footnote exists concerning the material he or she is reading; the reader can skip it or look for the footnote and read the extra material. Footnotes themselves can rest at the bottom of each page or can be collectively placed at the end of a chapter or document (where they are called *endnotes*).

Footnotes are usually numbered: Each footnote marker is a number that refers to its corresponding footnote. This is convenient if you use several footnotes and necessary if you use endnotes. If you use footnotes sparingly, you can use symbols rather than numbers. If you use, for example, an asterisk for the first footnote marker on a page, you can use double, triple, and even quadruple asterisks for additional footnote markers on the same page.

Word separates footnotes at the bottom of the page from the body of the text by inserting a *separator* between the body of the text and the footnotes. This separator is usually a horizontal line about two inches long, but you can change it to any string of characters you want.

As you add footnotes to a page, the footnote area expands from the bottom margin, pushing up into the text area. If the footnote area pushes up far enough to reach a footnote marker in the text area, it must stop expanding—there is no more room on the page for footnotes. If expansion stops and there isn't enough room in the footnote area to include the entire contents of the last footnote, Word splits the footnote and continues it on the next page. It uses a *continuation separator* on the new page to separate the text area from the extended footnote.

The continuation separator is usually a horizontal line stretching across the entire page, but you can change it to any string. If you want to make it even clearer that the footnote is continued from the previous page, you can add a *continuation notice*—text that Word places at the top of each continued footnote area.

INSERTING A FOOTNOTE

To insert a footnote in a Word document, move the insertion point to the location you want and choose Footnote from the Insert menu. The Footnote dialog box (shown in Figure 14-2) opens. Use it to set the type of footnote marker you want or to choose new separators or continuation notices.

If you choose OK without changing anything in the dialog box, the box closes, and Word inserts a numbered footnote marker at the insertion-point location. (Word keeps track of footnote numbers, so it inserts the proper sequential number as the marker.) Word then opens the *footnote pane,* a partition (shown in Figure 14-3) that appears at the bottom of the window.

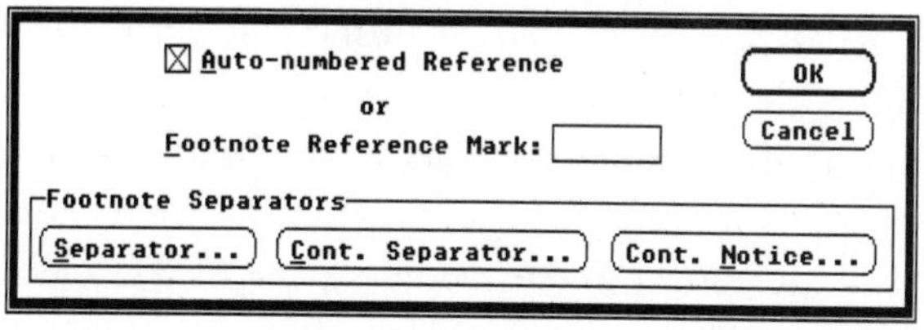

Figure 14-2. *The Footnote dialog box.*

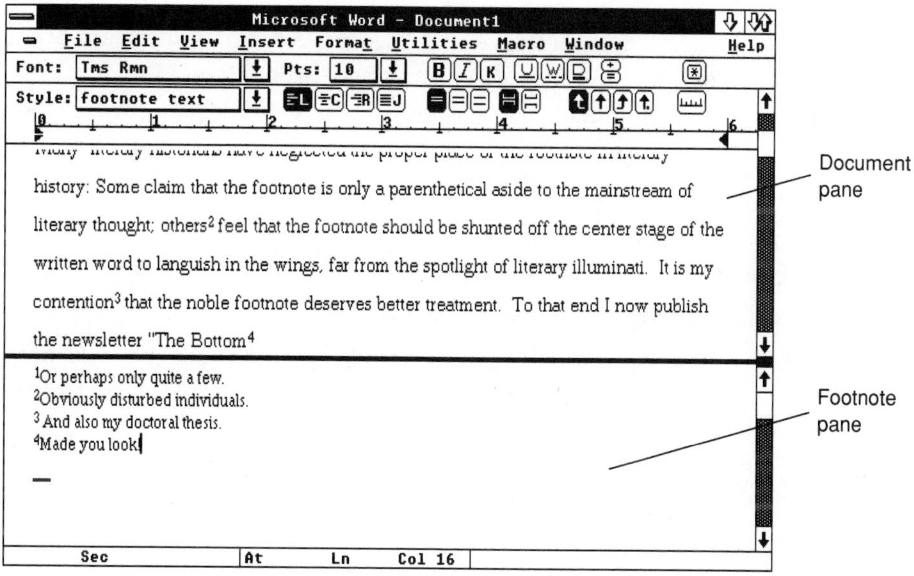

Figure 14-3. *The footnote pane.*

The Footnote Pane

The footnote pane is divided from the rest of the document by a thick horizontal bar. It contains all the footnotes you enter in a document and has its own vertical scroll bar you can use to scroll through those footnotes. Any text in the footnote pane does not appear in the body of the document; you see the footnote (or endnote) text only when you print or use page view.

When you insert a footnote marker in the document, Word places a copy of the marker at the beginning of a line in the footnote pane. The insertion point moves to the footnote pane so that you can enter the contents of your footnote there. As you enter, you can format characters and paragraphs as you do in the body of the text. The only limitation is that you can't delete or move the footnote marker; you must change the marker in the body of the text (as you'll learn to do later in this chapter).

When you finish entering the footnote contents, press F6 to return to the main text pane. The insertion point returns to its previous location there; the footnote pane remains open. To return to the footnote pane to edit or add to footnote text, press F6 again. The insertion point jumps to its previous location in the footnote pane. If you have a mouse, you can jump between the footnote pane and the main text pane by pointing to the pane you want and clicking.

To close the footnote pane and have more room in the main text pane, choose Footnotes from the View menu. The pane closes. Don't worry—the footnotes are still in memory! To see the footnote pane again, you can insert a new footnote or choose Footnotes from the View menu again. The footnote pane opens to show all the footnotes you entered.

A Footnote Entry Example

Try entering footnotes in the sample document:

1. Set the paragraph to center aligned, with the font set to 18-point boldface Tms Rmn, and then enter the title: *The Footnote In History.*
2. Turn off boldface, reduce the character size to 14 points, and then enter the next two lines: *by* followed by *Waldo Ambergris.*

3. Set the paragraph alignment to left, with double spacing and an open line before each paragraph. (As the scholarly Waldo Ambergris, you naturally want this treatise to take up as many pages as possible.) Reduce the character size to 12 points, enter the first word of the treatise—*Many*—and stop.
4. Choose Footnote from the Insert menu. The Footnote dialog box opens.
5. Choose OK to close the dialog box and use automatic footnote numbering. A superscript 1 appears after "Many," the footnote pane opens, and a 1 appears in the first line of the footnote pane.
6. Enter the footnote contents *Or perhaps only quite a few.*
7. Press F6 to return to the main text pane and continue typing the document up to the end of the word "others." Skip footnote 2 shown after "Some" in the sample document. You'll add it later.
8. Choose Footnote from the Insert menu; choose OK when the Footnote dialog box appears to insert a second numbered footnote. A superscript 2 appears after "others," and a 2 appears in the second line of the footnote pane.
9. Enter the footnote contents *Obviously disturbed individuals.* Then press F6 to return to the main text pane.
10. Continue entering the first paragraph. Enter the footnotes you see in the sample document after the words "contention" and "Bottom." Stop after you enter the word "acme." (Text doesn't need to be verbatim for this example, so abridge the body and footnote text if you like.)

Changing the Footnote Marker

Word usually numbers footnotes. To use your own, unnumbered footnote marker, enter the symbol you want in the Footnote Reference Mark text box of the Footnote dialog box and choose OK. Word inserts that symbol as a superscript character in the body of the text and then adds the character with its own footnote line to the footnote pane. Try entering the "@" symbol as a footnote marker.

1. Choose Footnote from the Insert menu to open the Footnote dialog box.
2. Type @ to enter it in the Footnote Reference Mark box and choose OK. The symbol appears as a superscript character following the word "acme" and again at the beginning of a new line in the footnote pane.
3. Enter the footnote contents *Trademark of the Acme Corporation, "We go out of our minds so you won't mind going out!"*
4. Press F6 to return to the main text pane and enter the rest of the document with footnotes as you find them in Figure 14-1. Use automatic numbering for the rest of the footnotes. (Again, you can abridge any of the text as you enter the rest of the document.)

EDITING A FOOTNOTE

When you enter a footnote in the footnote pane, it remains in that pane and doesn't appear in the body of the document. The only part of the footnote that appears in the main text pane is the footnote marker. It's important to realize that the footnote marker and its footnote are linked; the footnote marker in the main text pane controls the existence and location of the footnote in the footnote pane. If you cut, copy, or paste the footnote marker in the document, the footnote attached to the marker disappears or moves within the footnote pane to match the new location of the footnote marker. It's also important to realize that you can't cut, copy, or paste entire footnotes in the footnote pane. You must edit the footnote marker to affect the entire footnote.

Deleting a Footnote

To delete a footnote, move the insertion point to either side of its footnote marker in the main text pane and use Delete or Backspace to remove the marker. After the marker is gone, its footnote disappears from the footnote pane, and Word renumbers all other markers (if they're numbered) following the deleted footnote. If you immediately choose Undo from the Edit menu to restore the footnote marker, Word restores its footnote to the footnote pane.

Moving a Footnote

To move a footnote from one location to another, select the footnote marker in the main text pane as a text block and use Cut to remove it from the text. Paste the marker in its new location using Paste. The footnote changes its order in the footnote pane to match, and Word renumbers the footnotes and markers (if they're numbered) to reflect the new order.

Copying a Footnote

Some footnotes—such as "Ibid." references—are repetitious. Use Copy to make copies of a repetitious footnote. First select the footnote marker and then choose Copy from the Edit menu. Move the insertion point to the next location at which you need the footnote and choose Paste. Word inserts a footnote marker at that location and adds a copy of the original footnote to the footnote pane. Word correctly numbers the copy so that it doesn't repeat the number of the original footnote.

Finding Footnote Markers

Finding a specific footnote marker for editing is easy. Scroll through the footnotes in the footnote pane until you find the one you want. As you scroll, the main text pane scrolls to keep up with the footnote pane. When a footnote is at the top of the pane, the main text pane scrolls to show you that footnote's marker and the text surrounding it. You can then move the insertion point back to the main text pane to cut, move, or duplicate the footnote marker.

You can also use Go To to find a footnote marker: Choose Go To from the Edit menu (or Press F5). Enter *f* in the Go To text box (or on the status bar if you pressed F5), and follow it with the number of the footnote you want to find. For example, enter *f6* to jump to footnote number 6. Press Enter. The insertion point jumps to the footnote marker you specified. Note that the number you enter specifies the actual sequence number of the footnote. For example, if you enter *f6* in the Go To box, Word jumps to the sixth footnote in the document whether or not the footnote is numbered 6.

Editing Footnote Contents

You can edit the contents of a footnote exactly as you edit text in the main text pane, by cutting, pasting, copying, deleting, and formatting to get the result you want. Remember, however, that you can't delete or move the footnote marker in the footnote pane. You must do that in the main text pane.

A Footnote Editing Example

After reading the sample document, you decide that the footnote you applied to the word "others" actually applies to the people you described with the word "Some." Move the footnote from "others" to "Some" and then insert a new footnote to describe "others":

1. Scroll through the footnotes in the footnote pane until footnote 2 is at the top of the pane. The main text pane scrolls to show footnote marker 2.
2. Move the insertion point to the main text pane and select the footnote marker "2" as a text block.
3. Choose Cut from the Edit menu to cut the footnote marker from the main text. Footnote 2 in the footnote pane disappears, and Word renumbers the remaining footnotes accordingly.
4. Move the insertion point to the space following the word "Some" and choose Paste from the Edit menu to insert the cut footnote there. The footnote number appears in the body of the text, the footnote itself reappears in the footnote pane, and Word renumbers the footnotes.
5. Move the insertion point to the space following the word "others" and choose Footnote from the Insert menu. A footnote marker appears in the body of the text and in the footnote pane.
6. Enter the footnote contents *Mostly disreputable persons.*

The sample document is now complete. Use page view (by selecting Page from the View menu) to look at the results of your work. You see footnotes at the bottom of each page, separated by a short horizontal line from the body of the text.

CHANGING FOOTNOTE CONVENTIONS

Word's default footnote system uses numbered footnotes at the bottom of each page. This works well for most documents, but if you want to use a different footnote system, you can easily change these conventions.

Setting a New Footnote Starting Number

If a document is a continuation of previous work—perhaps one of many chapters in a book—the footnotes you use might need to start at a number other than 1. To set the starting number, choose Document from the Format menu. The Format Document dialog box (shown in Figure 14-4) opens. The settings in the Footnotes area (in the lower left corner of the dialog box) change the way footnotes work in a document.

Select the Starting Number text box, and change the number there from 1 to the starting number you want. Choose OK to close the dialog box; Word numbers the footnotes in your document starting with the number you entered.

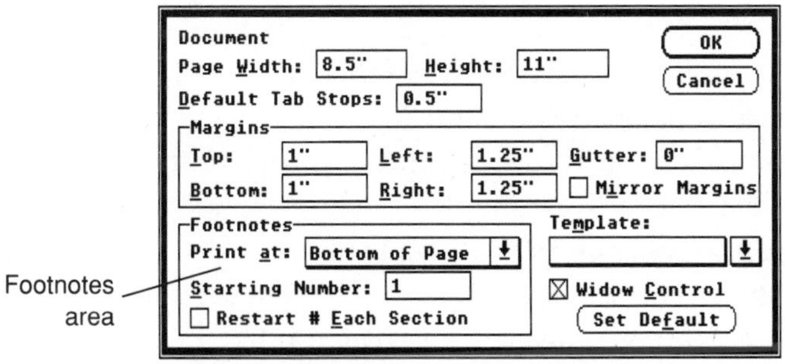

Figure 14-4. *The Format Document dialog box.*

Changing the Separators and the Continuation Notice

To change the horizontal line that separates footnotes from the body of text, choose Footnote from the Insert menu. Choose the Separator button in the lower left corner of the dialog box. A new pane labeled Footnote Separator (shown in Figure 14-5 on the following page) appears in the text window.

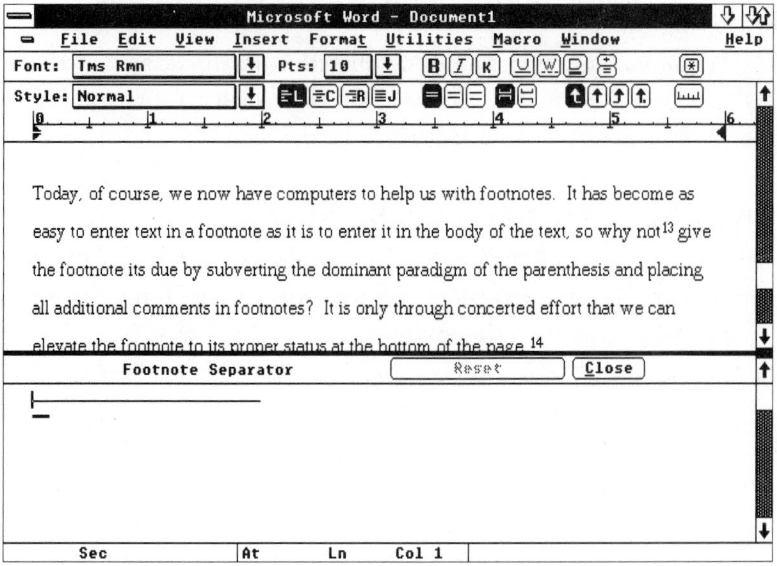

Figure 14-5. *The footnote separator pane.*

Use the keyboard to replace the horizontal line in the pane with your own string of characters. You can enter any characters you think appropriate and add character formatting such as boldface and italic. You can also use paragraph formatting to center the separator, add paragraph borders to it, and make other changes. Short and simple is usually best, however. Large separators take up space that could be better used for text and footnotes.

After you enter the separator characters you want, choose the Close button. (Press Shift-F10 and then C if you're using the keyboard.) If you decide you don't want your new separator, select the Reset button (Shift-F10 and then R) and then choose the Close button. The separator resets to the original short horizontal line before the pane closes.

To change the continuation separator or to create a continuation notice, choose Footnote from the Insert menu. Then choose either the Cont. Separator button to change the separator or the Cont. Notice button to change the continuation notice. A pane similar to the separator pane opens in the text window. Enter the text in the pane, and then choose the Close button when you finish.

Changing Footnote Location

To change footnote location, choose Document from the Format menu to open the Format Document dialog box. The list box labeled Print At in the Footnotes area offers four different footnote locations:

- End of Section: This setting turns footnotes into endnotes but places them all at the end of a section of a document. (You learn to create document sections in Chapter 16.) This setting is useful if you use sections to define chapters within a document. Footnotes then print at the end of each chapter.
- Bottom of Page: This is the default setting. Word places footnotes at the bottom of each page, building up from the bottom page margin until the footnotes reach the body of the text. If the last page of a document has only a small amount of text in the body, a large blank space appears between the text body and the footnotes below.
- Beneath Text: This setting places footnotes at the bottom of each page, starting from the bottom of the text body and working down to the bottom page margin. If the last page of a document has only a small amount of text in the body, the footnotes move up to the bottom of that text, leaving a large blank space between the end of the footnotes and the bottom page margin.
- End of Document: This setting turns footnotes into endnotes by collecting all footnotes and placing them at the end of the document.

To choose a footnote location, select one of the settings in the Print At list box and choose OK to close the dialog box and change the footnote location. Try turning the footnotes into endnotes in the sample document:

1. Choose Document from the Format menu to open the Format Document dialog box.
2. Select End of Document from the Print At list box in the Footnotes area and choose OK to close the dialog box.

3. Turn on page view (if it's not already on) by choosing Page from the View menu, and scroll through the document to see the change. Notice that footnotes are no longer at the end of each page; they're all collected as endnotes at the end of the document.

A QUICK SUMMARY

In this chapter you learned how to enter footnotes by using the Insert Footnote command and how to enter and edit footnote contents in the footnote pane. You saw how to move back and forth between the footnote pane and the main text pane and how to use editing commands to move, copy, and delete footnotes by moving, copying, and deleting their footnote markers. The last part of the chapter showed you how to create your own separators and continuation notices, how to control footnote numbering, and how to set footnote placement. In the next chapter you learn about one of Word's most powerful and unique features: styles.

Chapter 15

Styles Made Simple:

Formatting with Speed and Power

Styles is one of Word for Windows' most powerful features. You use styles to format paragraphs and characters with minimal effort and to easily change the appearance of similar elements throughout a document without changing each element individually.

In this chapter, you learn what styles are and how they work to your benefit. You see how to set a style by using an example paragraph or by creating your own style definition. Next, you learn how to apply the styles to existing text or to new text as you type. You also learn how to change existing styles and the text they control and how to move styles from one document to another using style sheets.

SETTING UP WORD

Keep the settings you've used in the preceding chapters as you work through the examples in this chapter.

- Full menus
- A text window that shows the ruler, ribbon, and status bar
- The Display as Printed option turned off (in the View Preferences dialog box)

Figure 15-1 on the following page shows the first two pages of an article on unicycle racing that includes elements you control with styles: a title, two levels of section headings, text body, and callouts for pictures.

Unicycle Racing: The Forgotten Sport

"There's nothing like the smell of bearing grease, the flash of sun on the seatpost, and 50 uniyclists straining for the finish line!" Howard Dutilleux is reminiscing, leaning back against the bar railing as he finishes another boilermaker. "You'll never see anything like that today--young punks all use two wheels now. Line me up another one, Jimbo...." Rob Formass nods in agreement and adds, "A shame. It's a damn shame." They raise their glasses in leathery hands, salute each other with a loud clink, and toss back their drinks in fond remembrance of better times past. They are the last of a dying breed: the professional unicycle racer.

The Beginnings Of Unicycle Racing

Although barely remembered now, unicycle racing started with much fanfare at the Auxiliary World's Fair of 1928 in Moscow, Idaho. Billed as a spectacle with "Chills, Thrills, and Spills--With Half The Wheels!", the world's first unicycle race had a purse of $500 to draw hungry unicyclists from around the country. The course, a seven-mile circuit with a steep 500-foot hill, was set up around the fairgrounds. The organizers built an upturned ramp on the descent of the hill so descending unicyclists could leap 15 feet through the air before the main grandstands--a guaranteed audience pleaser!

Picture: The Moscow race course, complete with mechanics' pits.

A Hit

This first experiment in professional unicycle racing was an immediate success. There were, of course, numerous accidents as unscrupulous unicyclists used their free hands to harass their opponents. A favorite trick was quickly spinning a neighboring unicyclist around 180 degrees so he would start pedaling in the wrong direction. Many cyclists continued pedaling in the wrong direction until they met the pack coming in the opposite direction (or until they came up to the wrong end of the ramp)!

(continued)

Figure 15-1.
Use styles to set and control the elements of this document.

Figure 15-1. *continued*

Unicycle Racing Spreads

Unicycle racing soon spread like heat rash under a cheap cycling jersey. Soon the entire Palouse area became the mecca for unicyclists from around the world. Special training camps sprang up, offering specialties like endurance unicycling (the 200-kilometer road race was especially popular at the time) and uphill sprints. Designers began to introduce specialty unicycles: 1935 saw the introduction of both the AeroAce 10-foot unicycle (effective for falling toward the finish line at the last moment) and the Marauder, a competitive unicycle built of solid cast iron. It didn't climb hills well, but its descents were murderous, and nobody wanted to collide with a Marauder. That was indeed the Golden Age of Unicycling.

Picture: The AeroAce and Marauder unicycles, ridden by unicyclist greats Arto deFeur and Simon Durst.

Women's Unicycling

Unicycling soon spread beyond the confines of male domination: League after league of women's amateur unicycle racing teams sprang up and spawned a corps of professional women racers. Although the governing board of the International Unicycle Committee tried to limit women's racing by ruling that all women's unicycle wheels must use no ball bearings or axles, the plucky women responded by eliminating unicycle seats and standing directly on the rim of the wheel, propelling their unicycles by rapidly running in place on the rim.

The Quest For Olympic Respectability

As popular as unicycle racing became, avid athletes and fans realized that it would not become a truly legitimate sport until athletes from around the world came together to race their unicycles at the Olympic Games. A committee quickly formed to promote unicycling as an Olympic sport, and soon recruited some of the most prestigious names in unicycling to perform in an exhibition during the 1937 Sub-Olympics in tiny Barbados. Although the Olympic sports selection committee was impressed with the

AN OVERVIEW OF STYLES

In the preceding chapters, you set character and paragraph formatting as you entered sample documents. This usually involved using several commands. For example, to create a title, you centered a paragraph, enlarged the point size of the text, and turned on boldface. When you moved on to the body of the text, you changed to left alignment, smaller text, and no boldface. Even if you're adept at using keyboard shortcuts, there is a significant pause while you stop to change formatting. Using a single instruction to set up the formatting for a title or normal text would be much quicker. Styles enable you to do just that.

A style stores information about combinations of formatting within a paragraph so that you can apply them later in a single step. A style stores both paragraph formatting (including tab stops and positioning) and character formatting. To create a style, you show Word the formatting you want by selecting an example paragraph, or you define the formatting you want using a dialog box. You then give the style a name; Word stores the style and its definition under this name. For example, you might define a style named "Section" as italic and underlined, with a half-inch left indent, and use it for section headings throughout a document.

To apply a style, you first select one or more paragraphs, as you do for paragraph formatting. You then select the style by name from either the ruler or a dialog box. The style you apply changes the formatting of any selected paragraphs to match the style's formatting definition. Styles also work as you enter text. When you choose a style during text entry, the style conforms your current paragraph and character formatting to the style's formatting. For example, after you define a style, such as the Section style, you can choose it before you type a section heading. When you enter the heading, it appears italicized and underlined with a half-inch left indent.

Automatic Styles

Word comes with predefined styles (called *automatic styles*) that you can use in any document. The most common style is "Normal," the default style. Normal is defined as a 10-point Tms Rmn font with left paragraph alignment and no character emphasis. Other automatic styles control common elements of documents. For example, when you open the header window, Word uses the style "Header," which includes a centered and right-aligned tab stop to help you align page numbers and titles.

Changing Style Definitions

After you apply styles to various elements, you can redefine the styles to quickly change the formatting of the elements. When you change the definition of a style, all elements in a document controlled by that style change their appearances to match the new definition. For example, if every section heading in a document is formatted by the Section style, you can change all the headings at once by changing the Section style definition. If you change it to centered boldface, all the section headings become centered and boldface. Without using styles, you would have to select each section heading individually to change it.

Style definition changes are even more powerful when you realize that every style, with the exception of Normal, is based on another style. This means that a style such as Section is defined as "Normal plus italic, underlining, and a half-inch left indent." When you change a base style, all its derivative styles change as well. For example, changing Normal's definition to use the Helv font instead of Tms Rmn changes the font in all styles based on it (including a style such as Section) to Helv. The only exceptions are derivative styles that specify their own fonts. If you create styles by building on a single base style, you can easily change the aspects of all those styles by simply changing the base style.

SETTING A STYLE

You can set a style in either of two ways: by using an example or by using your own definition. To set a style by example, you first select an example paragraph in a document and then use the ruler or the Format Define Styles command to capture the paragraph's formatting. To set a style by defining it yourself, you use the Format Define Styles command to open a dialog box, where you set all the formats you want included in the style's definition.

Using an example paragraph is the fastest and easiest method of setting a style and is useful if you format elements of a document as you write. Once you format a paragraph in a way you think you'll use again, capture its formatting in a style. Setting styles by definition is useful if you plan a document carefully before you start writing. Define a style for each kind of element you'll use in the document; later, as you write, you can apply your styles to enter the elements you want.

Selecting an Example Paragraph

To select a single example paragraph for setting a style, use the same rules as you use when selecting a paragraph for paragraph formatting: Select a single block of text in the paragraph, select the entire paragraph, or simply move the insertion point into the paragraph. You can also select more than one paragraph, but if you do, Word looks at the first paragraph in the selection and ignores all the others. (Note that if you select a text block that includes parts of other paragraphs, Word considers the other paragraphs selected whether they're entirely within the text block or not.)

Setting a Style by Example

After you select an example paragraph, use the ruler or the Format Define Styles command to set a style. To use the ruler, select the Styles combo box using the mouse or press Ctrl-S. Then replace its text by typing a new style name and pressing Enter. If no style exists for the name you enter, Word asks whether you want to define a style based on your selected paragraph. Choose Yes to set a new style or No to escape without setting a style.

To set a style by example using the Format Define Styles command, choose Define Styles from the Format menu to open the Define dialog box. Enter a name for the style you want to set in the Define Style Name text box and choose OK to close the dialog box and set the style.

When you set a style using either of these methods, Word checks the paragraph and character formatting of your example paragraph and assigns them to the style name you entered. If your example paragraph contains mixed character formatting, Word determines the character format used most often and assigns that formatting to the style you set.

Try setting a style now using an example paragraph and the ruler:

1. Enter the title of the article without formatting and press Enter.
2. Select the entire first paragraph (the title). Change character formatting to 18-point boldface and paragraph formatting to center alignment.
3. Select the Style combo box on the ruler by pressing Ctrl-S.
4. Enter the new style name *Title*, and press Enter. A dialog box asks whether you want to define the style "Title" based on your selection.
5. Choose Yes to close the dialog box and to set and apply the new style "Title."
6. Move the selection point to the end of the document (just below the title) to prepare for further text entry.

Setting a Style by Definition

To set a style by defining it yourself, open the Define dialog box (shown in Figure 15-2) by choosing Define Style from the Format menu. When the dialog box opens, choose the Options button to see the full Define dialog box. Note that the list box shows the Title style you created as an available style.

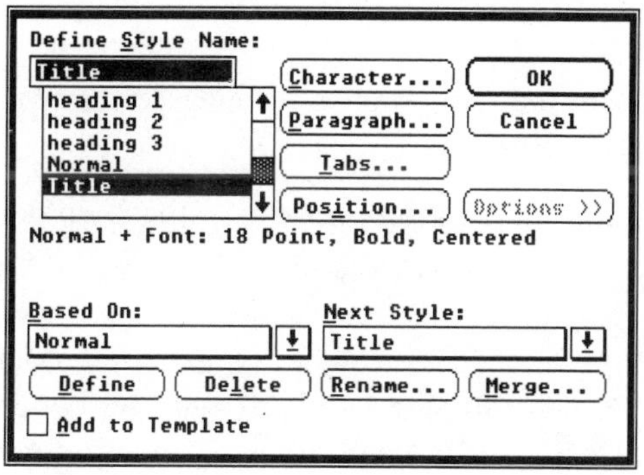

Figure 15-2. *The Define dialog box.*

The Define dialog box

The Define dialog box has many controls for setting styles. Use the Define Style Name text box at the top to enter a new style name. The list box below shows the currently available styles; you can choose any of them to examine or redefine a style. The area below the list box shows the style definition of any style you select from the list. When you first open the dialog box, this area lists the style of the currently selected paragraph in the document, showing any additional formatting such as new paragraph alignment, tab stops, or character emphases.

To set a new style by definition, enter a new style name in the Define Style Name box, and then change the style definition by using the four buttons in the middle of the dialog box: Character, Paragraph, Tabs, and Position. Each button opens a dialog box where you make formatting changes. These dialog boxes are the same ones you open by choosing Character, Paragraph, Tab, or Position from the Format menu. They offer different formatting options:

- The Character dialog box changes font, character size, typestyle, and other character formatting.
- The Paragraph dialog box changes alignment, indention, spacing, borders, and other paragraph formatting.
- The Tab dialog box changes tab-stop positions, tab-stop alignment, and tab leaders.
- The Position dialog box sets the paragraph's absolute or relative position on a page. (See Chapter 19 for more details.)

Any changes you make in these dialog boxes appear in the style definition after you close the dialog box by choosing OK.

The Based On combo box

As you learned earlier, every style definition is based on another style (with the exception of Normal). Use the Based On combo box to choose any currently available style as a base style for the selected style. The combo box descends to list every available style; any style you choose here appears as the base style in the style definition.

The Next Style combo box

Whenever you apply a style to a paragraph and press Enter at the end of that paragraph, you create a new paragraph that uses the same style (in the same way as you copy paragraph formatting whenever you press Enter at the end of a paragraph). Some styles work best when they apply only to a single paragraph. For example, when you press Enter at the end of a section heading, you want to return immediately to Normal style to enter regular text. Use the Next Style combo box to create a single-paragraph style.

When the Next Style combo box is empty, the style continues each time you press Enter. If you choose a new style in the Next Style combo box, Word changes to that style when you press Enter. For example, you can set a section heading style and define Normal as the next style. When you press Enter after entering a heading, Word starts the next paragraph using Normal style.

The Define, Delete, Rename, and Merge buttons

The four buttons below the Based On and Next Style combo boxes offer more style definition options. The Define button adds the name in the Define Style Name box (with its current definition) to the style list, creating a new style. The Delete button deletes any existing style from the style list except automatic styles, which can't be deleted. To delete a style, first select a name from the style list, and then choose the Delete button. The Rename button opens a small dialog box where you can rename a style. To rename a style, select a name from the style list, choose the Rename button, enter a new style name, and choose OK to close the Rename dialog box. The last button, Merge, transfers styles from one document to another, a feature described later in the chapter.

The OK, Cancel, and Close buttons

The OK and Cancel buttons in the Define dialog box work for the most part as they do in other dialog boxes. When you choose OK, you set the style currently entered in the Define Style Name box and close the dialog box; when you choose Cancel, you close the dialog box without setting a new style. If you set styles in the dialog box using the Define button, it adds new styles to the style list without closing the dialog box; consequently, the Cancel button changes to Close. Choosing Close closes the dialog box without setting a new style, but it doesn't do away with the styles you've already set. (To get rid of these styles, use the Delete button.)

An example

The sample article includes two different section headings: a level-one heading with boldface, double underlining, and a half-inch left indent; and a level-two heading with single underlining. The article also uses a picture callout with italic characters. Define three new styles named Head1, Head2, and Pict to use for these three elements. (Note that Word already has automatic styles labeled Heading 1, Heading 2, and Heading 3. Ignore them and create your own styles for this example.)

1. Choose Define Styles from the Format menu to open the Define dialog box, and then choose the Option button to expand the box.
2. Enter the name *Head1* in the Define Style Name text box.
3. Choose the Character button to open the Character dialog box.
4. Turn on the Bold and Double Underline options and choose OK to close the Character dialog box. The style definition now includes boldface and double underlining.
5. Choose the Paragraph button to open the Paragraph dialog box.
6. Set the Indents From Left setting to 0.5" and turn on the Keep Paragraph With Next option. Choose OK to close the dialog box. The style definition now includes a half-inch left indent and an option that ensures the heading won't be separated by a page break from the text that follows.
7. Choose Normal from the Next Style combo box.
8. Choose the Define button to add Head1 and its definition to the style list.
9. Enter *Head2* in the Define Style Name text box.
10. Select Head1 from the Based On combo box to use as a base for Head2. The base name in the style definition changes to Head1.
11. Choose the Character button to open the Character dialog box.

12. Turn on the Underline option and then choose OK to close the dialog box and return to the Define dialog box. The style definition now includes single underlining. Because it's based on Head1, it contains boldface, a left indent, and the Keep With Next Paragraph option.
13. Choose the Define button to add Head2 and its definition to the style list.
14. Enter the name *Pict* in the Define Style Name box.
15. Choose the Character button to open the Character dialog box.
16. Turn on the Italic option and choose OK to close the dialog box and return to the Define dialog box. The style definition now includes italic.
17. Choose OK to add Pict to the style list, close the dialog box, and return to the document.

APPLYING A STYLE

After you've defined useful styles for a document, apply them whenever possible to save yourself work in formatting. You can apply a style as you type or, if you prefer, you can enter a paragraph (or more) and then go back to apply a style to it. However you apply them, try to use styles consistently. If you conscientiously apply the same style to an element whenever it appears in a document, you can redefine the style later to change all the elements it controls.

Applying Styles During Text Entry

The fastest method for applying a style during text entry involves three steps: (1) Press Ctrl-S to select the Style combo box on the ruler, (2) enter the name of the style you want, and (3) press Enter. Word changes the formatting of the paragraph you're entering so that it matches the new style's definition. If you forget the names of the available styles, select the Style combo box and use the up and down cursor keys to scroll through the style names. If you have a mouse, click on the down arrow of the combo box to see a list of the style names and select the one you want.

You can also apply a style by choosing Styles from the Format menu to open the Styles dialog box (shown in Figure 15-3). Scroll through the style list to select the style you want. Any style you select appears in the Style Name text box, and its definition appears below the style list. Choose OK to close the dialog box and apply the style to your current paragraph, or choose Cancel to close the dialog box without applying a new style. (The Define button below OK and Cancel opens the Define dialog box if you want to define a new style.)

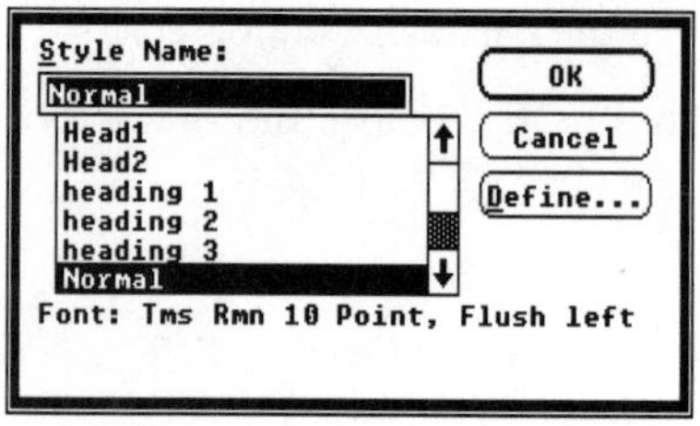

Figure 15-3. *The Styles dialog box.*

Applying Styles to Existing Text

You can apply a style to existing text by first selecting the text as a text block. Word looks at your text block as a selection of full paragraphs, as it does when you select text for paragraph formatting. This means that even paragraphs that are only partially selected will be changed by the style you apply.

After you select text, apply the style you want: Enter or select the style from the Styles combo box on the ruler or select the style from the Styles dialog box. All the text within the selected paragraphs changes to match the style definition.

Adding Manual Formatting to a Styled Paragraph

After you apply a style to a paragraph, you can go back to the paragraph and change its formatting using the ruler or the Format command. Doing this is called *manual formatting*; Word recognizes it as an addition to the paragraph's style formatting.

When you apply a new style to a paragraph that contains manual formatting, Word replaces all the manual formatting with the style's formatting, with one exception: Word *toggles* character emphasis—that is, Word adds emphasis to characters that don't have it and takes the emphasis away from characters that have it. For example, if you italicize several phrases in a paragraph and then apply a style including italic to the paragraph, the style turns all the plain text to italicized text and all the italicized text to plain text. This ensures that the words you emphasized using italic are still emphasized, this time by not being italic. To change text back to the style's own formatting without toggling, select the text and press Ctrl-Spacebar. For example, if you select a text block that contains both italicized and plain text and then press Ctrl-Spacebar when the style specifies plain text, all selected text turns to plain text whether or not it's italicized.

A Style Application Example

Use the styles you created earlier—Head1, Head2, and Pict—as you enter the rest of the sample article. (It's not important that you enter the normal text paragraphs verbatim, so feel free to enter gobbledygook to speed entry. Try to keep the paragraphs as long as those in the sample document, however.)

1. Type the first full paragraph of the document and press Enter. (Enter the paragraph in the Normal style; check the style name on the ruler to be sure you do so.)
2. Press Ctrl-S, type *Head1*, and press Enter to apply the Head1 style.
3. Enter the heading *The Beginnings Of Unicycle Racing* and press Enter. The heading appears boldface, double-underlined, and indented. When you press Enter, the style becomes Normal because the Head1 style definition includes Normal as its next style.
4. Enter the next paragraph of the article and press Enter. It appears in normal formatting.
5. Press Ctrl-S, type *Pict*, and press Enter to apply the Pict style.
6. Enter the picture callout *Picture: The Moscow race course, complete with mechanics' pits*. Press Enter. The line appears in italic. Notice that when you press Enter, the style doesn't change; the Pict style definition doesn't set the next style.

7. Enter the rest of the document using Normal style for the main text, Head1 style for all headings that have double underlining, Head2 style for all headings that have single underlining, and Pict style for all picture callouts. (You will run out of text before the article ends, but you don't need more than two pages for this example.)

REFORMATTING WITH STYLES

After you enter a document using different styles, you can reformat different elements in the document by redefining their styles. These changes can be specific or all-encompassing. By changing a base style, you change all the elements in a document that use derivative styles; by changing a style that has no derivative styles, you change only the type of element controlled by that style.

Redefining a Style

Redefining a style is much like defining a new style. You can redefine by selecting an example paragraph or by setting your own definition in the Define dialog box.

Redefining by example

To redefine by example, first select an example paragraph. An example paragraph for redefining a style must already have that style applied to it and contain some additional manual formatting such as italic, new indents, additional tab stops, and so on. Press Ctrl-S to select the Style combo box on the ruler, enter or select the name of style you want to change in the combo box, and then press Enter. If Word recognizes the name as an existing style and the example paragraph as the same style plus additional formatting, it opens a dialog box asking whether you want to redefine the style based on the selected paragraph. Choose Yes to redefine the style by example or No to stop the style redefinition.

Setting your own redefinition

To set your own style redefinition, choose Define Styles from the Format menu to open the Define dialog box. Choose Options to expand the dialog box. Next, select the name of the style you want to redefine from the style list.

Use the Character, Paragraph, Tabs, and Position buttons to set new formatting for the style, and then choose the Define button to redefine the style. Choose OK or Close to close the dialog box.

An example

Try changing the appearance of your sample article by changing its styles. Change the line spacing throughout the document by changing the Normal style. Then change the indention of the headings by changing Head1:

1. Choose Define Styles from the Format menu to open the Define dialog box, and choose the Options command button to expand the dialog box.
2. Select Normal from the style list.
3. Choose the Paragraph button to open the Paragraph dialog box.
4. Set alignment to Justified, enter *1 li* in the Spacing Before box, enter *2 li* in the Spacing Line box, and choose OK to close the dialog box. The definition of Normal now shows that it uses full justification with double spacing and an open line before the paragraph.
5. Choose the Define button to redefine Normal with its new spacing. All the lines in the document now change to double spacing and full justification, including those in the derivative styles Head1, Head2, Title, and Pict.
6. Select Head1 from the style list.
7. Choose the Paragraph button to open the Paragraph dialog box.
8. Enter *0* in the Indents From Left box and choose OK to close the dialog box. The Head1 style definition changes from a left indent of 0.5" to 0".
9. Choose OK to close the dialog box and apply Head1's new style definition. Both first-level and second-level headings move a half inch to the left. Head2 followed Head1's change because it is a derivative style of Head1.
10. Save this document under the name UNICYCLE for use in the next chapter.

Viewing Styles Within a Document

When you redefine a style to change document elements, you might find that some of the elements don't change because you forgot to apply the proper style to them. To see whether this is the case, you must find out which styles are applied to which paragraphs. One way to do this is to place the insertion point in a paragraph; the Style combo box on the ruler changes to show the style that applies to that paragraph. By moving the insertion point around through the document, you can see which styles are applied to which paragraphs.

The Style Name area

Word offers a more comprehensive method of viewing styles in a document: the Style Name area, shown in Figure 15-4. This area isn't normally open in the document window, but when you open it, it appears as a vertical strip along the left edge of the text, where it lists the style name for each paragraph to its right. As you scroll through the document, the style names scroll to match the paragraphs. Use the Style Name area to see the style applied to each paragraph in the document.

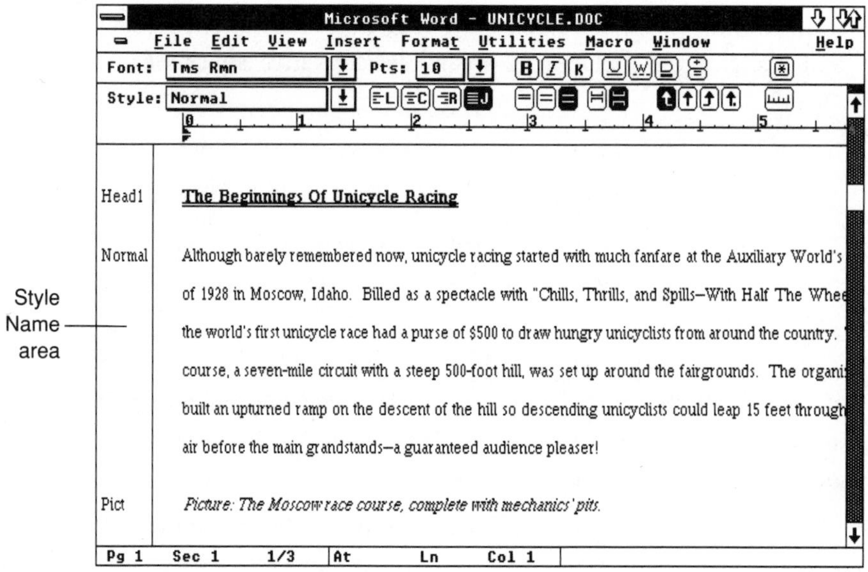

Figure 15-4. *The Style Name area appears along the left edge of the window.*

To open the Style Name area, choose Preferences from the View menu to open the Preferences dialog box. The value in the box labeled Style Area Width sets the width of the Style Name area. If you enter a positive value in inches, Word opens the Style Name area at that width. Choose OK to close the dialog box and see the Style Name area in the text window.

To change the width of the Style Name area, use the View Preferences command to enter a new width or, if you have a mouse, move the pointer to the line separating the area from the rest of the window. When the pointer changes to two vertical bars with arrows pointing left and right, drag the line left or right to the width you want.

To close the Style Name area, enter a width value of *0* in the Preferences dialog box or, if you have a mouse, drag the area's dividing line all the way to the left of the window and release it.

STYLE SHEETS

As you create new styles and add them to the style list, Word remembers them as a collection of styles called a *style sheet.* Each document you create has its own style sheet. When you save a document, Word saves its style sheet along with the document.

After you've worked to create useful styles for one document, you might want to use them again in another document. For example, the title and heading styles you created might be useful in other reports or articles you write. To transfer them to a new document, you merge style sheets in the Define dialog box. To do so, first open the document into which you want to bring the styles. Then choose Define Styles from the Format menu to open the Define dialog box. Choose the Options button to expand the dialog box, and choose the Merge button. The Merge dialog box (shown in Figure 15-5 on the following page) opens, and there you can select the document that has the styles you want.

The Merge dialog box works much like the Open Document dialog box: You use the Directories list box to look through directories and drives, and you use the Files list box to choose the document you want. Note that the Files list box normally shows all files ending with the extension DOT, files that are *document templates.* (Document templates are a way to store styles and other formatting for easy access when you start a new document; you

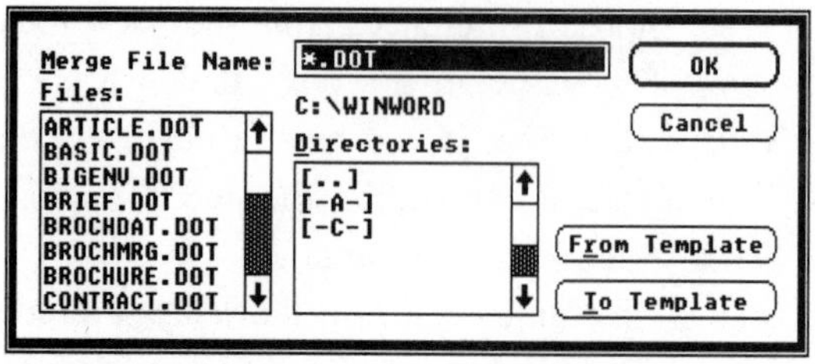

Figure 15-5. *The Merge dialog box.*

learn about templates in Chapter 17.) To see documents instead of templates in a directory, change the characters in the Merge File Name box to **.DOC* and press Enter. When you find the document you want in the Files list, select its name and then choose OK to close the dialog box and merge style sheets.

When Word merges the style sheet with the style sheet of the current document, it adds all the styles from the incoming style sheet to the style sheet of the current document. If an incoming style has the same name as a style in the current style sheet, a dialog box appears asking if you want to continue. If you choose yes, Word replaces the current style with the incoming style. For example, if you have a document open with a Normal style that uses Tms Rmn and you bring in styles from a document with a Normal style that uses Helv, Word replaces the Tms Rmn Normal style with the Helv Normal style.

A QUICK SUMMARY

You now know how to use styles as a powerful formatting tool. You learned how to set a style using the ruler and an example paragraph or by using the Define dialog box and a style definition. You then learned how to apply the styles to text as you type or to selected text that you entered previously and how to reformat document elements by changing style definitions. The last part of the chapter taught you how to transfer styles from one document to another. In the next chapter, you learn even more about formatting as you see how to divide a document into sections, set up columns of text, control page positions, and control other types of section formatting.

Chapter 16

Formatting by Section:

Vertical Alignment, Columns, and More

Not all formatting in Word for Windows occurs at the character and paragraph levels; Word also offers *section formatting* to control larger sections of a document. In this chapter, you learn how to divide a document into sections and learn about the different formatting options available in a section. You see how to change headers and footers from one section to another, accumulate endnotes in a section, add line numbers to pages, and control *vertical alignment,* the way Word fills in a page from top to bottom. You also learn to use perhaps the flashiest section-formatting option: columns, a feature that prints your text in columns like those in newspapers and magazines.

SETTING UP WORD

Use the same settings as you've used in the past few chapters:

- Full menus
- A text window that shows the ruler, ribbon, and status bar
- The Display as Printed option turned off (in the View Preferences dialog box)

Use the article you created and saved in the preceding chapter; you should find it under the name UNICYCLE.DOC. When you finish, the article will look like Figure 16-1 on the following page.

Unicycle Racing: The Forgotten Sport

"There's nothing like the smell of bearing grease, the flash of sun on the seatpost, and 50 uniyclists straining for the finish line!" Howard Dutilleux is reminiscing, leaning back against the bar railing as he finishes another boilermaker. "You'll never see anything like that today--young punks all use two wheels now. Line me up another one, Jimbo...." Rob Formass nods in agreement and adds, "A shame. It's a damn shame." They raise their glasses in leathery hands, salute each other with a loud clink, and toss back their drinks in fond remembrance of better times past. They are the last of a dying breed: the professional unicycle racer.

The Beginnings Of Unicycle Racing

Although barely remembered now, unicycle racing started with much fanfare at the Auxiliary World's Fair of 1928 in Moscow, Idaho. Billed as a spectacle with "Chills, Thrills, and Spills--With Half The Wheels!", the world's first unicycle race had a purse of $500 to draw hungry unicyclists from around the country. The course, a seven-mile circuit with a steep 500-foot hill, was set up around the fairgrounds. The organizers built an upturned ramp on the descent of the hill so descending unicyclists could leap 15 feet through the air before the main grandstands--a guaranteed audience pleaser!

Picture: The Moscow race course, complete with mechanics' pits.

A Hit

This first experiment in professional unicycle racing was an immediate success. There were, of course, numerous accidents as unscrupulous unicyclists used their free hands to harass their opponents. A favorite trick was quickly spinning a neighboring unicyclist around 180 degrees so he would start pedaling in the wrong direction. Many cyclists continued pedaling in the wrong direction until they met the pack coming in the opposite direction (or until they came up to the wrong end of the ramp)!

Unicycle Racing Spreads

Unicycle racing soon spread like heat rash under a cheap cycling jersey. Soon the entire

(continued)

Figure 16-1.
Column formatting prints the text of this article in two columns.

Figure 16-1. *continued*

Palouse area became the mecca for unicyclists from around the world. Special training camps sprang up, offering specialties like endurance unicycling (the 200-kilometer road race was especially popular at the time) and uphill sprints. Designers began to introduce specialty unicycles: 1935 saw the introduction of both the AeroAce 10-foot unicycle (effective for falling toward the finish line at the last moment) and the Marauder, a competitive unicycle built of solid cast iron. It didn't climb hills well, but its descents were murderous, and nobody wanted to collide with a Marauder. That was indeed the Golden Age of Unicycling.

Picture: The AeroAce and Marauder unicycles, ridden by unicyclist greats Arto deFeur and Simon Durst.

Women's Unicycling

Unicycling soon spread beyond the confines of male domination: League after league of women's amateur unicycle racing teams sprang up and spawned a corps of professional women racers. Although the governing board of the International Unicycle Committee tried to limit women's racing by ruling that all women's unicycle wheels must use no ball bearings or axles, the plucky women responded by eliminating unicycle seats and standing directly on the rim of the wheel, propelling their unicycles by rapidly running in place on the rim.

The Quest For Olympic Respectability

As popular as unicycle racing became, avid athletes and fans realized that it would not become a truly legitimate sport until athletes from around the world came together to race their unicycles at the Olympic Games. A committee quickly formed to promote unicycling as an Olympic sport, and soon recruited some of the most prestigious names in unicycling to perform in an exhibition during the 1937 Sub-Olympics in tiny Barbados. Although the Olympic sports selection committee was impressed with the sport, back-room maneuvering by the powerful bicycle-spoke industry--worried about losing half its business if unicycling took over--soon killed unicycling's Olympian aspirations.

CREATING SECTIONS

To use section formatting effectively, you should first divide a document into sections. Although you can apply section formatting to an entire document (Word treats the document as a single section), many section-formatting options aren't truly effective unless you use them on separate and contrasting sections.

To create a section, simply place the insertion point where you want one section to end and another to begin. Then choose Break from the Insert menu. The Insert Break dialog box (shown in Figure 16-2) opens, where you can choose a page break, a column break, or one of four types of section breaks.

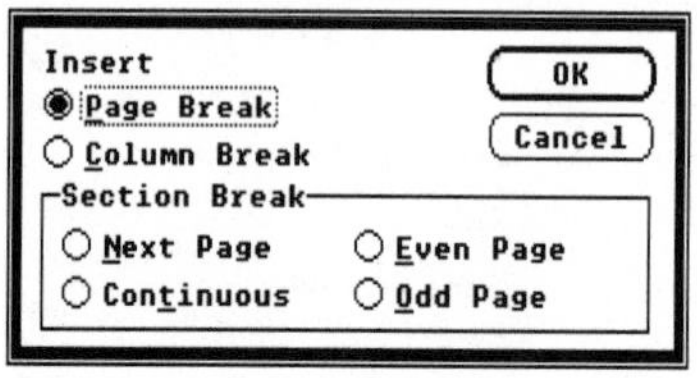

Figure 16-2. *The Insert Break dialog box.*

Types of Section Breaks

Each type of section break determines where the next section starts when you print your document:

- Next Page tells Word to start printing the next section at the top of a new page.
- Continuous tells Word to start printing the next section as a new paragraph on the same page (unless the page is full).
- Even Page tells Word to start printing the next section at the top of a new even-numbered page (leaving a blank odd-numbered page if necessary).
- Odd Page tells Word to start printing the next section at the top of a new odd-numbered page (leaving a blank even-numbered page if necessary).

Select the section break most appropriate for your needs. For example, if you use section breaks to divide chapters from one another, you might use New Page breaks to start each new chapter on its own page. If you're printing in book form with facing odd and even pages, you might want to use the Odd Page option to start each chapter on a right-hand page in the book. The Continuous break is useful for creating a section that you don't want to be obvious when you print the document.

After you select the section break you want, choose OK to close the dialog box and insert a section break at the insertion point's location. The break appears in your document as a double dotted line extending across the text window. As the paragraph marker contains all the paragraph formatting for the paragraph that precedes it, the section break marker contains all the section formatting for the section that precedes it. (The end of the document contains section formatting for the last section in that document.)

Word treats a section break marker as a single character (even though it looks like a series of dots) that you can select, copy, paste, and delete. When you copy or move a section break marker, you copy or move the section formatting with the marker. If you delete a section break marker, all the text preceding the marker uses the section formatting of the next section.

To format a section, you must first select it by simply placing the insertion point in the section or by selecting a text block in the section. To select more than one section, select a text block that includes text in each section you want to select. To help you see where each section lies, the status bar tells you the section number in which the insertion point is located, listing it as Sec 1, Sec 2, Sec 3, and so on.

Types of Section Formatting

You can set many types of section formatting to make sections look different from each other when you print a document:

- Headers and footers (including page numbers)—You can set headers and footers so that each section has its own set and so that page numbers either continue sequentially from section to section or start anew at the beginning of each section.
- Endnotes (footnotes)—You can set footnotes to print at either end of a section or at the end of a following section.
- Number of columns—You can tell Word to arrange the text to print in one column (the usual method of printing), two columns, three columns, or more. Each section can have a different number

of columns for printing, which is useful for creating newsletters, bulletins, and similar documents.

- Line numbering—Word can number the lines of text on each page to the left of the text, a convenient feature for contracts or similar documents in which readers need an easy reference to individual lines. You can turn line numbering on or off and set different line-numbering increments in each section.
- Vertical alignment—Word can print the contents of each page so they're flush against the top margin (occasionally leaving extra blank space at the bottom of the page), centered between the two margins so that any blank space is split equally between top and bottom margins, or stretched out to fit flush against both the top and bottom margins. You can set vertical alignment for each section of the document in any one of these three ways.

SETTING HEADERS AND FOOTERS

If you have the Special Edition with disks included, consult the Introduction

Whenever you create a new section, Word duplicates any existing headers or footers and uses them in the new section. Word then *links* the headers and footers of the new section to the headers and footers in the following section. This link keeps the headers and footers consistent throughout the document; whenever you change a header or footer, you change the linked headers and footers in the sections that follow.

For example, if you created a document with a header that listed the page number, and you then split the document into five sections, all five sections would include headers that listed the page number. The first header would be linked to all the duplicate headers that followed. If you changed the first section header to include the date as well, all the linked headers in the following sections would also change to include the date.

To create a section header or footer that isn't linked to the preceding section's header or footer, position the insertion point in the section you want, choose Header/Footer from the Edit menu, and then choose the header or footer you want to change from the list in the Header/Footer dialog box. The header or footer pane opens (shown in Figure 16-3), showing the header or footer contents. Change the contents as you like, and then choose Close to close the pane and set the header or footer.

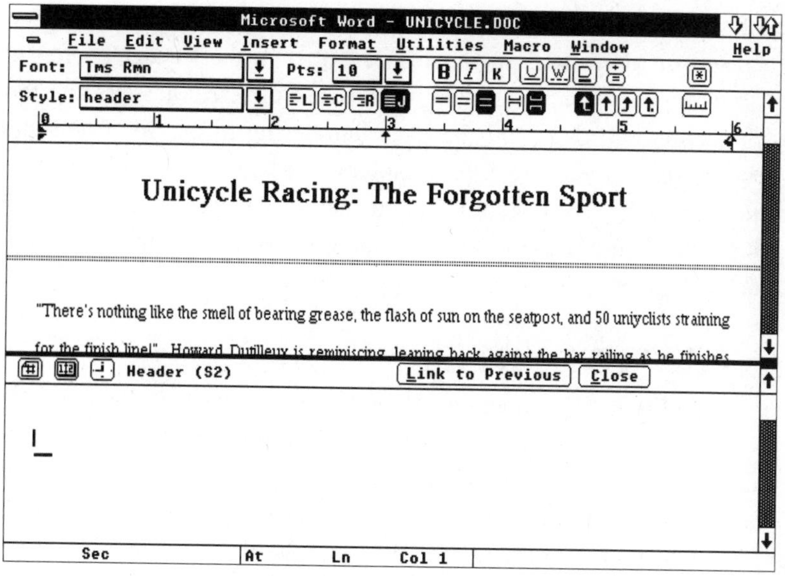

Figure 16-3. *The header/footer pane.*

After you change a section header or footer, Word breaks the link between that section and the preceding section so that any changes in preceding sections won't affect the new header or footer you set. Of course, if the new header or footer is linked to sections that follow, the following sections change to include the revisions. For example, consider the document with five sections that uses headers containing the page number and date. If you added the document title to the header of the third section, the fourth and fifth section headers would also change to include the document title. The first and second section headers would remain the same. If you then changed the first section header, the second section header would change because it's linked, but the third, fourth, and fifth sections would remain unchanged because the link would have been broken between the second and third sections.

You can reestablish a link between sections by opening the header/footer pane and using the Link to Previous button. After you break the link between a section and the preceding section, the Link to Previous button becomes active. When you choose the button, the contents of the header or footer change to match the preceding section's header or footer, and the link is reestablished between the two sections.

You can control the page numbering in a section by selecting the section and then setting your own starting page number in the Header/Footer dialog box. There might be times when you want to use different headers and footers for each section but also want the page numbering to continue sequentially between sections (as you might for chapters in a book, for example). To continue numbering between sections, open the Header/Footer dialog box from the Edit menu, choose the Options button, and delete any number that appears in the Page Numbers Start At box.

PRINTING ENDNOTES

If you use the Format Document command to set footnotes to print at the bottom of each page or as endnotes at the end of the document, section formatting has no effect on footnotes. If you set footnotes to print as endnotes at the end of each section, you can control them with section formatting. To do so, choose Section from the Format menu to open the Format Section dialog box (shown in Figure 16-4).

The middle of the dialog box contains the Include Footnotes option. When this option is on (as it is by default), any footnotes in the section print at the end of the text in the section. If you turn off the option, any footnotes in the section then pass on to the next section for printing there, unless that section also has the Include Footnotes option turned off. Word continues to collect the footnotes until it encounters a section with Include Footnotes turned

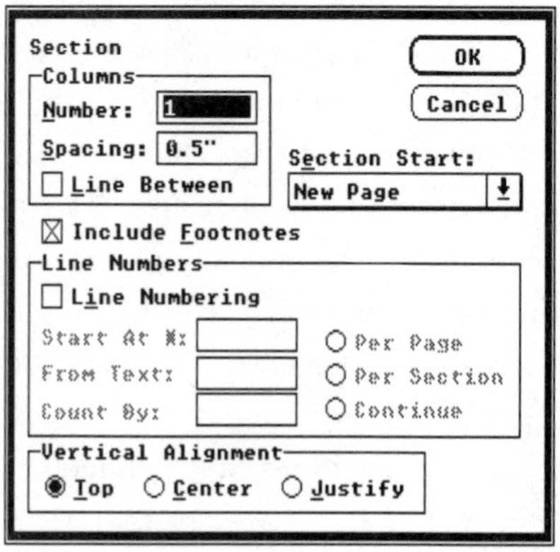

Figure 16-4. *The Format Section dialog box.*

on. It prints the collected footnotes at the end of this section. If every section passes on the footnotes, Word prints the footnotes at the end of the document. Note that if you set a section break to Continuous and set footnotes to print at the end of the section, you might have endnotes appearing in the middle of a page.

USING COLUMNS

When you use section formatting to create columns, you create *snaking columns,* which are different from the columns you create by using tab stops or inserting tables. Snaking columns divide each page into parallel vertical columns that Word treats as "narrow pages"; it fills each column with text and then jumps to the top of the next column to continue. If you change, add, or delete text, Word adjusts the text from column to column to avoid leaving holes in the copy.

To set up columns in a section, move the insertion point to the section you want and choose Section from the Format menu to open the Format Section dialog box. The top of the dialog box contains a Columns area (shown in Figure 16-5) to set the number and format of columns in the section.

Set the number of columns per printed page by entering a number in the Number box. Most documents look good with two or three columns; you might use more columns if you print on wide paper. If you set too many columns for your page width, the columns will be too narrow, resulting in excessive hyphenation.

The Spacing box sets the amount of space between columns. The default setting is 0.5 inch, but you can increase or decrease this width by entering a new value in inches. Again, use good judgment. Widths too wide leave no room for text in the columns, and widths too narrow run the columns so close together that text is hard to read.

To put a definitive separator between columns, turn on the Line Between option. It inserts a vertical line midway between columns.

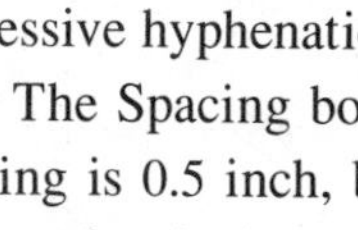

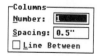

Figure 16-5. *The Columns area of the Format Section dialog box.*

Mixing the Number of Columns on the Same Page

Occasionally, you'll want to mix the number of columns on one page. For example, the UNICYCLE.DOC document title covers the width of one page (a single column) and rests over text printed in two columns. To mix column formats, choose the Continuous section break when you want to change from one column format to another. Because the Continuous break doesn't start a new page, you can set different column formatting in each section to create different numbers of columns on the same page.

Divide your sample document into two sections now, so that you can apply different column formatting to each section:

1. Move the insertion point to the beginning of the line following the title. The line begins, "There's nothing like the smell."
2. Choose Break from the Insert menu to open the Insert Break dialog box.
3. Select the Continuous break and then choose OK to close the dialog box. A section break marker appears across the text window between the title and the text that follows.
4. Be sure the insertion point is in the second section (where it should be after you insert the section break). Choose Section from the Format menu to open the Format Section dialog box.
5. Enter *2* in the Number box to specify two columns, leave the Spacing option at 0.5 inch, and turn on the Line Between option to put a vertical line between the two columns. Choose OK to close the dialog box. The text in the second section appears in a narrow column against the left side of the text window. The right side of the text window is empty.

Viewing Columns

You don't see columns lying side by side in Word's normal view mode; instead, you see the text as one long column, stretching vertically down the text window. You can scroll vertically to see the entire document. As you do, you see breaks of spaced, dotted lines at points where one column ends and another begins. These are called *column breaks*. To set a column break of your own (a *hard column break*), choose Break from the Insert menu to open the

Break dialog box. Select Column Break and then choose OK. A hard-column-break line appears in the document, forcing Word to start a new column there when you print.

To see columns side by side, turn on page view by choosing Page from the View menu. Try it now to look at the columns you set in your document. As you move from page to page, you see the way your text fits into columns. You can edit the text if you want while you're using page view or readjust the column width and margins. Return now to normal view to edit as you normally do.

RESETTING SECTION STARTS

When you insert a section break in a document, you choose New Page, Odd Page, Even Page, or Continuous. To change the type of section start, select the section you want, open the Format Section dialog box, and then move to the Section Start list box at the right side of the dialog box. It offers five types of section starts, but the fifth type of section start, New Column, is not available when you first insert a section break. Select the type of section start you want and choose OK to close the dialog box. Word changes the section so that it prints according to the option you selected. The New Column start works like the New Page start but uses columns instead of pages: Word prints the section at the top of a new column, leaving blank space at the bottom of the previous column if necessary.

NUMBERING LINES

A line number before each line makes it easy for readers to refer to the specific line by number, a convenience in conversations such as: "Can we change the phrase on page 43, line 7 to read '$10 per gross' instead of '$10 is gross'?" To add line numbers to a section, select the section, open the Format Section dialog box, and use the Line Numbers area, shown in Figure 16-6.

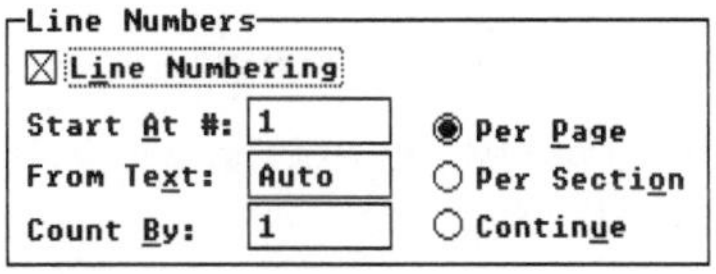

Figure 16-6. *The Line Numbers area of the Format Section dialog box.*

Select the Line Numbering button at the top of the area to turn on line numbering for the section. When you do, the entire Line Numbers area becomes active so that you can set line numbering options. The buttons at the right side of the section offer three numbering systems:

- Per Page—Word begins numbering lines at the top of each page, so the line numbers get no larger than the length of one page allows.
- Per Section—Word begins numbering lines at the beginning of the section and continues numbering to the end of the section.
- Continue—Word takes the last line number of the preceding section and uses the next consecutive number to start numbering lines in the current section. It continues numbering to the end of the section. For example, if the preceding section ended on line 1527, Word begins numbering the lines in the selected section with 1528.

If you choose either Per Page or Per Section, you can set the beginning number Word uses by entering the number in the Start At # box.

If you don't want to see a line number before every line, you can skip lines by entering a value in the Count By box. For example, if you want to see a line number only before every fifth line, enter *5* in the Count By box.

The From Text box controls the position of the line numbers. They usually appear 0.25 inch to the left of each line (0.13 inch in a multiple-column section); any measurement you enter here moves the line numbers that far to the left of each line. (Use judgment; if you enter too large a number, the line numbers disappear off the left edge of the page!)

SETTING VERTICAL ALIGNMENT

Use the three options in the Vertical Alignment area at the bottom of the Format Section dialog box to set vertical page alignment for a selected section:

- Top tells Word to print page contents flush against the top margin.
- Center tells Word to center page contents between the top and bottom margins.

- Justify tells Word to print page contents flush against both top and bottom margins. To achieve this effect, Word adds blank space between lines to fill out the page.

After you set the option you want, choose OK to close the dialog box and apply the alignment to the selected section.

A QUICK SUMMARY

This chapter showed you how to divide a document into sections and apply section formatting to them. You saw how to create, link, and unlink section headers and footers and how to control where endnotes print. You learned about snaking columns—how to set them up and view them. And you saw how to add line numbers to your document. In the last part of the chapter, you saw how to set vertical page alignment for a document. In the next chapter, you learn about formatting at the highest level: document formatting.

Chapter 17

Formatting by Document:

Page Size, Margins, Templates, and More

Document formatting is Word for Windows' top level of formatting: It controls the way the entire document looks on the printed page. In the first half of this chapter, you learn to use document formatting to set different page sizes, set margins, set the default tab stops that appear on the ruler, and turn Word's widow and orphan control on and off.

The second half of the chapter introduces you to a powerful formatting tool: document templates. You learn what document templates are and how they work, and you see how to create a template and use it to create a new document. You also learn how to modify a template and use it to store new styles, glossary items, and other document elements as you create them.

SETTING UP WORD

This chapter doesn't require any special settings—simply use the settings you've used in the past few chapters:

- Full menus
- A text window that shows the ruler, ribbon, and status bar

- The Display as Printed option turned off (in the View Preferences dialog box)

Load the article you created in Chapter 15 as the sample document for this chapter. You should find it under the name UNICYCLE.DOC. As you follow the examples in this chapter, you will change the document's overall appearance and use it to create a template.

DOCUMENT FORMATTING OPTIONS

When you use document formatting to control a document's appearance, you set different options:

- The page width and height options set the dimensions of the paper you use for printing. You can set the page size for printing on envelopes, labels, legal-sized paper, and more.
- The margin options set your document's top, bottom, left, and right margins. Use these options to control the amount of blank space surrounding the text on a page.
- The Default Tabs option sets the distance between default tab stops on the ruler (the tab stops that appear along the ruler before you set your own tab stops).
- The Footnotes option that you learned to use in Chapter 14 sets footnotes to appear in different locations throughout a document.
- The Widow Control option lets you avoid separating a single line from the rest of a paragraph when Word paginates a document.

Most of these options are independent features, but two of them—page size and margins—work together to control the size of the text area on the printed page.

PAGE SIZE

When you set page size, you tell Word the size of the paper you print on. It's a simple process. First, choose Document from the Format menu to open the Format Document dialog box shown in Figure 17-1. Two text boxes control the page size: Page Width and Page Height, which set the width and height of the page in inches. Enter your paper's measurements in these two boxes and choose OK to change the page size. Be sure the measurements actually match

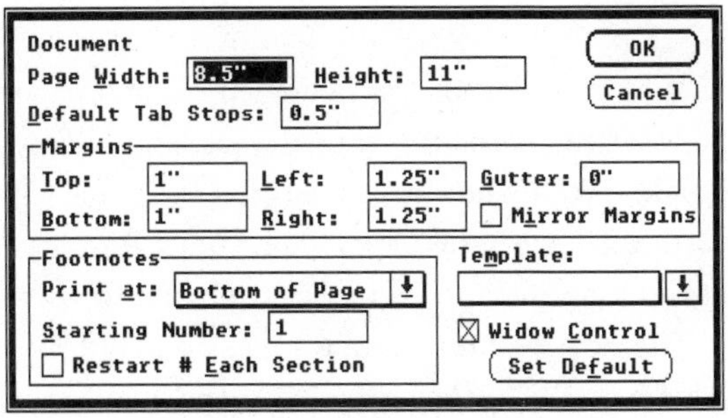

Figure 17-1. *The Format Document dialog box.*

the size of your paper, or you could be in for some unpleasant surprises when you print! The printer could run off the sides of the paper, place page breaks in the middle of a page, run text through a page break onto the next sheet, or surprise you with other printing tricks.

Try setting a new page size for the UNICYCLE.DOC article and then view the article normally and in page view to see the changes:

1. Choose Document from the Format menu to open the Format Document dialog box.

2. Enter a page width of *5.5* inches and a height of *8* inches. Choose OK to close the dialog box and set the new page size. The text in the text area changes to fit into the new, smaller page size.

3. Choose Repaginate Now from the Utilities menu to repaginate the document. Then scroll through the article and look for page breaks. Word moves the page breaks to create shorter page lengths. The new page size can accommodate a text area only six inches deep.

4. Choose Page from the View menu to see the document again. Notice that you can now see the right edge of the page on the screen because it's smaller. As you scroll, notice that each page in the article is much shorter.

5. Choose Page from the View menu again to turn off page view.

6. Choose Document from the Format menu and restore the page width to 8.5 inches and the height to 11 inches.

MARGINS

Word uses the margins you set to surround the text on each printed page with a blank area. The size of the text area is the result of the page size minus the size of the margins. For example, Word's normal page size is 8½ inches by 11 inches, the size of a standard U.S. sheet of paper (shown in Figure 17-2). Word normally uses left and right margins of 1¼ inches each and top and bottom margins of 1 inch each. This leaves a text area 6 inches wide (8½ inches minus 2½ inches) and 9 inches high (11 inches minus 2 inches). Word shows you the size of the text area by setting the normal margins on the ruler to give you 6 inches across and by paginating your text so that it fits into an area 9 inches high.

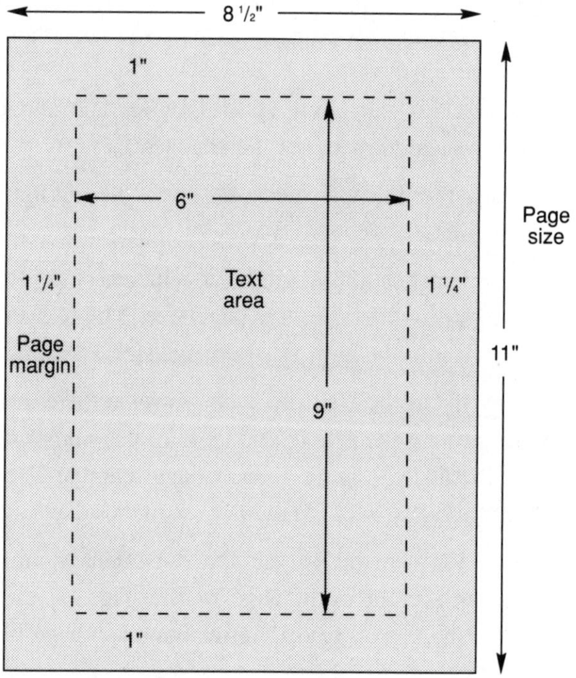

Figure 17-2. *The text area on a sheet of paper is the page size minus the page margins.*

Setting Top and Bottom Page Margins

The Margins area of the Format Document dialog box (shown in Figure 17-3) includes four text boxes to set the margins you want. Any values you enter here measure margins in from the edges of the paper. In the Top and Bottom text boxes, enter positive values in inches to set *flexible* margins. Enter negative values in inches to set *fixed* margins.

Headers and footers normally print above and below the top and bottom margins, but since fixed top and bottom margins don't move, large headers and footers might descend (or ascend) and overlap the text area. If you set flexible margins, the margins move farther toward the center of the page to accommodate large headers and footers. For example, if you set a flexible top margin of 1 inch and then create a large header that descends 1½ inches from the top of the page, Word moves the top margin down far enough to avoid overlapping the text with the header.

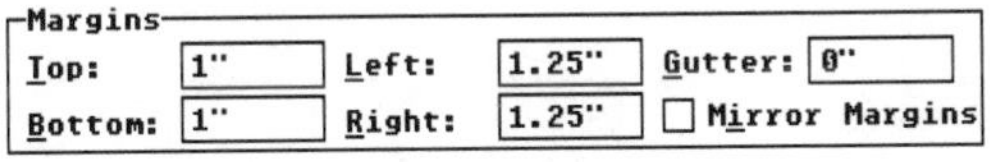

Figure 17-3. *The Margins area of the Format Document dialog box.*

Setting Left and Right Margins

To set left and right margins in the Format Document dialog box, enter their values in inches in the Left and Right text boxes. Always use positive values in these boxes.

When you change left and right margins or the page width, the ruler shows the new constraints of the text area. The 0 mark on the ruler shows the edge of the left margin and remains at the same place on the ruler. The right margin marker (shown in Figure 17-4 as a thin vertical line) moves left or

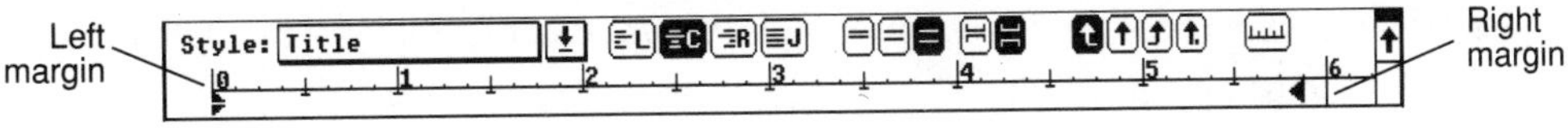

Figure 17-4. *The ruler shows the width of the text area by starting the left side at the 0 mark and marking the right side with the right margin marker. (Notice that the right indent has been moved in slightly to reveal the right margin marker.)*

right to show you the total width of the text area. (Because the right paragraph indent marker is usually on top of the right margin marker, move the indent marker aside to see the margin marker.) For example, you can reduce the width of the text area from 6 inches to 4½ inches by increasing both the left and right margins from 1¼ inches to 2 inches. (The 8½-inch page width is decreased by 2 inches on the left side and 2 inches on the right side to yield a 4½-inch text area.) When you do so, Word moves the right margin marker to the 4½-inch mark to show that the width of the text area has been reduced to 4½ inches.

You can set left and right margins on the ruler if you have a mouse. Click on the Ruler View icon on the ruler to turn on margin view (shown in Figure 17-5). The ruler changes to show the entire width of the current page size. The margins appear as brackets on the left and right sides of the ruler. To change the margins, simply drag the brackets to new locations along the measure.

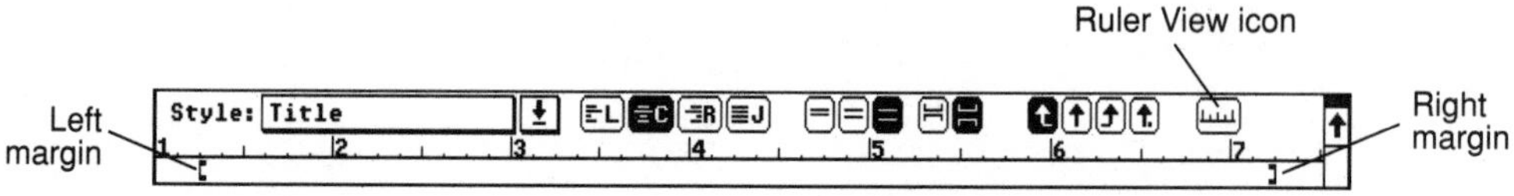

Figure 17-5. *The ruler in margin view shows the left and right margins along the width of the page.*

Using paragraph indents with margins

The paragraph indents you set are based on the left and right margins. Although you normally keep the indents within the margins, you can extend paragraph indents *into* the margins. To move a right paragraph indent into the right margin, move the right paragraph indent marker past the right margin measurement. To move a left paragraph indent into the left margin, move its marker past the 0 mark into the negative numbers. To do so using the Format Paragraph dialog box, enter negative values in the Indents text boxes. To move the indent using the mouse, hold down the Shift key and drag the marker to the new position.

Margins and laser printers

One hint if you use a laser printer: Most laser printers won't print within a half inch of the edge of a sheet of paper. If you set margins of less than a half inch or move the text too close to the edge of the paper, you might lose a few characters when you print on a laser printer.

Creating a Gutter

Whenever you bind printed pages together—whether you stitch them at a bindery, insert them in a folder, or simply staple them together along one edge—you lose some of each page to the binding. If your text falls too close to the binding, the reader is forced to pry the pages apart to read it. A *gutter* is an extra margin on the binding edge of each page. By adding a gutter, you ensure that text won't be lost in the binding. To add a gutter, use the Gutter text box of the Format Document dialog box to enter the size (in inches) of the gutter you want. Word adds the gutter space to the binding edge of the page, further reducing the width of the text area.

Creating Mirror Margins

When you print a document on both sides of a sheet and then bind the sheets together (like the pages of this book), you have different requirements than you do when you use only one side of each sheet. The gutter must alternate on odd and even pages to remain on the binding edge of the sheet, and any uneven left and right margins you set must alternate to retain their uneven quality.

Word offers *mirror margins* to accommodate double-sided printing. When you turn on the Mirror Margins option in the Format Document dialog box, the Left and Right text boxes change to Inside and Outside boxes. The Inside box controls the left margin of odd pages and the right margin of even pages; the Outside box controls the right margin of odd pages and the left margin of even pages. Word adds any gutter you set to the inside margin of the page. Turn on mirror margins whenever you print a document for reproduction on both sides of a page.

Setting Margins in Print Preview

You can easily set all four margins in the Print Preview window. First, choose Print Preview from the File menu to open the Print Preview window, and then choose the Boundaries button to see the margins as four dotted lines on the page, as shown in Figure 17-6. (If you set a gutter, Print Preview shows the gutter and the inside margin combined as a single blank area.)

Move any of the margin lines to reset a margin. The right side of the icon bar at the top of the window tells you the margin's distance in inches from the edge of the paper. To move a margin line with the mouse, drag the margin handle (the small black box at the end of the margin line) to the location you want. To move a margin line with the keyboard, press Tab until you select the margin line you want; then use the cursor keys to move the line to the location you want. When you finish, press Enter. After you have the margins set the way you want them, choose the Boundaries button to turn off the margin-setting mode. Then choose the Close button to exit the Print Preview window.

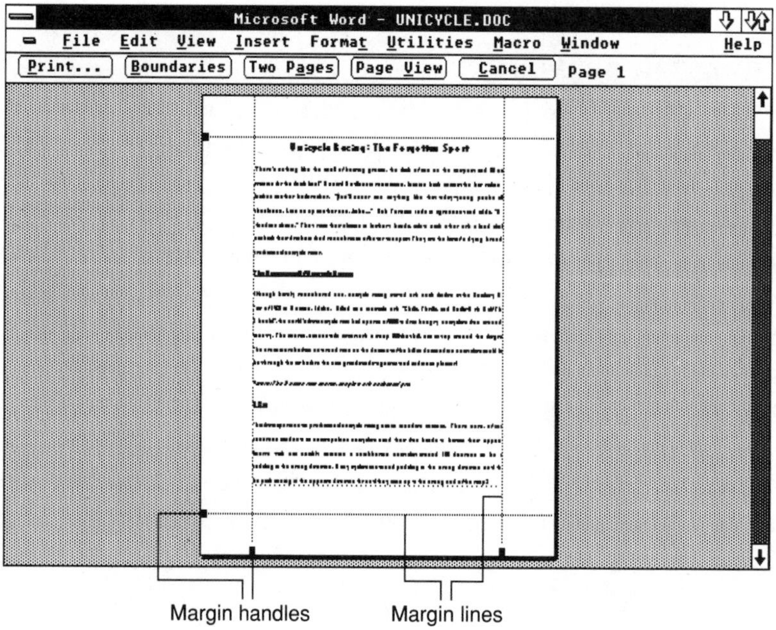

Figure 17-6. *Set margins in Print Preview by choosing the Boundaries button and moving the four margin lines.*

DEFAULT TAB STOPS

Word normally sets default tab stops every half inch along the ruler. The default tab stops remain in effect until you set your own tab stops (as you learned to do in Chapter 8). To change the default tab-stop interval, enter a new interval value in inches in the Default Tab Stops text box of the Format Document dialog box. Word changes the default tab stops on the ruler to fall at the interval you set.

WIDOWS AND ORPHANS

When Word paginates a document, it might occasionally split a single line from a paragraph, marooning the line at the top or bottom of a page. A single line moved from the end of a paragraph to the next page is called a *widow*. The first line of a paragraph left at the bottom of one page with the rest of the paragraph on the next page is called an *orphan*.

Word normally avoids widows and orphans by using an option called widow control. When this option is on, Word checks each page break during pagination to see whether it creates a widow or an orphan. If the page break would create a widow, Word moves a second line of the paragraph to the next page to give the widow some company, leaving an additional empty line at the bottom of the page. If the page break would create an orphan, Word moves the orphan to the next page to rejoin its paragraph, again leaving an empty line at the bottom of the page. Unfortunately, widow control doesn't work for paragraphs of three lines or less because there is no way to split the paragraph without creating a widow or an orphan. If you must keep a paragraph this size from splitting, use the Keep Paragraph Together option (as you learned to do in Chapters 7 and 10).

Some documents, such as legal documents, must contain the same number of lines on each page, and so widows and orphans must be left alone. To ignore widows and orphans, open the Format Document dialog box and turn off the Widow Control option.

DOCUMENT TEMPLATES

When you create a document, you also create a working environment for it by using styles, headers, footers, glossary entries, and other elements tailored specifically to the document. These document elements can also be useful if you go on to create similar documents, so there's no sense in confining them to a single document. Use a *document template* to save a document's working environment so that you can use it with other similar documents.

An Overview of Document Templates

A document template is much like a document. It stores text, styles, glossary entries, formatting, and other important elements. To see a template, you can open it as a document window on the screen. It looks no different from a document: You see the ruler and the ribbon (if you have them turned on), text in the window, the menu bar, and a template name at the top of the screen. You can save a template to disk in the same way that you save a document and recall it for later use. You can edit, revise, and format anything in a template in the same way that you manipulate text in a document. If you want, you can also print a template on the printer in the same way that you print a document.

So what's the difference between a template and a document? The difference is mainly one of use. When you create a document, you create a specific body of text and set of elements for a single piece of work. When you create a template, you create a general set of elements useful in any number of similar documents. After you create a template, you can use it with any new document to recreate the working environment you found so useful in other documents of that type.

For example, you might create a template for business letters that includes a header for numbering pages, a standard closing with your name and title, glossary entries containing the names and addresses of the people you commonly write to, and styles to set formatting you commonly use in a business letter. When you create a new business letter, you can tell Word to start a new document using the business letter template. The new document appears with the standard text already in place, the styles you need in the style list, the header already set, and useful business glossary entries in the glossary. You do not need to create new styles, headers, and other elements.

One other important difference between documents and document templates is that Word stores each on disk using a different file format and distinguishes between the two by giving them different filename extensions. All document filenames end in DOC, and all template filenames end in DOT.

Creating a Document Template

Whenever you create a document template, you save specific elements of a document's working environment to disk:

- Standard text (text used at the same place in each document)
- Styles
- Headers and footers
- Section formatting
- Document formatting
- Glossary entries
- Macros and macro key assignments
- Custom menus

You've read about most of the elements in previous chapters, but you haven't yet been introduced to macros and custom menus, advanced features that are discussed later in this book. In brief, a macro is a series of actions, such as choosing menu items and pressing keys, that you record in the computer's memory. Pressing a key combination or choosing the macro by name executes the series of actions. Custom menus are menus that have your own commands added and seldom-used commands removed. You'll learn to use both these features and include them in templates later; for now, it's enough to know that they are part of a template.

You create a new document template in one of three ways:

- Create a template from scratch
- Turn a document into a template
- Modify an existing template to create a new *derivative template*

The easiest method is to turn a document into a template.

Turning a document into a template

To turn a document into a template, first open the document. Check to be sure it has all the elements you want to save in the template. If it doesn't, add the text, styles, and other elements you want, and change or delete other elements that might be too specific for the template. For example, to turn a business document into a template, you might delete all the text in the document except your name and title at the end of the letter. You could then check the styles and glossary entries you have available, delete those you don't need, and add any you think you'll use.

Once you have the elements you want, including any text and headers or footers you want to use in every document created with the template, choose Save As from the File menu to save the document. When the Save As dialog box opens, choose the Options button to expand it, and choose Document Template in the File Format list box. Enter a filename such as BIZLET to remind yourself of the template's purpose. When you choose OK to close the dialog box, Word saves all the elements of your document as a template and appends the extension DOT to the filename. To remove the template from the screen, close it exactly as you would close a document.

Creating a template from scratch

To create a document template from scratch, choose New from the File menu to open the New dialog box (shown in Figure 17-7). Choose the Template option and then OK to close the dialog box and open a new template. Word labels the new text window Template1 (or Template2, Template3, and so on, depending on the number of templates you've opened during your Word session). The template looks and works like a document; you can add text, create styles, define glossary entries, set formats, and change elements until you get the results you want. When you finish, choose Save As from the File menu to open the Save As dialog box, where you save the template as you would save a document: Simply enter a filename and choose OK to save the template.

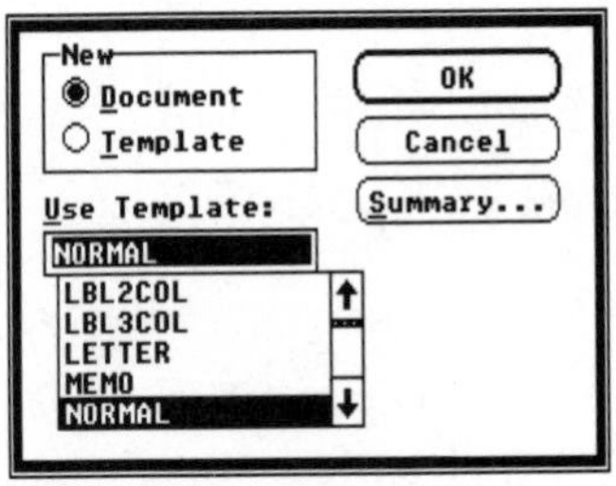

Figure 17-7. *The New dialog box.*

Modifying an existing template

Two methods enable you to create a new template from an existing one. In the first method, you create a new template based on an old template and then alter the new template to your needs. In the second method, you open an old template, make any changes you want, and then save it as a new template with a new template name.

To create a new template based on an old template, choose New from the File menu to open the New dialog box, choose New Template, select the template name of the existing template you want to change, and then choose OK to close the dialog box and open the new template. When the new template appears, it contains all the elements of the base template. Simply change the elements you want to modify and then save the template under a filename of your choice.

To alter an old template and save it under a new name, choose Open from the File menu to see the Open dialog box. Word shows you all the available documents in the Files list. To see a list of templates, change the name in the Open File Name text box to *.DOT and press Enter. Word shows you the templates available in your current directory. Select the template you want to alter. Then choose OK to close the dialog box and open the template in a new text window. Make any changes you want, choose Save As from the File menu, and then enter a new filename in the Save As dialog box. Finally, choose OK to save the template under a new name.

An example

Use UNICYCLE.DOC to create a template for future articles. You must first set the styles and other elements the way you want them and then save the article as a template:

1. Close UNICYCLE.DOC now without saving changes and then open it again. This gets rid of the formatting changes you made earlier.
2. Select the title paragraph. Choose Define Styles from the Format menu to open the Define Styles dialog box and choose the Option button to expand the dialog box.
3. Select Title from the style list and select Normal as the Next Style. Choose OK to close the dialog box. (This sets the Title style to return to normal text when you press Enter at the end of the title.)

4. Select all the text in the document and then delete it. (You have no common text to include in every article you write.)
5. Set the style of the first paragraph (now empty) to Title. (This ensures that the first style in a new article will be Title, used for entering the title.)
6. Choose Header/Footer from the Edit menu to open the Header/Footer dialog box. Select Header from the list box and then choose OK to open the header pane. Create a header that includes your name and the page number. Close the pane when you finish.
7. Change any other elements you want to set for future articles. Then choose Save As from the File menu and choose the Options button to expand the Save As dialog box.
8. Enter the name FEATURE in the Save File Name text box. Select Document Template in the File Format list box and choose OK to save the document as a template named FEATURE.DOT.
9. Complete the summary information if you wish; then choose OK.
10. Choose Close from the File menu to remove the template from the screen.

Now that you've created a feature-article template, you can use it whenever you want to create an article. The template has a paged header; contains styles for normal text, headings, a title, and pictures; and includes normal section and document formatting for printing your article.

Using a Template to Create a New Document

To use a template when you create a new document, simply select the template you want as you open the new document. When you choose New from the File menu, Word offers you a choice of templates in the dialog box that opens. Select the template you want from the Use Template list and choose OK to open the document. (Be sure the Document option is selected, or else you'll open a new template based on the template you selected.) The document that opens uses all the styles, formats, and other elements stored in the template you selected. (This template is called the *base template* of your document.) Use the elements to create your new document, and then print and save it as you would any other document. Don't worry that you'll alter the base template; Word saves your document as a DOC file and leaves the template unchanged.

Once you create a document using a template, you can change the document's base template by using the Format Document dialog box. The Template combo box offers all the available templates and shows you the current base template. (Use the combo box to see the template that a document is based on if you open a document you're unsure of.) When you select a new template in the combo box and choose OK, Word assigns the new template to your document.

How templates control documents

Templates don't control documents the way styles control paragraphs. When you use a template to start a new document, the template sets the working environment of the document but does not establish an active link between the template and the document. This means that when you change the definition of a template, none of the documents you've already created are affected by your changes. Only documents that you create later using the template are affected by the changes you make. The same is true of a template based on another template. When you change a base template, its derivative templates don't change.

Another important difference between styles and templates is that when you change a paragraph's style, the paragraph changes its appearance to match the new style; however, when you change a document's base template, the document's appearance doesn't change. Word ignores the new template's text, formatting, and headers and footers. The new base template simply adds its tools to the working environment: new styles, glossary entries, macros, and menu items. For example, if you start writing a business letter based on a business letter template and then decide to use some of the styles from a report template, you can change to the report template. Nothing you've entered changes, but the styles available in the report template now appear in the styles list.

An example

Use the article template you created to start a new article:

1. Choose New from the File menu to open the New dialog box.
2. Select FEATURE from the Use Template list and then choose OK. A new document based on the template appears.
3. Enter the title *Cargo Cults in Minnetonka* and press Enter. The title appears using the Title style, which changes to Normal style after you press Enter.
4. Enter any text you want after the title. It appears in Normal style.
5. Choose Styles from the Format menu to see the styles you can use in your article. Notice that you have the same styles available as the ones you used in UNICYCLE.DOC. Close the dialog box when you finish looking.
6. Open the header pane to see how the header is set for the document. Notice that it is the same header you set in the template. Close the pane when you finish.
7. Choose Document from the Format menu to open the Format Document dialog box. When it appears, notice that the Template combo box lists FEATURE as the base template.
8. Select NORMAL as a new base template in the combo box and choose OK. You now have a new base template—but notice that the appearance of your article hasn't changed at all.

Modifying a Template

As you develop and change your documents, you might want to modify your templates to include new elements or change old ones. The most straightforward way to do this is to open the template, make the changes you want, and save the template with your changes. There are times, however, when you'll want to add a new element (such as a new style) to a template without stopping to open the template.

Five template elements—styles, document formatting, glossary entries, macros, and custom menus—have options that save them directly to the base template's file on disk without opening the template. Use these options whenever you need to add an element you created or changed to a template. For example, if you create a business letter using a business letter template and then define a new glossary entry that contains the name and address of a new client you think you'll write to again, you can tell Word to add the glossary entry to the template. Word adds the glossary entry to the business letter template, where you can use it in future letters.

The Template and Global options

Three elements—glossary entries, macros, and custom menus—offer (in their dialog boxes) two options in an area labeled Context (as shown in Figure 17-8) that let you save the elements directly to a template file. These two options are Template and Global. If you choose Template when you define a glossary entry, macro, or custom menu command, Word saves the element directly to the current base template's disk file.

If you choose Global, Word saves the element so that you can use it globally—that is, in any document, no matter which base template you use. Any element defined using the Template option appears only in documents using the base template to which you saved the element.

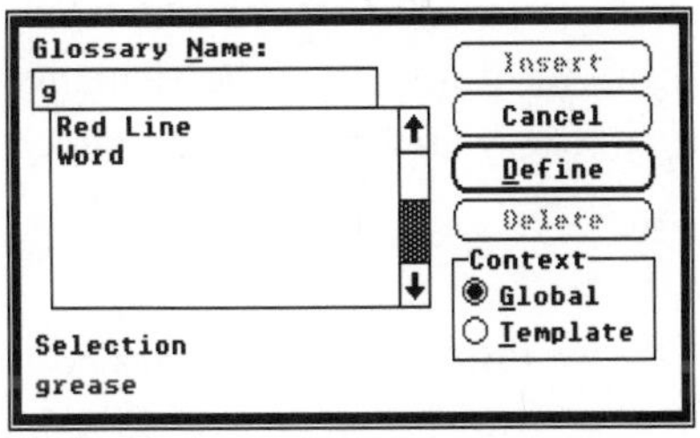

Figure 17-8. *The Glossary dialog box offers Global and Template contexts when you define a new entry, as do the macro and custom menu features.*

Saving styles to a template

Styles don't offer the Global and Template options, but you can save a style directly to a template disk file: Open the Define Style dialog box from the Format menu, and choose the Options button to expand it. Then select an existing style or create a new style to add to the base template. Turn on the Add to Template option at the bottom of the dialog box. When you choose OK, Word adds the style to the current base template.

Saving document formatting to a template

When you use the Format Document dialog box, you can save all the document formatting directly to the current base template by choosing the Set Default button in the dialog box. This button saves all the current settings in the dialog box to the base template as soon as you choose it, so be sure you have the settings you want before you choose the button.

The Default Document Template

All Word documents are based on templates. Therefore, if you open a new document without specifying a template, Word uses a default template, named NORMAL, as the base template. You can change NORMAL in the same way that you change other document templates—and you should, especially if you don't like the default font, emphasis, or character size you get when you start an average document. Any changes you make to the NORMAL template (including font, emphasis, and character size) affect the text you enter in a default document.

NORMAL is more than a default base template—it also stores global elements: the glossary entries, macros, and custom menus you define using the Global option. If you change any of these global elements in NORMAL, they change in every document you work on. It's a good rule of thumb whenever you change the NORMAL template to think carefully about the elements you change; you'll live with the consequences in every document you create.

A QUICK SUMMARY

This chapter taught you how to use document formatting: You learned to set page size and margins, to control widows and orphans when Word paginates, and to set the default tab stops on the ruler. This chapter also taught you how to use document templates: You learned how templates work—how they save the elements of a document's working environment—and saw how to create your own templates by converting documents into templates or by starting from scratch. You learned how to use a template as a base for a new document and then how to modify a template by opening it and changing it or by saving new elements to it directly from a document. In the next chapter, you learn how to find documents you might have lost in the vast, unexplored directories of your hard-disk drive.

Chapter 18

Document Summaries:

Finding Your Documents with Ease

As you create and save more and more documents, sooner or later you'll have trouble finding a saved document on your hard-disk drive. It might be hidden in a seldom-used directory, or it might be under a filename that gives you no clue to its contents. Because it would be impractical to open and look at each document on your disk, Word for Windows offers two tools that make storing and retrieving documents easier: document summaries and the File Find command.

In this chapter, you learn how to create a summary for each document you create and how to read a summary for information about a document. You also see how to edit existing document summaries and set the default information that Word inserts in every document summary. The second part of the chapter teaches you how to use the File Find command to look for documents stored on your hard-disk drive, sort a list of documents by different standards, and search documents and their summaries to find any documents that match your search criteria.

SETTING UP WORD

This chapter has no special printing or formatting needs, so use the same settings you used in the preceding chapter:

- Full menus
- A text window that shows the ruler, ribbon, and status bar

- The Display as Printed option turned off (in the View Preferences dialog box)

You create four sample documents for this chapter, but each document contains no more than five characters of text. Because this chapter deals with document summaries and document retrieval, your documents need nothing more than token contents. Your important creations are the summaries you fill out to go with the documents when you save them. The examples in the chapter tell you the information to use in each summary.

CREATING DOCUMENT SUMMARIES

Creating a document summary is a simple matter of filling in information in the Summary Info dialog box (shown in Figure 18-1). You've seen this dialog box many times; it appears each time you save a document for the first time. In the examples up to this point, you've ignored the dialog box and chosen the OK button to save the document without filling in any information. This section of the chapter shows you how to create a summary by filling in the blanks.

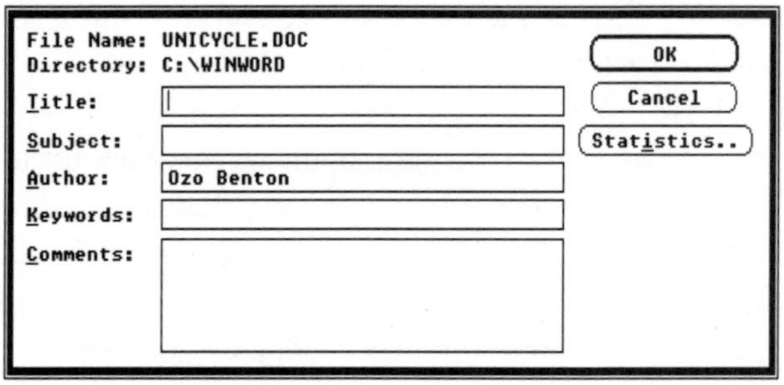

Figure 18-1. *The Summary Info dialog box.*

Opening the Summary Info Dialog Box

You can open the Summary Info dialog box in one of three ways. To create a summary before you start working on a document, open the dialog box by choosing the Summary button in the New dialog box that appears when you open a new document. To create a summary when you finish working on a document for the first time, choose Save; Word opens the Summary Info dialog box before it saves your document. To create or change a document summary while you're working on the document, choose Summary Info from the Edit menu to open the Summary dialog box.

The Parts of the Summary Info Dialog Box

The first two lines in the Summary Info dialog box are labeled File Name and Directory. They tell you the filename of the document currently open in the text window and the directory in which the document is saved (or in which it will be saved). You can't change the information in these two text boxes; to change the document's filename or directory, use the Save As dialog box.

You enter information about your document in the five text boxes below the filename and directory lines. Each information box accepts up to 255 characters, and you can enter and edit that information as you can in any standard text box. The first three boxes—Title, Subject, and Author—are the same headings most libraries use to catalog their books. The last two boxes—Keywords and Comments—are for adding additional information that would be useful in retrieving the document later.

The three buttons on the right side of the dialog box let you leave the box: OK closes the box and saves the information you entered; Cancel closes the box without saving the information you entered; and Statistics opens the Statistics dialog box, where you can see more information about the document. When you close the Statistics box, you return to the Summary Info dialog box.

Filling In the Summary Information

When you create a document summary, think about the information that will help you identify that document later. Fill in the Title box with the title of your document or, if your document has no title, invent one that reflects its contents. Make the title more descriptive than the filename: A file named "AAINV6.DOC" might have the title "Allied Ant Farms June 1989 Inventory." Enter a short subject in the Subject box, and use a subcategory if it's helpful; for example, the subject for a contract with a carpenter might be "Contract, building." Word fills in the Author box with the name you entered when you ran Word for the first time. To change the name of the author, select the Author box and enter a new name.

Keywords are single words or phrases that remind you of the important parts of your document. Enter them in the Keywords box with a space separating each word. For example, a business letter to Oliver Aukvert about the rising price of chicken fat used for making tallow might bring to mind "Aukvert tallow chicken fat inflation." Comments need not be as succinct as keywords. Use the Comments box to enter a description of the document's contents that helps you remember the document with a quick reading.

The Statistics Dialog Box

If you choose the Statistics button, you see the Statistics dialog box, shown in Figure 18-2. You learned in Chapter 11 that these statistics give you important information about your document—filename, drive, and directory; template used and summary title; dates and times when the document was started, last saved, and printed; revision and editing information; and the number of pages, words, and characters the document contains. Word updates the statistics every time you save the document except for the date and time last printed and the number of pages, words, and characters. These are updated when you print the document. To update without printing, choose the Update button. Word repaginates the document and updates the statistics.

Statistics depend entirely on the current state of the document. You can't change any statistics by entering new information in the Statistics dialog box—you must change the document itself. The statistics then change to reflect the new state of the document.

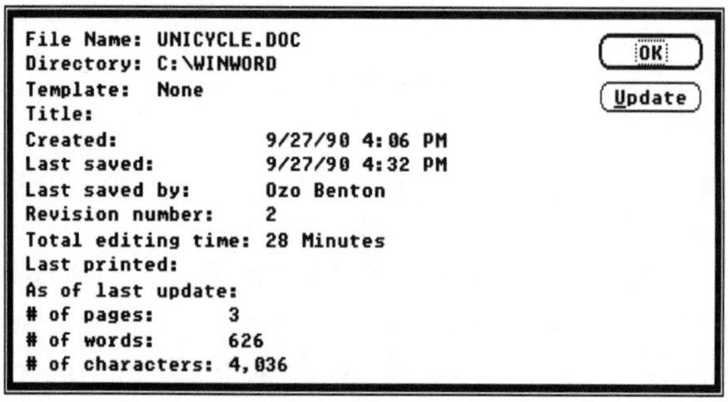

Figure 18-2. *The Statistics dialog box.*

Changing Summary Information

When you save a document, you also save its summary. To change the document summary, open the document, choose Summary Info from the Edit menu, and then change the contents of the information boxes any way you want. When you finish, choose OK to close the dialog box. Word remembers your changes and saves them when you save the document.

Changing Summary Defaults

Word takes care of two summary details for you: It opens the Summary Info dialog box when you first save a document, and it fills in the author's name in the Author information box. To change these defaults, choose Customize from the Utilities menu to open the Customize dialog box, shown in Figure 18-3.

To stop Word from opening the Summary Info dialog box when you first save a document, turn off the Prompt for Summary Info option. (For the following example, you'll want to leave this option on.) To change the name that Word inserts in the Author information box, change the contents of the text box labeled Your Name. To leave the Author information box blank, delete the entire contents of the text box. (If a document has already been opened, changing the name in the Your Name text box does not change the Author Name in the Summary Info dialog box; the new name will appear in subsequently opened documents, however. To change the Author Name in an opened document, make the change in the Summary Info dialog box.) You can also change the author initials, which Word uses for other purposes

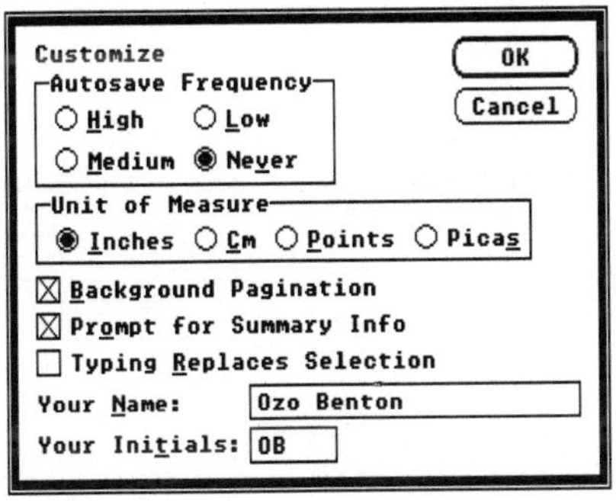

Figure 18-3. *The Customize dialog box.*

(such as filling in fields) by changing the contents of the text box labeled Your Initials. Once you set the options as you want them, choose OK to close the dialog box.

An Example

In this example, you create four documents that each contain a single word—the name of a number. You create summaries for the documents describing their contents and then save the documents to disk to use for later examples in this chapter. Figure 18-4 shows the contents of the Summary Info dialog box for each of the four documents.

1. Open a new document if you don't have one already on the screen, and enter the word *One*.
2. Choose Save from the File menu to open the Save dialog box, enter the filename *ONE*, and choose OK to close the dialog box and open the Summary Info dialog box.
3. Enter the contents of this document's Summary dialog box as shown in Figure 18-4 and choose OK when you finish. Word saves the document and its summary to disk.

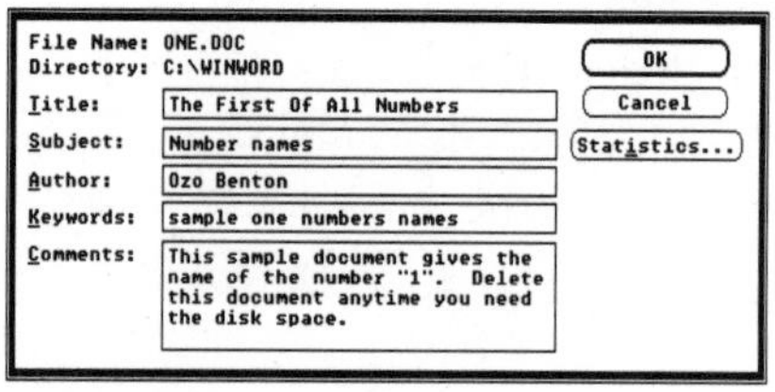

Document one

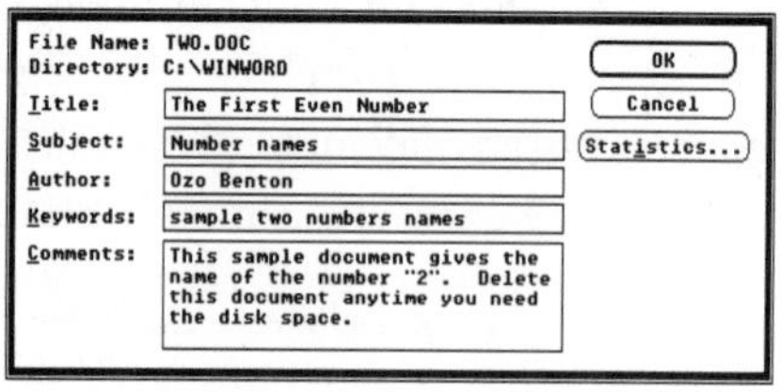

Document two

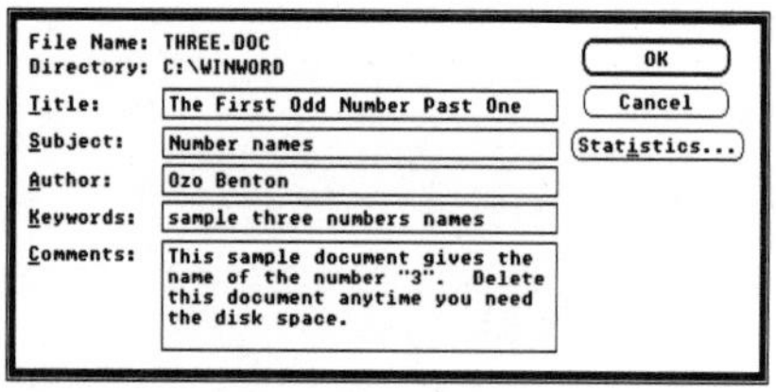

Document three

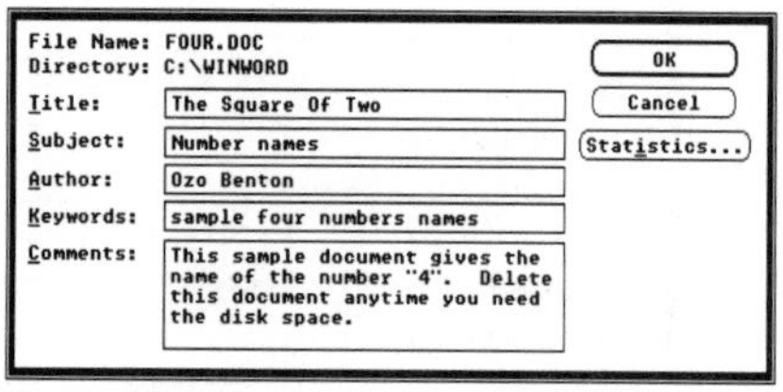

Document four

Figure 18-4. *These dialog boxes show the summary information to enter for the four documents you create.*

4. Choose Close from the File menu to close the document.
5. Repeat this procedure for the second, third, and fourth documents. Enter the word *Two* as text for the second document, enter its summary information according to Figure 18-4, and then save the document under the name "TWO." The third document contains the word "Three" and is saved under the filename "THREE"; the fourth document contains the word "Four" and is saved under the filename "FOUR." Use the appropriate summary information from Figure 18-4 for the documents.

FINDING DOCUMENTS

The File Find command provides you with a convenient tool for seeing a list of all the Word documents saved on your home disk drive. (The home disk drive is the drive where Word resides.) When you choose File Find, Word searches every directory on your home disk drive for document files (those ending in "DOC") and then shows them to you in a file list, where you can choose the document (or documents) you want. Word normally lists the documents in alphabetical order by document name, but you can also tell it to list them by author, creation date, size, or other criteria.

If the number of documents in the list is too large to navigate successfully, you can tell Word to search for documents that have special characteristics that match only the information you're looking for. For example, you might want to see only the documents created in the past week that include the keyword "fiscal" in their summaries. Word can easily search for all the documents that fit those criteria and display only those files in the file list.

The File Find Dialog Box

The File Find dialog box (shown in Figure 18-5 on the following page) shows you the document file list and gives you the options of sorting or searching through the documents in the list. To open it, choose Find from the File menu. The first time you do, Word displays a message that it is searching for document files as it looks through every directory on the home disk drive. If there are many documents on your disk, it might take some time for Word to find and sort all the files. Later searches are much faster because the list remains in memory until you change the search criteria or quit Word.

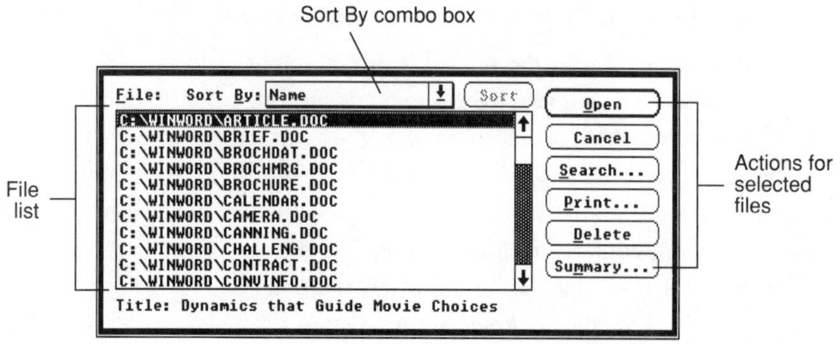

Figure 18-5. *The File Find dialog box.*

When Word finishes sorting, the File Find dialog box appears.

The file list fills most of the dialog box. It lists every document file Word found stored on the home disk drive, showing each file's full pathname and filename. Use the scroll bar on the right side of the dialog box to scroll through the file list.

You can select any document name in the file list by clicking on it using the mouse or by moving the selection bar up and down using the up cursor and down cursor keys. To select more than one document in the list using the mouse, hold down the Shift key while you click. If you use the keyboard, hold down the Shift key as you press the up cursor and down cursor keys; Word highlights all documents the selection bar passes over. If you hold down the Ctrl key, you can scroll through the list with the cursor keys and select and deselect individual files by pressing the Spacebar.

To sort the files in the file list by different criteria, use the Sort By list box at the top of the dialog box. When you open it, it offers these sort options:

- Name—Word lists the files in alphabetic order by pathname.
- Author—Word lists the files in alphabetic order by the author name entered in the document summary.
- Creation Date—Word lists the files in the order of the date they were first created, working from the newest document to the oldest. Word finds this information in the documents' statistics.
- Last Saved Date—Word lists the files in the order of the date they were last saved, working from the first saved to the most recently saved. Word finds this information in the documents' statistics.

- Last Saved By—Word lists the files in alphabetic order by the name of the person who last saved the document. Word finds this information in the documents' statistics.
- Size—Word lists the files in the order of their size in bytes, working from smallest to largest. Word finds this information in the documents' statistics.

Once you select the sort criterion you want in the Sort By list box, choose the Sort button to sort the files in the file list. The message line below the file list shows the criterion you selected and the way that the first document selected fits that criterion. For example, if you sort the list by Author and have a document selected, the line might show Author: Orval M. Lavro.

The buttons along the right side of the File Find dialog box act on the document (or documents) you select in the file list in the following ways:

- Open opens the document in a text window and closes the dialog box. If you have more than one document selected, Word opens them all, up to a limit of nine documents on the screen at once.
- Cancel closes the dialog box without opening any documents.
- Search opens the Search dialog box, where you can tell Word to search for specific documents.
- Print opens the File Print dialog box to print the selected documents without closing the File Find dialog box. The next chapter describes how to use this button to print more than one document at a time.
- Delete deletes the selected documents from the disk without closing the dialog box. Word asks for confirmation before it deletes the files. Deleting documents here is a convenient option; you can search for useless documents in this dialog box and then use Delete to remove them from disk without leaving Word.
- Summary shows the summary information for the selected document without closing the dialog box. If you have more than one document selected, Word shows the summary for the first document selected. You can, if you like, change the summary information. If you do, Word saves your new summary information to disk when you leave the Summary dialog box by choosing OK. This is a convenient way to edit summaries without opening documents.

An Example

This example uses the File Find dialog box to find the four documents you created earlier and to open the third document. You first sort by size because you know that these four documents are probably the smallest ones saved on your disk:

1. Choose Find from the File menu to open the Find File dialog box.
2. Choose Size in the Sort By list box and then choose the Sort button to sort the files by size. After sorting, you will see the four sample documents at the top of the file list (unless you have other documents with fewer than five characters in them).
3. To be sure the file named THREE.DOC is the one you want, select it and then choose the Summary button to see the summary information about that file. The Summary Info dialog box opens, where you read that this is a test document that gives you the name of the number "three."
4. Choose the Cancel button to close the Summary dialog box and return to the File Find dialog box.
5. Choose the Open button to close the File Find dialog box and open THREE.DOC in its own document window.

The Search Dialog Box

To search for specific documents saved on disk, first open the File Find dialog box and then choose the Search button to open the Search dialog box (shown in Figure 18-6). Fill in the text boxes in this dialog box to tell Word

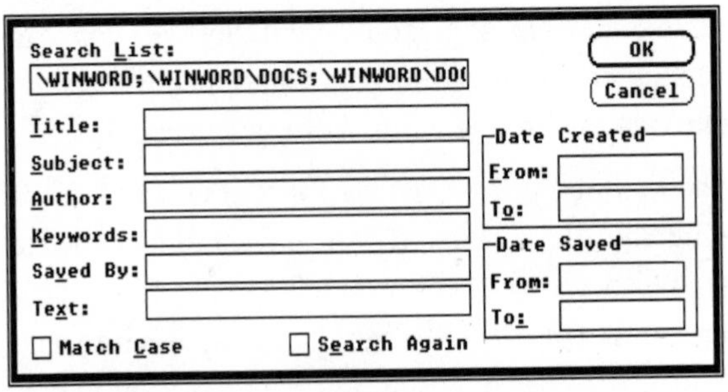

Figure 18-6. *The Search dialog box.*

where to search and what information to search for when it looks through the documents on your disk. This information is called the *search criteria.* Word finds any documents that match your search path and criteria and lists them in the file list of the File Find dialog box.

The search list

When you first open the File Find dialog box, Word searches through all the directories on your home disk drive for documents that have filenames with the extension "DOC." When you open the Search dialog box, the Search List text box shows all the directories in which Word found documents; the directory pathnames are separated by semicolons. To alter the way Word searches for documents when you first open the File Find dialog box, enter a new search list in the text box. Word searches through any directories whose pathnames you enter here.

To create a new search list, enter directory pathnames separated by semicolons. Word searches in these directories for filenames ending in "DOC." To look for different types of filenames, add a filename at the end of each pathname in the search list, using wildcards if necessary, to find the types of files you're looking for. For example, if you add *.DOT to the end of each pathname, you tell Word to search through each directory in the search list for documents that have the extension "DOT" (document templates). To make Word search through every directory on your home disk drive for "DOC" filenames (as it normally does), delete everything from the search list. If you want to search a different disk drive, enter the drive name as part of the search path.

Note that when you quit Word, it saves any search list you create and uses it the next time you open Word and use the File Find dialog box for the first time; your search list becomes the default search list. If you use specific directories for your Word documents, you can specify those directories in the search list so that Word never checks outside those directories. This is particularly useful if you have documents from other word-processing programs stored on your disk. Those document filenames might also end in "DOC," but if you set the search list to avoid their directories, they won't show up in your file list.

Entering Search Criteria

The next four text boxes for entering search criteria are Title, Subject, Author, and Keywords. Any text you enter in these boxes tells Word to search for that text in the corresponding fields of the document summaries. If you enter a name in the Saved By text box, you tell Word to look for documents saved by that person. Any text you enter in the Text box tells Word to look through the text within each document for the text you entered.

The areas labeled Date Created and Date Saved each contain two text boxes, where you enter a beginning and an ending date to define a date range. For example, if you enter *1/9/90* in the Date Created From box and *9/9/90* in the Date Created To box, you tell Word to find all the documents created between January 9, 1990, and September 9, 1990.

When you enter text in the text boxes, Word searches the appropriate summary element or document part for that text, no matter where it occurs in the element or part. For example, if you enter *two* in the Title box, Word looks for the word "two" anywhere in the titles of the documents it searches through. It would find documents with the titles "Tea for Two," "Two Are Quite Enough," and "Marcy Eats Two Squid." You can enter phrases as well as words. For example, Word searches for the phrase "fiscal disaster" entered in the Text box by looking through the text of every document it searches.

Wildcards and logical operators

You can use standard wildcard characters in text items to look for a range of text. An asterisk (*), as usual, stands for any number of characters, and a question mark (?) stands for any single character. Because you might want to search for text that actually contains an asterisk or a question mark, you can use a caret (^) before an asterisk or question mark if you want Word to read it as a literal character. For example, you would enter the item "blintzes?" as *blintzes^?* to make Word recognize the question mark as a true question mark rather than a wildcard character. To enter a caret that Word reads literally instead of as a character verifier, use two carets (^^). Word reads the first caret as a character verifier, verifying the second as a literal caret.

If you enter more than one text item in a criterion box, separate the items using a *logical operator*. A logical operator tells Word how to use the separate items as it searches. The three logical operators are listed on the next page.

- comma (,)—OR. When you use this operator between items, Word looks for documents that contain either one or the other item. For example, entering *mushrooms, sausage* in the Keywords box tells Word to find all documents whose summaries contain either the keyword "mushrooms" or the keyword "sausage."
- ampersand (&)—AND. When you use this operator between items, Word looks for documents that contain both items. For example, entering *pepperoni & mushrooms* in the Keywords box tells Word to find all documents that include both of those keywords. Word ignores documents that contain only one of the keywords.
- tilde (~)—NOT. When you use this operator before an item, Word looks for all documents that don't include that item. For example, entering *~anchovies* in the Keywords box asks Word to find all documents that don't contain the keyword "anchovies."

You can combine logical operators in a text box. For example, entering *pepperoni & ~anchovies* tells Word to find all documents that include the keyword "pepperoni" but don't include the keyword "anchovies." If logical operators are confusing to you, try reading them aloud: "Pepperoni AND NOT anchovies." They sometimes make more sense that way and help you decide which logical operators to use.

Search Options

The two options at the bottom of the Search dialog box change the way Word searches for the criteria you set. If you turn on the Match Case option, Word matches the case of the characters you enter in the text boxes. This means, for example, that Word won't match "Two" and "two." If the option is off, Word pays no attention to case when it searches for matches.

When you choose OK to start searching, Word normally searches through the documents listed in the file list of the File Find dialog box. To make Word conduct a fresh search through the directories in the search list, turn on the Search Again option and choose OK. Word searches through all the directories in the search list instead of the documents it already knows about.

Starting the Search

Once you set the search criteria, options, and search list as you want them, choose OK to start the search. Word closes the Search dialog box, returns to the File Find dialog box, and then begins looking through all the documents in the directories of the search list for any that match the search criteria. Whenever it finds a match, Word makes note of the matching document. When the search is finished, Word replaces the contents of the file list with the matching documents it found in its search. (To close the Search dialog box without searching, use the Cancel button.)

If you enter a search criterion in the Text box, the search takes longer because Word must look through all the text in each document instead of limiting its search to document summaries. Note that a text search through documents you saved via a fast save (with the Save command) isn't thorough because new text added to the document isn't integrated with the rest of the text when the document is saved. If you plan to search regularly for document text, be sure to save all your documents using the Save As command to perform a full save.

An Example

Try using the Search dialog box to search for documents. In your first search, you find all the sample documents except ONE.DOC. In the second, you find all the sample documents and then delete them.

1. Choose Find from the File menu to open the File Find dialog box.
2. Choose the Search button to open the Search dialog box.
3. Enter *sample & numbers & ~one* in the Keywords box. (This asks Word to search for documents with the keywords "sample" AND "numbers" AND NOT "one.")
4. Choose OK to start the search. Word closes the Search dialog box, searches, and then returns to the File Find dialog box with documents TWO.DOC, THREE.DOC, and FOUR.DOC showing in the file list. (These files' document summaries all have the keywords "sample" and "numbers" but not "one." Document one, which has the keywords "sample" and "numbers," didn't make the list because it also has the keyword "one.")

5. Choose Search to open the Search dialog box again.
6. Replace the contents of the Keywords box with *sample & numbers* and choose OK to start the search. Word closes the Search dialog box and searches, returning to the File Find dialog box with all four sample documents in the file list.
7. Select all four of your sample documents and then choose Delete to delete them from the disk. When Word asks whether you're sure, choose Yes. Word deletes all four documents from your hard disk.
8. Choose Cancel to close the dialog box.

A QUICK SUMMARY

This chapter showed you how to save and find documents on your hard-disk drive. You first learned how to create meaningful summaries to use later with the File Find command. You then learned how to find documents in the file list of the File Find dialog box and how to sort the documents in the list by different criteria. You also learned how to select one or more documents from the list and open, print, delete, and find summaries for the selected documents. The last part of the chapter showed you how to use the Search dialog box to set search criteria and use them to find a specific set of documents. In the next chapter, you learn some of Word's special printing techniques.

Chapter 19

Printing Variations

Printing most Word for Windows documents is a straightforward task: You choose Print from the File menu and then wait for the document in the text window to emerge from your printer on 8½-inch-by-11-inch paper. Many Word users never need to do more than this, but some users have special printing needs. Word offers advanced printing tools to help.

In this chapter, you learn how to handle odd sizes of paper and how to print on standard business envelopes. You also learn about Spooler, a Windows program that you can use to print an entire batch of documents by using a single command. The last part of the chapter shows you how to print the elements of a document that you normally don't see—style sheets, glossaries, summary information, hidden text, and so on.

SETTING UP WORD

The sample document for this chapter uses hidden text, so set Word to show hidden text. Because you'll print the examples in this chapter, you must also set Word to show text on the screen in the same way as it will look when printed. Use these options:

- Full menus
- A text window that shows the ruler, ribbon, and status bar
- The Display as Printed option turned on (in the View Preferences dialog box)
- The Hidden Text option turned on (also in the View Preferences dialog box)

The first part of this chapter shows you how to print an address on a standard business envelope. Figure 19-1 shows the final result, an envelope with a return address in the upper left corner and the main address in the center of the envelope.

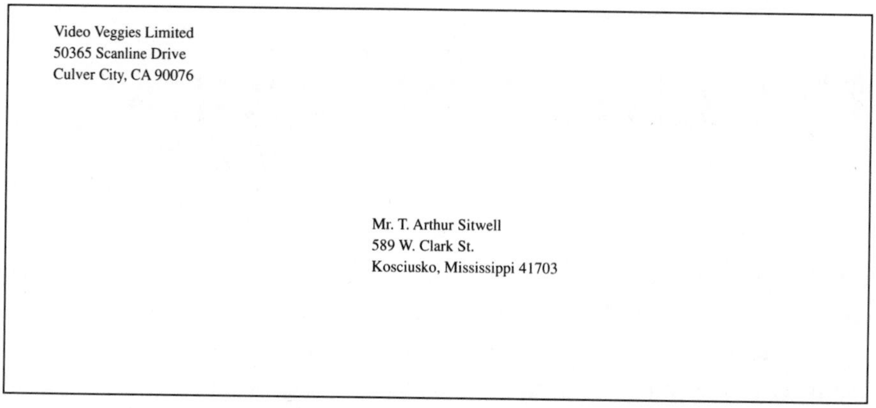

Figure 19-1. *Use Word to print an address on a standard business envelope.*

PRINTING ON DIFFERENT SIZES OF PAPER

Not everything you need to print can be done on 8½-inch-by-11-inch paper. Lawyers, for example, print documents on legal-size sheets of paper, and European businesses might need to print using A4 European standard paper (8¼ inches by 11⅔ inches). And almost everybody at one time or another must print an address on an envelope—a rectangle quite different in size and proportion from standard paper.

To print on nonstandard paper, you must first tell Word that you're using a different size of paper. Enter the dimensions of your paper as the page size, and then set new page margins, if necessary, to work with the new page size. (You learned to do both these tasks in Chapter 17.) If your printer automatically feeds the new paper (via a tractor or a sheet feeder), you might also need to set a new page size in your printer driver so that the printer knows when to eject one sheet of paper and move on to the next. You learn to do this later in the chapter.

When you use a laser printer to print on a long, narrow sheet of paper (such as an envelope), the printer might feed it through from the left side to the right instead of the standard way (from top to bottom). If so, you must use the File Printer Setup command to rotate the printing 90 degrees to match the orientation of the envelope.

Creating a Business Envelope Template

Standard American business envelopes measure 9½ inches wide by 4⅛ inches tall. If you create a template for this size of paper, you can use the template to print an address on most business envelopes. The template should use common text to print a standard return address in the upper left corner (unless you print on envelopes that have the return address already printed) and should print the main address 2 inches down from the top edge and 3½ inches in from the left edge of the envelope.

Use two tools to make entering the main address easier: hidden text and the Format Position command. If you enter a line of hidden text that explains how to enter the main address just before the main address paragraph, anyone who uses the template (including you) can easily read what to do. When you print the envelope address, the hidden text won't print. If you find the hidden text distracting in the template, you can turn it off using the View Preferences dialog box.

The Format Position command easily positions a paragraph of text at the exact location you want on a sheet of paper. This advanced page-layout feature has many options that you can read more about in the Word for Windows *User's Reference*. For this example, all you need to know is how to use Format Position to put your main address in the correct location on the envelope.

Using the Format Position command

To use Format Position, select a paragraph and then choose Position from the Format menu to open the Format Position dialog box (shown in Figure 19-2 on the following page). Use this dialog box to anchor the position of the selected paragraph to a set location on the page. A paragraph so positioned won't move from the spot even if you alter the text before and after it—normal text flows around the anchored paragraph like a river around a boulder.

Set a paragraph position in the dialog box using the two combo boxes in the areas labeled Horizontal and Vertical. Any value you enter in the Horizontal combo box sets the left edge of the paragraph that number of inches from the left side. Any value you enter in the Vertical combo box sets the top of the paragraph that number of inches from the top. The Relative To options in each area determine the top and left side from which Word measures when it sets the paragraph position: Margin measures in from the page margin, Page measures in from the edge of the page, and Column measures in from the left edge of a column.

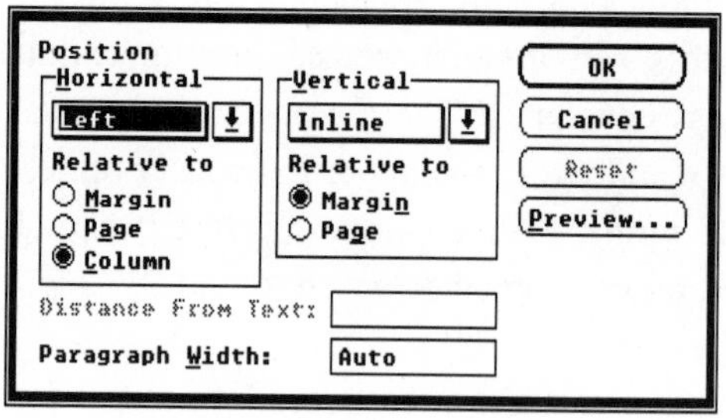

Figure 19-2. *The Format Position dialog box.*

An example

This example creates a template for addressing a business envelope.

1. Use the File New command to open a new template (not a document).
2. Choose Document from the Format menu to open the Format Document dialog box.
3. Enter *9.5* as the page width and *4.125* as the height to set the size of the page to match the envelope.
4. Enter top, bottom, left, and right margins of *0.5* to put a half-inch border around the entire envelope. A half-inch margin ensures that every printer (including a laser printer) will be able to print text located flush against the margins. If your printer can print closer to the edges, set a smaller margin if you want.
5. Choose OK to close the dialog box and return to the template in the document window.
6. Enter the return address (the first three lines of the sample document in Figure 19-1). Press Enter at the end of each line.

7. Use the Format Character dialog box to turn on hidden text, and press Enter. Then enter a fourth line that reads *Enter the address on the next line. Use Shift-Enter at the end of each line.* Turn off hidden text at the end of the line and press Enter. The insertion point now rests at the beginning of a new paragraph where you'll type the main address.
8. Choose Position from the Format menu to open the Format Position dialog box.
9. Enter *4* in the Horizontal combo box and *2* in the Vertical combo box to set the new location of the main address paragraph. Choose the Page option in both the Horizontal and Vertical areas to tell Word to measure the location from the edges of the envelope. Then choose OK to close the dialog box.
10. Choose File Save to save the template; enter the name *ENVELOPE* to save it.
11. Choose File Close to close the template text window.

Creating and Printing an Envelope Document

Now try using your new envelope template to create an envelope address document:

1. Use the File New command to open a new document based on the ENVELOPE template. The new document appears in the window with the return address in the upper left corner, followed by instructions in hidden text for entering the main address. Move the insertion point to the beginning of the main address paragraph.
2. Enter the three-line main address shown in the sample document, pressing Shift-Enter at the end of each line. (Remember that Shift-Enter starts a new line without starting a new paragraph.)

Although the main address appears directly below the return address in the text window, the main address will appear in the center of the envelope when you print. To see the full page layout before you print, turn on page view.

Printing on a horizontal envelope

If your printer accepts envelopes horizontally (so that you feed the top of the envelope directly into the printer), follow these instructions to print the address you created:

1. Insert the envelope in your printer so that it's ready to print. (Different printers work differently, so read your owner's manual to find the correct position for an envelope. If you can't find the information, try positioning the upper left corner of the envelope where you'd position the upper left corner of a standard 8½-inch-by-11-inch sheet of paper.)
2. Be sure your printer is on and selected, and then choose Print from the File menu to open the Print dialog box.
3. Choose the Options button to expand the Print dialog box, and check that the Include Hidden Text option is off so that your instruction line in the envelope doesn't print out.
4. Choose OK to start printing. Word opens a dialog box containing a message that your page size doesn't match the page size set on your printer; tell it to go ahead anyway. Mismatched page sizes won't affect printing on a single, hand-fed envelope.

Printing on a vertical envelope

If your printer accepts envelopes vertically (so that you feed the left end of the envelope directly into the printer), you must rotate the text by 90 degrees. To do so, follow the printing steps of the previous example, but add these steps before you choose Print from the File menu:

1. Choose Printer Setup from the File menu to open the Printer dialog box, shown in Figure 19-3.

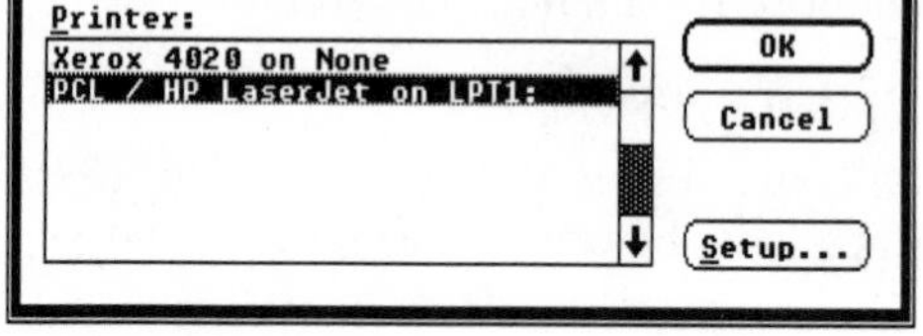

Figure 19-3. *The Printer dialog box.*

2. If the box lists more than one printer, select the printer you'll use. Then choose Setup to open the Setup dialog box. This dialog box varies according to the printer you are using. Figure 19-4 shows the Setup dialog box for Hewlett-Packard laser printers.

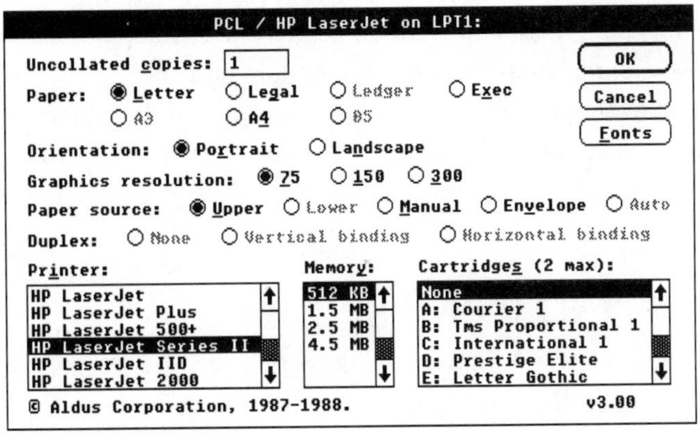

Figure 19-4. *The Setup dialog box for Hewlett-Packard laser printers.*

3. Move to the area labeled Orientation and turn on the Landscape option. Then choose OK to close the Setup dialog box.
4. Choose OK to close the Printer dialog box.
5. Choose Print from the File menu to open the Print dialog box, choose the Options button to expand the box, and check that the Include Hidden Text option is off. Then choose OK to print the envelope.

The Landscape setting tells your printer to rotate the text 90 degrees to match the orientation of the envelope you feed into it. (Portrait orientation is Word's normal setting.)

Setting printer page size

Because you hand-fed your envelope for the previous examples, it wasn't important to match Word's document page size with the page size set for the printer. However, if you ever use envelopes attached to backup pinfeed paper, you must set your printer for the size of the envelopes. If you don't, the printer will eject the length of an 8½-inch-by-11-inch sheet of paper at the end of each address it prints, hopelessly fouling up your printing.

To set the printer's page size, choose the Printer Setup command from the File menu and choose your printer. Then open the Setup dialog box, where you can choose the page size (if the printer driver for your particular printer allows different page sizes). The Windows manual gives you more information about setting up your printer for different page sizes. (Note when you enter page size that height is measured from the top of one envelope to the top of the following envelope, not from the top to the bottom of a single envelope.)

If you have an envelope feeder that feeds envelopes into the printer one at a time, you might want to set the paper size to match your envelope when you print, although it might work without change. Experiment to see how your printer works with envelopes.

BATCH PRINTING USING SPOOLER

If you have the Special Edition with disks included, consult the Introduction

When you print using Word's Print command, you print the document in the active document window. This can slow you down if you have more than one document to print at a time. For example, if you use Print to print a batch of documents, such as all the weekly reports of the past two months, you must load one document and print it, load another document and print it, and so on, until you have printed all the documents you want. There is an easier solution—use the File Find dialog box to feed all the documents to Spooler.

Spooler

Spooler is a Windows application that handles all printing in Windows. Whenever you print a Word document, Word first translates the contents of your document into a stream of data to send to your printer. Instead of sending the data directly to your printer, however, Word creates a temporary *print file* on your hard-disk drive and sends the data to that file. It then runs the Windows Spooler and tells it that it has a document to print. (If Windows' default settings in the WIN.INI file have been set to include the line "spooler=no," Spooler won't run. Consult your Windows manual to learn how to turn Spooler on.)

To print a Word document, Spooler finds the print file that Word created on disk, opens and reads it, and sends the data directly to the printer (a process called *spooling*). When it finishes printing the document, Spooler deletes the printer file from the disk drive. All this happens while Word is running, because Spooler is a multitasking application—that is, it can run at the same time as other applications. To see it running, look under Word's full-size document window: The Spooler icon appears in the lower left corner of the Windows screen while Spooler runs.

Spooler can save you time. Because printers are quite slow (compared with computers), Word has to wait a long time to print a document by sending data directly to the printer, especially if the document runs over two or three pages. By sending data to a print file instead, Word can finish its printer obligations in seconds, and Spooler then works in the background to spool the printer data from the disk to the printer. The result is that you can go back to work with Word while Spooler busily prints documents. Note that on some occasions either Word or Spooler will slow down when the other program accesses the disk or performs a similar complex task.

The print file queue

If you tell Word to print a second document while Spooler is still printing your first one, Spooler creates a *print file queue*, a waiting list of documents to be printed. Your second document appears just below the first in the queue. Spooler works through the print file queue, printing the document at the top of the list and adding documents to the end of the queue as you designate them to be printed.

Sending a Batch of Documents to Spooler

To print a batch of documents, open the File Find dialog box. Select all the documents in the file list that you want to print, and then choose the Print button to start printing them. Word turns each document you selected into a print file on disk and then starts Spooler. If you try to print more documents at one time than Spooler can handle, it displays a message that it will not print that many documents at a time. You can try printing the batch again after the print file queue has decreased enough to accept the new documents.

Controlling Spooler

Once Spooler starts printing, you can control its functions by starting it, stopping it, and canceling print jobs in its queue. To see the queue and work with Spooler's menu, open the Spooler window (shown in Figure 19-5 on the following page) by opening the Spooler icon. (If you don't see the icon, press Alt-Esc until it appears on the screen.)

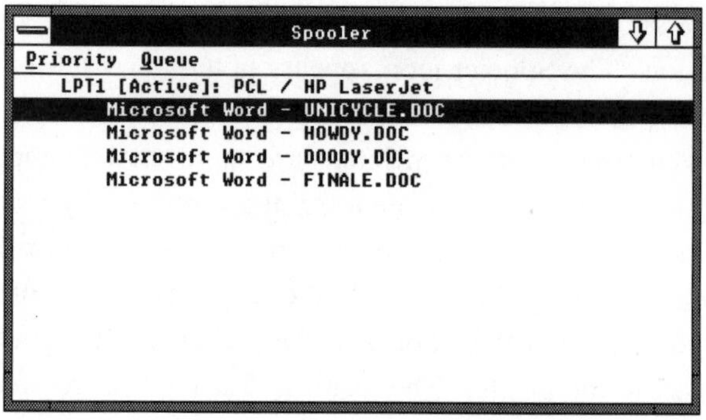

Figure 19-5. *The Spooler window.*

The main part of the Spooler window shows the print file queue. The print jobs are listed from top to bottom in the order in which they're to be printed; the top of the print queue shows the printer (or printers) being used. The menus in the menu bar offer commands you use to control Spooler.

Pausing a print job

To temporarily pause printing, choose Pause from the Queue menu. Spooler stops sending data to the printer until you choose Resume, also from the Queue menu.

Canceling a print job

To cancel any print job in the queue, first select the name of the job (or jobs) you want to cancel, and then choose Terminate from the Queue menu. Spooler removes all the selected jobs from the queue. If you cancel the job at the top of the list (the document currently being printed), Spooler stops printing, removes the document from the queue, and moves on to the next job (if there is one).

Quitting Spooler

To quit Spooler, choose Exit from the Priority menu. Spooler closes, canceling all jobs in its queue. Normally, you don't need to quit Spooler; it turns itself off when it finishes printing the jobs in its queue.

PRINTING DOCUMENT ELEMENTS

Every Word document and template has its own set of elements such as glossary entries, styles, custom menu items, and summary information. These tools remain conveniently in the background; you don't normally see them on the screen, and you use them only when you need them. There are times, however, when you want to see a list of the elements available to you in a document or template. For example, if you have a printed list of styles available for a given template, you don't have to open the Styles dialog box every time you want to choose a style. You can also use the list to teach others how to pick styles when they create a document using the template.

Word prints the elements of a document if you tell it to. To do so, choose Print from the File menu to open the Print dialog box (shown in Figure 19-6), and use the Print list box to select the element you want. When you choose the OK button, Word prints the element you selected.

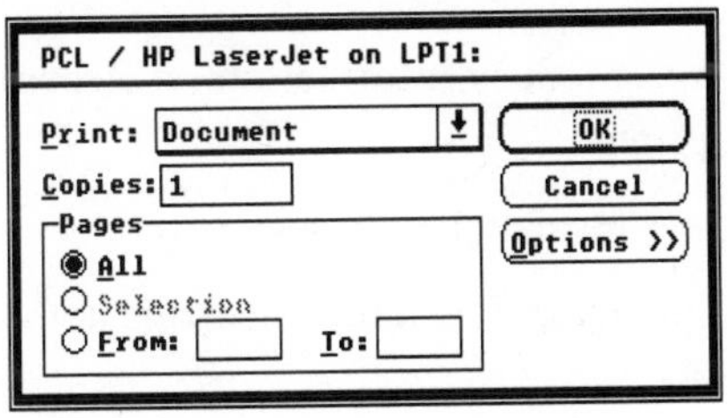

Figure 19-6. *The Print dialog box.*

Your element choices are:

- Document, which prints the current document or template.
- Summary Info, which prints any summary information you added to the document or template when you saved it.
- Annotations, which prints any annotations added to a document or template without printing the rest of the text. (Annotations allow readers to add comments to a document without changing it. You learn more about them in Chapter 20.)
- Styles, which prints the full style list of the document or template so that you can see each style available.

- Glossary, which prints all the glossary entries available in the document or template, including both global and template entries.
- Key Assignments, which prints the names of any macros you create followed by the keys you assign to them and short descriptions of the macros. (Chapter 23 gives more details about creating macros.)

Printing Hidden Information

Word documents and templates often include hidden information that doesn't normally print. To print the hidden information with the rest of the document, use the four options in the Include area of the Print dialog box (shown in Figure 19-7). To see the options, choose Print from the File menu to open the Print dialog box, and then choose the Options button to see the full dialog box. The Include area is at the bottom of the dialog box.

The four options are:

- Summary Info, which prints any summary information on a separate page after the document is printed.
- Hidden Text, which prints any text formatted as hidden text.
- Annotations, which prints any annotations on a separate page at the end of the document.
- Field Codes, which prints any fields in the document as field codes instead of field results. For example, if you insert a date in a header and then turn on the Field Codes option, you see the field code instead of the actual date the field creates.

To use one of these options, turn it on in the Include area and choose OK to start printing. Word prints your document (or element if you choose that instead), adding the hidden information you requested. Keep in mind that you can't include hidden information when you print some elements. For example, if you print Styles, the style sheet doesn't include hidden text, annotations, fields, or summary information.

Figure 19-7. *The Include area of the expanded Print dialog box shows options for printing hidden information.*

A QUICK SUMMARY

In this chapter, you learned how to set page size and margins to create an envelope template and then learned how to create an address document and print an envelope horizontally or vertically. You also learned about batch printing and how Spooler uses a print file queue to print a batch of documents in the background while you work with Word. The last part of the chapter showed you how to print the normally invisible elements of a document or template and how to include hidden information in your printout.

This chapter ends the third section of this book, in which you've learned about some of Word's most useful tools. In the next section, you learn about advanced features—the power tools you use for some of the most difficult tasks in word processing.

SECTION FOUR

Power Tools

This section introduces you to some of Word for Windows' most advanced features. You use them to add comments to a document, to show revisions, and to see a document in many different forms, including outline form. These features help you create easily adjusted tables of information, reduce a complicated set of commands and actions to a single keystroke, give Word special directions in a document, and print personalized form letters.

The chapters in this section don't go into great detail about these advanced features, which would be beyond the scope of an introductory book. Still, you learn enough to see how advanced features work and to pick up some useful techniques, both of which might pique your interest in learning even more about the power of Word for Windows.

Chapter 20

Sharing Documents with Other People

Some documents, such as contracts and legal documents, are shared with people for suggestions and review. These documents pass from person to person, gathering little yellow stickers and rashes of red ink containing comments about the document. Each time you incorporate the comments into the document, the revision shows recent changes—deleted text with a line drawn through it and new text underlined—so that readers can easily see the changes.

In this chapter, you see how to share a document electronically without its gathering red ink and yellow stickers. You learn to lock a document file so that other readers can't change its contents, and you see how to save the document and transfer it on disk (or over a computer network if you have one) to other readers, who can add their own comments as Word for Windows annotations. You also learn how to incorporate annotations into your document (or ignore them if appropriate) and how to create a revision of the document that shows deleted text, added text, and sections that have been changed.

SETTING UP WORD

Annotations require little in the way of intricate formatting, and they don't require printing for you to see how they work. Use the standard Word setup:

- Full menus

- A text window that shows the ruler, ribbon, and status bar
- The Display as Printed option turned off

The sample document for this chapter (shown in Figure 20-1) is the copy for a one-page magazine advertisement. There are two versions: The first is

Walter Wiggam's House of Digital Doodads
12846 Tomorrow Street
Friedmont, CA 93754

Modem Mutt: This handwoven slipcover slips on your modem to make it look just like an adorable puppy! Watch it wink as the front lights on your modem show incoming data, see its "tail" (your data cable) send valuable information to your computer, but watch out for its "byte!" Made of colorful and durable acrylic yarn. Available in fawn, mauve, and chartreuse. Weight 6 oz.................. $5.95

Floppy-Disk Holder: Tired of searching through piles of floppy disks for your system disk and other commonly used disks? Search no more! Our new floppy-disk holder sits vertically next to your computer where you can simply set disks against its smooth plastic surface. Powerful magnets behind hold each disk in place so you can easily retrieve it the next time you need it. Save time and trouble with this convenient tool! Available in red, green, blue, and the secondary luminous colors. Weight 4 lbs, 2 oz..$15.95

Digital Doodad Gold Disk, Collector's Edition: You've never put a floppy disk like this in your computer's disk drive! Made of genuine 24 carat gold, this disk puts a gleam in your eye and says "Wealth!" to the computer users around you. Weight 9 oz...$24.95

Br'er Rabbit Security Keyboard: If you're bothered by data snoops in the office who use your computer while you're gone, why not try out Br'er Rabbit Security Keyboard? Just unplug your keyboard before you go and replace it with the security keyboard. When a data snoop sits down at your computer and begins to type, he'll find his fingers stuck fast to the keys while an alarm rings loudly! Great also as a practical joke! Available in cream or buff. Weight 2 lb, 14 oz...................................$44.95

"Always Hot" Coffee Cup Holder: Get the most out of the overheated chips in your computer console: use them to keep your coffee hot! The "Always Hot" Coffee Cup Holder hangs over the fan vent of your computer console, where hot blasts of air keep your mug of coffee or tea toasty! Available in big blue or apple red. Weight 7 oz... $3.49

Print Head Perfume: Add your own personal touch to those letters you write on your word processor with Print Head Perfume. Just put a drop of this on the print head of your printer, and your letter takes on "the sweet smell of success!" Specify dot-matrix or laser printer. (Laser printer version comes as a toner additive.) Weight 3 oz.. $7.95

To order, call 1-800-555-1212. Operators are standing by!

Figure 20-1. *The original draft of the ad copy is on the left, and the revised version is on the right.*

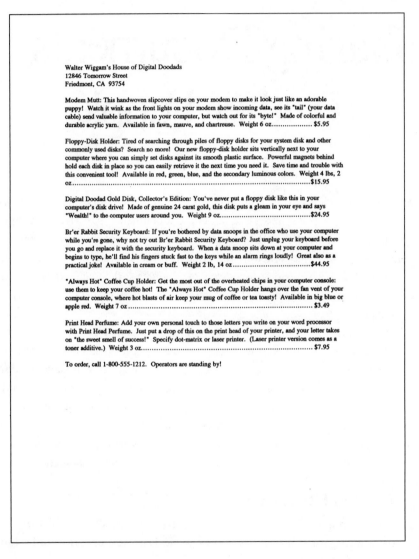

the original draft you write as the ad copywriter for Walter Wiggam's House of Digital Doodads. The second is the revised version of the draft, which includes the production manager's suggestions and which passed muster with Walter Wiggam himself.

Walter Wiggam's House of Digital Doodads
12846 Tomorrow Street
Friedmont, CA 93754

Modem Mutt: This handwoven slipcover slips on your modem to make it look just like an adorable puppy! Watch it wink as the front lights on your modem show incoming data, see its "tail" (your data cable) send valuable information to your computer, but watch out for its "byte!" Made of colorful and durable acrylic yarn. Available in fawn, mauve, and chartreuse. Weight 6 oz.................. $5.95

Digital Doodad Gold Disk, Collector's Edition: You've never put a floppy disk like this in your computer's disk drive! Made of genuine 24 carat gold, this disk puts a gleam in your eye and says "Wealth!" to the computer users around you. You might be able to save data onto this disk, but we make no guarantees. Weight 9 oz..$24.95

Br'er Rabbit Security Keyboard: If you're bothered by data snoops in the office who use your computer while you're gone, why not try out Br'er Rabbit Security Keyboard? Just unplug your keyboard before you go and replace it with the security keyboard. When a data snoop sits down at your computer and begins to type, he'll find his fingers stuck fast to the keys while an alarm rings loudly! Great also as a practical joke! Available in cream or buff. Weight 2 lb, 14 oz...................................$44.95
Br'er Rabbit Glue Solvent. Weight 1 oz.. $4.95

"Always Hot" Coffee Cup Holder: Get the most out of the overheated chips in your computer console: use them to keep your coffee hot! The "Always Hot" Coffee Cup Holder hangs over the fan vent of your computer console, where hot blasts of air keep your mug of coffee or tea toasty! Available in big blue or apple red. Weight 7 oz... $3.49

Print Head Perfume: Add your own personal touch to those letters you write on your word processor with Print Head Perfume. Just put a drop of this on the print head of your printer, and your letter takes on "the sweet smell of success!" Specify dot-matrix or laser printer. (Laser printer version comes as a toner additive.) Weight 3 oz.. $7.95

To order, call 1-800-555-1212. Operators are standing by!

ANNOTATIONS

Word's annotations are the electronic equivalent of comments on yellow tags stuck to the pages of a document. People using Word to read your document on their computers can insert an annotation with their comments at any point; you can later read and discard those comments with ease, making changes in the document as you see fit. The annotations don't change the document's contents, and you don't see them in the main body of the text or in a printout unless you want to see them.

Creating annotations is very much like creating footnotes: To insert an annotation, choose Insert Annotation. An annotation mark appears at the insertion-point location as hidden text, showing the annotator's initials and an annotation number. The annotation pane opens at the bottom of the document window, where the same annotation mark appears. Enter any comments here, and then return to the main document window to read more of the document and insert additional annotations.

You read annotations in the same way as you read footnotes: You open the annotation pane and scroll through the annotations, or you look for annotation marks in the main body of the document as the annotation pane scrolls to match. You can delete annotations by deleting the annotation marks, and you can incorporate suggested changes by cutting and pasting text from the annotation into the main body.

Locking a Document for Annotations

Before you hand over a document file to another person, you might want to lock it for annotations, a feature that prevents anyone but you from changing the document itself. To lock a document for annotations, choose Save As to save the document, and then select Options to fully extend the Save As dialog box. Turn on the Lock for Annotations option and save the document. Word notes that the file is locked and establishes that you are the author by reading your name in the Utilities Customize dialog box. (Be sure it shows your name!) Only you, as the document's author, can lock or unlock the document for annotations.

If you save a locked document onto a floppy disk, you can give that disk to another Word user to read. If you're part of a computer network, you can post the document file on the network for other readers to download and read using Word. When they open the document, Word informs them in the status bar that you have locked the document, and it prevents them from altering the contents of the document. The readers can't add or delete text or use many of the editing, insertion, formatting, and utilities commands. (The commands are dimmed and unavailable.) All the readers can do is add annotations and resave the document onto disk with those added annotations.

To unlock your document when it returns to you, reopen it on your computer, choose Save As, turn off the Lock for Annotations option, and resave the document onto disk. Locking or unlocking the document for annotations has no effect on what you, the author, can do. Word allows you to make any changes you want, whether the document is locked or not.

Inserting an Annotation

Anyone can insert an annotation, no matter who the document's author is or whether the document is locked. First, move the insertion point to the location at which you want to make a comment. Then choose Annotation from the Insert menu (the only functional command on the menu when the document is locked) to insert an annotation mark and open the annotation pane.

When you choose Insert Annotation, Word turns on hidden text (if it is not already on) so that you can see the annotation mark it inserts. The mark includes your initials as shown in the Utilities Customize dialog box, followed by an annotation number. The mark is formatted as hidden text.

The annotation pane shows the annotation mark followed by an empty line where you can enter comments. Enter characters here as you do in a footnote pane. Your comments can be as long or short as you like, and you can edit and format them as much as you want. To return the insertion point to the main document window, click on the location you want, or press F6. Pressing F6 again returns you to the annotation pane.

You can enter as many annotations as you want—Word keeps them in sequential order in the annotation pane. If other people add annotations, you can see their initials in the annotation marks so that you know who made the comments. When you finish adding annotations, save the document onto disk. Word appends all your annotations to the document file for later reading.

An example

To see how annotations work, first enter the text of the original draft of ad copy. When you finish, save the document onto disk, substitute the production manager's name for yours, reopen the document, and insert your comments as annotations:

1. Enter the text of the original draft as shown in the left side of Figure 20-1. You need no special formatting (this is only ad copy), but you might want to add a decimal tab stop with a dotted leader at 5.5 inches to position the prices at the end of each blurb. (If you get tired of typing, you don't need to enter the last two product descriptions for this example.)
2. Choose Save As from the File menu to open the Save As dialog box, and then choose Options to fully expand the dialog box.
3. Turn on the Lock for Annotations option, enter the name *ADCOPY*, and choose OK to save the document onto disk as a locked document.
4. Close the document.
5. Choose New from the File menu to open a new document. (You don't really need a new document—you only want the Utilities menu to appear. It won't appear without an open document.)
6. Choose Customize from the Utilities menu to open the Utilities Customize dialog box, enter the name *Fenster Whelp* and the initials *FW* in the Your Name and Your Initials text boxes, and choose OK to close the dialog box.
7. Close the new document, and reopen ADCOPY. You are now Fenster Whelp, reading the document to add comments. Notice that the status bar tells you the document is locked and that you can't make any changes to the document text. Many of the commands in the menus aren't available.
8. Move the insertion point directly before the $5.95 price of the Modem Mutt, and choose Annotation from the Insert menu. Word turns on hidden text, inserts your initials and the number 1 (for the first annotation), and opens the annotation pane. The insertion point is in the annotation pane following the annotation mark there.

9. Enter this comment: *The price of acrylic has gone up. The new price should be $7.95.*

10. Press F6 to return to the main document window and move the insertion point to the beginning of the "Floppy-Disk Holder" blurb.

11. Choose Insert Annotation to insert an annotation. An annotation mark appears, and the insertion point moves to the annotation pane.

12. Enter the comment *This item has been discontinued due to customer complaints.* Then press F6 to return to the main document window. Figure 20-2 shows your annotations.

13. Enter a third annotation at the end of the "Br'er Rabbit" blurb that says *Please add Br'er Rabbit Glue Solvent here ($4.95) so that customers know they need the solvent to unstick fingers.*

14. Move back up to the "Digital Doodad Gold Disk" blurb, and enter a fourth annotation just before the phrase "Weight 9 oz." Add the comment *Please add the sentence "You might be able to save data*

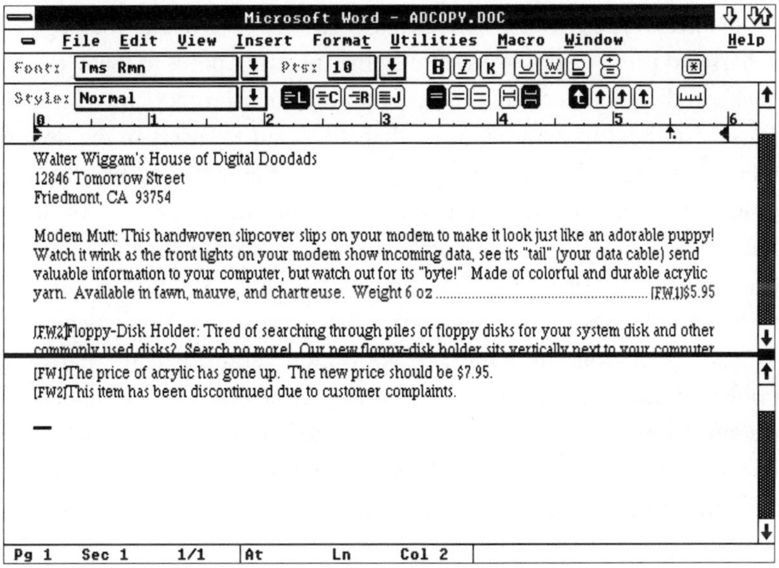

Figure 20-2. *The annotation pane shows comments. The annotation marks appear as hidden text in the document.*

onto this disk, but we make no guarantees." The FTC has complained to us about customers' lost data. Note that Word makes this the third annotation and that the annotation in the "Br'er Rabbit" section becomes the fourth. Word keeps the annotations in consecutive order.

15. Now that you're finished, save the document onto disk under the same filename and close the document.

Reading an Annotated Document

When you receive an annotated document, read the annotations in much the same way as you read footnotes. First open the document, and then open the annotation pane by choosing Annotations from the View menu. Word turns on hidden text to let you see the annotation marks in the document. Press F6 to return the insertion point to the document. As you scroll through the text in the main document window, the annotations in the annotation pane scroll to match the location of the view in the main text window.

To find annotations quickly in a large document, press F5 to turn on the Go To feature. Type *a* (for "annotation") in response to the message in the status bar, and press Enter. Word moves the insertion point to the next annotation mark in the document, and the annotation pane scrolls to match.

If you find text in an annotation that you want to insert in the document, press F6 to move to the annotation pane, select the text, and use the Cut (or Copy) and Paste commands to move the text into the document. To delete an annotation, simply delete its annotation mark in the document: The annotation's comments disappear from the annotation pane. To close the annotation pane when you finish, choose Annotations again from the View menu.

To see annotations in print, use the options described in Chapter 19 to print only the document's annotations or the document with its annotations. If you choose to print hidden text, you can read the annotation marks in your document printout to see where each annotation belongs. If you print a document without setting any print options, neither the annotation marks nor the annotations appear in the printout.

MARKING DOCUMENT REVISIONS

Documents that undergo frequent revision (such as contracts) often require that all additions and deletions appear marked so that readers can easily see the parts that have changed. Added text is traditionally shown underlined; deleted text is shown with a *strikethrough,* a line through the middle of each character.

Word offers a revision-marking feature that uses these traditional marks to show changes you make to a document. When you turn on the feature, any text you add to a document appears underlined, and any text you cut or delete from a document appears with a strikethrough instead of disappearing from the document. You can print the document with revision marks for other readers to review, and later go through the document again to accept or reject the proposed changes.

Setting Revision Marks

To turn on revision marking, choose Revision Marks from the Utilities menu to open the Revision Marks dialog box, shown in Figure 20-3. Turn on the Mark Revisions option in the upper left corner of the box, and then choose OK to close the box and start marking revisions.

After you turn on revision marking, any text you add to the document, whether you type it or paste it from another location, appears underlined. Any text you delete or cut does not disappear but appears with a strikethrough. Word also adds a vertical *revision bar* in the margin beside any line of text that contains a change. The revision bar makes it easy to find changes in a document by simply scanning the page margins.

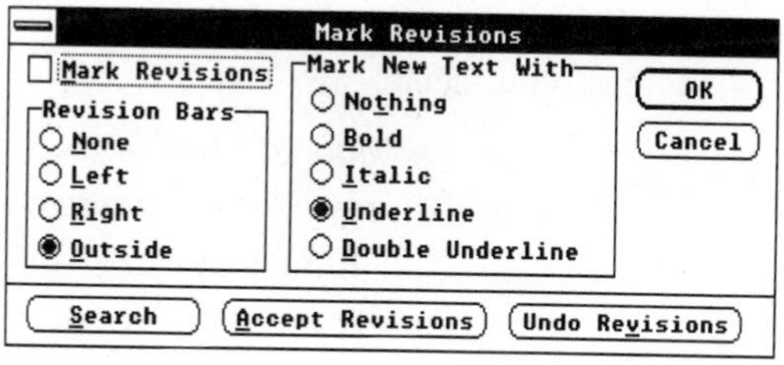

Figure 20-3. *The Utilities Revision Marks dialog box.*

Turn off revision marking by turning off the Mark Revisions option in the Utilities Revision Marks dialog box. After you do so, any text you add is not underlined, and any text you cut or delete disappears from the document. However, all the revision marks you added earlier remain in place. To get rid of them, you accept or reject the revisions (as you learn to do later in the chapter).

An example

Now go back to your role as copywriter. Change to your real name, and then open your document to read the annotated comments from Fenster Whelp. Make marked revisions to your text to create a copy that Walter Wiggam can read:

1. Open a new document to make the Utilities menu appear.
2. Choose Utilities Customize to open the Utilities Customize dialog box, enter your own name and initials in the Your Name and Your Initials text boxes, and choose OK to close the dialog box.
3. Close the new document and reopen ADCOPY. You can now edit your document and use commands that weren't available to you as Fenster Whelp. Word recognizes you as the document's author, so the document lock has no effect.
4. Choose Revision Marks from the Utilities menu to open the Utilities Revision Marks dialog box.
5. Turn on the Mark Revisions option, and choose OK to close the dialog box and start revision marking.
6. Choose Annotations from the View menu. Word turns on hidden text and opens the annotation pane. You see the first annotation mark and read the first annotation comment.
7. The first comment asks you to change the Modem Mutt price, so select the price in the main document and press Delete to remove it. The price remains but appears with strikethroughs to show that it's been deleted.
8. Enter a new price of *7.95* following the old price. The new price appears underlined to show that it's been added.

9. Press F5 to turn on Go To in the status bar, and enter *a* to search for the next annotation. The insertion point moves to the second annotation, at the beginning of the "Floppy-Disk Holder" blurb.
10. Delete the entire blurb to comply with the annotation comment. The entire paragraph appears with strikethroughs.
11. Use F5 and *a* to jump to the next annotation, and then press F6 to move to the annotation pane.
12. Select the sentence "You might be able to save data onto this disk, but we make no guarantees." Choose Copy from the Edit menu to copy the sentence.
13. Press F6 to return to the text window and choose Paste from the Edit menu to insert the sentence into the blurb. (Add spaces as necessary to make the sentence fit properly.) The sentence appears underlined as new text.
14. Use F5 and *a* to jump to the last annotation.
15. Add a new line of text below the "Br'er Rabbit" price that reads *Br'er Rabbit Glue Solvent. Weight 1 oz........$4.95*. The new sentence appears underlined.
16. Now that you're finished, choose View Annotations to close the annotation pane and turn off hidden text. The revised document should look like the one in Figure 20-4 on the following page.

Changing Revision Marks

Word's standard revision marks don't always work well if your document contains a lot of character formatting. For example, if you have underlined text in a document, then underlining new text is confusing. To change Word's standard revision marks, open the Utilities Revision Marks dialog box and change the revision-mark settings.

To change the way Word marks new text, choose any of the five options in the area labeled Mark New Text With. These options set new text to show as boldface, italic, underlined, double-underlined, or with no emphasis at all. To change the way Word places revision bars beside altered text, choose any of the four options in the Revision Bars area. Three of these options put the revision bar beside the left, right, or outside margin of altered text. The outside

Walter Wiggam's House of Digital Doodads
12846 Tomorrow Street
Friedmont, CA 93754

Modem Mutt: This handwoven slipcover slips on your modem to make it look just like an adorable puppy! Watch it wink as the front lights on your modem show incoming data, see its "tail" (your data cable) send valuable information to your computer, but watch out for its "byte!" Made of colorful and durable acrylic yarn. Available in fawn, mauve, and chartreuse. Weight 6 oz.................. $~~5.95~~7.95

~~Floppy Disk Holder: Tired of searching through piles of floppy disks for your system disk and other commonly used disks? Search no more! Our new floppy disk holder sits vertically next to your computer where you can simply set disks against its smooth plastic surface. Powerful magnets behind hold each disk in place so you can easily retrieve it the next time you need it. Save time and trouble with this convenient tool! Available in red, green, blue, and the secondary luminous colors. Weight 4 lbs, 2 oz...$15.95~~

Digital Doodad Gold Disk, Collector's Edition: You've never put a floppy disk like this in your computer's disk drive! Made of genuine 24 carat gold, this disk puts a gleam in your eye and says "Wealth!" to the computer users around you. You might be able to save data onto this disk, but we make no guarantees. Weight 9 oz..$24.95

Br'er Rabbit Security Keyboard: If you're bothered by data snoops in the office who use your computer while you're gone, why not try out Br'er Rabbit Security Keyboard? Just unplug your keyboard before you go and replace it with the security keyboard. When a data snoop sits down at your computer and begins to type, he'll find his fingers stuck fast to the keys while an alarm rings loudly! Great also as a practical joke! Available in cream or buff. Weight 2 lb, 14 oz..............................$44.95
Br'er Rabbit Glue Solvent. Weight 1 oz.. $4.95

"Always Hot" Coffee Cup Holder: Get the most out of the overheated chips in your computer console: use them to keep your coffee hot! The "Always Hot" Coffee Cup Holder hangs over the fan vent of your computer console, where hot blasts of air keep your mug of coffee or tea toasty! Available in big blue or apple red. Weight 7 oz.. $3.49

Print Head Perfume: Add your own personal touch to those letters you write on your word processor with Print Head Perfume. Just put a drop of this on the print head of your printer, and your letter takes on "the sweet smell of success!" Specify dot-matrix or laser printer. (Laser printer version comes as a toner additive.) Weight 3 oz.. $7.95

To order, call 1-800-555-1212. Operators are standing by!

Figure 20-4. *Word shows all the revisions with revision marks. Note the revision bars in the left margin.*

option is for documents that have mirror margins: The revision bars appear on the outside margins of both odd and even pages. You can also choose not to show revision bars at all.

Word uses only one type of mark to show deleted text: a strikethrough. You can't change this type of marking.

Incorporating Revisions

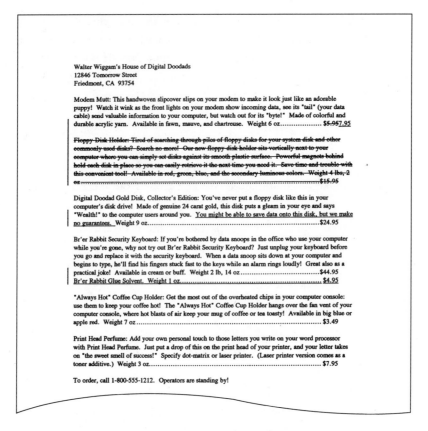

The Utilities Revision Marks dialog box includes three buttons along its bottom edge that you use to find revisions and then accept or reject them. When you choose the Search button, Word searches through the document for a revision. When it finds one, it selects the entire revision as a text block. If you think the revision is worth keeping, choose the Accept Revisions button: Word removes from the selection all text marked with strikethroughs and revision bars and keeps new text after removing the new text marks. If you don't like the revision, choose the Undo Revisions button: Word removes from the selection all new text and revision bars and keeps deleted text after removing the strikethroughs.

The Accept Revisions and Undo Revisions buttons work on the entire document if you have no text selected. Using Accept Revisions accepts changes throughout the whole document; using Undo Revisions gets rid of them throughout the document.

An example

You've shown your ad copy with marked revisions to Walter Wiggam, who decides that he likes all the changes except the new price for the Modem Mutt, which isn't competitive with similar products on the market. Now go through the ad copy and incorporate the revisions where appropriate:

1. Move the insertion point to the beginning of the document and choose Revision Marks from the Utilities menu to open the Utilities Revision Marks dialog box.
2. Choose the Search button to find the first revision. Word selects the price change for the Modem Mutt.
3. Choose the Undo Revisions button. Word changes the price of the Modem Mutt to $5.95.
4. Choose the Search button to find the next revision (the deleted blurb), and then choose Accept Revisions. Word removes the entire blurb from the document.
5. Choose Search to find the next revision (an added sentence) and choose Accept Revisions to keep the added line.
6. Use Search and Accept Revisions to accept the next added sentence.
7. Save and print your final ad copy to send to the page-layout department, and then close the document.

A QUICK SUMMARY

In this chapter, you learned how to add comments to a document by using annotations. You saw how to lock a document so that other readers can add annotations without altering the document's contents. You learned how to insert annotations and also how to read, change, and include annotation comments as document contents. The second part of the chapter showed you how to mark document revisions. You learned how to set the types of revision marks Word uses and how to search for and accept or reject document revisions. In the next chapter, you learn how to look at a single document in many different ways and how to work with many different documents at once.

Chapter 21

Views, Outlines, and Document Windows:

Working Efficiently with Long and Multiple Documents

This chapter introduces you to different ways to look at a Word for Windows document. You learn to use Word's draft, normal, and page views to see a single document in rough, partial, or full formatting. You also learn to use the outline view to create an outline from scratch or to view an outline of an existing document. In the last part of the chapter, you see how to open as many as nine different documents on the screen at once and how to split a document window into panes to view two parts of a single document at one time. All these tools make it easier for you to see the contents of a long document and to work with material spread through many different documents.

SETTING UP WORD

Use the standard setup for the examples in this chapter:

- Full menus
- A text window that shows the ruler, ribbon, and status bar
- The Display as Printed option turned off

You use two documents for the examples in this chapter. The first is the article you created earlier in Chapters 15 and 16 and saved under the name UNICYCLE.DOC. You use it to look at different views. The second document is an outline you create in outline view that shows the structure of a user's manual for a piece of entertainment software called "Stellar Sawbones." Figure 21-1 shows the outline document.

Introduction
  Welcome to a world of medical thrills and excitement! As Dr. Thralnor Fefnikal of the Assimilated Lowculture Planetary Association, you will have the opportunity to practice surgery and larceny on unsuspecting denizens of planets throughout the known galaxy. Before you start your career, take a few minutes first to fill in the warranty card.
- The Warranty Card
- Other Digidilly Games

Setting Up
- Computers with the IRS Card
  - With One Floppy-Disk Drive
  - With Two Floppy-Disk Drives
  - With a Hard-Disk Drive
- Computers with the GTI Card
  - With Test Drive
  - With Overdrive
  - With Drive and Determination

Playing the Game
- Choosing a Planet
  - Ice Planets
  - Desert Planets
  - Surf 'n Turf Planets
- Finding a Patient
  - Listening to the Police Scanner
  - Waiting Around the Race Track
  - The Bad Part of Town
- Your Surgical Tools
  - The Laser Scalpel
  - The SuperGlue Sutures
  - The Neutrino Nail Clipper
  - The Framborzhdulnibluck
- Malpractice Insurance
  - Cut-Rate Firms
  - Forging Coverage Certificates
- Intergalactic Flight
  - Avoiding Police
  - Paying Bribes
  - Your Safe Hiding Place
- Scoring

Figure 21-1. *Word's outline view makes it easy to create document outlines.*

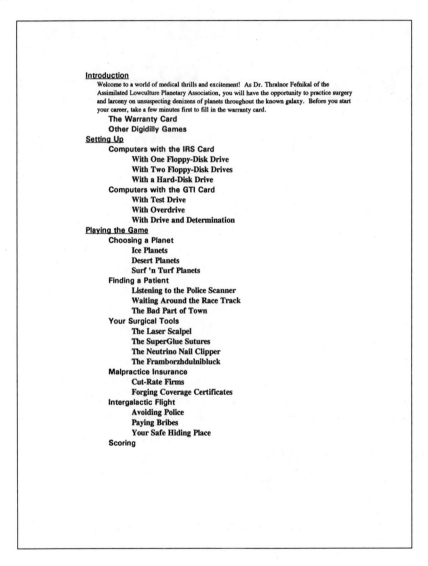

DOCUMENT VIEWS

Word offers you four different views of any document:

- Draft view
- Normal view
- Page view
- Outline view

The first three views—draft, normal, and page—offer varying degrees of *display speed* and *visible formatting*. Display speed is the amount of time Word takes to update the document window when you change text or scroll. Visible formatting is the amount of formatting Word shows you on the screen. The more formatting you see, the closer the screen document is to the document that actually prints on paper. However, the more visible formatting a view shows, the slower the display speed becomes. This is because showing formatting makes your computer work harder to keep track of all the various types of elements. The more formatting you see, the more time Word takes to update the screen each time you change text or scroll through the document.

Draft view is the speediest: It shows little character formatting and doesn't bear much resemblance to the text you finally print, but it's speedy when you scroll and edit text. Normal view is the view you've used throughout most of this book. It balances display speed with visible formatting: You can see full character and paragraph formatting, you can get a good idea of the way section and document formatting will look on a printout, yet the display speed is still acceptable (although not as fast as that of draft view). Page view shows all formatting: You see footnotes, headers, and footers where they occur on the page, and you see each page as a white rectangle on a colored background, with fully formatted text placed within the page margins. Because page view shows all formatting, its display speed is slow.

Outline view isn't designed with display speed or visible formatting in mind; it instead shows the underlying structure of a document. It displays different levels of headings by using different indentions on the screen: Outline view recognizes nine different levels of headings, and it indents them appropriately in half-inch intervals. It also recognizes body text and indents it slightly under its heading.

Draft View

To turn on draft view, choose Draft from the View menu. Draft is a toggle command, so when you first choose it, a check appears before the command on the menu. When you choose Draft again, you turn off draft view, and the check disappears.

Draft view uses only one font to display text—the system font (the font Windows uses for menu text)—and displays only limited character formatting. You apply character formatting as you do in normal view, but if you change fonts or point size, you don't see any changes in the text. If you change typestyle, draft view usually shows it as an underline, no matter which typestyle you choose. Boldface, italic, underlining, word underlining, and double underlining typestyles all appear as single underlining in draft view. Small caps appear as full-sized uppercase letters, and superscript and subscript characters appear above or below the line. Figure 21-2 shows part of a document in draft view.

You edit and scroll through text in draft view as you do in normal view. You edit headers, footers, and footnotes in a separate pane and don't see them

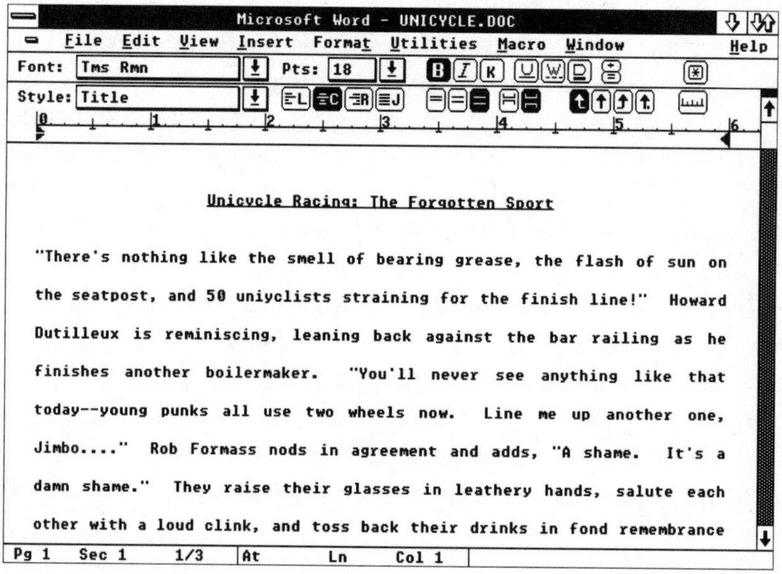

Figure 21-2. *Draft view shows limited character formatting and uses only the system font.*

on the page until you print the document. Any formatting changes you make in draft view that don't show up—such as font changes and other character formatting—are still incorporated in the document. When you change to normal or page view, all the formatting appears where you placed it.

Use draft view when formatting isn't important and you want Word to respond as quickly as possible to your editing and scrolling. Draft view is particularly useful if you run Word on a low-powered computer system—you'll find the speed refreshing.

Page View

To turn on page view, choose Page from the View menu. This command is also a toggle command that turns on and off when you choose it. Page view and draft view can't both be on at the same time, so choosing one turns off the other. If you turn off both page and draft views, Word uses normal view.

Page view shows your document as close to the way it will be printed as your monitor allows. Although you don't see an entire page at one time, you can scroll to see all parts of the page. In addition to character and paragraph formatting, you see section and document formatting as you scroll. You see the edges of the page and the page margins you set. You also see footnotes, headers, and footers where they appear on each page. A page break appears not as a dotted line across the document window but as a break from one page to another with the top and bottom page margins in between. If you create multiple snaking columns in a document, you see them side by side, and if you set a fixed-position paragraph, you see it in its specified location.

Scrolling in page view using the mouse works a little differently than it does in other views. The vertical scroll bar (shown in Figure 21-3 on the following page) includes two additional controls—*page icons*—above and below the scrolling arrows. To use the page icons, click on them. The bottom icon moves the view forward to the same location on the next page. The top icon moves the view back to the previous page. To scroll within a page and between pages, use the rest of the scroll bar as you do in draft and normal views.

Move the insertion point through the text by using the keyboard as you do in draft and normal views. Two additional keyboard combinations let you move to elements that aren't normal parts of the text. Alt-down cursor moves the insertion point to the beginning of the next document element, and Alt-up

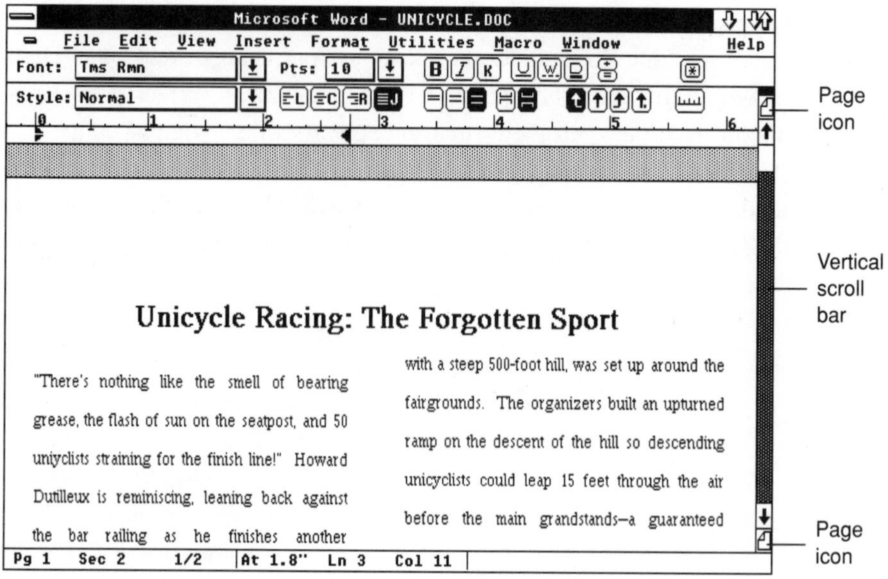

Figure 21-3. *Page view shows all formatting, including headers, footers, and footnotes, but it doesn't show the entire page at one time.*

cursor moves to the beginning of the previous document element. For example, press Alt-down cursor to move from one column of text to another in a multiple-column page, or use it to move from the body of the text to a footer.

Editing in page view also has its own conventions. Although you edit body text as you do in normal view, headers, footers, and footnotes don't work the same way. Because these elements appear on the page instead of in their own panes, you simply select the text in a header, footer, or footnote where it appears on the page and then change it as you want. If you change a header or footer that's linked to other headers or footers, the text in the linked headers or footers changes accordingly.

The ruler also works differently in page view if you use multiple columns. When you move the insertion point to a column, the ruler changes the location of its 0 mark to match the left margin of the column. For example, if you select the right column of a pair of snaking columns and it starts halfway across a standard page, the 0 mark of the ruler moves to the middle of the screen. This convention makes it easier to set indentions in columns.

Use page view after you finish most of a document and want to concentrate on final formatting before you print. You'll find that page view can be painfully slow if you have a low-powered computer system and is not as fast as you're used to even if you have a high-powered computer. Using normal and draft views for heavy editing and saving page view for touch-ups will make your work go much faster.

A View Example

Try using draft, normal, and page views to view the unicycle article you created earlier. To see how page view handles multiple columns and a footer, set the document to include multiple columns and a footer before you change the views:

1. Open the document named UNICYCLE.DOC. It appears in normal view.
2. Choose Section from the Format menu to open the Format Section dialog box.
3. Enter *2* in the Columns Number text box and choose the OK button to close the dialog box and set the text in two snaking columns.
4. Choose Header/Footer from the Edit menu to open the Header/Footer dialog box, and then select Footer from the list box. Choose OK to open the header/footer pane. Enter *Unicycle Footer* and close the pane.
5. Choose Draft from the View menu to turn on draft view. The text in the document window changes to the system font, and special character formatting in the titles and headings appear only as underlines.
6. Scroll up and down through the document. Notice that Word updates the display very quickly as you scroll.
7. Choose Page from the View menu to turn on page view and turn off draft view. All the character formatting appears as you set it originally, and you see both columns on the page at one time. If the insertion point is in the first column of text, you see the ruler's 0 mark on the left side of the page.
8. Move the insertion point to the second column by clicking on it or by pressing Alt-down cursor. The ruler shows the 0 mark in the middle of the page.

9. Scroll to the bottom of the page. Notice that the footer appears below the body of the text and that when you scroll far enough, you see the bottom edge of the page. Continue scrolling if you want to see the next page. Notice that scrolling is much slower than it is in draft view.
10. Choose Page from the View menu to turn off page view. You see the document in normal view once again.

OUTLINING

An outline is a traditional tool for arranging concepts in hierarchical order. Main (high-level) concepts are set flush against the left margin, and lesser (lower-level) concepts are indented to the right under the concept they amplify. You can easily see the main points of an outline by reading only the high-level concepts and can easily rearrange a document's structure by moving a concept with all its associated lower-level concepts. To promote a lower-level concept to a higher level, you simply move the concept line to the left; to demote a concept to a lower level, you move the concept line to the right.

Outline view offers useful features for creating and changing outlines. You can do the following:

- Enter concepts as different levels of headings
- Add associated text (called *body text*) to any heading
- Change a heading's level by moving it left or right
- Change the order of concepts by moving headings, subheadings, and body text up or down in the outline (without using the Cut and Paste commands)
- Hide any subheadings and body text under a heading to clear up the outline
- Set the display level to hide all body text and any headings below a certain level so that you can view only the main points of an outline

You can use outline view for many tasks, but you should find the three uses listed on the following page particularly helpful.

- Creating an outline from scratch: Use outline view to create a hierarchical structure of headings and to set the basic structure of your document. Then return to any other view to fill in text below each heading.
- Viewing the structure of an existing document: Turn on outline view for an existing document to show its headings in their hierarchical structure with body text below each heading. By setting the display level to show only important concepts, you can quickly see the overall document structure.
- Scrolling quickly through a document: Turn on outline view to see only headings at and above a certain level. This "shortens" a long document considerably, so you can quickly scroll to the location you want and then switch to another view to see all the text.

Heading Styles

To understand how outline view works, you must first know that Word offers nine automatic heading styles you can use. These heading styles are labeled, in order of importance, "heading 1," "heading 2," "heading 3," and so on down to "heading 9." When you apply a heading style to a paragraph, it sets formatting appropriate for a heading. For example, "heading 1" uses boldfaced and underlined characters in the 12-point Helv font. You can change any of these style definitions so that the headings appear in the formatting you want.

When you turn on outline view, all paragraphs change their indentions to show the heading hierarchy within a document. "Heading 1" is flush left, "heading 2" is indented ½ inch, "heading 3" is indented 1 inch, and so on to "heading 9," which is indented 4 full inches. Non-header styles are considered body text and appear indented ¼ inch to the right under the headings that precede them.

Consider this example: Suppose you have a level-1 heading followed by body text, a level-2 heading followed by body text, and a level-3 heading followed by body text. When you turn on outline view, you see the level-1 heading flush left with its body text indented ¼ inch, the level-2 heading indented ½ inch with its body text indented ¾ inch, and the level-3 heading indented 1 inch with its body text indented 1¼ inches.

Using Outline View

To turn on outline view, choose Outline from the View menu. This is a toggle command that you turn on and off by choosing it. You can use outline view with normal view, in which case you see character formatting, or with draft view, where you see all text in a single font with limited character formatting. Using outline view with draft view speeds up outline editing.

When you turn on outline view, an *outline icon bar* appears where the ruler usually appears, *heading icons* appear before each paragraph, and paragraphs are indented according to their heading levels. Figure 21-4 shows the sample outline as it appears in outline view.

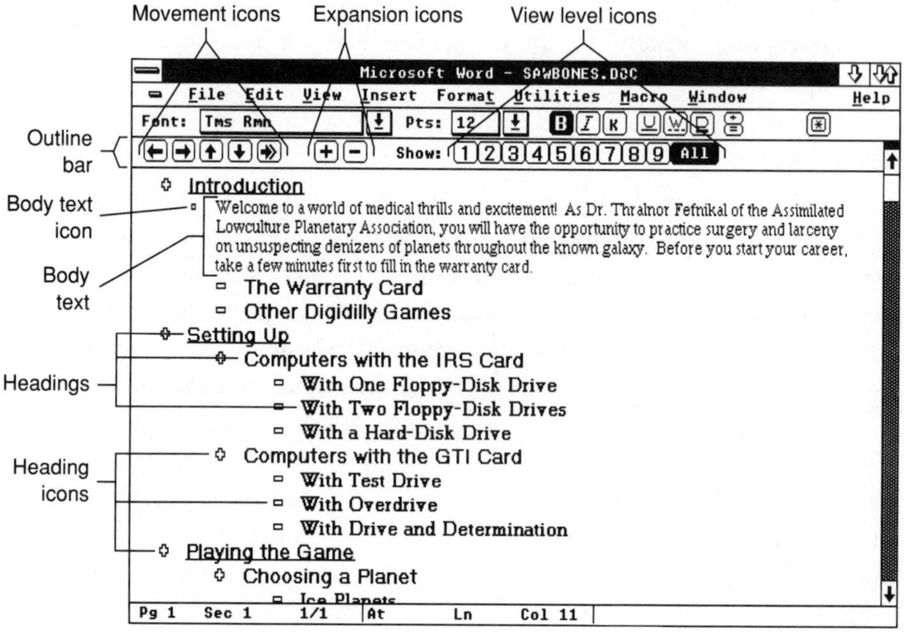

Figure 21-4. *Outline view shows the structure of headings in a document.*

Use the outline icon bar with the mouse. It contains different groups of icons that work on selected paragraphs:

- The movement icons move paragraphs up and down in the outline or left and right to promote or demote them.

- The expansion icons hide or display all subheadings and body text under a selected heading.
- The view level icons hide all headings and body text below the level you select.

Use the heading icons to see the status of a paragraph. If the icon is a plus sign, the paragraph is a heading that has subheadings or body text under it. If the icon is a minus sign, the paragraph is a heading that has no subheadings or text. If the icon is a small square, the paragraph is body text. You can also use heading icons with the mouse to drag a paragraph up, down, left, or right, or to hide or reveal any subheadings or body text associated with the paragraph.

Entering Text

Enter text in outline view as you do in other views. Any text you enter conforms to the style of the paragraph you're in. There are, however, some small differences in the way styles are applied in outline view: If you start a new document in outline view, the default style of your first paragraph is "heading 1" instead of "normal." When you press Enter at the end of a heading paragraph, the next paragraph uses the same heading style. If you do the same in any other view, the next paragraph uses the "normal" style because the heading style defines "normal" as the next style.

Selecting Text

Select text in a paragraph as you do in the other views. If you select a text block that includes text in more than one paragraph, Word selects all the text of any paragraphs in your text block. This makes it impossible (fortunately) to promote, demote, or move only part of a paragraph. If you have a mouse, you can easily select a heading with all its subheadings and body text simply by clicking on its heading icon.

Changing Paragraph Order

To move paragraphs up and down in the outline without promoting or demoting them, first select the paragraph(s) you want. (Remember that you can select a single paragraph simply by placing the insertion point in it.) If you have a mouse, click on the Up Arrow icon in the outline bar to move the paragraph up or click on the Down Arrow icon to move the paragraph down. To move a heading with all its subheadings and body text, point to the heading's icon and then drag the heading up or down to a new location. To move selected paragraphs up or down using the keyboard, press Shift-Alt-up cursor or Shift-Alt-down cursor.

Promoting or Demoting Paragraphs

To promote or demote a heading, use the mouse to select the Left Arrow icon or Right Arrow icon in the outline bar. To perform the same task via the heading icon, simply drag the icon left or right. To promote or demote a heading using the keyboard, press Shift-Alt-left cursor or Shift-Alt-right cursor.

To change a heading into body text, you demote it in a different way than you do to change it into a lower-level heading. If you have a mouse, select the Text icon on the outline bar. (It's the rightmost icon of the movement icons and looks like a right arrow with a second outline around its head.) To change to body text using the keyboard, be sure that Number Lock is turned off. Then press Shift-Alt-5 on the numeric keypad.

To promote body text to a heading, either select the Left Arrow icon or Right Arrow icon in the outline bar, drag the text's heading icon left or right, or press Shift-Alt-left cursor or Shift-Alt-right cursor.

Whenever you promote or demote a paragraph, you change its style. For example, if you demote a level-2 heading to a level-3 heading, you change its style from "heading 2" to "heading 3." If you demote a level-1 heading to body text, you change its style from "heading 1" to "normal."

Collapsing or Expanding a Heading

If you don't want to see subheadings or body text beneath a heading, you can collapse the text so that only the heading shows. Word adds a thick dotted bar beneath the heading to show that the heading has subheadings or body text beneath it, even though you can't see it.

To collapse subheadings and body text one level at a time from beneath a heading, first put the insertion point in the heading. If you have a mouse, click on the Minus icon in the outline bar. If you have a keyboard, press the

Minus key on the numeric keypad. Each click or key press collapses the lowest visible level of heading or body text beneath the selected heading. For example, if you put the insertion point in a level-1 heading that contains level-2, level-3, and level-4 subheadings, the first time you click or press, the level-4 headings disappear, collapsing into the level-3 headings above them. The next click or press collapses the level-3 headings, and the following click or press collapses the level-2 headings into the main heading.

To expand a heading that contains collapsed subheadings, move the insertion point into the heading and then either use the mouse to click on the Plus icon in the outline bar or press the Plus key on the numeric keypad. Each click or press expands the next lower level of heading beneath the selected heading. If you wanted to expand the heading you collapsed in the last example, the first click or press would reveal the level-2 subheadings, the next would show the level-3 subheadings, and another would show the level-4 subheadings.

If you want to collapse all levels of subheadings and body text with one action, either double-click on the heading's heading icon or select the entire heading, including the paragraph mark, and press the Minus key on the keypad. Double-clicking on the heading icon a second time expands all levels of subheadings. To get the same results with the keyboard, first select the heading, including the paragraph mark, and then press the Plus key on the numeric keypad.

Setting the Display Level

When you set the display level, outline view shows only the headings at and above the level you choose, collapsing lower-level headings and body text into the headings above them. If you select All, all heading levels and body text appear. To select levels using the mouse, click on the number icon in the outline bar for the heading level you want to see (1 to 9), or click on the All icon to see all headings and body text. To select levels using the keyboard, press Shift-Alt with a number key (1 to 9). Use the numbers above the regular keyboard, not those in the numeric keypad. To select the All level, press Shift-Alt-A.

An Example

As a documentation writer, you are asked to write a manual for the new medical adventure computer game "Stellar Sawbones" (published by Digidilly, Inc.). To start, you create an outline of the material you have to explain:

1. Open a new document and choose Outline from the View menu to turn on outline view. The outline icon bar appears, and the insertion point is in the first paragraph, a "heading 1" paragraph that has a Minus icon to its left.
2. Type *Introduction* and press Enter to start a new paragraph.
3. Enter two more paragraphs: *Setting Up* and *Playing the Game*. Each paragraph you enter appears as a level-1 heading. These are the three major parts of your manual.
4. Now enter a level-2 subheading under "Introduction." Move the insertion point to the end of the "Introduction" line and press Enter to start a new paragraph.
5. Select the Right Arrow icon on the outline bar (or press Shift-Alt-right cursor) to demote the new paragraph to a level-2 heading. Notice that the heading icon before "Introduction" changes to a plus sign to show that the paragraph now has a subheading.
6. Type *The Warranty Card*, press Enter, and then type *Other Digidilly Games*. You now have two subheadings below "Introduction."
7. Now add subheadings below "Setting Up." Move the insertion point to the end of "Setting Up," press Enter to start a new paragraph, and demote it to a level-2 heading.
8. Type *Computers with the GTI Card*, press Enter, and then demote the new paragraph to a level-3 heading.
9. Enter three new paragraphs as level-3 headings: *With Test Drive*, *With Overdrive*, and *With Drive and Determination*.
10. Continue to enter outline elements, promoting and demoting paragraphs as necessary until the outline matches Figure 21-5.

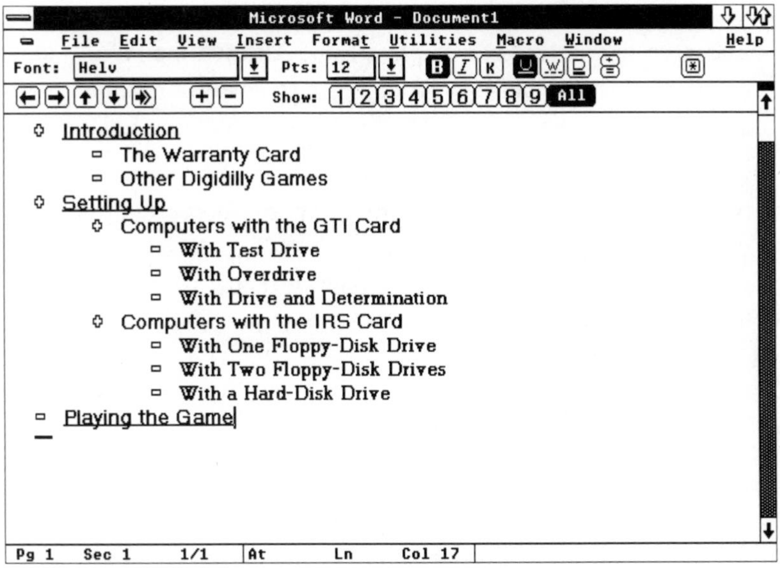

Figure 21-5. *Enter this outline for the example.*

11. Now switch the order of two headings—"Computers with the IRS Card" and "Computers with the GTI Card"—so that the "IRS" heading and all its subheadings appear before the "GTI" heading. If you have a mouse, drag the "IRS" heading icon up until it appears directly above the "GTI" heading, and then drop it there. If you use the keyboard, move the insertion point to the "IRS" heading, and press the Minus key on the numeric keypad to collapse the heading. Press Shift-Alt-up cursor until the "IRS" heading moves directly above the "GTI" heading. Expand the heading again by pressing the Plus key on the numeric keypad.

12. Enter the rest of the outline as you see it in the sample document in Figure 21-1, but leave out the body text paragraph following "Introduction."

13. To enter the body text paragraph, move the insertion point to the end of "Introduction," press Enter, and demote the new paragraph to body text by selecting the Text icon on the outline bar or by pressing Shift-Alt-5 on the numeric keypad. (Be sure that Number Lock is off.)

14. To see the outline with only level-1 and level-2 headings, select the 2 icon on the outline bar or press Shift-Alt-2 on the regular keyboard. The outline shows only the first two levels of headings, with a thick dotted line under each heading that contains hidden subheadings or body text.
15. Now look at your outline in normal mode. Choose Outline from the View menu to turn off outline view. The document appears with headings, subheadings, and body text all in place. All you have to do to write the manual is fill in more (much more!) body text. Good luck!

DOCUMENT WINDOWS

Word enables you to open up to nine different documents on the screen at one time to let you compare text and formatting and cut, copy, and paste text among the documents. Each document you open appears in its own text window; as you open new ones without closing ones already on the screen, Word displays the document windows in layers, one on top of another, with the most recently opened document on top. Although they appear similar, a document window isn't a full-blown Windows program window: It's a window within a window, a text window within Word's program window.

When you first open a document window, it's hard to see that it's a separate entity on the screen because it stretches all the way from the menu bar and the ribbon down to the status bar in the Word window. To see a document window on its own, choose Restore from the Document Control menu (the short dash on the left edge of the menu bar). The document window shrinks and detaches itself from the menu bar and ribbon so that it appears with its own border and title bar (as shown in Figure 21-6). It also includes its own ruler and scroll bar (if they are turned on) and has its own Document Control menu in the upper left corner and a Maximize box in the upper right corner.

When more than one document window is open, only one window is active—the window on top. Only the active window has an insertion point and an operating scroll bar, so it is the only window in which you can enter text. To make an inactive window active, click on the desired window (if any part of it is visible) or press Ctrl-F6 to activate each window in turn and bring it out in front of the others.

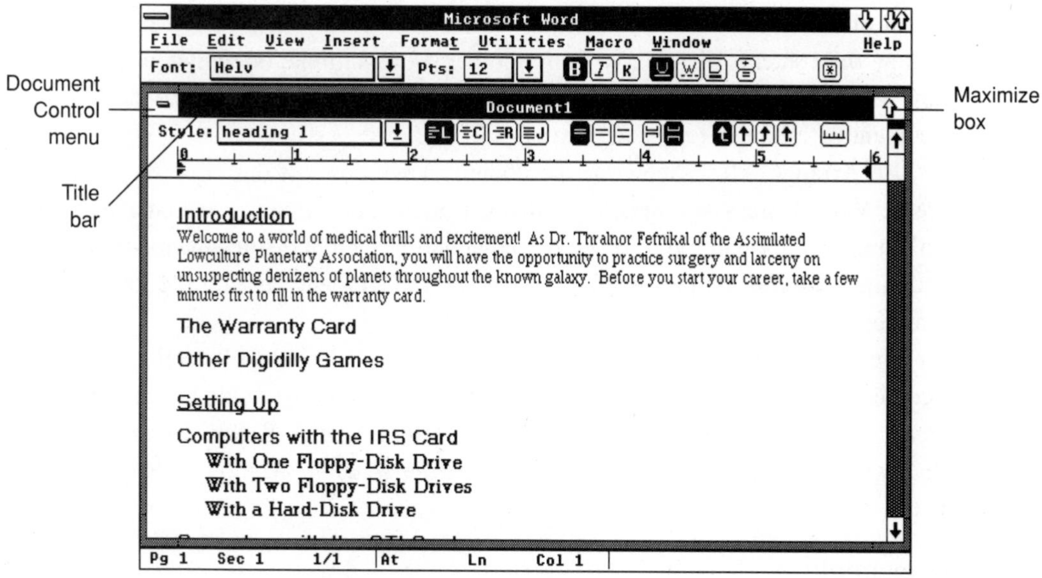

Figure 21-6. *Use the Restore command to shrink a document window and detach it from the Word program window.*

Controlling Document Windows

You can move and control the size of document windows in much the same way as you do program windows. If you have a mouse, you can drag a window to a new location by its title bar, change its size by dragging one of its borders or corners, return it to maximum size by clicking on the Maximize box, and close it by double-clicking on its Document Control menu. If you use only the keyboard, you can perform the same functions by using the commands on the Document Control menu. To open the menu, press Alt and then the hyphen key (-).

The Window menu

Word offers a Window menu that contains commands for controlling document windows. Use the New Window command to open two or more windows showing the same document. Choosing the command opens a new window showing the same document as the one in the currently active document window. With multiple windows showing the same document, you can look at different locations in the document simultaneously or set one window to show the contents differently from another. For example, one window can show a document with hidden text hidden, and the other can show the same document with hidden text made visible.

Use Arrange All to show all the document windows at one time on the screen. Word resizes and arranges all open document windows so that they don't overlap, allowing you to see the contents of each. This arrangement is particularly useful if you need to compare the contents of all the open document windows.

The bottom part of the Window menu shows the title of each open document. Choose any title to bring that document's window to the top of the screen and make it active. This is a useful tool when all the document windows are at full size and you can't see the inactive windows beneath the top one.

An example

You should still have open the outline you created earlier. Try opening a second window for the outline and a third window showing a different document:

1. Choose Restore from the Document Control menu to reduce the outline window in size and detach it from the Word program window.
2. Choose New Window from the Window menu to open a second window showing the outline. The second window appears, overlapping the first window.
3. Use File Open to open UNICYCLE.DOC. It appears, overlapping the first two windows.
4. Press Ctrl-F6 to bring one of the outline windows to the top and make it active.
5. Choose UNICYCLE.DOC from the Window menu to return that window to the top and make it active.
6. Choose Arrange All from the Window menu. Word shrinks and arranges the three document windows so that they all appear on the screen as shown in Figure 21-7.

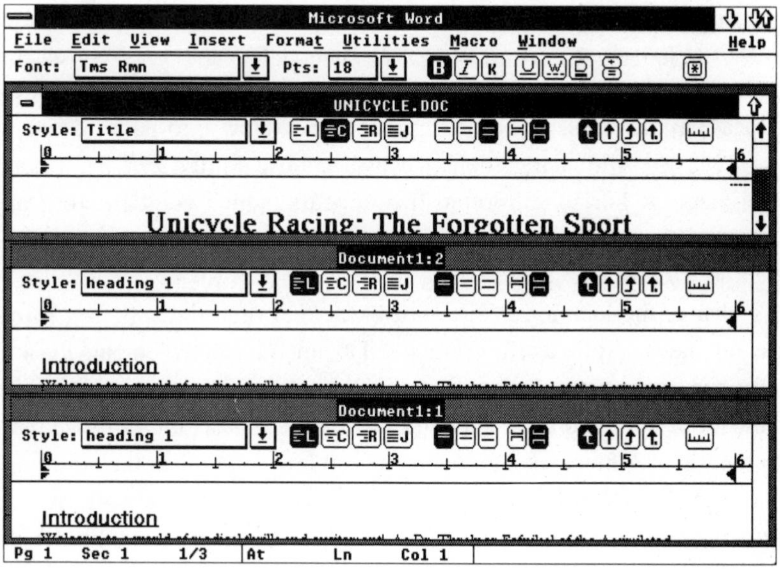

Figure 21-7. *Arrange All organizes document windows so that they all appear on the screen without overlapping.*

7. Close the UNICYCLE.DOC window and one of the outline windows. If you have a mouse, simply double-click on the Document Control menu in each window. If you use the keyboard, choose Close from each window's Document Control menu.

8. Maximize the outline window so that it fills the entire screen. If you have a mouse, click on the Maximize box. If you use the keyboard, choose Maximize from the Document Control menu.

Window Panes

To compare different sections of the same document without opening a second window, you can split a window into two panes. These panes are separated from each other by a horizontal *split bar*. You can adjust the split bar up or down to resize the panes. Each window pane has its own scroll bar, and you can set each pane to show a different view, so you can use panes to look simultaneously at different locations in a document, using a different view for each. For example, one pane could show the outline view of a document while the second pane showed the normal view of the same document.

To split a window into panes using a mouse, find the *split box,* a tiny black box at the top of the vertical scroll bar. Drag it down. As you drag, a horizontal dotted line appears across the window. When you drag it to the split location you want, release it to split the window into panes as shown in Figure 21-8. To split using the keyboard, choose Split from the Document Control menu. A horizontal dotted line appears, which you can move up and down with the cursor keys. When you reach the position you want, press Enter to split the window into panes.

To change the location of the split bar, either drag the split box using the mouse or choose Split again from the Document Control menu to activate the split bar, use the cursor keys to move it to a new location, and press Enter. To remove the split and close the panes using the mouse, either move the split bar to the top or bottom of the document window or point to the split box and double-click. To close the pane using the keyboard, choose Split again, use the cursor keys to move the split bar into the upper or lower border of the document window, and press Enter.

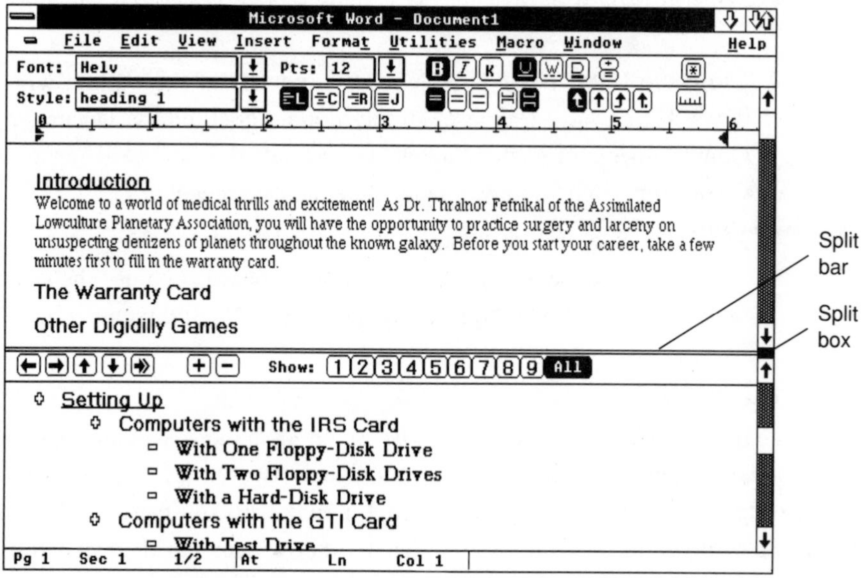

Figure 21-8. *When a window is split into two panes, each pane can show the same document in a different view.*

After you split a window into two panes, you can move the insertion point between panes by pressing F6 or, if you have a mouse, by clicking on the pane you want. If you set a new view by using a View command, Word turns on the view only in the pane you have selected. For example, if both panes show the normal view, you can move the insertion point to the bottom pane and turn on outline view. The top pane then shows the document in normal view, and the bottom pane shows it in outline view.

Word normally allows independent scrolling of each pane to let you see different sections of a document in each pane. However, if you set one pane to show the outline view and the other to show draft, normal, or page view, then the other pane scrolls to match the outline view. You can use this idiosyncrasy to good advantage: Scroll the outline pane to easily find the location you want and then jump to the other view (which will be in the same location) to edit or add text.

An example

Try working with the outline document window when it's split into two panes. Start with the document in normal view:

1. Split the window into two panes either by dragging the split box halfway down the window or by choosing Split from the Document Control menu and pressing Enter.
2. Choose Outline from the View menu. The bottom pane appears in outline view, while the top pane remains in normal view.
3. Scroll the bottom pane down by one screen. The top screen scrolls to match: The top line of the outline pane controls the view location of the normal pane.
4. Close the pane by moving the split bar all the way to the bottom of the window. (Either drag the split bar or use the Split command and press Enter.) The bottom pane disappears.

A QUICK SUMMARY

In this chapter, you learned to view a document in any of four views. You learned how draft, normal, and page views differ in their display speeds and in the amount of formatting they show, and you learned how to use outline view to create and edit outlines and to scroll quickly through text. The last part of the chapter showed you how to use document windows to see several documents at once and how to use window panes to see different views and different parts of the same document simultaneously. In the next chapter, you learn how to put the flexibility of Word's tables to good use.

Chapter 22

Creating Tables

Arrange information in a table, and you're guaranteed to draw your reader's eye to it. Take too much time and trouble creating the table, and you'll roll your eyes every time you see it. In this chapter, you learn to create tables in Word for Windows that both you and your reader can easily look at. You start by inserting a table in a document and setting the table's dimensions. You go on to move the insertion point from place to place in the table, entering and formatting text. You then learn how to move material from one part of the table to another and how to add and delete rows and columns. The last part of the chapter shows you how to control the appearance of the table: how to set column widths, align the table rows between the page margins, and add borders.

This chapter isn't an exhaustive account of Word's tables. It is instead an introduction that gives you enough working knowledge to create your own tables. The end of the chapter tells you about more table possibilities you can read about in Word's *User's Reference*.

SETTING UP WORD

Use the standard setup to work through the examples in this chapter:

- Full menus
- A text window that shows the ruler, ribbon, and status bar
- The Display as Printed option turned off

Also be sure that Word is set to show table gridlines (which it should be by default). The Table Gridlines option is in the View Preferences dialog box.

The sample document for this chapter (shown in Figure 22-1) is a single-page letter written to drum up subscriptions for a national newspaper. The document includes a table comparing the newspaper's features to those of other papers; you create the table, fill it in, and edit it using Word's table features.

1/9/90

Dear Friend:

The mid-winter doldrums--we all get them! That's why Leander Mylarivek, the man who brought you mail-order pizza, is expanding his services to include home mail delivery of The New Midnight Star Tattler. You may know the Star Tattler as the weekly newsmagazine guaranteed to deliver the stories you want, but did you know that it now has double the writing staff to bring you even more of these great stories? From Alzorno, our spirit-channeling astrologist/hairdresser columnist, to Zachary Ansadahl, our roving reporter on the lookout for Elvis, we've beat the competition across the board when it comes to the features we *know* you'll want to read. The table below tells it all:

Number of Features from October to December, 1989

	The New Midnight Star Tattler	The Gossip Rag	USA Enquirer	Lifestyles of the Sinful and Wicked
Psychic predictions of natural catastrophes and changing presidential hairstyles	22	19	6	11
Inspiring stories of recovery from drug dependency, bulimia, or a vague feeling of unrest	35	8	29	13
I-was-there accounts of UFO abductions for interstellar checker tournaments	12	2	4	7
Accurate reports on Elvis's new career as a topless mud wrestler in Sheldon, Iowa	49	37	26	47

Well, what are you waiting for--more hours of tedious boredom?! Get out your Visa or MasterCard and call us *now* at the number on the enclosed subscription card. Your copies of the Star Tattler will be on their way *immediately!!!!*

Yours sincerely,

James T. Ardentheffer
Subscription Manager

Figure 22-1. *Word's table features create the table in this sales letter.*

AN OVERVIEW OF TABLES

In Chapter 8, you learned to arrange information in columns by using tab stops. That method works well as long as you don't put more than a few words of text in each location. The text is hard to revise, however; when you try to do so, entries often jump forward or backward by a tab stop, misaligning information and moving it from the end of one line to the beginning of another. To overcome these problems, use Word's *tables*.

A table is a grid that divides the page into rows and columns as shown in Figure 22-2. If you're familiar with spreadsheet software such as Microsoft Excel, you'll find that a table looks much like a small spreadsheet. Each location within the table is called a *cell;* you can move the insertion point from cell to cell in a table and enter text or graphics in each cell.

Each cell in a table is an independent text-entry area: It has its own margins, indents, and tab stops. You can set character and paragraph formatting within a cell exactly as you do outside the table. You set the width of each cell when you create or modify the table. The height of each cell is set by its contents: As you enter text and graphics, the cell, along with all the other cells in the same row, grows downward to accommodate its contents.

After you enter text or graphics in a cell, you can easily edit the cell's contents and move contents from one cell to another. You change a cell's contents by moving the insertion point into the cell and editing, the same way you do in regular text. To move the contents of one cell to another, you use

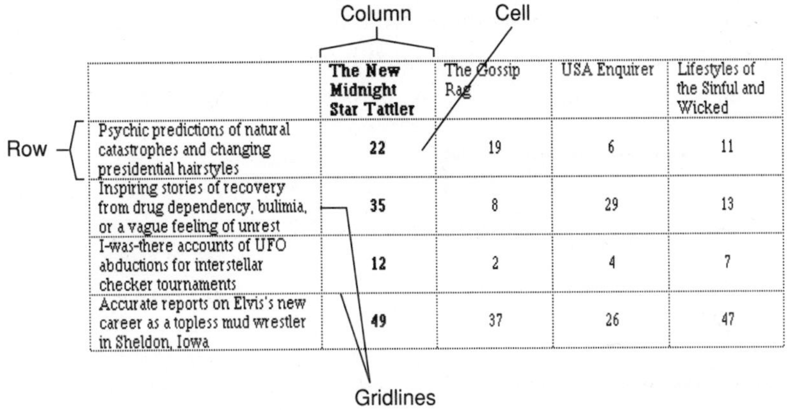

	The New Midnight Star Tattler	The Gossip Rag	USA Enquirer	Lifestyles of the Sinful and Wicked
Psychic predictions of natural catastrophes and changing presidential hairstyles	**22**	19	6	11
Inspiring stories of recovery from drug dependency, bulimia, or a vague feeling of unrest	**35**	8	29	13
I-was-there accounts of UFO abductions for interstellar checker tournaments	**12**	2	4	7
Accurate reports on Elvis's new career as a topless mud wrestler in Sheldon, Iowa	**49**	37	26	47

Figure 22-2. *A table divides the page into rows and columns of cells.*

the Cut, Copy, and Paste commands. If you need more rows and columns in the table, you can easily add them. You can also delete rows and columns. And finally, you can control the appearance of a table by changing the width of its columns and by adding borders either around groups of cells or around the entire table. When you print the table, only the borders and contents of the table print; the dotted gridlines that help you see cell boundaries don't appear.

INSERTING A TABLE

To insert a table, move the insertion point to the location in the document where you want the table to be. Choose Table from the Insert menu to open the Insert Table dialog box (shown in Figure 22-3).

The default values in the dialog box create a table that stretches across the width of the page, with two columns across and one row down. To set different numbers of columns and rows in the table, change the numbers in the Number of Columns and Number of Rows text boxes.

The Initial Col Width text box controls the width of each column. Its default value is Auto, which tells Word to create column widths by splitting the distance equally between the left and right page margins so that the resulting columns stretch from the left page margin to the right page margin. To set your own column width, enter a value in inches in this text box. If your width creates columns that don't fill the width of the page, Word leaves the extra space to the right of the table. If your width is too wide for the page, the right side of the table runs off the page.

The Convert From area in the bottom of the dialog box governs conversion of regular text to a table. If you select a text block and then choose Insert Table, you can choose any of the three following options: Paragraphs converts

```
┌──────────────────────────────────────────┐
│ Insert Table                               │
│ Number of Columns:  [2      ]  ( OK     )  │
│ Number of Rows:     [1      ]  ( Cancel )  │
│ Initial Col Width:  [Auto   ]  ( Format...)│
│ ┌─Convert From──────────────┐              │
│ │ ○ Paragraphs              │              │
│ │ ○ Tab Delimited           │              │
│ │ ○ Comma Delimited         │              │
│ └───────────────────────────┘              │
└──────────────────────────────────────────┘
```

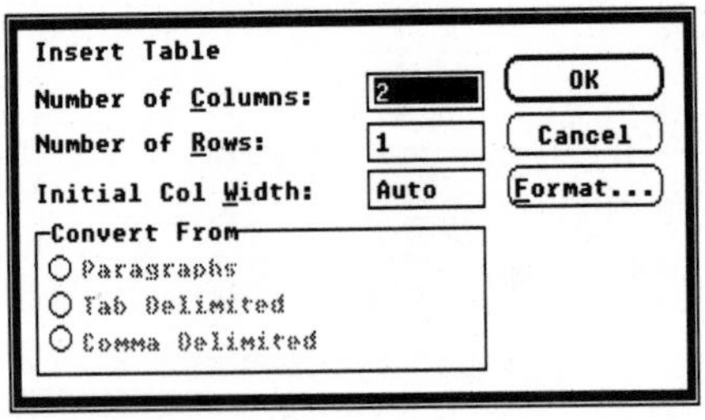

Figure 22-3. *The Insert Table dialog box.*

each paragraph of the text block to a separate cell; Tab Delimited converts each piece of text separated by a tab to a separate cell; and Comma Delimited converts each piece of text separated by a comma to a separate cell. The Word *User's Reference* tells you more about this feature.

Use the buttons on the right to move out of the dialog box: OK closes the dialog box and inserts the table with the dimensions you set; Cancel closes the dialog box without inserting a table; and Format opens the Format Table dialog box, where you can control the table's appearance.

An Example

Enter the sample letter so that it includes a table:

1. Open a new document. Set paragraph formatting to include an open line before each paragraph and then enter the first three paragraphs of the sample letter, ending with the sentence "The table below tells it all." (It isn't important to enter this text verbatim, so abridge it if you like.) When you finish, press Enter to start a new paragraph.
2. Set paragraph formatting to center alignment and character formatting to bold and type the table's title: *Number of Features from October to December, 1989*. Press Enter.
3. Set paragraph formatting to left alignment with no open line before the paragraph. (Word uses the paragraph formatting you have in effect as the paragraph formatting for each cell of the table you insert.)
4. Press Enter to add one blank line below the title.
5. Choose Table from the Insert menu to open the Insert Table dialog box.
6. Set a dimension of five rows by five columns by entering *5* in both the Number of Columns and the Number of Rows text boxes.
7. Press Enter to close the dialog box and insert the table. The table appears beneath the title paragraph, and the insertion point appears in the top left cell.

MOVING THE INSERTION POINT WITHIN A TABLE

Any text you type in a cell fills only that cell—it doesn't extend to adjacent cells. When you reach the right border of the cell, the insertion point jumps to the beginning of a new line within the cell instead of moving to the next cell. To move to another cell using the mouse, simply click in the cell you want. The insertion point appears there, and you can begin entering text.

To move the insertion point from cell to cell using the keyboard, press Tab. Each time you do so, the insertion point jumps one cell to the right unless you're at the end of a row, in which case it jumps to the beginning (left end) of the row below. To jump in the opposite direction, press Shift-Tab. Note that if you press Tab when you're in the bottom right cell, Word creates a new row of cells and moves the insertion point to the beginning of the new row.

You can also move from cell to cell using the cursor keys: If you press the up cursor key when the insertion point is at the top of the cell or the down cursor key when the insertion point is at the bottom of the cell, the insertion point moves up or down into the adjacent cell. If the insertion point is at the beginning of the cell's contents, press the left cursor key to move it to the cell on the left; if the insertion point is at the end of the cell's contents, press the right cursor key to move it to the cell on the right.

Word also offers keyboard shortcuts for jumping to different cells within a table:

- Alt-PgUp moves to the top of the current column.
- Alt-PgDn moves to the bottom of the current column.
- Alt-Home moves to the beginning of the current row.
- Alt-End moves to the end of the current row.

To leave the table entirely, simply click outside the table. To reenter the table, click in any cell. To leave the table using the keyboard, press the up or down cursor key until the insertion point moves out of the table. To reenter the table, use the up or down cursor key to move back into the table.

WORKING WITHIN A CELL

After you move the insertion point into a cell, you can enter text and graphics there as you do in regular parts of the document. The ruler shows the indents and margins of the cell you're in. As you type, the text fills in from the left to the right indent and then begins a new line below the current line. If there isn't room in the cell for the new line, the cell stretches down to make room, and all the other cells in the row grow with it to maintain the same height across the entire row.

You can set character formatting within a cell as you normally do, choosing different fonts, sizes, and typestyles. You can also set paragraph formatting by choosing alignment and spacing and by setting tab stops. To use tab stops within a cell, press Ctrl-Tab to jump from stop to stop: If you press Tab, you'll jump to the next cell.

Cell Margins and Indents

You can set paragraph indents within a cell, but you set them relative to *cell margins* instead of page margins. To understand cell margins, compare them to page margins: Just as Word sets page margins to keep text from running off the edge of the page, Word sets cell margins within each cell to keep text from running into the border of the cell. These left and right cell margins are usually a fraction of an inch wide. The ruler shows their location with margin markers (shown in Figure 22-4). The first-line indent and left indent of each

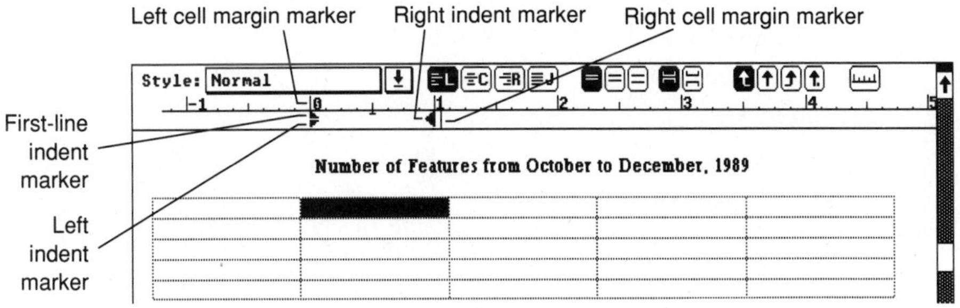

Figure 22-4. *The ruler shows the margins and indents for the currently selected paragraph in the selected cell. The 0 mark is set at the cell's left margin. The right indent marker has been moved to the left to reveal the right cell margin marker.*

paragraph are set relative to the left cell margin, and the right indent is set relative to the right cell margin. To set paragraph indents in a cell, select the paragraph(s) you want. Then drag the indent markers on the ruler or set the indents in the Format Paragraph dialog box.

Editing and Formatting

After you've entered text in a cell, you can edit and format it: First select a text block and then apply editing or formatting commands to alter the text. When you select text, you must remain within the cell; if you extend the selection to an adjacent cell, Word selects the entire contents of both cells. Any editing or formatting command you choose affects the entire text block.

An Example

Enter some text in the cells of your sample table. Start with the insertion point in the upper left cell of the table:

1. Move to the right one cell (click in it or press Tab) and enter *The New Midnight Star Tattler.* The row expands to accommodate the text.
2. Move to the right one cell and enter *The Gossip Rag.*
3. Move to the right one cell and enter *USA Enquirer.*
4. Move to the right one cell and enter *Lifestyles of the Sinful and Wicked.*
5. Move to the first cell of the next row (click in it or press Tab) and enter *Psychic predictions of natural catastrophes and changing presidential hairstyles.*
6. Move through the rest of the cells and enter the contents as shown in the sample document in Figure 22-1. (To center the numbers in their cells, turn on centered alignment and press Enter once before typing each number.)
7. Move to the end of the document (out of the table) and enter the rest of the letter.

EDITING AND FORMATTING MULTIPLE CELLS

To edit or format the contents of more than one cell at a time, you must first select all the cells you want. Selection techniques vary for mouse and keyboard:

- To select the entire contents of a single cell using the mouse, move the pointer into the left margin of the cell (the pointer turns into a right-pointing arrow) and click. To use the keyboard, move the insertion point to the beginning of the cell's text; then hold down Shift and use the cursor keys to move the insertion point to the end of the cell's text.
- To select a row of cells using the mouse, move the pointer into the left page margin beside the row you want (the pointer turns into a right-pointing arrow) and double-click. To use the keyboard, move the insertion point into the leftmost cell of the row you want, hold down Shift, and use the cursor keys to move the insertion point into the rightmost cell of the row.
- To select a column of cells using the mouse, move the pointer to the top border of the top cell in the column you want. When the pointer turns into a small, black, down-pointing arrow, click. To use the keyboard, move the insertion point into the top cell of the column you want, hold down Shift, and use the cursor keys to move the insertion point to the bottom cell of the column.
- To select a block of cells using the mouse, drag the pointer from one corner of the block to the opposite corner of the block. To use the keyboard, move the insertion point to the upper left cell of the block you want, hold down Shift, and use the cursor keys to move the insertion point to the bottom right cell of the block.
- To select the entire table, press Alt-5 on the numeric keypad. (Be sure Num Lock is off.)

After you select a block of cells, you can cut, copy, and paste their contents. If you choose Cut, the contents of the cells in the block are cut and put onto the Clipboard, leaving empty cells behind. If you choose Copy, the contents of the cells in the block are copied to the Clipboard, leaving the cell contents intact. To paste the contents of multiple cells from the Clipboard to the table, select a single cell and then choose Paste. Word pastes the contents of the Clipboard into the table using the selected cell as the upper left cell of the block and working to the right and down as it pastes. The pasted cell contents replace any previous cell contents.

Note that if you extend the selection to include part of the table *and* part of the document above or below the table, cutting cell contents also cuts the actual cells along with the contents.

An Example

Format the *Star Tattler's* column so that the text appears in boldface. First, select the second column from the left. If you have a mouse:

1. Move the pointer to the top of the column, where it turns into a small, black, down-pointing arrow.
2. Click to select the column.
3. Turn on bold character formatting. All the characters in the column appear in boldface.

If you use the keyboard:

1. Move the insertion point to the top cell of the column.
2. Hold down Shift and use the down cursor key to extend the selection to the bottom of the column.
3. Turn on bold character formatting. All the characters in the column appear in boldface.

EDITING A TABLE

After you create a table, you can add or delete cells. To do so, first select a cell or block of cells and then choose Table from the Edit menu to open the Edit Table dialog box, shown in Figure 22-5.

The first three options in the upper left quarter of the dialog box set the section of the table that your editing actions affect. If you turn on Row, Word works on full rows; if you turn on Column, Word works on full columns; and if you turn on Selection, Word works only on the selected cells. If you use the

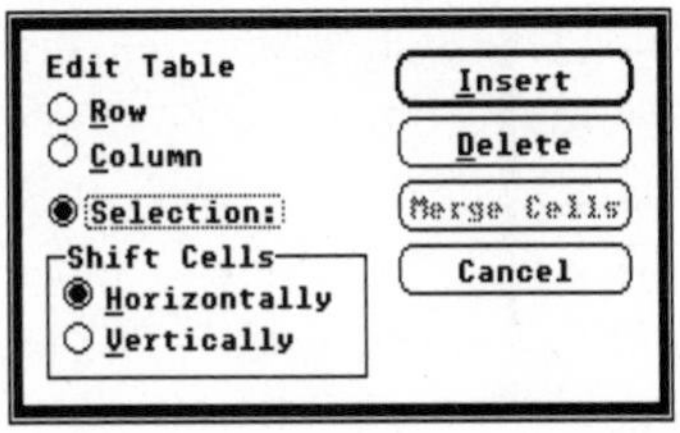

Figure 22-5. *The Edit Table dialog box.*

Row or Column option when you don't have a full row or column selected, Word extends the effective selection to include the full row or column. For example, if you select two side-by-side cells in the middle of the table and then set Column, Word extends the effective selection to include the full columns containing both cells.

The buttons on the right side of the dialog box initiate editing actions: Insert inserts a new column if the Column option is on, a new row if the Row option is on, or a new block of cells next to the selected block if the Selection option is on. Delete cuts the selected columns if the Column option is on, the selected rows if the Row option is on, or the selected block if the Selection option is on.

The options in the Shift Cells area determine how Word inserts and deletes around a selected cell block. If you turn on Horizontally, Word moves existing cells to the right of the selected block to make room for new cells and moves existing cells to the left to fill in a deleted block. If you turn on Vertically, Word moves existing cells down from the selected block to make room for new cells and moves existing cells up to fill in a deleted block.

FORMATTING A TABLE

To change the appearance of cells within a table, select the cells you want to format, and choose Table from the Format menu to open the Format Table dialog box (shown in Figure 22-6 on the following page).

The first text box in the dialog box is labeled Width of Columns *n–n*, where *n–n* are the numbers of the columns selected in the table. For example, if you select cells in columns 2 through 4 before you open this dialog box, the text-box label is Width of Columns 2–4. This text box sets the cell width of all the selected cells. Enter a value in inches to set the cell width you want.

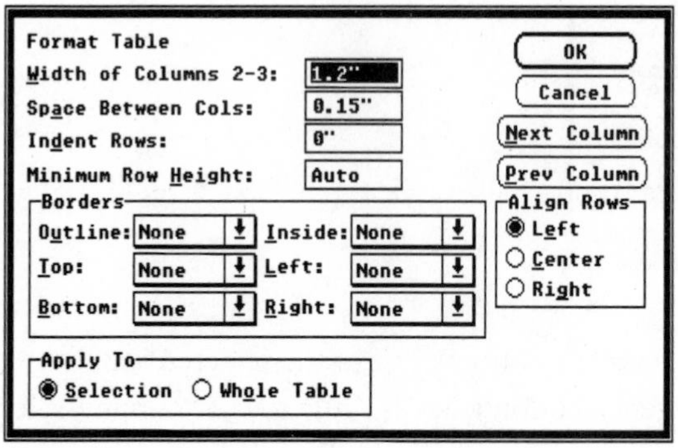

Figure 22-6. *The Format Table dialog box.*

The next text box, Space Between Cols, sets the cell margins. Any value in inches you enter here determines the amount of space used for the cell margins in the selected cells. Word divides the Space Between Cols value by two to set the cell margins. For example, if you set a value of 0.2 inch in Space Between Cols, Word puts 0.1 inch of space on both the left and right edges of the cell. Figure 22-7 shows the relationship between cell width and cell margins.

The Indent Rows text box sets an indention for the currently selected rows. This indention moves the rows to the right of the left page margin. Enter a value in inches here to indent selected rows to the right.

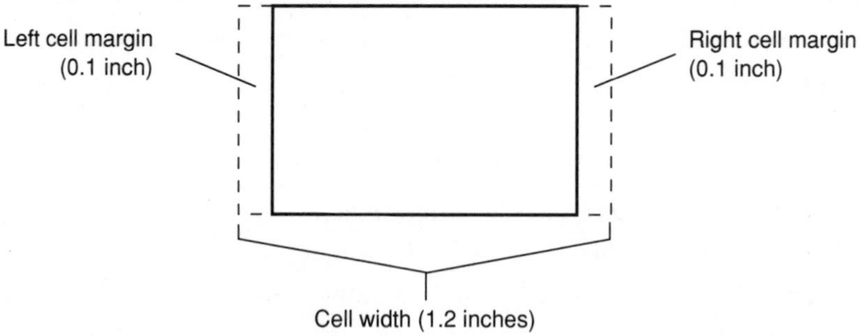

Figure 22-7. *A 1.2-inch cell with a Space Between Cols setting of 0.2 inch has 0.1-inch cell margins.*

Borders

The Borders area of the Format Table dialog box sets borders around selected cells. These list boxes control different areas of the selected cell block:

- Outline puts a border around the outside edge of the selected block. It adds no borders to any cells in the interior of the block.
- Top puts a border on the top edge of the selected block.
- Bottom puts a border on the bottom edge of the selected block.
- Inside puts a border on all the interior cell edges in the selected block. It adds a border to all cell edges not affected by the Outline list box.
- Left puts a border on the left edge of the selected block.
- Right puts a border on the right edge of the selected block.

Each list box offers the same options you have for bordering a normal paragraph: None, Single (a single thin line), Thick (a single thick line), Double (double thin lines), and Shadow (a thick line that is cornered to give a shadowed effect). Set the list boxes to the options that give you the effect you want.

Setting Row Alignment

The three options in the Align Rows area of the Format Table dialog box align selected rows between the left and right page margins: Left aligns the rows flush against the left page margin; Center centers the rows between the left and right page margins; and Right aligns the rows flush against the right page margin.

Changing the Cell Selection and the Affected Area

Use the Next Column and Previous Column buttons to change the selected cells in the table without closing the dialog box. If you select Next Column, Word selects the next single column to the right of the currently selected cell block. If you select Previous Column, Word selects the next single column to the left of the currently selected cell block.

You can also format the entire table instead of only the selected cell block: Turn on the Whole Table option in the Apply To area. To affect only the selected cell block once again, turn on the Selection option. After you choose formatting and the areas to be affected, choose OK to close the dialog box and apply the formatting to the selection (or the whole table).

Viewing the Table

When you format a table to include borders, the gridlines you see on the screen can mar the effect. To see the table without gridlines, choose Preferences from the View menu to open the View Preferences dialog box. Turn off the Table Gridlines option and choose OK to close the dialog box. The table appears as it will print—without gridlines.

An Example

Add borders to your table to make it easier to read, and then change column widths to more easily accommodate the text in the first column:

1. Move the insertion point inside the table if it isn't already there.
2. Choose Table from the Format menu to open the Format Table dialog box.
3. Turn on the Whole Table option in the Apply To area to make your border settings affect the whole table.
4. Set the Outline list box in the Border area to Thick.
5. Set the Inside list box in the Border area to Single.
6. Choose OK to close the dialog box. The table appears surrounded with a thick border. The interior cells are outlined with single thin lines.
7. Select the entire rightmost column of the table.
8. Choose Format Table to open the Format Table dialog box.
9. Enter *1* in the Width of Column 5 text box to reduce the cell width of column 5 to 1 inch.
10. Choose the Previous Column button to change the cell selection to column 4.
11. Enter *1* in the Width of Column 4 text box.

12. Use the Previous Column button to move to column 3 and then to 2, and change their widths to 1 inch.
13. Choose the Previous Column button to change the cell selection to column 1.
14. Enter *2* in the Width of Column 1 text box to set its cell width to 2 inches.
15. Select Double in the Right list box in the Borders area.
16. Choose OK to close the dialog box. The table appears with the first column 2 inches wide and the rest of the columns 1 inch wide. The right side of the first column has a double line border.
17. Select the entire top row of the table.
18. Choose Format Table to open the Format Table dialog box.
19. Select Double in the Bottom list box in the Borders area.
20. Choose OK to close the dialog box. The table appears appears in its final form, with a double border along the bottom of the first row.

MORE TABLE FEATURES

The table features you've read about so far are only the basics. If you explore tables more fully in Word's *User's Reference*, you'll find you can do much more. For example, you can:

- Calculate among cells as you can in a spreadsheet
- Convert existing text into a table (including a text file generated by a database program)
- Convert a table into text
- Set table cell widths using the ruler
- Place tab stops within a cell
- Split a table into two parts
- Insert a page break in the middle of a table
- Set a minimum row height to expand rows with minimal contents
- Merge the contents of several cells into a single cell
- Split a previously merged cell into several separate cells

- Position a table on the page so that text flows around it
- Create irregular tables containing partial rows and columns

A QUICK SUMMARY

In this chapter, you were introduced to Word's tables. You learned to insert a table, set its dimensions, and move from cell to cell to fill it in. You saw how to edit and format cell contents and then how to select and edit the contents of multiple cells. The chapter went on to show you how to edit a table by changing the number of columns, rows, and cells and how to format a table by setting cell width and margins, adding borders, and setting alignment. The last part of the chapter gave you some ideas about further table features. In the next chapter, you learn about a timesaving feature: macros.

Chapter 23

Macros:

Repetitive Tasks Made Simple

This chapter introduces you to macros, one of Word for Windows' most powerful tools. You learn what macros are and what they can do, and you see how to record and run your own macros. You learn how to edit a macro and how to assign it so that you can run it by choosing a menu command or pressing a key combination. You also see how to change Word's standard key combinations to work the way you want and how to customize menus by adding or deleting commands. At the end of the chapter, you'll find some further ideas for using macros.

SETTING UP WORD

Use standard Word settings for this chapter:

- Full menus
- A text window that shows the ruler, ribbon, and status bar
- The Display as Printed option turned off

There is no sample document for this chapter—you create a macro rather than a document in the examples.

AN OVERVIEW OF MACROS

A macro is a set of actions that plays back with a single command. You typically create a macro by recording a set of repetitive actions as you perform a Word task. You can play the macro back later when you want to repeat the task. To understand how this works, think of the keyboard, the mouse, and the parts of the Word window as controls you use to issue orders to Word. When you type a sentence on the keyboard, you issue an order to Word to insert a sentence at the insertion point. If you click on the Bold icon of the ribbon or press Ctrl-B, you issue an order to Word to turn bold character formatting on or off. Some parts of the Word window might actually issue a series of orders. For example, when you choose Annotation from the Insert menu, you issue a series of orders to insert an annotation mark, open the annotation pane, move the insertion point into the pane, and add an annotation mark in the pane.

Recording and Running a Macro

When you create a macro, you create a list of orders that Word stores in memory. The simplest way to do this is to record your actions by choosing Record from the Macro menu and carrying out the actions you want to record. When you finish recording, choose Stop Recorder from the Macro menu. Between the time you start and stop the recording process, Word records every action issuing an order that you take with the keyboard or mouse, including:

- Typing text using the keyboard
- Using special keys such as the cursor keys, the function keys, the Delete key, and the Backspace key
- Pressing a key combination to turn a feature, such as italic character formatting, on or off
- Choosing a menu command using the keyboard or the mouse
- Filling in box information
- Using the mouse on any of the on-screen tools such as the scroll bars, the ribbon, the ruler, window sizing boxes, and others. (Note that mouse editing actions—such as selecting text—can't be recorded. During recording, the pointer becomes transparent to show this.)

After you record a macro, Word stores it in memory under the name you give it and, at the end of your session, stores it on disk if you want to use it again later. You can run a macro by choosing its name from a dialog box or—if you take the time to assign the macro to a menu or a key combination—by choosing it as a menu command or by pressing its key combination.

Record a macro whenever you find yourself performing repetitive actions. For example, if you add annotations to a document and find that you're constantly using the same annotation text—such as "This costs entirely too much!"—you can turn the whole process into a macro. You first start the macro recording. You then insert an annotation, type the standard text, move the insertion point back to the main text window, and close the annotation pane. Finally, you stop the macro recording. The next time you want to insert an annotation that reads "This costs entirely too much!" you simply run the macro. Word then inserts the annotation, fills in the text, returns the insertion point to the main text window, and closes the annotation pane.

Editing and Programming Macros

You can edit any macro you create. Word shows the macro in its own window as a list of commands in a programming language called "Word Embedded Language." You can revise the macro by changing, adding, and deleting commands. You can also create a macro from scratch by entering your own list of commands. Editing at this level requires programming skills and a thorough knowledge of Word Embedded Language. If you don't want to program, you can use Word's macro editing tools to rename or delete a macro.

Customizing Menus and Key Combinations

After you create a macro, you can assign it to either a menu or a key combination. To assign a macro to a menu, you choose the menu to which you want to add it and then give the macro the name you want to appear on the menu. Word adds the name as a menu command so that you can run it by choosing the command from the menu. To assign a macro to a key combination, you show Word the key combination you want by pressing it. Word remembers the assignment so that you can run the macro later by pressing its key combination. To remove a macro command from a menu or a key combination, you can delete its menu command or remove the key-combination assignment.

If you have the Special Edition with disks included, consult the Introduction

In addition to the macros you create for yourself, Word includes a large set of built-in macros. You use these built-in macros every time you choose a regular menu command or press one of Word's regular key combinations. For example, when you press Ctrl-B, you run a built-in macro that turns on bold character formatting. Just as you add and remove your own macros from menus and key combinations, you can add and remove Word's built-in macros. In this way you can customize Word's menus and key combinations by removing normal commands from menus and reassigning standard key combinations. For example, if you never use the Annotation command on the Insert menu, you can remove the command from the menu.

When you customize Word's menus and key combinations, you can choose to use them globally—in all the documents you create—or in a template. When you customize in a template, you create a set of menu commands and key combinations that appear and work only when you work in that template or in a document based on that template. For example, if you create a template designed for writing simple memos, you can remove all the advanced menu commands (such as Insert Table of Contents) and add custom macro commands that insert a memo heading and add your initials at the end. When novice users create a memo using this template, no complex and unnecessary commands will be available to get them into trouble. If they create a document based on a different template, the menus return to the global menu settings so that they can choose advanced commands.

RECORDING A MACRO

To begin recording a macro, choose Record from the Macro menu. The Macro Record dialog box (shown in Figure 23-1) appears.

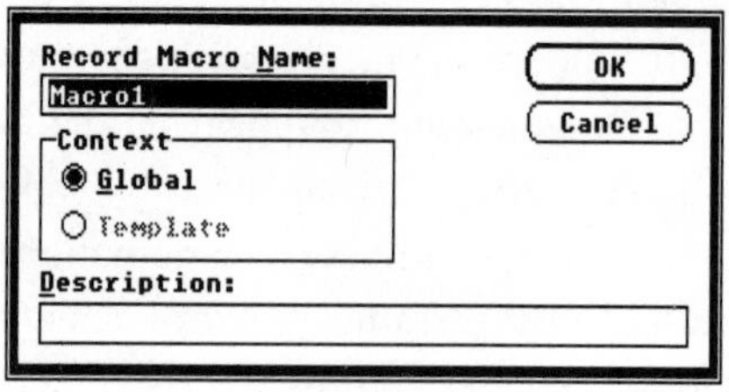

Figure 23-1. *The Macro Record dialog box.*

Before you start recording, use the Record Macro Name text box to enter a name for your macro. (If you don't enter a name, Word names the macros you create Macrol, Macro2, and so on.) If you create a macro in a template or in a document that uses a template, you can limit your macro to the template by choosing the Template option in the Context area. If you choose Global, the macro is available in all documents. Finally, fill in a short description of the macro in the Description text box to jog your memory about the macro's use. If you add the macro to a menu, your description appears on the status bar whenever you highlight its menu command.

To start recording, choose the OK button. (Choosing Cancel closes the dialog box without recording.) The dialog box closes, and Word begins recording your actions. Choose menu commands, press key combinations, type text, or change formatting on the ribbon and ruler—perform any actions you want recorded. When you finish, choose Stop Recorder from the Macro menu. Word stops recording your actions and stores them under the macro name you entered.

An Example

Create a new template designed to create fiscal reports, and then create a macro for the template that creates and titles a 5-cell-by-5-cell table:

1. Choose New from the File menu. When the dialog box appears, use it to open a new template.
2. Choose Record from the Macro menu to open the Macro Record dialog box.
3. Enter the name *AddTable* in the Record Macro Name text box.
4. Choose the Template option in the Context area to make this macro a template macro.
5. Enter *Adds a sales report table* in the Description text box.
6. Choose the OK button to close the dialog box and start recording.
7. Set paragraph formatting to center alignment and character formatting to bold, type the title *Sales Report*, and then press Enter.
8. Return paragraph formatting to left alignment and turn off bold character formatting.

9. Choose Table from the Insert menu to open the Insert Table dialog box.
10. Enter *5* in both the Number of Columns text box and the Number of Rows text box and then choose OK to close the dialog box. A 5-cell-by-5-cell table appears.
11. Choose Stop Recorder from the Macro menu to stop recording your actions.

RUNNING A MACRO FROM A MACRO LIST

The simplest way to run a macro you've just recorded is to choose it from the Macro Run dialog box, shown in Figure 23-2. To open the box, choose Run from the Macro menu.

The Macro Run dialog box shows a list of all the macros you've created, including both global and template macros, that are available for your current template. To see Word's built-in macros, turn on the Show All option on the right side of the dialog box. Word adds over 200 built-in macros to the list so that you can run any of them. Turn off the Show All option to see once more only your own macros.

To run a macro, select the macro from the macro list or enter the macro's name in the Run Macro Name text box. The Description area at the bottom of the dialog box lists the description of that macro. Choose the OK button; the dialog box closes and the macro runs. (Choosing Cancel closes the box without running any macros.)

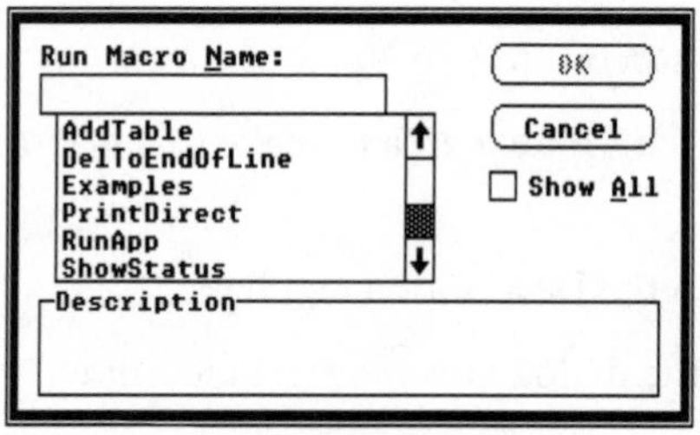

Figure 23-2. *The Macro Run dialog box.*

An Example

Try running the macro you just created. First, clear the template:

1. Select everything in the template and then press the Delete key to clear the template.
2. Choose Run from the Macro menu to open the Macro Run dialog box. You should see AddTable at the top of the macro list.
3. Select AddTable in the macro list. AddTable appears in the Run Macro Name text box, and its description appears in the Description area.
4. Choose OK to close the dialog box and run the Macro. The table title appears, and a 5-cell-by-5-cell table appears below it. (The Insert Table dialog box doesn't appear because Word doesn't need it to open dialog boxes when it runs a macro. Word already has the values it needs to execute the Insert Table command.)

EDITING A MACRO

If you want to change a macro you've recorded, choose Edit from the Macro menu to open the Macro Edit dialog box, shown in Figure 23-3.

The macro list in the dialog box shows the available macros, as the list in the Macro Run box does. To see only global custom macros, turn on the Global option in the Context area. To see only template custom macros, turn on the Template option. To also see Word's built-in macros, turn on the Show All option.

If you have the Special Edition with disks included, consult the Introduction

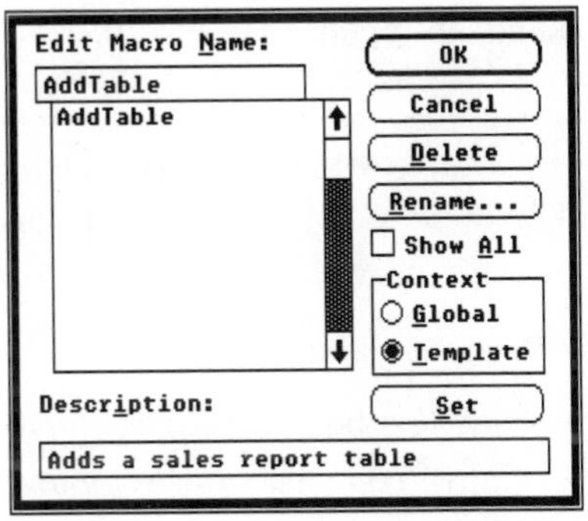

Figure 23-3. *The Macro Edit dialog box shown here lists the template macros.*

To edit a macro, first select it from the macro list or enter it by name in the Edit Macro Name text box. The Description text box then shows the macro's description (if it has one). After selecting a macro, you can perform simple editing changes in the dialog box. To change the macro's description, simply change the contents of the Description text box, and choose the Set button. To rename the macro, choose the Rename button; a second dialog box appears, where you enter a new name and choose OK. Word then renames the selected macro. To delete a selected macro, choose the Delete button. Word removes the macro from memory and from the macro list. Deletion is often the easiest form of editing a recorded macro: Once the macro's gone, you can use Macro Record to re-record it.

This kind of simple editing might be all you need if you record and run only simple macros. If so, choose Close to close the dialog box when you finish. Word remembers all the editing changes you made. To see the contents of a macro and change the Word Embedded Language commands, choose OK. Word opens a special window that lists the macro's contents. You can edit the contents as you see fit (read the Word *User's Reference* for a description of the Word Embedded Language), test them using the buttons in the Macro Edit icon bar at the top of the window, and then close the window and save your changes. Be sure you know what you're doing when you edit a macro: If you enter changes incorrectly, your macro might not work, or worse yet (in very rare cases), might delete files or close down Word in the middle of your work.

An Example

Change the name and description of your macro:

1. Choose Edit from the Macro menu to open the Macro Edit dialog box.
2. Select AddTable from the macro list. It appears in the Edit Macro Name text box, and its description appears in the Description text box.
3. Choose Rename to open the Macro Rename dialog box.
4. Change the text in the New Macro Name text box to *AddSalesTable* and then choose OK to close the dialog box. The macro name changes in the macro list.

5. Move to the Description text box and enter a new description: *Adds a 5-by-5 sales table.* Then choose Set to accept the description.
6. Choose Close to close the Macro Edit dialog box.

ASSIGNING A MACRO TO A KEY COMBINATION

To assign a macro to a key combination, choose Assign to Key from the Macro menu. The Macro Assign to Key dialog box (shown in Figure 23-4) appears.

The Assign Macro Name list shows all global macros if the Context area is set to Global, and it shows both global and template macros if the Context area is set to Template. Select Global in the context area to make the macro key assignment available in all documents or select Template to make the key assignment available only when using the current template. Global macros can have either Global or Template context, but template macros can have only Template context.

Select the name of the macro you want in the Assign Macro Name list. When you do, the Current Keys list shows any key combinations to which the macro is already assigned, and the description area displays the macro's description. Because you can assign a macro to more than one key combination, the Current Keys list has a scroll bar you can use to scroll through its list of key combinations.

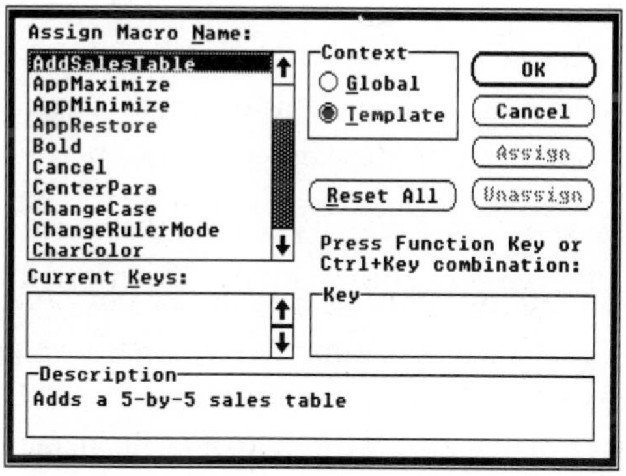

FIGURE 23-4. *The Macro Assign to Key dialog box shown here lists both global and template macros.*

To choose a key combination for assignment, try pressing any key combination you think will work. When you pick a key combination that Word can use, Word shows the combination in the Key area of the dialog box. If the combination is currently unassigned, the Key area says so. If the combination is already assigned to a macro, the Key area tells you which macro. Some of the key combinations to which you can assign a macro are:

- Ctrl plus another key
- Shift plus function keys 2 through 12, the Insert key, the Delete key, or some keys on the numeric keypad
- Ctrl plus Shift plus another key
- Any single function key, F2 through F12

Note that you can't use function key F1 for key combinations: It's reserved as a help key. If you press it, the Help window appears. Note also that most of the Ctrl-Shift combinations don't have built-in macros already assigned to them, so you can easily use them for your own macros.

To assign the selected macro to the key combination, choose the Assign button. If you assign a macro to a key combination already used for another macro, Word removes the first assignment and assigns the currently selected macro to the key combination. Although a key combination can run only one macro, a macro can be run from many different key combinations. Each time you assign a key combination to a macro, the combination is added to the Current Keys list.

To free a key combination from a macro, select the macro from the Assign Macro Name list and then select the key combination from the Current Keys list or press the key combination; it then appears in the Key area. Choose the Unassign button. Word removes the key combination from the Current Keys list and no longer runs a macro when you press the key combination.

Note that you can assign and unassign Word's default key combinations for built-in macros such as bold character formatting and centered paragraph alignment. If you think you've gone too far and want to return to the default key combinations, choose the Reset All button. Word reassigns the default key combinations to the appropriate built-in macros.

When you finish your macro assignments, choose the OK button or the Close button to close the dialog box. OK assigns the selected key combination to the selected macro. Neither the Close button nor the OK button affects any assignments or unassignments you made using the Assign and Unassign buttons.

To play back the macros you assigned, press the appropriate key combinations.

An Example

Assign your table macro to the key combination Ctrl-Shift-T:

1. Choose Assign to Key from the Macro menu to open the Macro Assign to Key dialog box.
2. Choose Template in the Context area to display both template and global macros.
3. Select the AddSalesTable macro from the top of the Assign Macro Name list. The Description area displays the macro's description. The Current Keys list shows no key combinations because you haven't yet assigned any to the macro.
4. Press Ctrl-Shift-T. The Key area shows the key combination and notes that it is currently unassigned.
5. Choose the Assign button to assign the key combination to the macro. The combination appears in the Current Keys list.
6. Choose OK to close the dialog box.
7. Clear the template by selecting all its contents and pressing Delete.
8. Press Ctrl-Shift-T. The macro runs, and a table appears in the text window.

ASSIGNING A MACRO TO A MENU

To assign a macro to a menu, choose Assign to Menu from the Macro menu. The Macro Assign to Menu dialog box appears (shown in Figure 23-5 on the following page).

Select the macro you want from the Assign Macro Name list. (Selecting template in the Context area shows both global and template macros.) The

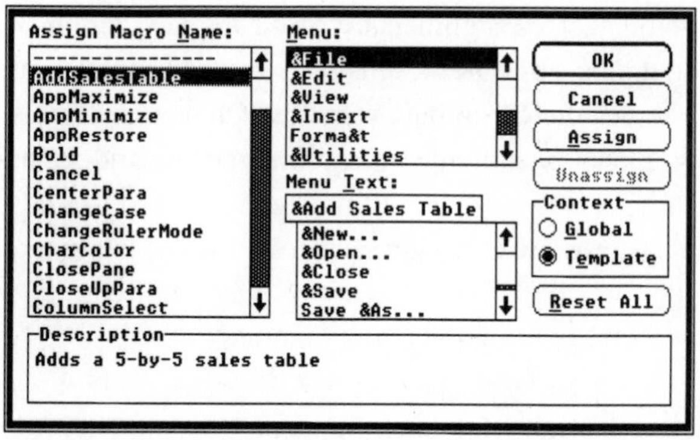

Figure 23-5. *The Macro Assign to Menu dialog box shown here lists both global and template macros.*

macro's name appears in the Menu Text text box, and its description appears in the Description area. Select the name of the menu you want from the Menu list. Its full contents appear in the menu contents list below the Menu Text text box. You can scroll through the list to see the commands in the menu. A dotted line represents a separator, one of the lines that divides a menu into groups of commands. The ampersand (&) in the command name appears immediately before the *key selection character*—the character that is underlined in the menu. When you select a menu command using the keyboard, you press this underlined character to choose the command.

When you select a macro from the Assign Macro Name list, the Menu Text text box shows the macro name and adds an ampersand before the first character. To change the text, enter your own command name and put the ampersand before any single character you want to use as the key selection character. Try to avoid a character already used in the menu. (Scroll through the menu commands to see what's available.)

To assign the selected macro to the selected menu using the menu text you entered, choose the Assign button. Word assigns the macro as a command at the end of the menu; you can see it if you scroll through the menu contents list. (Note that if you assign a template macro to a menu, it can have only Template context and appears only in the template's menus.) To add a separator to the menu, select it from the top of the Assign Macro Name list—it appears as a dashed line—and then assign it to the menu as you assign a macro.

To remove a command from a menu, select the command in the menu contents list. It then appears in the Menu Text text box. Choose Unassign; Word removes the command from the menu. Note that you can set the context to Global or Template so that Word removes the command from all menus or from only the menus that appear when you use the current template. Be careful, though, when you create custom menus. If you delete the Macro Assign to Menu command, you won't be able to get back to this dialog box to undo your changes. If you go too far changing menus and commands, you can always return to the default menus by choosing the Reset All button. If all else fails, you can quit Word, delete the WINWORD.INI file, and then restart Word. This resets all defaults so that Word appears as it did when you first installed and ran it.

Once you create custom menus for a template, those menus appear whenever you open that template or a document based on it. The custom menus remain in place as long as either the template or a document based on it is the active window. If you move to a window containing a different template, the menus change to fit that template.

To close the Macro Assign to Menu dialog box, choose OK. Word assigns the selected macro to the selected menu if the assignment hasn't been made and then closes the dialog box. Choosing Cancel (or Close) closes the dialog box without making an assignment. Neither the OK command nor the Close command affects assignments and unassignments you made with the Assign and Unassign buttons.

To use a macro assigned to a menu, open the menu and choose the macro's command; Word then runs the macro.

An Example

Assign your macro to the Insert menu as a command named "Sales Table":

1. Choose Assign to Menu from the Macro menu to open the Macro Assign to Menu dialog box.
2. Choose Template in the Context area to display both global and template macros.
3. Select the AddSalesTable macro from the Assign Macro Name list. It appears as &Add Sales Table in the Menu Text text box.

4. Select the Insert menu from the Menu list. Its contents appear in the list below the Menu Text text box.
5. Change the contents of the Menu Text text box to read *&Sales Table*. (No other command in the menu uses S as a key selection character, so S is a good choice.)
6. Choose the Assign button to add the macro to the insert menu. At the bottom of the menu contents list you will see &Sales Table.
7. Choose OK to close the dialog box.
8. Clear the template by selecting all its contents and pressing Delete.
9. Run the Macro by choosing Sales Table from the Insert menu. The 5-cell-by-5-cell table appears in the text window.

Now that you're finished with the macro examples, you can get rid of them by closing the template without saving it. To save the macro examples, simply save the template. Any time you use the template, the macro and the custom menus and key combinations reappear.

ADDITIONAL MACRO POSSIBILITIES

Using macros effectively is a matter of degree. If you watch for repetitive tasks and record them as macros, you'll soon create a library of custom macros that make your document creation much easier. If you take some additional time to create customized template menus and key combinations, you can make your work even easier.

You might want to learn to program macros in a macro editing window. By doing this, you can create macros that are impossible to record. The Word Embedded Language is structured much like the BASIC programming language, so you can create conditional loops to repeat an action many times or to test for certain conditions before executing the rest of the macro. You can also use a variety of special commands that aren't available using standard Word actions. For example, you can create a macro that opens another Windows program and returns data from that program.

You can create some macros that run automatically: These are a special set of macros called *auto macros*. One auto macro runs when you open a new document, another runs when you open an existing document, and a third runs when you start Word for the first time. Auto macros are good for performing standard preparatory work such as opening a document based on a favorite template or opening and arranging a set of documents in windows so that you have access to all the documents.

Macros can range from recordings of extremely simple actions to professional programming efforts. As you create more and more useful macros, you can trade them with other people by saving the macros in a template and swapping templates. You'll find a large library of macros (in addition to the built-in macros) on the Word for Windows disks, a good place to start a macro collection. As professional macros appear, you should be able to buy more programmed macros that add powerful capabilities to Word. Collect as many good macros as you can; they will save you a great deal of work.

A QUICK SUMMARY

This chapter introduced you to macros, showing you first the principles behind macros and then how to use them. You learned how to record a macro, run it from a macro list, edit it, assign it to a key combination, and assign it to a menu. The end of the chapter gave you some ideas for further macro uses. In the next chapter, you meet another important Word tool: fields.

Chapter 24

Fields:

Giving Special Instructions to Word

Fields are instructions embedded in a document; Word for Windows follows these instructions each time you print the document. This chapter introduces you to fields, explaining what they do and how they're constructed. You learn to insert your own fields in a document, view fields as a set of instructions or as the results of the instructions, and edit fields to get different results. The chapter goes on to introduce you to some simple field types and ends with suggestions for further field use.

SETTING UP WORD

Use standard Word settings for this chapter:

- Full menus
- A text window that shows the ruler, ribbon, and status bar
- The Display as Printed option turned off

The sample document for this chapter is a template you create as the owner of a chain of astrological-prediction outlets. Each outlet runs Word for Windows; the astrologer simply opens your template and enters the prediction for the client. The template uses fields to fill in the day's date, the astrologer's name, and the number of words in the prediction so that the cashier, who charges the client five cents per word, can ring up the total bill. Figure 24-1 on the following page shows a filled-in example of the template in use.

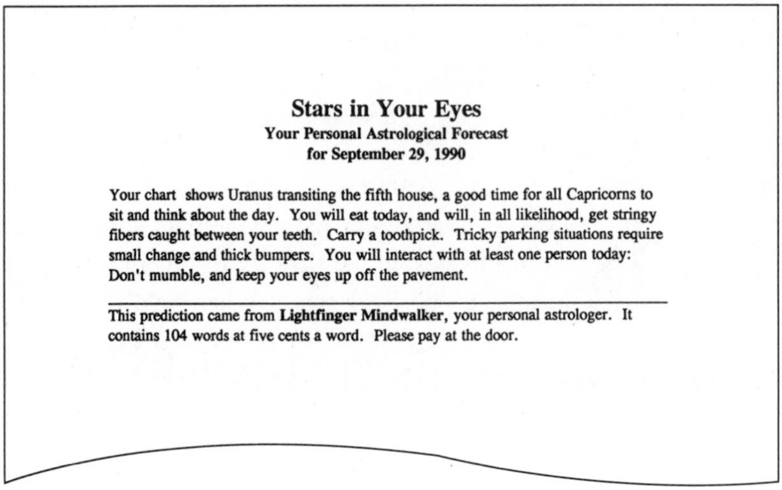

Stars in Your Eyes
Your Personal Astrological Forecast
for September 29, 1990

Your chart shows Uranus transiting the fifth house, a good time for all Capricorns to sit and think about the day. You will eat today, and will, in all likelihood, get stringy fibers caught between your teeth. Carry a toothpick. Tricky parking situations require small change and thick bumpers. You will interact with at least one person today: Don't mumble, and keep your eyes up off the pavement.

This prediction came from **Lightfinger Mindwalker**, your personal astrologer. It contains 104 words at five cents a word. Please pay at the door.

Figure 24-1. *Word fields fill in dates, names, and word counts in the template for this document.*

AN OVERVIEW OF FIELDS

A field instructs Word to fill in a piece of current information or to perform an action when you print or repaginate a document. In earlier chapters, you used fields to insert the day's date, the time, or the current page number in headers and footers. Fields can also provide information from the document's summary such as the author's name, the word count, the current filename, or the subject. If you need to import information from another Windows application, a field can pull out current data from compatible program files such as Microsoft Excel spreadsheets. Fields can also perform actions such as calculating mathematical expressions, numbering items in a document, compiling an index or a table of contents, controlling a printer with precise printer commands, or running a macro.

Using Fields

To use a field, you first insert it in a document by choosing the Insert Field command or by pressing Ctrl-F9. You have a choice of field types—each type performs a different task. After you insert the field, Word shows you the information the field produces (called the *field result*) and then does not update the result again until you print the document, repaginate, or tell Word to update the field. For example, when you insert a time field, Word shows the current time when you insert the field. As the seconds and minutes pass by, the time inserted in the document remains the same. When you print the document, Word replaces the old time with the current time.

Word usually shows the result of a field and not the field itself. If you ask to see *field codes* (the text that makes up the field itself), Word replaces field results throughout the document with field codes. When field codes are visible, you can see the location of each field in the document, the field type, and any further operating instructions the field contains. (Figure 24-2 shows an example of field codes within a document.) You can edit the contents of each field code to change the result of the field. When you're finished, you can then tell Word to show the field results again instead of the field codes.

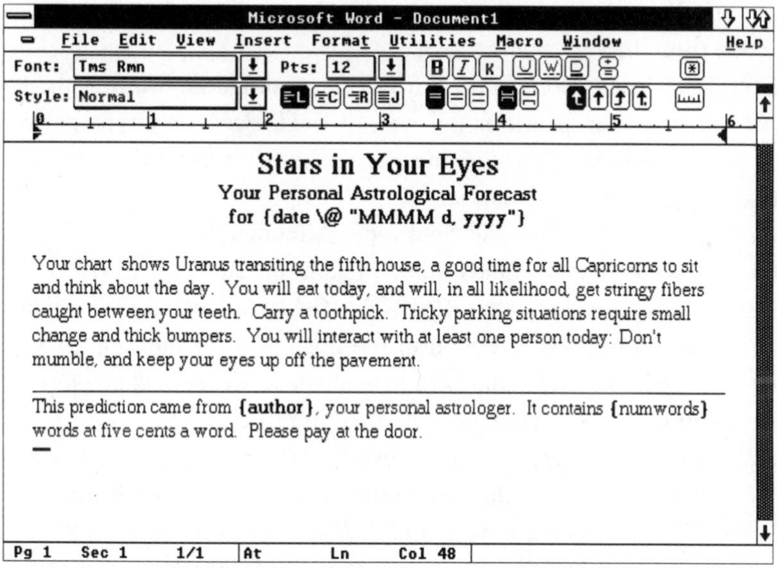

Figure 24-2. *When you ask to see field codes, Word shows the contents of each field instead of each field's result.*

The Parts of a Field

Each field code can include as many as four different field parts: *field characters, field type, field instructions,* and *field switches.* Figure 24-3 shows all of these parts.

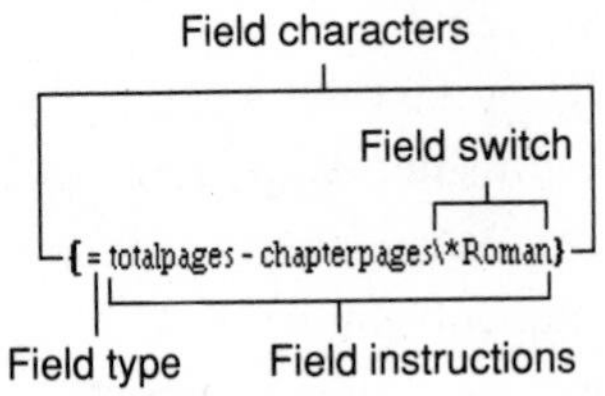

Figure 24-3. *A field code shows the parts of a field.*

Each field must be enclosed within two *field characters.* Although the characters look like braces, they aren't. You can enter them only by inserting a field, and they appear only in pairs. Field characters set off the enclosed field code from the surrounding text.

Each field must also contain a *field type,* a single keyword at the beginning of the field that identifies the type of field. Each field type performs a different function such as inserting a page number, inserting the author's name, or performing a calculation.

Field instructions follow the field type. Although field instructions aren't always necessary—many fields don't include instructions at all—you can use instructions to modify the effect of a field. An instruction might be a bookmark that designates a section of the document for the field to act in, a mathematical expression for the field to evaluate, a string of characters for the field to insert in the document, or other field modifiers.

Field switches change the field's default actions or set the field's formatting. Like instructions, switches are optional and need not be included in the field code. Each switch starts with a backslash (\) and is followed by a single character and sometimes by *arguments,* strings of characters that tell Word how to apply the switch to the field. An example is a switch that tells the date field how to display a date: Among other possibilities, it can show the date in the formats *1/9/90; January 9, 1990;* and *9-Jan-90.*

INSERTING FIELDS

You can insert a field in a document by using either of two methods: choosing Field from the Insert menu or pressing Ctrl-F9. The Insert Field command opens a dialog box that lists available field types, instructions, and switches. Use it when you want to see the choices available to you. If you know exactly the text of the field code you want to insert, use Ctrl-F9.

The Insert Field Dialog Box

Choose Field from the Insert Menu to open the Insert Field dialog box (shown in Figure 24-4).

The Insert Field Type list box shows all the field types available in Word. The three categories of field types are:

- Result field types, which insert information in a document. The date field, which inserts the date in a document, is a result field.
- Action field types, which tell Word to act on a document without inserting information. The macrobutton field, which tells Word to run a macro, is an action field type.
- Marker field types, which provide a reference for other fields to act on. The index entry field, which marks a section of text to be referred to in an index, is a marker field type.

When you select a field type from the list, the appropriate code for that field type appears in the Field Code text box in the bottom of the dialog box. The line below the text box prompts you for further information you might

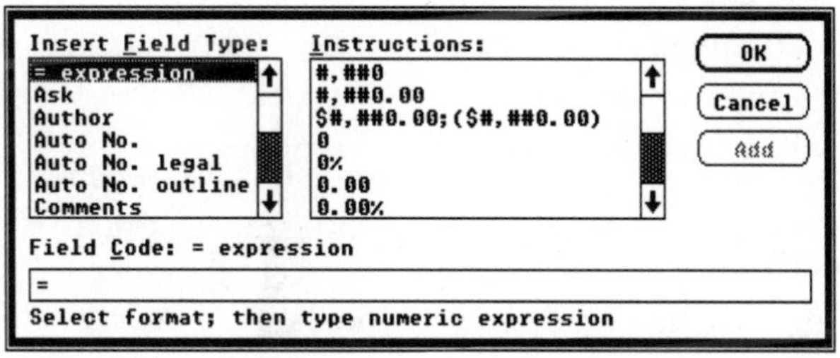

Figure 24-4. *The Insert Field dialog box.*

enter after the field type, and the line above the text box (following the Field Code label) shows the field type code in uppercase letters, followed by lowercase words that tell you the kinds of instructions and switches you can use with the field type.

For example, if you select Print from the field type list, the code "print" appears in the Field Code text box. The line below the text box reads "Type printer codes or PostScript code," telling you to enter literal codes or PostScript printer codes for Word to send directly to the printer for exact printer control. The line above the text box reads PRINT "printer-instructions," showing you that printer instructions are the kind of instructions used in the print field. Of course, this information is only a memory jogger. For exact information about the field type and the kinds of instructions and switches you use with it, consult the section on fields in the Word *User's Reference*.

To add instructions or switches to your selected field type, enter them directly into the Field Code text box following the field type name, or choose them from the Instructions list box. Each time you select a field type in the Insert Field Type list box, the Instructions list box shows possible variations on the effect of that field type. It doesn't list all possible variations and, in fact, doesn't list any variations for some field types, but it does show the most common ones available. To include a variation in the field code, select it in the Instruction list box and then choose the Add button. Word adds the appropriate instructions or switches for that variation to the Field Code text box. You can use the Instructions list box and the Add button to insert several instructions in the same field if you like.

After you enter the field type and any instructions or switches you want in the Field Code text box, choose OK to close the dialog box and insert the field at the current insertion-point location. If you insert a result field, Word shows the result of the field where you inserted the field. Choose Cancel to close the dialog box without inserting a field.

The Field Insertion Key

To type a field code directly into a document, type the field code where you want the field located and then select the field code text as a text block. Press Ctrl-F9: Word adds field characters on each end of the text block, turning it into a field. To leave the field and continue entering regular text, simply move the insertion point out of the field code. Word doesn't show the result of your field code until you update the field (as you learn to do later in the chapter), print, or repaginate the document.

Inserting a Field Directly from a Menu

Word offers three commands in the Insert menu that insert fields directly into a document: Index Entry, Index, and Table of Contents. These commands insert fields that create indexes and tables of contents. (You can read more about creating indexes and tables of contents in the Word *User's Reference*.) The commands are offered because these field types are used most often. If you have other fields you insert regularly, you can add them to the Insert menu using Word's macro feature.

An Example

Start the sample template and insert a date field to show the current date:

1. Use the File New command to open a new template.
2. Turn on bold character formatting and centered paragraph alignment, select 18-point Tms Rmn characters, and then type the line *Stars in Your Eyes* and press Enter.
3. Reduce the point size to 12 points and then type the line *Your Personal Astrological Forecast*. Press Enter.
4. Type *for* followed by a space.
5. Choose Field from the Insert menu to open the Insert Field dialog box.
6. Select Date from the Insert Field Type list box. A set of different date formats appears in the Instructions list box, and the Field Code text box shows the code *date*.
7. Select the date format *MMMM d, yyyy* from the Instructions list box and then choose the Add button. The Field Code text box now shows the code *date \@ "MMMM d, yyyy"*. (The date format is a switch that tells Word to show the date as the full name of the month followed by the day of the month, a comma, and the year in four figures.)

8. Choose the OK button to close the dialog box. Word inserts today's date in the field location.
9. Press Enter to start a new line. Then turn off bold character formatting and set left paragraph alignment.
10. Press Enter twice more to move to a new line. This leaves an open line at the top and a line below the open line for entering an astrological prediction.

VIEWING FIELDS

After you insert fields in a document, you can view either the field results or the field codes. To switch between seeing field results and field codes throughout the entire document, choose Field Codes from the View menu. This is a toggle command: The first time you choose it, you show field codes. The second time you choose it, you show field results. To change the view in a text block without changing it in the rest of the document, select the text you want and then press Shift-F9. This key combination toggles the view only within the text block.

Splitting a text window into two panes enables you to view field codes and results simultaneously. When you move the insertion point to a pane and use the View Field Codes command to show either field codes or field results, the command affects only the pane you're in. By scrolling each pane to show the same section of a document, you can view the fields in one pane as field codes and those in the other pane as field results. This is a useful editing feature when you want to change the field codes and check the field results.

Locating Fields

When fields are scattered throughout a long document, you can find them easily by making the insertion point and the view jump from field to field. Pressing F11 (or Alt-F1) moves the insertion point forward to the next field in the document. Pressing Shift-F11 (or Shift-Alt-F1) moves the insertion point back to the previous field.

An Example

Look at the field you inserted to see both the field code and the field result:

1. Split the window into two equal-sized panes.
2. Scroll the lower pane to show the same text as the upper pane and leave the insertion point in the lower pane.
3. Choose Field Codes from the View menu. The bottom pane changes to show the date field code. The upper pane still shows the actual date, not the field code that creates the date.
4. Choose Field Codes again from the View menu to see the field result and then close the lower pane.

EDITING AND FORMATTING FIELDS

You can edit and format field codes, or you can edit and format field results. When you edit a field code, you change the field and any information it inserts in the document. When you edit a field result, you change the information in the document, but you don't change the field, so the next time you print the document, repaginate, or update the fields, your changes disappear as the field reinserts the information.

Editing and Formatting Field Codes

To work on field codes, you must first set the view to show field codes in the text window. You can then change the contents of a field by moving the insertion point between the field characters and editing the text the way you would edit regular text. You can insert and delete characters, and you can also select text blocks and then cut and paste them. You can't delete the left or right field character using the Delete key or the Backspace key. You can't cut them individually, either: As soon as you select either the left field character or the right field character, Word selects the entire field code, including both field characters and the text in between. To delete an entire field, select it and then press the Delete key.

The first character following the left field character has a special role in the field. When you apply any character formatting to this character, Word applies the same formatting to all characters in the field result. For example, if you format the first character of the date field code for italic, when Word inserts the date in the document, it uses italic text. Any formatting you apply to the rest of the field code has no effect on the field result (unless you use a picture switch, which is a special field switch that fully controls the format of the field result). It's often easiest, however, to change the entire field code's format rather than only the first character of the field code.

Nesting fields

If you move the insertion point within the field characters, you can *nest* fields by inserting fields within the field code, exactly as you insert fields anywhere else in the document. For example, you can nest the numchars and the numwords fields within an = expression field: {= {numchars}/{numwords}} uses nested fields to calculate the average number of characters in each word of a document.

Editing and Formatting Field Results

When a field inserts information in a document, you can edit and format the inserted text if you set the view to show field results. When you select the inserted text, if you select either the first character or the last character of the text, Word selects all the inserted text. If you avoid the first and last characters, you can select individual characters between them and then format or cut and paste them. To remove the first character, place the insertion point directly after it and press Backspace. To remove the last character, place the insertion point directly before it and press Delete.

If you select the field result and then change its character formatting, Word changes the formatting in the field code to match. The next time the field inserts information during an update, the new information uses the same character formatting. For example, if you italicize the date that the date field inserts, Word changes all the characters in the date field code to italic. When you update fields or print a document, the field inserts a new date using italic characters.

An Example

Enter the first sentence in the bottom part of the template and use the author field to insert the author's name in the sentence. Enter a second sentence that uses the numwords field to insert the number of words in the document into the sentence. Format the author field so that the name appears in boldface:

1. Use the Underline key (Shift-Minus) to type a line across the width of the page. Press Enter.
2. Type *This prediction came from* and then type a space.
3. Type *author*. Then select it as a text block.
4. Press Ctrl-F9 to turn the block into a field code. Word encloses the word "author" in a pair of field characters.
5. Press End to move the insertion point out of the field code, just to the right of the last field character. Type a comma and a space, followed by *your personal astrologer*.
6. Type two spaces and start the next sentence by typing *It contains* followed by a space.
7. Type *numwords*. Then select it and press Ctrl-F9 to turn it into a field.
8. Move the insertion point out of the field, just to the right of the last field character.
9. Type a space followed by *words at five cents a word. Please pay at the door*.
10. Select the entire author field.
11. Turn on bold character formatting so that the field code appears in boldface characters. Figure 24-5 shows the result.
12. Save the template with the filename FORECAST.DOT.
13. Close the template.

Stars in Your Eyes
Your Personal Astrological Forecast
for {date \@ "MMMM d, yyyy"}

This prediction came from **{author}**, your personal astrologer. It contains {numwords} words at five cents a word. Please pay at the door.

Figure 24-5. *The sample template in the text window, showing field codes.*

UPDATING FIELDS

Every time you print or repaginate a document, Word updates most of the fields in the document. (Some special fields don't update in the same way as the regular fields do—the Word *User's Reference* explains how these work.) To update fields before you print or repaginate, be sure the view is set to show field results, select a text block that contains all the fields you want updated, and then press F9. Word updates all fields in the text block and inserts a fresh result for each result field.

To lock a field's result so that it won't be updated, select the field (or its result) and press Ctrl-F11 (or Ctrl-Alt-F1). If you then select the field and press F9, the field result doesn't change. To unlock the field for updating, select it and press Ctrl-Shift-F11 (or Ctrl-Shift-Alt-F1). If a field inserts information in a document that you want to keep without ever updating again, you can unlink that information from the field by selecting the field result and pressing Ctrl-Shift-F9. Word then turns the information into regular document text and deletes the field that inserted the information.

An Example

Try updating all fields in a document. First open a new document using the template you created earlier and then change the number of words in the document and update the fields to see the information change to match:

1. Open a new document based on the FORECAST template you created earlier. The last sentence contains a rough estimate of the number of words in the document.
2. Move the insertion point to the empty paragraph above the divider line, and type the astrological prediction as it's shown in the sample document. Notice that the numwords field doesn't change to show the new number of words.
3. Select the entire document and then press F9. The last sentence changes to show a new approximation of the number of words.

If you took time to count the words in your document yourself, you probably noticed that the word count in the numwords field was not too accurate. This is because Word has yet to count the number of words in the document, so it creates an estimate based on the number of characters in the document. Once you print the document or ask Word to update the statistics in the Statistics dialog box (opened through Edit Summary Info), Word knows the exact number of words in the document and can accurately update the numwords field. Before you print a document with a numwords field for the first time, you should first update the document's statistics using the Summary Info and Statistics dialog boxes so that the field results will be accurate when you print.

If you noticed that customers are being charged for words in the title and bottom paragraph, you're much too astute to pay Stars in Your Eyes for this astrological forecast!

SIMPLE FIELD TYPES

To use fields effectively, you should take time to read about the different field types listed in the "Fields" sections of the Word *User's Reference*. Although some of these field types are complex and take some time and experimentation to understand, most field types are simple and insert useful information in your documents. You'll find a whole family of field types—such as keywords, subject, and savedate—that insert different parts of a document's summary into the document. You'll also find three field types—date, time, and page—that you can use in the body of a document as well as in headers and footers to insert the current date, time, and page number.

Another field type, fillin, opens a box that asks you to enter needed information. You enter a prompt in the field code that Word repeats when it opens the box. When you enter a reply to the prompt, Word inserts the reply in the document. For example, you can use fillin to ask for a current invoice number in a shipping form. When you create the field, you add *"Invoice number?"* as a prompt instruction in the field code. When you print the shipping form, Word first opens a dialog box that asks "Invoice number?" After you enter the invoice number, Word inserts the number in the field location and then prints the shipping form.

The = expression field type resolves mathematical expressions and inserts the results into the document. It's especially useful when used with nested fields. For example, if you wanted the astrology template to compute and print the amount of money owed for the forecast, you would use the field code {= {numwords}*.05 \# $0.00}. The mathematical expression {numwords}*.05

uses a nested field to multiply the number of words in the document by five cents. The switch \# $0.00 asks the field to print the result with a dollar sign before it and two decimal places to the right of the decimal point.

ADDITIONAL FIELD POSSIBILITIES

As you learn to combine advanced fields, you can achieve some useful results:

- You can mark sections of text as index entries using the index entry field. The insert index field compiles all these entries, creating an index with entries and subentries. If you revise the document, the index changes, if necessary, to show new page numbers.
- You can compile a table of contents by using the table of contents field. It collects heading paragraphs throughout the document and shows them in order with page numbers. You can control the level of the headings the field collects, and you can also assign nonheading text to be collected by the field. As you revise the document, the table of contents changes, if necessary, to show new page numbers.
- You can insert text from a bookmark elsewhere in the same document or in another document.
- You can insert data from a Microsoft Excel spreadsheet or other compatible Windows application. As the data in the spreadsheet changes, the information the field inserts changes with it.
- You can go beyond the capabilities of the Renumber command to renumber paragraphs in different styles, including legal numbering and outline numbering. You can also set up independent series of numbering intermixed within the same text, so you can independently number a series of figure titles, a series of table titles, and a series of figure captions in the same document.
- You can calculate using the contents of table cells, turning a table into a simple spreadsheet within a document.
- You can use a field to test a condition in a document and then act on the result of the test. For example, a field can test to see whether

an outstanding balance is greater or less than $1,000. If the balance is greater, Word can print an urgent plea for money; if it's less, Word can print a polite request for payment.

- You can insert complex mathematical formulas on the screen and in the printout. The formula field creates and displays arrays, brackets, fractions, integrals, and other mathematical symbols and formulaic conventions.
- You can directly control a printer by using the print field to send printer *literals* (direct commands) to the printer. This feature is especially useful for creating special printing effects on PostScript-controlled printers.
- You can run a macro. The macrobutton field displays a string of text in the text window. If you click on the field or the display text, Word runs the macro you set in the field code. Use this feature to create "buttons" throughout a document that the user clicks on to run a macro.

A QUICK SUMMARY

This chapter introduced you to the basics of fields. You learned the four parts of a typical field and saw how to insert a field in a document. You also learned how to change the view to show either field codes or field results, saw how to edit and format both field codes and field results, and then learned how to update the fields without printing to see the result of your editing work. The last part of the chapter introduced you to some simple field types and went on to show you some of the possibilities available if you learn more about advanced fields. In the next chapter, you learn to use fields in combination with the File Print Merge command to create form letters and similar documents.

Chapter 25

Printing Form Letters by Merging Documents

Form letters are an integral part of life in the twentieth century. They call us directly by name; they inform, implore, and cajole us into action. Now you can strike back by using Word for Windows to send out form letters of your own—this chapter shows you how. You learn how to create a main document, inserting fields where you want text to change from letter to letter. You then learn how to create a data document containing the changing text and use the File Print Merge command to merge both documents to create a run of form letters. The last part of the chapter gives you some ideas for other print-merging possibilities.

SETTING UP WORD

Use the standard settings for this chapter (and also set Word to show field codes):

- Full menus
- A text window that shows the ruler, ribbon, and status bar
- The Display as Printed option turned off
- The View Field Codes option turned on

The four sample documents shown in Figure 25-1 on the following pages are brief form letters created using Word's print-merging features.

A

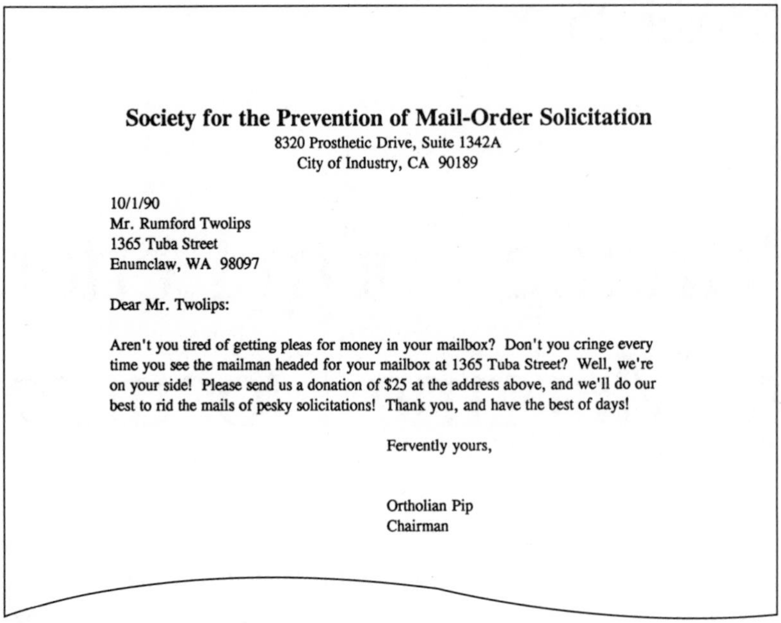

Society for the Prevention of Mail-Order Solicitation
8320 Prosthetic Drive, Suite 1342A
City of Industry, CA 90189

10/1/90
Mr. Rumford Twolips
1365 Tuba Street
Enumclaw, WA 98097

Dear Mr. Twolips:

Aren't you tired of getting pleas for money in your mailbox? Don't you cringe every time you see the mailman headed for your mailbox at 1365 Tuba Street? Well, we're on your side! Please send us a donation of $25 at the address above, and we'll do our best to rid the mails of pesky solicitations! Thank you, and have the best of days!

Fervently yours,

Ortholian Pip
Chairman

B

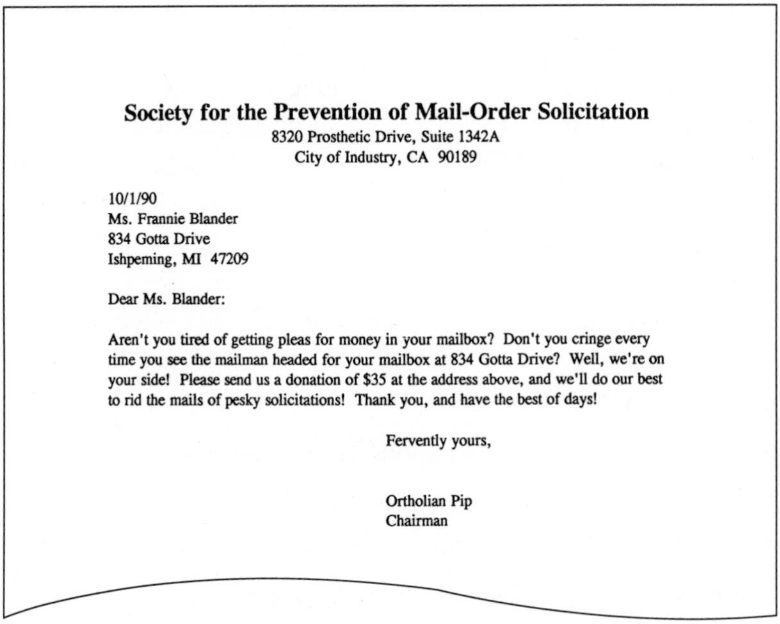

Society for the Prevention of Mail-Order Solicitation
8320 Prosthetic Drive, Suite 1342A
City of Industry, CA 90189

10/1/90
Ms. Frannie Blander
834 Gotta Drive
Ishpeming, MI 47209

Dear Ms. Blander:

Aren't you tired of getting pleas for money in your mailbox? Don't you cringe every time you see the mailman headed for your mailbox at 834 Gotta Drive? Well, we're on your side! Please send us a donation of $35 at the address above, and we'll do our best to rid the mails of pesky solicitations! Thank you, and have the best of days!

Fervently yours,

Ortholian Pip
Chairman

Figure 25-1. *Word merges two documents to create this run of four form letters.*

C

Society for the Prevention of Mail-Order Solicitation
8320 Prosthetic Drive, Suite 1342A
City of Industry, CA 90189

10/1/90
Rev. Ollie Bortalk
12 Wildside Walk, Apt. #2
Thibodaux, LA

Dear Rev. Bortalk:

Aren't you tired of getting pleas for money in your mailbox? Don't you cringe every time you see the mailman headed for your mailbox at 12 Wildside Walk, Apt. #2? Well, we're on your side! Please send us a donation of $10 at the address above, and we'll do our best to rid the mails of pesky solicitations! Thank you, and have the best of days!

Fervently yours,

Ortholian Pip
Chairman

D

Society for the Prevention of Mail-Order Solicitation
8320 Prosthetic Drive, Suite 1342A
City of Industry, CA 90189

10/1/90
Dr. John Smith
4321 Main Street
Anytown, PA 29303

Dear Dr. Smith:

Aren't you tired of getting pleas for money in your mailbox? Don't you cringe every time you see the mailman headed for your mailbox at 4321 Main Street? Well, we're on your side! Please send us a donation of $100 at the address above, and we'll do our best to rid the mails of pesky solicitations! Thank you, and have the best of days!

Fervently yours,

Ortholian Pip
Chairman

AN OVERVIEW OF PRINT MERGING

Creating form letters with Word is a three-step process called print merging. The three steps are:

- Creating a main document
- Creating a data document
- Choosing File Print Merge to merge the two documents and create a run of form letters

When you create a *main document,* you create the document that contains the fixed text of the letter. Fixed text doesn't change from one letter to the next—it's usually the main body of information within the letter. You show Word where to insert changing text (such as names and addresses) within the main document by inserting a field for each element of changing text.

When you create a *data document,* you create a second document that contains a set of *records* that Word uses to fill in the fields inserted in the main document. Each record in the data document contains the information for one version of the form letter. The information within each record is separated into discrete parts called *data items.* Each changing text field in the main document corresponds to one data item.

After you create both the main document and the data document and save them onto disk, you move to the main document and choose Print Merge from the File menu. Word inserts the first set of data items from the data document into the fields of the main document and then prints the letter. After printing, Word replaces the field results with the second set of data items from the data document and prints a second letter. It continues to work through all the records of the document, printing letters until there are no more records to insert.

CREATING A MAIN DOCUMENT

To create a main document, start a new document using the File New command. Insert a special field called a *data field* at the beginning of the document to prepare it for print merging. As you type the rest of your document, insert a *bookmark field* wherever you want Word to insert changing text.

The Data Field

The data field is an action field that tells Word to look for a data document and then retrieve information from that document during print merging. You must insert the data field in the beginning of the main document, in a location that precedes any bookmark field. Because the data field is an action field, it doesn't insert results, so you can insert it without interfering with the text around it.

To insert the data field, move the insertion point to a location somewhere in the beginning of the document and choose Insert Field or press Ctrl-F9. Enter the field code so that it starts with the field type "data" and then includes the data document filename as a field instruction. For example, {Data address.doc} is a data field that tells Word to look for data in a document named ADDRESS.DOC when print merging. If you don't insert a data field at the beginning of the main document, you'll have trouble when you print or update the fields—Word won't know where to find the data to fill the fields and will give you error messages.

Bookmark Fields

A bookmark field is a field that contains only a bookmark name—it has no field type. When Word updates a bookmark field, it looks for the contents of that bookmark and inserts them as the field results. To insert a bookmark field, move the insertion point to a location where you want to insert changing text and press Ctrl-F9. Then enter a suitable bookmark name as the field code. Use a single word that reminds you of the changing text to be inserted, but be careful to avoid the names of field types. For example, "name" and "address" work well as bookmark names, but if you use "title," Word will interpret it as the title field code and insert the title of your document instead of reading it as a bookmark and inserting changing text.

To insert the same changing text in different locations, use the same bookmark name. For example, if you want to insert a person's first name in the top of the form letter and then use it again in the body of the letter, use the same field for both places—perhaps something like {firstname}. You might also want to add nonbookmark fields—a date field, for example, to insert the date at the top of the document.

An Example

Create the main document for the sample form letter, using the screen contents of Figure 25-2 as a guide. The bookmark fields you use supply the name and address of the recipient and an estimate (a bookmark field named estsum) of the amount the recipient can donate.

1. Open a new document using the File New command.
2. Set paragraph formatting to centered alignment.
3. Use boldface 18-point Tms Rmn characters to enter *Society for the Prevention of Mail-Order Solicitation.* Press Enter.
4. Turn off bold formatting, reduce the character size to 12 points, and then enter the next two lines of text.
5. On a line of its own following the last two lines you entered, press Ctrl-F9 to enter a field.

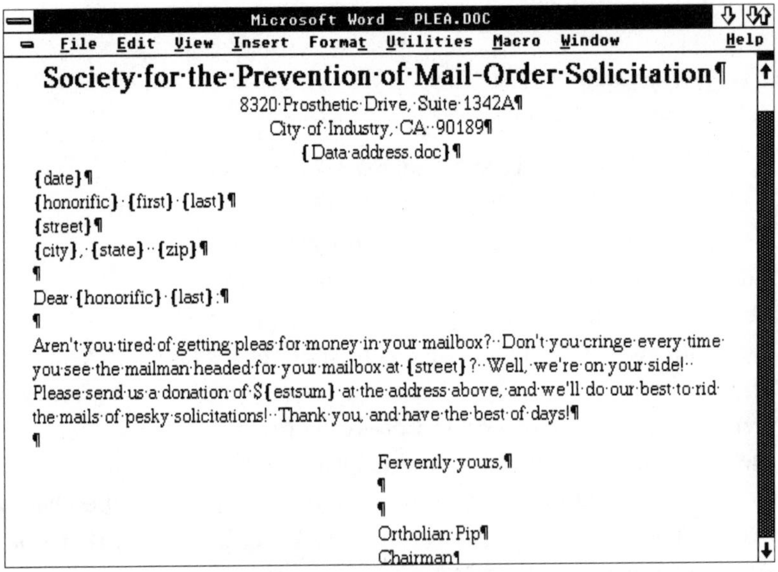

Figure 25-2. *This main document shows the field codes necessary for merging as well as spaces and paragraph marks for easy text entry. It's shown without the ruler, ribbon, and status bar so that you can see the full text in one screen.*

6. Enter the field code *Data address.doc* within the field characters. This sets up a data field that tells Word to look for the data document named ADDRESS.DOC.
7. Move the insertion point out of the field to the end of the line and press Enter to start a new line.
8. Set paragraph formatting to left alignment.
9. Enter the rest of the document as it appears in Figure 25-2. Be sure to put spaces and punctuation between fields as they are shown. Use a 3-inch left indent to align the closing (starting with "Fervently yours,").
10. Use the File Save As command to save the document under the name of PLEA.

CREATING A DATA DOCUMENT

The information in a data document is arranged as records and data items. The first record in the document is the *header record,* a record that lists the bookmark name for each data item in the records that follow it. The records that follow are called *structured data records.* Each data item within a structured data record contains the text for a single bookmark field in the main document, and each record contains the data items necessary to fill all the bookmarks in the main document.

Separators

As you enter data items, you must separate each one from the next by entering a comma or by pressing Tab. If you use commas as data-item separators, use them as separators throughout the data document. Likewise, if you use tabs, use them throughout the data document: You can't mix tabs and commas as separators. At the end of each record, press Enter. The paragraph mark separates each record from the following one.

As an example, the following line contains one structured data record with five data items separated by commas. The end of the line contains a paragraph mark (invisible here) that separates the record from any records following it in the data document:

Mark,Time,1276 Galaxy Way,Scranton,PA

Notice that there are no spaces preceding or following each comma separator. If you include a space, Word retrieves that space as the first or last character of the data item, which can throw off spacing when the item is inserted in the main document. Notice also that there are spaces in the middle of "1276 Galaxy Way." These spaces are part of the data item, and Word inserts them in the main document with the rest of the text. To enter a comma as part of a data item separated by comma separators, use a backslash before the comma. For example, "1276 Galaxy Way\, Apt. 34" is inserted in the main document as "1276 Galaxy Way, Apt. 34."

The Header Record

The first record in a data document *must* be a header record so that Word knows the bookmark name for each data item in the records that follow it. These bookmark names must exactly match the bookmark names you used in fields of the main document; otherwise, Word won't be able to find the information it needs in the data document. As an example, the header record for an address data document might be:

firstname,lastname,street,city,state

Word doesn't insert any of the names in the header into the main document during print merging—it moves to the structured data records to find the actual insertion data.

Structured Data Records

When you enter structured data records below the header record, it's very important that each record contain the same number of data items as the header record. If not, Word gives you an error message when you try to merge the records. If you're missing the information necessary for a data item, you can enter an empty data item by typing two separators, one after another. For example, if you didn't know Mark Time's street address, you could enter his record as:

Mark,Time,,Scranton,PA

Word then reads the third data item as empty during a print merge and inserts nothing at its bookmark field in the main document.

It's also important that you enter the data items in the same order as the names in the header record. It's not necessary, however, that the order of data items in the data document match the order of bookmark fields in the main document. For example, a main document might ask for data items in the order "firstname," "lastname," "address," "firstname." If the data document lists them in records using the order "lastname," "firstname," "address," it makes no difference. Word still retrieves the information it needs and inserts it in the proper bookmark field locations.

If you create an orderly data document, you can easily see where data is missing or misaligned. A simple way to do this is to use the Insert Table command to create a table with the same number of columns as you have data items. Enter the header record in the first row of the table, one data item per cell. Then fill in rows below with structured data records, lining up data items in the column below the appropriate item in the header record.

Once you finish creating the data document, you must save it under the name you used in the data field of the main document. If you don't save the document or if you save it under a different name, Word won't be able to find it for print merging.

An Example

Create and save a data document for the main document you created earlier. (In this example, you will not use the Insert Table command.)

1. Open a new document using the File New command.
2. Enter the header record as it's shown in Figure 25-3 on the following page. It must be the first line of the document, and you should be sure the spelling of each data-item name exactly matches the spelling you used in the main document bookmark fields. Press Enter at the end of the record.
3. Enter the four structured data records that follow, separating each data item with a comma and ending each record by pressing Enter. Notice that the third record uses a "\" to enter a comma in the data item and that the zip code is missing—its data item is simply two commas following "LA."

4. Use the File Save As command to save the document under the name ADDRESS, the filename you gave in the data field of the main document.
5. Close the data document and return to the main document.

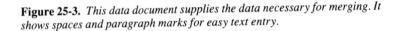

```
honorific,first,last,street,city,state,zip,estsum¶
Mr.,Rumford,Twolips,1365·Tuba·Street,Enumclaw,WA,98097,25¶
Ms.,Frannie,Blander,834·Gotta·Drive,Ishpeming,MI,47209,35¶
Rev.,Ollie,Bortalk,12·Wildside·Walk\,·Apt.·#2,Thibodaux,LA,,10¶
Dr.,John,Smith,4321·Main·Street,Anytown,PA,29303,100¶
```

Figure 25-3. *This data document supplies the data necessary for merging. It shows spaces and paragraph marks for easy text entry.*

THE FILE PRINT MERGE COMMAND

After you create a main document and a data document to go with it, be sure the main document is active, and then choose Print Merge from the File menu to open the Print Merge dialog box shown in Figure 25-4.

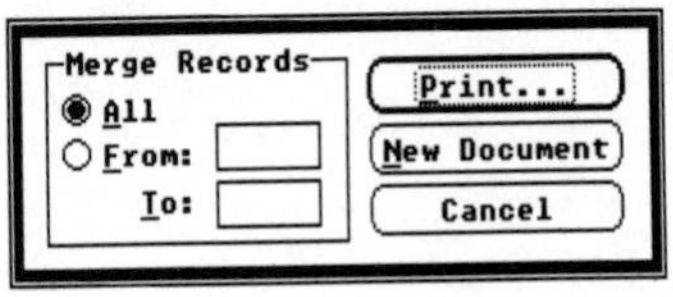

Figure 25-4. *The Print Merge dialog box.*

Setting a Range of Records

Word normally prints a run of form letters using every record in the data document. To limit the run to a smaller set of records, use the settings in the Merge Records area. Turn on the From To option and then fill in the From and To text boxes. Word counts the records in the data document by starting with the first structured data record after the header record and counting up to the last record in the document. To set a range in the From and To text boxes, enter the low record number in the From box and the high number in the To box. If you leave the From box empty, Word prints starting with record number 1. If you leave the To box empty, Word prints through to the last record. Turn on the All option if you want Word to merge all records.

Printing Form Letters

To print a run of form letters, select the Print button. The Print Merge dialog box closes, and the Print dialog box opens, where you can set printing options as you want them. (See Chapter 11 for details.) Choose OK to start printing. As Word prints, the status bar counts the records as Word merges them. When it finishes printing, you see the main document fields updated with the last set of records merged into the document.

Merging to a New Document

You might want to see the results of your print merge without printing documents. If so, select the New Document button in the Print Merge dialog box. Instead of sending the merge results to the printer, Word sends the results into a new document named FORM LETTERS1 (or 2, or 3, and so on, as the circumstances warrant). The new document appears in a text window on the screen. If you look through the new document, you'll find all the form letters created by the print merge, with a New Page section break separating each form letter. You can scroll through to look for irregularities created by the print merge (such as bad grammar). When you're finished, you can print the whole run by choosing File Print. The section breaks start each form letter at the beginning of a new page.

Error Messages

The merge won't work if you have bookmark fields in the main document without corresponding data items in the data document, if you don't have the correct number of data items in each record, or if you do not put a data field in the beginning of the main document or a header record in the beginning of the data document. If one of these conditions exists, Word puts an error message in the main document as field results for fields that didn't work. It's time then to check carefully that your spelling matches between bookmark fields and the header record and that the structured data records contain the correct number of data items, with no superfluous commas or tabs.

An Example

Use the main document and data document you entered to create the sample form letters you saw in Figure 25-1. For this example, simply put the results in a new document instead of printing them out—it takes less time and won't waste paper.

1. Be sure the main document text window (titled PLEA.DOC) is the active window. Then choose Print Merge from the File menu to open the Print Merge dialog box.
2. Choose the New Document button. The dialog box closes, and the status bar counts records as Word merges them. When the print merge is finished, a new window titled FORM LETTERS1 appears.
3. Scroll through FORM LETTERS1 to see the four form letters you created. They should match the four sample letters in Figure 25-1. Notice in the third letter that the comma in the street address made it into the letter and that the missing zip code caused no problems, because you entered it in the data document as an empty data item. The data field at the top of each letter will be filled in with the date when you print the document.
4. To print the form letters, choose Print from the File menu and then choose OK to close the Print dialog box.

ADDITIONAL PRINT-MERGE POSSIBILITIES

Although print merging itself is a simple process, you can obtain versatile results by using fields creatively in the main document. You might use a conditional field to test the data items for each form letter you create and then print different text depending on the data item. For example, you could add a field to the main document you created to check the amount of money that the record gives as an estimated donation. If the amount is over $25, the conditional field could add an extra paragraph discussing the obligation of generous (and well-to-do) people to contribute to good causes. If the amount is $25 or lower, the field could add a paragraph saying that every little bit helps.

Creating the data document can be the most arduous part of printing a form letter—you can spend hours at the keyboard typing long lists. Fortunately, many people keep names and addresses and other print-merge data in a database file. Most database programs offer a report-generation option that finds the addresses you need and sends them into a disk file instead of printing them out. It's a happy fact that almost all database programs separate data items in the disk file by a comma or a tab and that they separate each record with a return (a paragraph mark in Word). By spending a little time with your database program, you can create a text-only file with the data you need for print merging. All you need to do is open the file in Word, add a header record, resave the file, and then use the file's name in the data field in the main document.

Another time-saver for creating a data document: You might have data in a Word table that you want to merge into a main document. If so, you can use the table as data for a print merge. Word reads each cell as a data item and each row of cells as a record. The top row of the table serves as the header record.

Consider some variations on print merging. Although most people use it to create form letters, you can also use print merging for other projects. For example, you can create a document for printing addresses on mailing labels. If you use a data field and bookmark fields, you can then use a data document generated by your database program to enter all the addresses you need for the mailing labels. Your imagination is the limit.

A QUICK SUMMARY

This chapter showed you how to use print merging to create form letters. You learned to create a main document using the data field with bookmark fields to mark areas of changing text. You then learned how to create a data document by arranging information as data items within records, and you saw how to merge those records with the main document using File Print Merge. The last part of the chapter showed you some additional possibilities for using print merging with database programs and mailing labels.

With this chapter, you reach the end of this book. You now know how to use Word for Windows tools that range from simple to complex, from helpful to indispensable. Don't stop here! Word is a vast world of word-processing features. The more you explore, the more you'll find of value. Browse through the *User's Reference,* talk with other Word users, and experiment—you're sure to find tricks that make your documents better looking and easier to create.

Index

References to illustrations and tables are in italic.

D

J–K

L

M

N

O

P

Q–R

S

Michael Boom

Michael Boom is the author of two Microsoft Press books, *The Amiga* and *Music Through Midi.* He has worked as a software producer for Electronic Arts and as a music and software development consultant for Commodore-Amiga, Inc. He currently lives in the Bay area, where he works as a consultant for Sun Microsystems.

LEARN MICROSOFT® EXCEL NOW
PC Version
Ralph Soucie

LEARN MICROSOFT EXCEL NOW is a complete introduction to Microsoft Excel for the IBM PC, PC/AT, PS/2s, and compatibles. If you've never used Microsoft Excel, this step-by-step guide and example-packed tutorial is the quickest and easiest way to master this popular spreadsheet program. You'll quickly pick up how to use Microsoft Excel's worksheet, database, charting, and macro capabilities with this no-nonsense tutorial. You'll learn how to

- create worksheets and charts
- enter data
- use formulas and functions
- edit and revise worksheets
- develop databases
- analyze data
- work with linked files
- create and use macros
- print documents

LEARN MICROSOFT EXCEL NOW includes dozens of timesaving tips, practical examples, and screen illustrations. The fastest way to learn Microsoft Excel is with LEARN MICROSOFT EXCEL NOW.

352 pages, softcover   7 3/8 x 9 1/4 $22.95   Order Code LEEXNO

LEARN MICROSOFT® EXCEL NOW—*Special Edition*
PC Version
Ralph Soucie

This Special Edition is the ideal way to preview Microsoft Excel for Windows and discover the excitement of computing in a graphical environment before you upgrade to the full retail version. This unique book/disk combination includes a functional Working Model of Microsoft Excel for Windows that provides its own run-time version of Microsoft Windows and lets you create spreadsheets of up to 64 rows and 16 columns. It includes most of the features of the full-priced version with the exception of the Help system, the Dialog Editor, the on-line tutorial, and sample documents. Now you can learn how to create presentation-quality worksheets, charts, and databases with this Special Edition of LEARN MICROSOFT EXCEL NOW.

352 pages, softcover with two 5.25-inch disks   7 3/8 x 9 1/4 $29.95   Order Code LEEXND

RUNNING WINDOWS™
The Microsoft® Guide to Windows™ 2.0, Windows/286,™ and Windows/386™
Nancy Andrews and Craig Stinson

If you want a hands-on introduction to Windows 2, Windows/286, and Windows/386, turn to RUNNING WINDOWS. In an example-rich approach, the authors provide all the information you need to fully understand and successfully use Windows' built-in desk applications and accessories and the most popular Windows applications. Additional sections include step-by-step techniques for creating reports and proposals with popular MS-DOS applications and instructions for using Windows in color.

368 pages, softcover   7 3/8 x 9 1/4 $19.95   Order Code RUWI

Microsoft Press books are available wherever quality computer books are sold, or credit card orders can be placed by calling 1-800-MSPRESS.